Contents

Figures

Tables

Preface to first edition

There is no shortage of books available that set out to be introductions to sociology at A-level. The obvious questions must be 'Why write another one?' and 'What has this new book got that others have not?' The answers are clearly related to each other.

An introductory sociology text for the student at this level should:

1   be readable, in terms both of vocabulary and of intrinsic interest;
2   introduce as much of the examination syllabus as possible;
3   present a picture of sociology that is as faithful to the reality as is possible;
4   show how sociological insights relate to the world of everyday experience.

While there are books on the market which meet some of these criteria, none meets them all, and this is what we have tried to do in this text. Most especially, we have concentrated on the first criterion. Sociology is difficult, but it does not have to be obscure. As teachers (and we all teach, or have taught, A-level sociology), we have felt the need for a book which is genuinely sociological, and which we can recommend on the first day of the course, when our new students are still 'post O-level' rather than fully A-level. This is what we have tried to write.

Nine people have contributed to the book. The editors' job has been to integrate the contributions into a whole. This does not mean that the task has been to prevent or to cut out repetition. There are basic themes that run right through sociology, and these have been allowed to emerge and re-emerge as appropriate. Furthermore, particular examples have been used more than once, and this too is deliberate. Society has been described as a 'seamless web'. The problem with tracing the pattern of a web is to know where to start, and to recognize that it is impossible to avoid occasionally retracing your steps. We have regarded this as a positive advantage, in that it shows how the same concepts and ideas can be used in different ways and in different contexts, and how certain central concepts throw light on many areas of social life. In order further to encourage this integration, cross-references are provided throughout the text.

All the current syllabuses in A-level sociology encourage some degree of specialization. However, specialization in one area should not mean the total exclusion of others. While different teachers will pursue different themes in depth in their courses, students should have the opportunity to read through a chapter on those topics that are not being so studied. The chapters of this book have been written in such a way that a good general insight into their content can be gained from a single reading, if that is all that is required. This is essential for a broad understanding of sociology, and to improving examination answers, which often call for a wide-ranging approach.

For those areas which are chosen for specialist study, further reading is essential. A-level sociology cannot be studied from only one book, however long or thorough it might be. For this reason, advice for further reading is added to each chapter. In addition, the bibliography has been compiled not to justify what appears in the text, but to assist with follow-up study by both teacher and student. Some may find it difficult to obtain the books mentioned in the bibliography. We would remind you of the inter-library loan system that operates in Britain, which means that any book in any public library (and in many college and university libraries) can be obtained by application at any other library, even the smallest local mobile library.

Finally, we would collectively reaffirm our belief that the study of sociology has a great deal to offer to the student. As well as the obvious benefit of obtaining an A-level certificate, the best sociology enables us to increase our understanding of ourselves, of others, and of the social world that we experience. Such an understanding is essential if we are to retain or regain some degree of self-determination and control over what we do, what happens to us, and what is done in our name.

Acknowledgements
With nine contributors, it is impossible to list by name all those to whom we owe thanks. Nevertheless, we do thank all those relatives, friends, colleagues, students, teachers, librarians, and others who have helped us all so much over the years. They know who they are, and we are grateful.

Preface to second edition

The objectives of this new edition are the same as those of the first edition, that is, to provide a readable introduction to the major areas of sociology that are examined at A-level. In order to continue to meet the second objective of the first edition, this volume has been expanded to include new chapters on Gender and on Development, and the Population chapter has been extended and modified to incorporate the sociology of health. Other chapters have been altered to varying degrees by their authors, to take account of what they regard as the important new developments. It is in the nature of sociology that the extent of such developments varies very much from one area to another.

The acknowledgements we made in the first edition stand. There are now, however, even more people to whom thanks are due, and one more person to give them.

1 Sociology and the social sciences

Charles Townley

The systematic study of people in society

It seems reasonable to assume, since you are reading this book, that you are an inquiring, literate person. As such you will already have formed some ideas about the people around you in your daily life and about the society in which you live. Perhaps you feel that, by and large, people are quite co-operative, friendly and helpful, or maybe you feel that people are really very competitive and selfish. Perhaps you feel that, despite the occasional news headlines, life is a lot more stable and secure in our society than it is in many others. Or perhaps you feel that society is sick: that there are too many strikes; that there is too much vandalism; that unemployment is far too high; that the National Health Service is unsatisfactory; and that the violence in Northern Ireland will go on for ever.

One way or another you will already hold some views about 'people in society', particularly our society. In studying sociology you will have the opportunity to examine these views critically and to extend them. That is to say you will have the opportunity to examine your views and beliefs in the light of alternative explanations. For that is, in essence, what critical analysis involves: an examination of assumptions in the light of alternatives. Those of you who are following a course leading to an examination may very well be faced with examination questions which begin by asking you to 'Examine critically. . . .' or 'Discuss critically. . . .' and, even if the questions do not ask for this explicitly, one reliable way of displaying your understanding is to show that you understand more than one way of analysing or explaining something. So we can explain a film in terms of its plot, its characters, its underlying message or its direction. We can analyse a game in terms of its excitement, the players' skills or the tactics which the players adopt.

For example, if you live in a nuclear family you may come to take that system so much for granted that it never occurs to you that there may be alternative ways of living (see page 217). You may so take it for granted that marriage is monogamous, between one man and one woman, that you never consider that, in some societies, marriage may be polyandrous, involving one woman taking several husbands, or polygamous, when one man takes several wives. This is not to suggest that monogamous marriage is under threat. But it raises questions about the basis or functions of marriage which we may have forgotten, and it enables us to re-examine our sentiments about marriage and a marriage partner. Is love the only basis for marriage? Are arranged marriages any more or any less stable? Can they work in a culture where such marriages are not the norm?

Exactly the same may be true about our other beliefs, about social class, women's roles, educational opportunity, strikes, and many more. Is social class a thing of the past? Is it something that would disappear if only sociologists would stop talking and writing about it? Now that we have experienced our first woman prime minister is there equality of the sexes? Have comprehensive schools brought equality of educational opportunity? Do the trade unions have too much power? In this book we have set out to show that sociological analysis can extend our understanding of people in society. It can do this in several ways, for sociology itself has several ways of looking at all these subjects. We shall look at these different sociological 'perspectives' later. First let us discuss what sociology is.

What do you think it is? It is certainly a word that is used freely today, so freely and loosely, in fact, that it is often misused. You may sometimes hear people talk about 'sociological problems in our society' when they really mean social problems. As a result there are many misunderstandings. Is it about social welfare and the social services? Is it to do with government and making social policy? Is it concerned with prisons and penal reform? Or with crime and its treatment and the reform of criminals? Is it about socialism and changing society? Is it about industrial relations and preventing strikes? Or about town planning and building leisure centres? Or even about population and birth control? The short answer is that sociology is none of these things. However, all of them will have been studied by sociologists at one time or another and an understanding of sociology would almost certainly help people working in all of these areas.

Let us approach a definition by looking at the definitions which have been offered by previous writers. Morris Ginsberg, a founding father of British sociology, wrote, 'Sociology may be defined as the study of society, that is, of the web or tissue of human interactions and interrelations' (Bartlett 1939).* More recently Barry Sugarman has written, 'Sociology is the objective study of human behaviour in so far as it is affected by the fact that people live in groups' (Sugarman 1968). For

---

* See the bibliography at the end of this book for further details of any title mentioned in the text.

Salvador Giner, 'Sociology is one of the social sciences. Its purpose is the scientific study of human society through the investigation of the social behaviour of man' (Giner 1972). Three American sociologists recognize, like many others, that a brief definition is difficult. 'Nevertheless, we do need a brief definition to get us started. Sociology is the study of individuals in a social setting that includes groups, organizations, cultures, and societies; and of the interrelationships of individuals, groups, organizations, cultures, and societies' (Ritzer *et al.* 1979). More recently and in similar vein Ronald Fletcher (1984) has said, 'Sociology, quite simply, is the attempt to study as scientifically as possible all forms of association known to us: their nature, functions, interconnections and sequences of continuity and change, in all types of society.'

It is difficult to improve on these definitions in a few words so let us examine them for a moment. If we read them again it is clear that they all recognize three elements in sociology. It is a *systematic* study of *people* in *society*. By systematic we often mean 'scientific' or 'objective', something very different from the methods of a journalist or a poet. We shall examine this idea of systematic study in Chapters 2 and 3 when we ask the question, 'Is sociology a science?' (see pages 22 and 63) Let us focus first on the other two elements, people and society, which are the concern of all the social sciences.

The social sciences

A problem facing all students who come to study a discipline for the first time is that they must do two things simultaneously. They must familiarize themselves with the substance or content of their new subject and, at the same time, they must learn the methodology of the subject. That is, they must become familiar not only with the knowledge and research findings which fill the textbooks but also with the methods by which the knowledge is obtained and organized, that is, with the logical basis of the subject itself. In simple terms this means the way sociologists think and work.

These two elements are not separate; they are very closely related. The way social scientists organize their discipline, that is, the way they look at the social world they are studying and the way they choose the concepts they use to analyse and describe it, will determine the way the books are written and the way the knowledge is presented.

Because we are all familiar with social life through our everyday experiences we may feel that the social sciences are very largely a matter of commonsense. But, as a look at any textbook will quickly indicate, though each of the social sciences is concerned with people in society, each discipline goes beyond commonsense understandings. Each discipline focuses on a particular aspect of social life, each uses particular methods of study and each employs its own set of concepts. It is this set of concepts, the most basic ideas in a subject, which constitute the 'logical basis of the subject', which enables the social scientist to go beyond everyday commonsense and understandings and which distinguishes one discipline from another. 'The sociologist does not look at phenomena that nobody else is aware of. But he looks at the same phenomena in a different way' (Berger 1966). His way of looking is his *perspective*.

In building a house, for example, each craftsman concentrates upon one particular aspect of the building. Each uses his own particular methods and employs his own tools. So we are unlikely to find a bricklayer fitting electric cables with a plumber's wrench! So, too, in the social sciences, each discipline develops its own conceptual tools and its own perspective – its own way of looking at things. This perspective, in turn, determines which topics each discipline investigates, the kinds of questions it asks and, thus, the conclusions it reaches.

The economist focuses upon the production and distribution of wealth, often using statistical methods and employing concepts such as supply, demand, scarcity, production, distribution and costs. The psychologist focuses his study upon the individual, sometimes employing experimental methods, and using concepts like needs, drives, motivation, personality, traits, intelligence. The psychiatrist is concerned with mentally disturbed individuals; he works through case-studies and uses concepts like neurosis, psychosis, obsession, transference and therapy. Political scientists traditionally focus upon governments, often using statistical methods and the concepts of power, conflict, elite, democracy, parties and pressure groups. Anthropology comes closest to sociology in many respects, studying the culture of whole, often small-scale 'primitive' societies through ethnographic field studies (see page 68) and concepts such as culture, customs, rituals, institutions and values. In addition to sociology, which we shall look at in more detail below, we might also include social history and geography in our list of social sciences.

If we take football as an example we can see that each discipline has its own perspective on the subject, distinctive from every other in some way, and also different from that of the newspaper sports pages. A historian might put it in the context of how ball games developed in a society, where they originated and under what conditions they came to be played. A geographer might be interested in where it is played and under what climatic or economic conditions, or how leisure and sports facilities fit into a pattern of land use. An anthropologist would be interested in rituals, customs and beliefs and how they fit into the whole social system. Frankenberg, an anthropologist studying a Welsh village, showed how football had a cohesive function and brought people in that village together through committees, meetings, matches and other activities (Frankenberg 1957). A psychologist might well be interested in the personality characteristics associated with success in football; so an American psychologist compared Bobby Charlton's aspirations with his achievement in shooting. An economist might examine the 'economics of survival': what size of population is necessary to produce crowds large enough to support a professional club; what is the maximum size of playing staff that a club can afford. Frankenberg believed a sociologist 'would immediately wish to discover the distribution of age, sex, social class, ethnic origin and religion of those who played, watched or organized and, in no time at all, would produce a set of punched cards ready to feed through the computer and produce tabulations' (ATSS conference, 1975).

If we take the example of 'work' (see Chapter 10) we can see again that each discipline views it quite differently. Psychologists are interested in work because many people spend a lot of their time at work and their general psychological well-being will be related in some way to their work experiences. The psychologist will use concepts like motivation, aggression and anxiety. The economist regards work as labour, one of the four factors of production, and he uses concepts like wages, costs and profit. Political scientists are interested in the relationship between workers and the power structure. For example they will investigate the political party membership of different categories of worker, voting patterns and trade union membership. They will use concepts like power, authority, government and conflict.

These distinctions are rarely clear-cut and it will not be surprising to find that the sociologist's interest in work overlaps other disciplines. Sociologists, like psychologists, are interested in attitudes to work; like political scientists they are interested in the power which workers have and in the conflicts of interest which arise between, say, white-collar and blue-collar workers; and, like economists, they are interested in capitalism. Their main concern is with the relationship between work and the maintenance of order or the production of change in society. They use concepts such as the division of labour, function, conflict, meaning and alienation. Thus Talcott Parsons claimed that work was functional for society. For him it was the means by which society fulfilled its material needs to survive. For Marx, on the other hand, the development of capitalism was a process in which organizations grew in size and people became alienated from work.

Sociologists then, like all social scientists, are concerned with the systematic study of people in society. What distinguishes sociologists from other social scientists, although they sometimes overlap, is (i) the sorts of questions they ask and the issues they choose to think about, (ii) the concepts they use, such as culture, role, norm, class, authority, social action and meaning, and (iii) linking (i) and (ii), their own particular sociological perspectives. We can now look at these in more detail.

2 Sociological perspectives

Charles Townley and Mike Middleton

The variety of sociology

In the last chapter we quoted Ronald Frankenberg as saying that a sociologist interested in football 'would immediately wish to discover the distribution of age, sex, social class, ethnic origin and religion of all those who played, watched or organized and, in no time at all, would produce a set of punched cards ready to feed through the computer and produce tabulations'. However, Frankenberg was speaking some years ago and if only his words were still true then life for the student of sociology would be very simple, for his words suggest that sociologists have one distinct way of looking at the social world, one distinct set of concepts and one set of methods of carrying out their research.

Alas, life is not so simple! There is no such thing as *the* sociological perspective; there are several. Some, like symbolic interaction, phenomenology and ethnomethodology, have become more widely recognized in Britain only recently, and this has given rise to the impression that this pluralism is a fairly recent development. It is our intention in this chapter to outline some of the more important perspectives in British sociology, to indicate their founding authors and to show how they have been used to illuminate certain social phenomena.

Until very recently it would have been safe to treat sociology as we have treated the other social sciences. We would probably have said that sociology was the science of society. In 1966, Peter Berger wrote, 'The sociologist, then, is someone concerned with understanding society in a disciplined way. The nature of this discipline is scientific. This means that what the sociologist finds and says about the social phenomena he studies occurs within a rather strictly defined frame of reference.' That strictly defined scientific frame of reference determined the way the sociologist looked at society. It produced what was regarded as the 'distinctive sociological perspective' as opposed, for example, to a psychological perspective or a commonsense view of things.

The subject matter, or focus, was society. More precisely

If you were to insist that the basic problem to which sociology addresses itself be described in a single phrase, we would reply: it seeks to explain the nature of social order and disorder. Sociology shares with all other essentially scientific perspectives the assumption that there is order in nature and that it can be discovered, described and understood . . . sociology seeks to discover, describe and explain the order which characterises the social life of man. [Inkeles 1964]

This concern with the explanation of order has been the traditional concern of sociology since its early years and was central to the development of the first distinctive sociological approach or perspective.

This approach became known as 'positivist' sociology though it is sometimes referred to as the 'traditional' or 'macro' or 'structural' approach. It is described as traditional for historical reasons, as macro because it takes a large-scale look at society as a whole, and as structural because it involves analysing the structure of society. There are fine distinctions between these terms but they are not important to us, at this stage. We must recognize that they are often used interchangeably. Equally, there are differences between an 'approach', a 'perspective', a 'model', a 'theory' and a 'paradigm', but these terms are also often used interchangeably and it is sufficient for our purpose at this stage if we treat them as being approximately the same, although they are examined more closely in Chapter 3, pages 61–3.

Within this positivist approach, however, there were two distinct ways of looking at society and explaining the existence of order. Each produced its own model of society, its own theory or paradigm and, thus, its own perspective. These are called the 'functionalist' and 'conflict' perspectives. In addition there have developed over the past decades in British sociology what have come to be known as the 'new perspectives', the 'phenomenological', 'interpretive' or 'interactionist' perspectives. Thus the student coming to sociology for the first time has to recognize that there are several perspectives within the subject and that there are different ideas, different questions and different concepts associated with each.

All the social sciences have their origins in philosophy but the early philosophers did not distinguish between fields of knowledge. They focused upon any aspect of life that interested them: everything was merely a branch of philosophy. But, as knowledge increased, it became split up into separate fields or subjects. The natural sciences and physical sciences were the first to become separated. The social sciences only became distinct in the last two centuries; until then they were the province of philosophers. And it is far back in philosophy that we find the origins of the different perspectives within sociology. Philosophers since Aristotle and Plato have been concerned to discover the true nature of people, of society, and of the relationship between the two.

It is the relative importance given to 'society' which is the basis of positivist sociology and provides the foundation of the functionalist and conflict perspectives; it is the relative importance given to 'people' which provides the foundation for the interpretive or phenomenological perspectives. To use a crude over-simplification (which we shall elaborate upon as we proceed) we might say at this stage that the former perspectives emphasize people as the product of *society* while the latter emphasizes society as the product of *people*.

Positivist sociology

The first distinctive sociological perspective sprang from the work of Auguste Comte (1798–1857), who coined the word 'sociology' from the Latin *socius* and the Greek *logos*, in 1837. Comte believed that the scientific discipline of sociology was the result of a natural progression or development of human thought through three stages. In the first stage, thinking was theological or fictitious, when the 'will of God' was accepted as an explanation of virtually everything from the divine right of kings to rule, the class system in society or droughts and poor harvests. In the second stage it was metaphysical or abstract. In the final stage it was scientific or positive. At this third stage all phenomena are looked upon as subject to natural laws that can be investigated by observation and experimentation. Comte believed that the social world is like the natural, physical world. It is made up of objective facts, independent of individuals, just waiting to be discovered. So, for Comte, social life, people and society, should be treated in the same scientific manner as biological organisms. The parts should not be studied on their own but each element should be studied in the light of the whole system, using scientific methods of analysis to produce accurate, quantified data.

When people and society are subjected to this scientific analysis, Comte believed, sociology would become the positive basis of social and political action, providing the basis for reforms. Comte wrote during the period of social and political upheaval following the French Revolution and the rapid social and economic changes of the Industrial Revolution. He believed that sociologists would be like secular (i.e. non-religious) priests bringing a new order to society. They would depend not on divine inspiration but on scientific knowledge, which would be used to predict in order to control. The social order was no longer deemed to be God-given but would be changed and improved by men on the basis of their understanding.

This was Comte's 'positive philosophy' and the essence of positivism. In addition to its origins in Comte's term, 'The name "positivism" derives from the emphasis on the positive sciences – that is on tested and systematic experience rather than on undisciplined speculation' (*International Encyclopaedia of the Social Sciences* 1968). Thus it is closely identified with traditional scientific method, which is described in Chapter 3, pages 63–6.

So positivist sociology, rather than examining the way individuals construct the social world around them, assumes that society is an independent system, 'out there' waiting to be examined, analysed and understood like the natural world, rather like a biologist looking at an ant hill or an astronomer examining the stars. The ultimate aim is to produce a general theory of social action in the same way that physicists are trying to produce a single explanatory theory of the universe.

Functionalism

The functionalist perspective is rooted in the work of Emile Durkheim (1858-1917) who, like Comte before him, was preoccupied with understanding social order. Functionalism provides a perspective on society as a whole. It views society as an organism in which all the parts function in a way that ensures the continued well-being of the whole organism, like the various systems in the human body or the parts in a watch. The whole is greater than the sum of the parts. Society is regarded by functionalists as something which has an existence of its own and has a structure that serves to maintain it.

Functionalism is inextricably tied up with the question of order. It asks how is order maintained in society? How do we avoid Hobbes's war of all against all? The answer suggests that order, stability, cohesion and integration are maintained in society by its parts. These parts are social institutions, those permanent features of social life, like the family and the church, whose existence is 'useful' or functional in some way. The very permanence of such institutions is an index of their 'usefulness'. If they were not functional they would disappear and be replaced, like passing fashions; not all social phenomena are permanent. Clothing may be institutionalized in so far as we all wear clothes, but the mini-skirt was a temporary phenomenon. The people involved in these social institutions, people living in families, for example, may not be conscious of the functions which they and the institutions fulfil but, as a consequence of the institution existing, certain effects follow. No matter what parents may be conscious of doing, children are socialized in families. In this way the family is said to be functional in society, and socialization is said to be one of the functions of the family. Institutions are long lasting and, therefore, are functional.

Durkheim (1858-1917)

Durkheim used the term 'function' in his *Rules of Sociological Method* (1895). He argued that the sociologist's task was first, to explain the cause of any social phenomenon, like religion, and then to explain the function it fulfils. 'We use the word "function" in preference to "end" or "purpose" precisely because social phenomena do not generally exist for the useful results they produce. We must determine whether there is a correspondence between the fact under consideration and the general needs of the social organism. . . .' (Durkheim 1895). In other words Durkheim was saying the term 'function' is more suitable than the word 'purpose' because institutions are not always conscious of the consequences of their existence. Sociologists must try to understand whether there is a relationship between, for example, the existence of institutions like the family or the church and the need of society to have people socialized.

Social phenomena such as conventions, social rules and beliefs, and institutions like the family, religion, education and law, were regarded by Durkheim as 'social facts'. That is, they are external to the individual, and exist independently of that person, exercising constraint on his or her behaviour. Following Comte in the positivist tradition, it was important for the sociologist to study social facts scientifically as if they were 'things', rather than to study individuals. He practised what he preached and provided a classic example in his work on suicide. One might imagine that the decision to take one's own life was entirely personal and psychological in character. Without denying these elements, Durkheim made a detailed study of the statistics and showed that suicide rates varied widely but consistently with different social conditions. So it, too, was a social fact.

His work was essentially a reaction against the nineteenth-century doctrines of individualism, biologism and progressivism. Instead of believing that modern industrial society could be analysed in terms of contractual agreements between individuals motivated by self-interest, he stressed the collective aspects of social life. Central to his thinking is the importance of shared norms and values and this is expressed in his concept of the collective conscience which stresses the values, beliefs and normal patterns of behaviour that were common throughout society.

The word 'conscience' requires a brief explanation. The term 'collective conscience' is actually a rather literal translation of Durkheim's *conscience collective*. The specific French word *conscience* goes beyond the English meaning of the same word to include what in English is rendered as 'consciousness'. So the collective conscience is not a sort of mass guilt feeling but a set of norms and customs which are experienced as a social awareness by individuals. [Brown 1979]

Although Brown refers to social awareness, quite often we so take these norms and customs for granted that we are not aware of how much they do constrain us. If you are a man, will you put on a dress and high-heeled shoes tomorrow morning? If you are a woman, will you play rugby next Saturday?

Durkheim clearly has in mind the stable Roman Catholic societies of Europe up to the nineteenth century. But when a society is in a state of turmoil or undergoing rapid social change, conditions which typified Europe in the nineteenth century, then the norms and values are no longer so clear-cut and unambiguous. Then individuals find themselves faced by moral dilemmas rather than the moral certainty which characterized the earlier cultures Durkheim had in mind.

In our own time, for example, many individuals including highly religious people face uncertainty over the attitude they should adopt towards the use of violence in the pursuit of 'just causes'. Examples abound in the shape of guerrilla movements in Africa, the Middle East and Northern Ireland, and in acts of kidnapping and hijacking.

At a more personal level, people face predicaments over their attitude to speeding in motor cars, advice on contraceptives to school-children, abortion and tax evasion. Such a state of normlessness Durkheim called 'anomie', though he considered it to be a temporary state of affairs which must be replaced by consensus if society was to survive. It is interesting to speculate whether Durkheim would consider Britain in the 1980s to be in a state of anomie, given the personal difficulties associated with unemployment or technological change.

For Durkheim, the individual is very much the product of society. The values we hold and the normal patterns of behaviour we display are the result of pressures to conform exerted by society, and society must ensure that this conformity occurs. Without the certainty and predictability that order brings, life would be full of uncertainty, anxiety and chaos. His work on education provides a good example. In order to reach a satisfactory definition of education he regards it as a social fact and considers it in all societies at all points in time. He concludes that

Education is the influence exercised by adult generations on those that are not yet ready for social life. Its object is to arouse and to develop in the child a certain number of physical, intellectual and moral states which are demanded of him by both the political society as a whole and the special milieu for which he is specifically destined. [Durkheim 1922]

All education is a continuous effort to impose on the child ways of seeing, feeling and acting which he could not have arrived at spontaneously. [Durkheim 1938]

Education consists of a methodical socialisation of the young generation. [Durkheim 1922]

Education is the moral agent of society, external to the individual and constraining him or her to conform to collective norms and values. In simple functionalist terms the main function of education is socialization (see Chapter 9, page 247).

Radcliffe-Brown (1881-1955)

The foundations of functionalism laid by Comte and Durkheim were built upon by later writers, particularly the anthropologists Malinowski and Radcliffe-Brown. Radicliffe-Brown's work emphasized the structural analogy between social life and organisms even more clearly than

Durkheim's. It was this emphasis in his work which gave rise to the term structural-functionalism. He is quite clear about the meaning of the word 'function'.

As the word function is here being used the life of an organism is conceived as the functioning of its structure. It is through and by the continuity of the functioning of an organism that the continuity of the structure is preserved. If we consider any recurrent part of the life process, such as respiration, digestion, etc., its function is the part it plays in, the contribution it makes to the life of the organism as a whole. [Radcliffe-Brown 1952]

Parsons (1902-79)

The work of Durkheim and Radicliffe-Brown has been further developed by the American sociologist, Talcott Parsons. He began with the assumption that the complexity of any society must be based on some sort of systematic organization and that all societies must share some elements of organization in common. It is the sociologist's task to identify them.

For society to exist at all the individual must live as a social animal, that is, he or she must interact and co-operate with other individuals in order to survive and to develop. No man is an island; Rousseau's noble savage never actually existed and anybody who lives the life of a hermit or a recluse today is regarded as an oddity or a deviant. It is the pattern of interaction and co-operation which interested Parsons. He viewed it as a systematic response to certain basic needs or problems faced by all societies. Thus he began by looking upon society as a social system which develops sub-systems to resolve these needs or problems. Each sub-system can itself be viewed as a system in its own right with its own sub-systems functioning to maintain it (see Figure 5, page 101).

Parsons, using the work of Sigmund Freud in his own attempt to construct a general theory of action, believes that all social systems have to resolve two sets of problems, the 'instrumental' problems of achieving certain ends, for example, survival, and the 'expressive' problems of maintaining efficient co-operation between individuals. These two sets of problems are further refined, for 'any social system is subject to four independent functional imperatives or "problems" which must be met adequately if equilibrium and/or continuing existence of the system is to be maintained' (Parsons 1957). These four 'functional imperatives' or 'problems' make up the GAIL model. They are

> Goal attainment
> Adaptation
> Integration
> Latency

Each is resolved by one or more of the system's sub-systems. Goal attainment is concerned with the setting of goals and keeping the system moving towards its goals. Adaptation is concerned with procuring the means to achieve those goals, that is, adapting the material world to attain certain ends. Integration is concerned with maintaining harmony and solidarity, perhaps in the face of deviance, while latency (or pattern-maintenance) is concerned with 'tension-management' and stability, perhaps in the face of destabilizing strains. This is done usually through activities whose beneficial value is latent, beneath the surface, or not immediately apparent.

As societies become more complex, it also becomes more likely that each system will develop some degree of specialization. This takes the form of a division of labour between individuals and a division of function between sub-systems. So particular institutions or sub-systems tend to be concerned with particular 'problems'.

If we focus our attention on society as a whole then the sub-system which is most important in resolving the goal attainment problem is the 'polity', the political system or system of government. In Britain it is parliament and the cabinet who are responsible for setting goals concerning our survival, standards of living, inflation, health, the redistribution of income, equality of opportunity, and so on. The adaptation function is fulfilled mainly by the economic sub-system, industry, which produces and distributes the means by which we survive, progress, improve our standard of living, etc. (see page 275). The integration function is very largely concerned with the process of socialization, and with the maintenance of a system of shared norms and values, what Durkheim would have called the collective conscience. It is not possible to identify one particular sub-system which fulfils this need. All those institutions concerned with the inculcation of norms and values, for example, the family, religion, education and the media, are regarded as contributing to the resolution of this problem (see pp. 89–149). Latency does not, like the other three imperatives, focus on the needs of the system itself but on the units or individuals of which it is composed. It is concerned with what is latent or potential. Thus anything which is therapeutic or satisfying in one part of our lives may enable us to achieve our potential in another part. So going on holiday, watching television or doing the garden help sustain us as individuals and in so doing 'recharge our batteries' so that we may fulfil our potential as mothers, citizens, club members, workers, etc., in other sub-systems. These activities have a latent value for the social system as a whole, that is, society.

To appreciate the significance of Parsons's work it is important to understand his overall aim and to put it into the context of his work as a whole, which spans a period of more than forty years. He was trying to establish a general theory of action which linked the psychological elements and the socially determined elements in human behaviour. As a writer he is usually characterized as a 'die-hard functionalist' in the 'worst positivist tradition', simply because other sociologists focus, as we have, on that particular strand of his work. But we should remember that, however much he was a functionalist, that label is much too neat and simplistic to cover the variety in his work.

Merton (b. 1910)

Robert Merton, too, is an American sociologist who has made very important contributions to sociological theory, particularly in relating the work of eighteenth-century European philosophers, like Hegel, to twentieth-century American sociology. Here we want to pick out only one small part of his work which contributed to the development of functionalism.

Merton refined this analysis when he distinguished between 'manifest' and 'latent' functions. He acknowledged that people are to a great extent conscious and aware of the purpose of many activities. Thus he defined manifest functions as those consequences which are both intended and recognized, and latent functions as those which are neither intended nor recognized. For example, one manifest function of education is learning. As a consequence of attending school from the age of 5 to 16 pupils learn things which they did not know before. At the same time the schools are providing a free 'baby-sitting' service to parents and increasing the manpower available for employment; these are some of the latent functions of education.

Merton also observed that consequences which are 'favourable' or functional for one institution or system may be unfavourable for another, so he developed the concept of 'dysfunction'. Thus bingo may be recreational and functional for society. It may be functional for the firms which organize it commercially and for most of those who attend the sessions and enjoy them, but it may be dysfunctional for some families if it becomes obsessive and leads to conflict and tensions. If it did this on a large scale it would be dysfunctional for society.

The application of functionalism

Functionalists, then, view society as an integrated, harmonious, cohesive whole where all the parts function to maintain equilibrium and consensus. Thus a functionalist looking at any institution in society would ask what functions that institution performs. What are the functions of the family? of religion? of education? of crime? of stratification? How do they serve to maintain equilibrium and consensus? This is a good example, referred to in our opening paragraphs, of theoretical perspective determining the questions which are asked, the kind of knowledge which is produced and the way it is presented.

For example, the American sociologist, Kingsley Davis, in his book *Human Society* (1948), explained the universality of the family as a form of social organization in these terms. The family serves a host of functions including the stable satisfaction of the sex need, the production and rearing of children, socialization, the provision of recreation, the maintenance of health, the inculcation of religious beliefs, education and the economic function of producing sufficient to provide food, clothes and a home.

But, as society has changed and developed, particularly western society over the past 200 years, some of these functions have been fulfilled by other institutions. The state has taken on much of the responsibility for health and education. Commercial interests and the state (via the BBC) provide entertainment and fill leisure time which would once have been more the province of the family. Economic functions have clearly shifted from the family, as the basic unit of production in pre-industrial Europe, to capitalist and state organizations. Yet only the family can successfully combine the basic functions of satisfying the sex need, producing and rearing children and socialization. In this way, says Davis, the family is functional to all societies, though the form it takes varies from one society to another (see pages 217–9).

This perspective can be applied to other institutions in exactly the same sort of way. If we take religion, for example, a typical American sociology textbook asks explicitly, 'What functions do religious institutions fulfil in the life of the community?' (Lundberg 1963). In terms of Talcott Parsons's social systems theory and GAIL model, its functions are clearly 'expressive' rather than 'instrumental'. Sapir believed the most general function of religion was to help an individual to overcome fear and anxiety and to find peace of mind. Perhaps the function which is most commonly identified by sociologists is that of social control through the propagation and legitimation of values. The maintenance of social order is heavily dependent on a high degree of value consensus and 'by adding divine sanction to human values, religion buttresses the norms of society and unites its adherents into a moral community whose members feel a deep common bond because they share a belief in what is morally true' (Broom and Selznick 1968). According to Max Weber, if the Protestant revolution had not occurred, the Protestant ethic with its emphasis on salvation through personal strivings and achievement could not have developed. And without the development of these values capitalism would not have developed either (see page 36).

Equally, the functionalist perspective can be applied to education. Durkheim, emphasizing the relationship between education and society, focused upon the function of socialization. Parsons, writing over half a century later, agreed. 'From the functional point of view the school class can be treated as an agency of socialization. That is to say it is an agency through which individual personalities are trained to be motivationally and technically adequate to the performance of adult roles' (Parsons 1959). But he goes further. In an industrial society education has at least one other important consequence. While on the one hand it is an agency of socialization, 'on the other hand, it is, from the point of view of the society, an agency of manpower allocation' (Parsons 1959) (see pages 246–7).

If we apply the same perspective to stratification it yields similar results. Stratification, or social inequality, is both inevitable and functional; it fulfils a societal need.

The main functional necessity explaining the universal presence of stratification is precisely the requirement faced by any society of placing and motivating individuals in the social structure. As a functioning mechanism a society must somehow distribute its members in social positions and induce them to perform the duties of these positions. [Davis and Moore 1945]

If all the jobs in society were equally pleasant, equally rewarding, equally important, required equal talent or skill and received the same wage, then it would not matter who got into which job. But this state of affairs obviously does not exist. Some jobs or positions offer more intrinsic satisfaction, demand more skill and more training and, say the functionalists, are more important than others. So how do we ensure that all these jobs are filled in the most efficient manner? In the words of Davis and Moore, it is social inequality which is the 'unconsciously evolved device by which societies ensure that the most important positions are conscientiously filled by the most qualified persons' (Davis and Moore 1945). And, as we have noted earlier, the education system is actually responsible for the act of differentiating between children and allocating them to these occupational roles (see page 181).

We could go on applying this perspective to all sorts of phenomena almost indefinitely, but we shall restrict ourselves to two brief examples of a slightly different kind, the Royal Wedding in 1981, and deviance. The wedding is a good example of ritual, and ritual is functional in several ways. It has a cohesive function in so far as it brings people together in a common act and so reinforces their common bonds and social solidarity. In Durkheim's words, 'Rites are, above all, means by which the social group reaffirms itself periodically' (Durkheim 1912). It has a revitalizing function, for 'if a society is to be kept alive its members must be made keenly aware of their social heritage. Traditions must be perpetuated, faith must be renewed, values must be transmitted and deeply embedded' (Nisbet 1965). And it has a euphoric function in so far as it establishes a pleasant feeling of well-being, happiness, satisfaction or contentment. It is easy to apply all these functions to an analysis of the Royal Wedding.

In the same way we can ask what are the functions of deviance: crime, for example? We might well imagine that criminal activities like robbery, violence or vandalism must be dysfunctional in so far as they threaten social order and harmony. They must surely be disruptive rather than integrative. But for Durkheim deviance from norms only serves to highlight the existence of those norms and to confirm them in the minds of individuals. If nobody broke the existing laws then new standards and laws would emerge. If there were no assault or grievous bodily harm it might well become an offence to swear or to look aggressive. Deviance thus reinforces and sustains the collective consciousness of consensus. The deviants themselves are seen as individuals who have failed to internalize fully the commonly held or 'shared' values of society and are in need of correction (see pages 314-8).

Conflict theory

Whereas functionalism emphasizes consensus, shared norms and shared values, and uses concepts like order, harmony, cohesion, integration and equilibrium, conflict theory takes a different view of society. This perspective emphasizes differences between interest groups, and uses concepts like control, conflict, power, constraint, domination, exploitation, coercion, dissensus and change. Whereas a functionalist perspective offers us a view of society made up of parts, all contributing to the harmonious operation of the whole, a conflict perspective offers us a view of society split into essentially two groups, aggregates, or classes, whose interests conflict (see page 183).

The central theme or thesis of conflict theory is that conflict is inherent in the structure of society. It is an inevitable fact of life. 'The notion that wherever there is a social life there is conflict may be unpleasant and disturbing. Nevertheless, it is indispensable to our understanding of social problems.... Not the presence but the absence of conflict is surprising and abnormal, and we have good reason to be suspicious if we find a society or social organization that displays no evidence of social conflict' (Dahrendorf 1968). Conflict does not necessarily imply violence and bloodshed, of course; it may range from civil war on the one hand to parliamentary debate and letters to a newspaper on the other. In each case, however, we can identify people with differing interests pursuing their own interest.

This indicates a very significant difference from the functionalist or systems perspective. Functionalism reifies society; that is, it treats society as something which has an existence in its own right and so has needs of its own. This is something you will need to think about as you continue your study of sociology. Is it helpful to think about society as a system with needs? Is it more realistic to think about it that way? Can we ever separate society from the people of whom society is composed? Conflict theory on the other hand denies the existence of society as a thing and treats it as being made up of individuals, groups and classes, each with needs, interests and goals of their own.

It was first articulated as a sociological theory by Dahrendorf in 1968.

He identified its historical origins in Plato's *Republic* and in the debate
between Socrates and Thrasymachus (Dahrendorf 1968).

Marx (1818-83)

Its real foundations, however, must be in the works of Karl Marx and
Frederick Engels in the nineteenth century. Marx was one of the most
powerful and influential thinkers of that century. So influential was he,
in fact, that approximately half the world's population now live under
governments described as Marxist. His work draws upon several fields
of knowledge and he demonstrated his own intellectual ability in the
disciplines of philosophy, history, economics and politics, as well as
sociology. Like Comte, Spencer and Durkheim, he could be described as
a product of his time for, like them, he wanted to develop 'a science of
society on the basis of which men could first understand, and then
deliberately change and improve the nature of their social order'
(Jordan 1971). Like the others, too, 'he believed that the efforts to
understand the social processes which were afoot, and the political
efforts to create such a society, required a rigorous scientific study of
man and society' (Fletcher 1971).

The purpose of such rigorous scientific study was to uncover the
invariable laws which governed human activity just as much as they
governed the natural world. To this extent his work can be labelled
positivist and, according to Bottomore (1975), 'Marx considered his own
social theory was closer to being a positive science than was Comte's
positivism.' However, because we are focusing upon the aspect of Marx's
work which underpins the conflict perspective, we should stress that it is
only one aspect of his work and not all his writing is positivist. In fact,
there are two main strands to his work:

1 the individual conquering nature, mastering the environment and
  developing a capacity to control his or her own destiny;
2 the individual being subjected to forces which men have created but
  can no longer control, e.g. capitalism.

Marx based his analysis of society on the materialist conception of
history. In this view history is not a record of wars, monarchs or great
statesmen, but is more a record of how people organize themselves to
satisfy their material needs for food, clothing and shelter. 'The determining factor in history is, in the last resort, the production and
reproduction of material life' (Engels 1884). In other words, the economic
system, the way people organize themselves to 'keep body and soul
together', to produce, determines their whole way of life. Production
involves social relationships. As long as each individual is not doing
everything alone there exists a division of labour, and this will lead to
divisions between skilled and unskilled workers, manual and non-
manual workers, those who produce and those who provide services,

those who give orders and those who do not, those who make decisions and those who do not, and, most fundamental, between owners of capital and those with only their labour to sell. These social relations are 'the real foundation on which legal and political superstructures arise and to which definite forms of social consciousness correspond' (Marx 1859).

Thus, for Marx, work is the sub-structure of society, the foundation upon which the superstructure of family type, conjugal roles, religious beliefs, system of government, laws, etc., is built. The sort of work a society undertakes is the mode of production, and the way people organize themselves to do it constitutes the relations of production. 'The mode of production in material life determines the general character of the social, political and spiritual processes of life. It is not the consciousness of men that determines their existence but, on the contrary, their social existence determines their consciousness' (Marx 1859). Put very simply, it is not the way people think that produces their way of life, but their way of life that produces the way they think.

This can be illustrated at a very elementary, or elemental, level. Imagine that you were one of a dozen people who had been marooned on a desert island or were the sole survivors of some natural disaster. In order to survive you need food but the only food available is a species of nocturnal rabbit. In the first instance your 'mode of production' will be hunting, and, if everybody is required to hunt, your conventional pattern of living by day and sleeping by night must be reversed. Then the way you decide to organize yourselves to catch the rabbits will produce the 'relations of production', that is, who does what. Will everybody fend for themselves, or will there be a division of labour? If so, who will do what? Will the best hunters keep all they catch, or get the biggest share, or will the 'catch' be divided up equally? How will decisions be made? Will the most successful hunters become the leaders, or have higher status? Will they develop more power? What will the position of women be? What will the group value most? Will these values be shared by everybody?

The answers to all these questions would describe the relations of production, but the answers would themselves depend upon the mode of production. That is, they would be different depending upon whether the group decided to gather food, hunt it, grow it or make things which they would exchange for it.

As the mode of production develops and becomes refined, for example as the division of labour increases, then some categories or classes of people will have more influence, more power and more wealth than others. The self-interest of different categories or classes will lead to conflict.

For Marx, history could be divided into different periods, each of which was characterized by a different mode of production. The main periods were ancient civilization, feudalism and capitalism, though he sub-divided these even further. In the period of ancient civilization the dominant mode of production could be described as slavery, and the means were slaves. During feudalism the mode was agricultural and the means land; under capitalism the mode is industrial and the means capital, in all its many forms.

The result of applying this view of history, for Marx, was to conclude that 'The history of all hitherto existing society is the history of class struggles. Freeman and slave, patrician and plebeian, lord and serf, guild-master and journeyman, in a word, oppressor and oppressed, stood in constant opposition to one another, carried on an uninterrupted, now hidden, now open fight. . . .' (Marx and Engels 1848). In any society there are differences of interest stemming from the division of labour and the mode of production. The most fundamental conflict of interest is between those who own the means of production and those who do not. In feudal society the conflict was between those who owned land and those who did not. In capitalist society it is ultimately between owners and non-owners of capital.

Thus, in seeking general laws through which he could understand society and which he could use as a tool for political action, Marx reached several conclusions. Classes exist in all societies. They are aggregates of people (not 'groups' in the usual sociological sense) who share the same relationship to the means of production. In any society there are the 'haves' and the 'have nots', those who own the means of production, land and capital, and those who do not. This fundamental conflict of interest is an inherent part of the structure of any society. In nineteenth-century capitalist Britain Marx wrote, 'the interests of capital and the interests of wage labour are diametrically opposed' (Marx 1848). Basically there were only two classes which he designated 'the bourgeoisie' and 'the proletariat'. He recognized that there existed other classes of people like managers, professionals such as accountants, and small shopkeepers but, ultimately, they would recognize where their 'true interest' lay.

Those who owned the means of production, the bourgeoisie, became the ruling class. They had the power to decide what would be produced, where factories would be built and who would be employed. Their economic power became the basis of political power and they made the law, which would reflect their own interest. But their power went even further. Marx believed that the ruling class also controlled the ideas, the values, the beliefs and philosophies in society. He wrote,

The ideas of the ruling class are in every epoch the ruling ideas: i.e. the class which is the ruling material force of society, is at the same time its ruling intellectual force. The class which has the means of material production at its disposal, has control at the same time over the means of mental production, so that thereby, generally speaking, the ideas of those who lack the means of mental production are subject to it. [Marx 1845]

This is ideology, the notion that the dominant ideas, values and beliefs of a society derive from the dominant class. At the same time they support and reinforce the position of the dominant class by legitimating the *status quo*, that is by ensuring that the population as a whole accepts the inequalities of wealth and power as being justified and proper. Examples might include laws which frustrated the trade unions at different times, religious beliefs which make up the Protestant ethic, with its emphasis on salvation through personal strivings, or the education system being thought of as an avenue of social mobility. Elsewhere we see examples of a ruling class being identified by its colour. So, in South Africa, certain 'cultural' facilities are denied by the ruling whites to other ethnic groups; they contend, for example, that blacks 'are not interested in opera' so a new opera house will be for whites only.

Drawing upon the work of the German philosopher, Georg Hegel, Marx elaborated his view of social change and developed the theory of dialectical materialism. The internal conflicts in society produced not only conflicting social classes but also change from one mode of production to another. Marx was convinced that there was a pattern to these changes, and wrote, 'In broad outline we can designate the Asiatic, the ancient, the feudal and the modern bourgeois methods of production as so many epochs in the progress of the economic formation of society' (Marx 1859). Using Hegel's process of dialectical change, in which thesis and antithesis produce synthesis, Marx claimed that in any of these 'epochs' one class could be regarded as thesis, the other as antithesis, and the outcome of the conflict between the two as synthesis. Each new synthesis contained the seeds of the next conflict and thus further change. Marx provided few concrete illustrations from earlier 'epochs' but concentrated on feudalism and capitalism. He recognized that it was in the interests of both the bourgeoisie and the proletariat to destroy feudalism, but at that point their shared interest ended and self-interest would lead to conflict. In the early stages those sharing the same class position, that is, the same relation to the means of production, would not recognize their common interest because the ruling class ideology is effective. A 'class in itself' would only become 'a class for itself' as class consciousness developed. This would occur as the development of capitalism created large impersonal factories, like those caricatured in Charlie Chaplin's *Modern Times*, which would, in turn, create 'alienation'. A revolution would follow and the new synthesis would be the communist state: 'What the bourgeoisie, therefore, produces, above all, is its own gravediggers. Its fall and the victory of the proletariat are equally inevitable' (Marx and Engels 1848). But until class consciousness develops a person is living in a state of 'false consciousness', not realizing his 'true' class position.

The revolution which Marx predicted for the capitalist Britain he was examining has not occurred and it is not part of our task here to speculate why, interesting though that is. (See pages 37-8 and 170-8). Instead we have to recognize that he has contributed to sociological perspectives a view of society which is dynamic rather than static. It is a view in which changes occur as a result of internal conflicts and, if these changes are subjected to empirical research, the pattern of change which emerges allow us to formulate theory or general propositions in the tradition of positivism.

Weber (1864-1920)

Max Weber's contribution to conflict theory, like Marx before him, represents only one part of his enormous contribution to sociological theory. He is sometimes referred to as 'the bourgeois Marx' because so much of his work was concerned with testing, reassessing or developing Marx's ideas. Like all the other major theorists of class structure, Weber began with Marx's formulation of the question and accepted that class is economic in origin. For Weber, however, stratification was much more than an economically determined class position; it also involved a consideration of status, power and parties. In addition, he showed that class itself was more complex than Marx had described.

Social class was more than just 'relationship to the means of production'. For Weber it was determined by 'market situation'. He begins by accepting that ' "Property" and "lack of property" are the basic categories of all class situations.' He continues, 'Within these categories, however, class situations are further differentiated. . . .' (Weber 1924). There are important distinctions between different kinds of capital or property. A man with a large amount of liquid capital, that is, cash, is in quite a different position from a man with a small amount of fixed capital, for example, a mine or a factory in a remote geographical position. And there are equally important distinctions between different kinds of labour. There are differences between skilled, semi-skilled and unskilled labour, for example, but there are also differences within these categories. A mining engineer cannot easily transfer his skills to, say, carpet manufacture. What is important, says Weber, is the kind of capital or labour which is available in relation to the kinds of capital or labour which are being sought in any particular place. In his own words, '. . . the kind of chance in the market is the decisive moment which presents a common condition for the individual's fate. Class situation is, in this sense, ultimately "market situation" ' (Weber 1924). So in Weber's analysis there is even more scope for conflict.

His analysis not only refines the idea of classes but the whole concept of stratification. For Weber stratification is more than economically determined social class; it extends to differences in status and power. Status is very much a question of the 'social estimation of honour', and although this may very well be based upon property and wealth, it is not necessarily so. In our own society, for example, a pools winner does not necessarily increase the 'social honour' in which he is held by others, but a priest or clergyman may well have little money and high status. Equally there are others who, by virtue of their status, say, 'councillor' or 'professional', or because of particular achievements, may be highly esteemed.

Status groups reinforce their position by developing particular life-styles. Sometimes they sustain their distance by excluding those with certain social characteristics, for example religion, earning a living through manual labour, or expressing certain political views. In addition, 'stratification by status goes hand in hand with a monopoli-zation of ideal and material goods or oppportunities in a manner we have come to know as typical' (Weber 1924). So, in Britain, one status group maintains its exclusiveness through a particular form of educa-tion: prep school, public school and sometimes Oxbridge. This pattern of education then becomes a 'qualification' for certain occupations.

Dahrendorf (b. 1929)

More recently Ralf Dahrendorf, who prefers the term coercion theory to conflict theory, has developed the ideas of Marx and Weber. His argument is simple. 'It is not voluntary co-operation or general consensus but enforced constraint that makes social organization cohere' (Dahrendorf 1959). In coercion theory change and conflict are found throughout society. They are the norm rather than the exception. 'Change and conflict have to be assumed as ubiquitous, all elements of social structure have to be related to instability and change, and unity and coherence have to be understood as resulting from coercion and constraint' (Dahrendorf 1959).

While accepting that Marx's analysis was largely correct he analyses the changes which have occurred in the structure of industrial societies since Marx's day. Capitalism has given way to modern industrial, post-capitalist society. This is due largely to:

1 The decomposition of capital – where companies' capital is more widely spread and managers exercise more control (see page 172).
2 The decomposition of labour – where the division of labour has created many differences between groups of workers (see page 173).
3 The emergence of a 'new middle class' of salaried employees in industry, commerce and government service (see page 176).
4 The institutionalization of social mobility as 'one of the crucial elements in the structure of industrial societies' (see page 178).

(These four factors are particularly important in accounting for the absence of revolution in Britain. They prevented the development of class consciousness which was so necessary in Marxist theory if the class struggle was to succeed.)

5 The growth of equality through progressive taxation and social rights such as pensions, unemployment benefit and health insurance.
6 The 'institutionalization of class conflict', when capital and labour negotiate formally, using agreed procedures to reach compromise solutions.

As a result of these changes class conflict is unlikely to take the form of massive class struggles envisaged by Marx. Instead, in a theory which is intended to cover both capitalist and post-capitalist societies, Dahrendorf highlights authority relationships as the key to understanding conflict. Those who have authority and give orders, on the one hand, and those who are subject to authority and who obey orders, on the other, may be regarded as interest groups. Through their common interest, deriving from authority structures, they become a class. Class conflict, then, is any conflict of groups having different places in the authority structure. It is likely to occur in a variety of institutions. It may occur in industry between owners or management and workers, in politics between parties, in religion between different faiths or sects, in geographical contexts between regions, or in communities between areas. In most cases the conflict will be channelled and institutionalized, in the form of debate or negotiation, but, because of the interrelationship between institutions, there will be occasions when conflicts become superimposed upon one another. Northern Ireland and southern Africa must constitute two such examples.

Application of conflict theory

When this perspective is applied to social phenomena and institutions, as we applied the functionalist perspective earlier, quite different results emerge. The obvious example is stratification. From this perspective social class is the most significant form of stratification, and in any society there will be two fundamentally antagonistic aggregates of people, that is, classes. They are distinguished, by economic factors, into those who have most of the wealth, power and authority and those who do not. There may well be other classes in between but this fundamental distinction remains a basic difference of interest which will keep the classes separate. It produces differences in life-styles, values and attitudes that have been the subject of much research over the past twenty years (see pages 167–8). Some of these differences have been presented in the form of an 'ideal-type' model by Goldthorpe and Lockwood (*see opposite*). This model gives us two sharply contrasting social perspectives, each of which comprises a set of internally consistent beliefs, values and attitudes.

Working-class perspective   Middle-class perspective

General beliefs

The social order is divided into 'us' and 'them': those who do not have authority and those who do.

The division between 'us' and 'them' is virtually fixed, at least from the point of view of one person's life chances.

What happens to you depends a lot on luck; otherwise you have to learn to put up with things.

The social order is a hierarchy of differentially rewarded positions: containing many rungs.

It is possible for individuals to move from one level of the hierarchy to another.

Those who have ability and initiative can overcome obstacles and create their own opportunities. Where people end up depends on what they make of themselves.

General values

'We' ought to stick together and get what we can as a group.

You may as well enjoy yourself while you can instead of trying to make yourself 'a cut above the rest'.

Everyone ought to make the most of their own capabilities and be responsible for their own welfare.

You cannot expect to get anywhere in the world if you squander your time and money. 'Getting on' means making sacrifices.

Attitudes to specific issues
On the best first job

'A good steady job.'

'Learn a trade.'

'As good a start as you can get.'

'A job that leads somewhere.'

Towards people needing social assistance

'They have been unlucky.'
'They never had a chance.'
'It could happen to any of us.'

'Many of them had the same opportunities as others who have managed well enough.'
'They are a burden on those who are trying to help themselves.'

On trade unions

'Trade unions are the only means workers have of protecting themselves and of improving their standard of living.'

'Trade unions have too much power in the country.' 'The unions put the interests of a section before the interests of the nation as a whole.'

SOURCE: Goldthorpe and Lockwood (1963).

At the same time the data concerning the distribution of wealth in Britain indicate, for example in 1977, that 1 per cent of the population owned 23 per cent of the personal wealth, that 5 per cent owned 46 per cent of the wealth, that 10 per cent owned 62 per cent of the wealth, while 80 per cent of the population owned only 18 per cent of the personal wealth in the country (RCDIW, 1979). The stability of these figures, together with the limited amount of social mobility, is taken to indicate the existence of a dominant group which perpetuates the *status quo*. It may do this by using methods which range from open confrontation in industrial disputes, like that of the coal miners in the long strike of 1984/5, to using the police to control pickets or demonstrators, thus 'upholding the law'. Or it may do so through ideology via the church, education and mass media. The more the 'ruling class' becomes conscious of the consequences of its actions the closer we come to the idea of a conspiracy and 'conspiracy theory'

When this perspective is applied to the study of education it is easy to conclude that the education system serves to maintain the existing inegalitarian social and economic arrangements in society, (see pages 246–51). It serves the interests of an elite in two ways: firstly through the structure of the system itself, and secondly through the content and organization of the curriculum. When examining the structure of the education system in Britain, conflict theorists maintain that the private sector is the means by which the elite educates its children and prepares them for elite status. A public school education may still be sufficient 'qualification' for certain jobs, and it is certainly an important avenue to Oxford and Cambridge. Of men entering Oxbridge in the 1960s 54 per cent came from public schools, 16 per cent from direct grant schools and 30 per cent from grammar schools. (The percentage of Oxbridge women from public schools has nearly always been lower.) Oxbridge is also a very important road to certain occupations. 'The civil service [is] very much an Oxbridge – and particularly an Oxford – affair' (Sampson 1965). In addition Sampson has shown that approximately 80 per cent of Church of England bishops, judges and QCs, directors of the Bank of England and members of the Conservative party cabinet (in 1966) attended public and direct grant schools (Sampson 1971). The situation was neatly summed up in the Newsom Report (1963), which said, 'The public schools are not divisive simply because they are exclusive. An exclusive institution becomes divisive when it arbitrarily confers upon its members advantages and powers over the rest of society.'

Conflict theory, in addition to providing this analysis of the system of education, also lends itself to an analysis of the content of education. The school curriculum has come under close scrutiny in recent years and Michael Young has examined the notion of education as knowledge management (see page 264). He sees education as an important agent of social control in so far as it is involved in both the creation and transmission of values and in the institutionalization of knowledge which maintains the social order. Those in positions of power identify certain forms of knowledge as more important than others. Thus, for Young (1971), 'high status knowledge' is characterized by

literacy, or an emphasis on written as opposed to oral presentation; individualism (or avoidance of group work or co-operativeness. . . .); abstractness of the knowledge and its structuring and compartmentalising independently of the knowledge of the learner; finally and linked with the former, the unrelatedness of academic curricula, which refers to the extent to which they are 'at odds' with daily life and common experience.

According to Althusser (1971), education is an 'Ideological State Apparatus'. If 'the ideas of any age are the ideas of the ruling class' then the curriculum, and particularly the high status knowledge which dominates it, can be regarded as a ruling-class view of knowledge. The curriculum is thus a tool of the ruling class, a factor in social control which helps to maintain the *status quo*, including class dominance.

According to the conflict perspective, what counts as valid school knowledge has no relevance in the lives of many pupils, but is imposed on them by 'those who know best'. And if those pupils are low achievers they believe themselves to be unintelligent and accept lower paid work as their legitimate reward.

Religion, too, may be analysed from a conflict perspective, using the concept of ideology (see page 135). For Marx religion was 'the opium of the masses'; it dulled people's senses to the inequalities and rigours of capitalism. Beliefs about salvation and achievement led people to accept such inequalities and hardship as 'legitimate' and normal. No matter what deprivations people suffered in this life they were led to believe that if they accepted their lot and worked hard they would achieve salvation – in the next world if not in this one. This was the only system; capitalism was the God-given way of things, and few thought of challenging it. It is little wonder then that the Church of England has been referred to as 'the Tory party at prayer'.

A conflict theorist's view of crime would emphasize the origin of the laws that have been broken and the interest of those who made them (see pages 331-6). Many laws are concerned with the protection of property, but there are those who would say that 'property itself is theft'. A good example is the statutory claiming, registration and exploitation of land in North America which, until settlement by Europeans, had been held and used communally by native Indian tribes. Other examples include the subjection of blacks to the white man's law of apartheid and their direction to designated 'homelands' in South Africa, or the British land-owners in Ireland in centuries past; when the victims objected they were regarded as criminals.

Conflict theorists would also point to the different treatment which members of different social classes experience in the administration of law enforcement and justice. In most western societies where the police have legitimate discretion, a middle-class white has a much greater chance of avoiding prosecution than a coloured working-class youth, for example.

It is when we come to apply the conflict perspective to the family that it becomes clear that this body of theory has not been developed systematically and coherently in the way that functionalism has. Because conflict theory operates mainly at a macro level, with a view of society as a whole, it has rarely focused on social forms or institutions like the family, and very little has been written on this particular topic. Nonetheless, the application is clear and is described in Chapter 8 (pages 220–21).

The family, like education and religion, is an agent of socialization. In socializing the young the family is, in fact, inculcating values, beliefs and a view of the world which are ideological, that is, which represent the ideas, values and beliefs and world view of the dominant social class.

At the same time if we look at the works of Marx and Engels (1884) then the form of the family to be found in any particular society at a particular point in time will be determined by the mode of production. Whilst we may regard the nuclear family as the most natural thing in the world, this is far from being the case; it has developed with industrialization. In Marxian terms it is part of the superstructure which is determined by the sub-structure of economic activity. Thus in some societies we still find polyandry being practised, in others polygyny, and in every case the form of the family and the mode of production will affect the roles of husbands and wives and the norms of behaviour outside the family.

What emerges from a study of these two perspectives is, especially, that each is focused upon a different question. Functionalism is concerned with the question of *order*, whilst conflict theory is concerned with *control*. Each employs its own set of concepts to analyse its own concern. Where functionalism uses harmony, cohesion, integration, system, consensus and equilibrium, conflict theory uses conflict, coercion, domination, power, dissensus and change.

Drawing upon Dahrendorf we can summarize them in the following manner:

Functionalist/integration theory	*Conflict/coercion theory*
1 Every society is a relatively persistent, stable structure.	1 Every society is, at every point, subject to change.
2 Every society is a well-integrated structure.	2 Every society displays, at every point, dissensus and conflict.
3 Every element in a society has a function, i.e. contributes to the	3 Every element in society makes a contribution to social disinte-

maintenance of the social system.
4 Every functioning social structure is based on a consensus of its members' values.

gration and change.
4 Every society is based on the coercion of some of its members by others.

SOURCE: Dahrendorf (1959).

Phenomenology and interpretive sociology

The approaches discussed so far have been concerned with 'macro' sociology, concentrating on the structures of society and trying to show how even so individual and private an action as suicide can be explained by locating it within these social structures and the connections and interrelationships between them. The emphasis has been on the individual in *society* rather than the *individual* in society. It is this latter emphasis that it now to be considered. Our question is 'How do we create and maintain the society in which we live?' Social facts, rather than being things that should be counted and explained, are seen as *actions that need to be interpreted*. Looking back at Durkheim's work we might ask, 'How reliable are the statistics that he used?' Is it not the case that Catholics are more likely than Protestants to regard suicide as shameful and therefore to disguise its incidence? Will all coroners define it and treat it in the same way? Rather than the statistics themselves it is the method by which they were collected that becomes the focus of interest, and this in turn suggests alternative interpretations and approaches (see pages 68–73).

In the past two decades a number of new perspectives have appeared in sociology, and have led to some new and very important developments in theory and in research. Among the perspectives which have emerged are symbolic interactionism, phenomenology and ethnomethodology. We would like to suggest that, for the purposes of this book and for students coming to the study of sociology for the first time, it is helpful to think of these perspectives as a group, which may be called 'phenomenological' or 'interpretive' sociology. Just as positivist approaches are sometimes called 'macro' or 'structural', so phenomenological approaches sometimes attract the labels of 'interpretative' or 'action'. In this book, several of the authors prefer to use the term 'interpretive'.

These perspectives have reappeared comparatively recently but their origins go back a long way. This serves to remind us that they represent a theoretical controversy about what constitutes a proper method in social science, which goes back an equally long way.

On the one hand there are those who argue that social science should follow as closely as possible the well tried methods of the natural sciences and look for general laws in social life. . . . On the other hand are those who claim that the social sciences differ from the natural sciences either in the character of their subject matter or in their methods or both. [Outhwaite 1975]

Phenomenological or interpretive sociologists fall into the second category. Their work has several roots but an important one lies in Max Weber's notion that sociologists ought to develop an understanding of social action. He actually defined sociology as 'a science which attempts the interpretive understanding of social action in order thereby to arrive at a causal explanation of its course and effects' (quoted in Bendix 1966). By social action Weber meant 'all human behaviour when and in so far as the acting individual attaches subjective meaning to it', (Bendix 1966). It was the sociologist's task to understand and interpret this behaviour and the meaning attached to it. Stated like this it sounds very psychological, and to some extent it is. The sociologist needed to understand what motivated people, what meanings situations had for them, that is, how things appeared to them, and how they subjectively interpreted what they experienced. It is essentially sociological, however, in that it focuses upon the context of meanings, and the context can only be understood as a social context; that is, one in which individuals interact, interpret situations and share meanings. So Saturday night in a pub is usually a time for relaxation, not work, for the customers. When a teacher is talking about a forthcoming exam it's time to listen; examinations have a meaning which most people in the examination class share.

To succeed in this task of understanding what things meant to people the sociologist had virtually to 'stand in other people's shoes'. The sociologist had to try to understand the social forces that caused people to act in a particular way. This is the method called, in German, *Verstehen*. Roughly translated it means 'understanding' but there is no literal translation; hence, we still use Weber's original German word.

Phenomenology is really a school of philosophy which developed in Germany under the inspiration of Edmund Husserl about the time that Mead and the Chicago school (see page 49) were writing in the United States. The word comes from the Greek root, originally meaning 'appearances'. Today phenomenological sociologists are concerned with the 'way things appear' to people, with what Weber would have called 'understanding'. When it is applied by sociologists in practice, however, studying pupils in schools, patients, in hospitals or drug users in the community, it can take many forms. It is not a single, simple, uniform approach. This allows us to suggest a diagrammatic framework for considering the variety of sociological perspectives, as shown in Figure 1.

We are not suggesting for one moment that these are absolute, separate and unrelated categories. As this figure stands it represents an over-simplified view of the relationship between the elements. It does not indicate the subtle blends and mixes that characterize the best

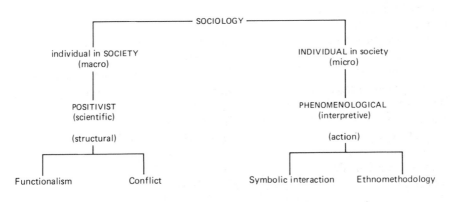

Figure 1 *The variety of sociological perspectives*

sociology. As an ex-A-level student put it, 'an enormous amount of sociology doesn't fall into any of the elements but floats around in the middle'. In this chapter, for example, we have indicated that Parsons's work encompasses more than functionalism, although we located him in the section on functionalism. We have also cited Marx's contribution to conflict theory under macro, positivist approaches, but his work also contributes to phenomenological perspectives. At the same time some concepts employed by phenomenologists lend themselves to the analysis of macro phenomena. And on page 53 we indicate that ethnomethodology is often regarded as a branch of symbolic interactionism. However, we believe this framework is a useful analytical tool for placing concepts, theories and authors into some sort of coherent framework. We hope you will enjoy extending it and investigating its complexities.

You might find the following lists of terms helpful. We hope they will indicate some of the ideas you will encounter and enable you to locate them in different perspectives, at the same time thinking about the connections between them.

Traditional	**Alternative**
Positivist	Interpretive
Structuralist	Interactionist/Phenomenological
Macro	Micro
Normative	Individual
Nomothetic	Idiographic
Quantitative	Qualitative
Measurement	Understanding
Static	Process

Predictive	Responsive
Behaviour	Action
Subjects/respondents	Actors
Generalization	Illumination
Causal explanation	Description
Survey	Case study
Questionnaires	Observation/participant observation
Interview schedules	Open/unstructured interviews
Abstract/universal theory	Grounded theory
Experiment	Ethnography
Objective	Subjective
External	Internal
Publicly verifiable	Unique
Replicable	Negotiable

Although there are differences between them, phenomenological perspectives share many features in common, not least an anti-positivist stance. 'Phenomenological approaches in sociology may be usefully viewed in terms of a reaction against one of the major characteristics of traditional "mainstream" sociology, namely the positivist methodology that the latter emphasizes' (Vulliamy 1973).

In addition they also share the following assumptions:

1 Individuals actively interpret and construct their world.
2 Interpretive research procedures can supplement quantification and surveys.
3 Categories that we usually take for granted should be treated as problematic.

As we have seen, these perspectives are also known as the 'interpretive paradigm', because they emphasize the way individuals interpret their world (and, to some extent, the way researchers themselves interpret a subject's actions).

For these phenomenological approaches to have any validity, it is of course necessary to assume that people are not mere automatons, to be studied as if they were simply very complex machines. Ants and bees cannot help but do what their instincts demand, what they are 'programmed' to do. Their actions are not to be explained as the result of conscious thought, or of likes and dislikes, but as the operation of instinctual responses that preclude the possibility of choice. Human beings, on the other hand, are to be thought of as pre-eminently creatures of choice. They are able to think about the future, imagine the consequences of actions and hence to choose to do this rather than that. Their actions can only be understood if we appreciate the choices they have made and the consciousness of those choices.

Symbolic interactionism

A man who stops his car because he sees a solid brick wall in front of him is reacting to the physical property of the obstruction. If, on the other hand, he stops his car because he sees a red light or a warning sign, he is responding not to the physical property of the sign, but to the meaning that his society has given to that sign. We are always interacting with our environment and with other people, directly when we fall off a cliff, or bump into someone in the dark, and through the medium of symbols when we write a letter, react to the length of someone's hair or the style of their clothes. The physical and the symbolic are always around us and inextricably mixed together, as when we endow material things such as gold with great human value. But as the name implies, that sociological perspective known as symbolic interactionism is concerned primarily with the way that the individual interacts with the symbolic rather than the physical universe.

Symbolic interactionism is American in origin, its basic ideas being found in the work of such men as William James (1842-1910), John Dewey (1859-1952), Charles Horton Cooley (1864-1929), W. I. Thomas (1863-1934) and George Herbert Mead (1863-1931). In different ways and with different emphases they were concerned to assert the importance of the social group for understanding the nature not only of human society but also of human beings. Human beings are social creatures, always to be found in groups, and therefore the study of human behaviour should begin with the fact of human association. The individual separated from society is not typical of human beings – solitary confinement and isolation have long been regarded as the most severe of punishments – and society without individuals is meaningless. If, therefore, we wish to understand either the individual or the society, it must be on the interaction between people that we focus our attention.

Mead, undoubtedly the most influential figure in the development of symbolic interactionism, regarded the existence of society as essential for the 'development of the self' in the individual. It is only as children become aware of other people as individuals that they are able to think of themselves as individuals in their own right, so that an important aspect of play to the human child is that of learning the skill of imaginatively being someone else. This empathetic understanding, of knowing what the other feels, not only enables them to understand the actions of others but also enables them to anticipate how they will react to actions of their own. As they become more aware of other people and how they think and act, so do children become more aware of themselves and of their place in society. It is our membership of a group that gives us our individuality. Becoming a member of society is rather like becoming a member of a team. To behave appropriately as a team member it is not enough to know how to perform your own part thoroughly, you must also have a good understanding of the roles of all the other members of the team. You must be able to anticipate what they are likely to do. An understanding of what is possible for them to do, taking into account both the rules of the game and the abilities of the players, enables you as team member to put your own role in context.

Similarly in society we do not simply react to the gestures that people make towards us, but we interpret them and then select the best response for the occasion. Someone we know waves to us from across the street. Their intention may be to give a friendly greeting, to invite us to stop for a chat, or to insult us. Before we can respond appropriately we must decide what their gesture meant to them, what they intended, as we must try to ensure that the gesture we make in response is understood in the way that we intend: we wish to acknowledge the greeting, but also indicate that we have no time to stop to chat. Our interaction with other people is a series of responses mediated by this self-conscious monitoring process. It is contrasted with the way we blink our eyes when something is thrust towards us or the way our leg will jerk if the knee is tapped in the correct place, and it depends upon our being able to put ourselves 'inside the head' of the other person.

However, our responses are never completely predictable. We may intend to make a friendly remark, but the words that come out might well be tactless, and we then become conscious of the meaning of our actions after they have taken place. In fact it is only at that point that we might become fully aware of what we intended, as we contemplate what we actually did.

From the interactionist perspective, therefore, the study of society is based on the assumption that human beings make sense of the world through their interaction with other human beings. If we do not eat then we will die; that is a fact of our existence, of the chemistry of our bodies. But what we choose to eat, what we define as food, is the result of our participation in a society, and we may end up dying rather than eat something that nutritionally is perfectly adequate food. Despite Britain's involvement in the Common Market many English people find it difficult to think of snails as a delicacy to be eaten. We act towards things on the basis of the meanings that things have for us and not simply on the physical properties of those things. But although those meanings are created by the interaction of members of our society, they are not the same for us all. We interpret the situations in which we find ourselves on the basis of our past experience, and in this respect every individual is unique. Consequently meanings change as new interpretations are reflected back to us from the response of others and from our perceptions of our own actions as we live in the world.

The interactionist perspective, therefore, seeks to explain a situation by taking into account the actor's definition of it; behaviour becomes explicable when it is understood from the point of view of the actor.

Unfortunately there is no simple way of discovering the point of view of the actor. M. H. Kuhn, who worked at the University of Iowa from 1946 until his death in 1963, approached the problem of developing questionnaires and attitude scales on the principle that the best way to find out what someone thinks of themselves is to ask them. His most famous test, variously known as the TST (twenty statements test) or the WAI (who am I?), consists of asking the subject to write down twenty statements in answer to the question 'Who am I?' – without spending too much time thinking about it. The results are then subjected to various statistical techniques, and hence the self-concepts of various groups can be established. However, this approach is more in accord with the techniques of traditional mainstream sociology; its ultimate aim is to derive scientific laws that will explain the facts that research has accumulated, and which will enable the social scientist to predict and so to control. It is in the positivist tradition, modelled on the methods of the natural scientist.

But as has long been recognized there are important differences between studying the properties of, for example, metals and the properties of societies. With metals the problem is one of the isolation of variables, and of accurate measurement; the scientist does not have to consider what attitude the metal takes to his experiment, whether it minds being heated up, for example. But this is precisely what the social scientist does have to consider. The work of the linguist, Labov, provides a good illustration. He demonstrated that attempts to measure the speech of children were crucially affected by the nature of the testing situation. A black child when given a language test – such as being asked to identify and describe a toy aeroplane – by a white-coated doctor in the clinical environment of a hospital or university might well refuse to speak at all. But this should not be taken to mean that he cannot express himself in language – as Labov was able to show by getting a black interviewer to talk to the child in a park near his home (Labov 1969). Clearly, the results of any pencil and paper test must be affected by the attitudes of the people being tested to the fact of their being tested, who is testing them, and where the test is taking place. Tests produce quantifiable data, but at the expense of over-simplifying complex situations.

In fact the bulk of work that is clearly influenced by the symbolic interactionists lies outside this mainstream of American sociology, and has been particularly associated with the University of Chicago, where Mead himself was a professor of philosophy, and where his work was carried on and developed by H. G. Blumer. The Chicago school, in contrast to pencil and paper tests and questionnaire techniques, laid great stress on the use of observational procedures, such as interviews (particularly of the open-ended or non-directive type where the respondent is encouraged to talk rather than simply answer set questions), auto-biographies, case-studies and, pre-eminently, participant observation (see pages 69–71).

For this to be successful it is necessary for sociologists to engage in a task not dissimilar to translating from a foreign language. They must be sufficiently familiar with the group they are studying to make sense of their behaviour, or rather to understand what their behaviour *means* to the group, and they must then find a way of making these discoveries intelligible to people who have a different perspective. The language of academic journals and textbooks of sociology is far removed from that of, say, a Glasgow street corner gang. To understand what is is like to be a member of such a gang, to find out what they do and what their activities mean to them, and then to explain it all in academic English without losing the essential flavour of the experience, requires a considerable literary as well as sociological talent.

Our understanding of minority groups and deviants has been profoundly affected by studies attempting this task of interpretive understanding, and it is in these ethnographic studies that the close relationship of sociology and anthropology can most easily be seen. Perhaps the most vivid writer in this tradition is Erving Goffman, who is virtually a school on his own. Goffman is associated with what has been called the 'dramaturgical approach' to the study of interaction. Social encounters are described in theatrical terms – the people involved are following scripts, they know what are appropriate things to say to the doctor when he says 'How are you?' just as they will all be part of a different play when a friend asks them the same question on the street. Goffman is an acute observer of all these encounters and his descriptions of how people cope with shame – how do you face your friends immediately after being reprimanded by the teacher? – and of how people generally present themselves in public are always interesting and full of insights. In latter years, however, he has been more concerned to provide us with concepts for analysing social encounters than to provide us with analyses of actual situations. In his book *Asylums* (1961), for example, he uses the concepts of 'depersonalization', 'mortification' and 'stigma'.

Phenomenology and ethnomethodology

Sitting in a darkened theatre, watching the actors on stage, it is easy to become so immersed in the action of the play that we forget it is not 'real life'. At the cinema, similarly, we may so identify with the action on the screen that we may feel fear, laugh out loud or even cry; only afterwards do we say, 'It was only a film!' Even in the familiar surroundings of our own home, in the company of family or friends, the pictures produced on a small screen can so engage our attention that we begin to believe in the reality of the characters – to be concerned about what happens to them, to have hopes and fears for their future. A popular series, such as *EastEnders*, clearly involves many people in just this way.

How is this illusion created? What must the playwright, actor, producer and cameraman do to make us forget that the words spoken are learned, not spontaneous, that the actions are rehearsed and that we are looking at pictures, not life?

Confronted by a poor play or bad acting it is easy for us to become aware of these things. If an actor forgets his lines or a fight is clumsily staged the illusion is shattered and we see the play for what it really is – not real life but a pretence. The theatre critic is one who, while watching the drama, must retain total awareness of the parts played by the script, the techniques of the actor, and the understanding of the producer in creating the play. The critic tries to reduce the action on the stage, the object of his or her consciousness, to the phenomena out of which it is constituted – script, acting, etc. – and then to appraise the importance of each part. Is it a good play ruined by bad acting? A good play, good actors, but badly produced? And so on.

Perhaps we can analyse real life in a not dissimilar way. We tend to take the world around us for granted. We are not constantly amazed that water is available at the turn of a tap, that buses arrive at predictable times, nor that the shops sell the things that we need. We have the 'illusion' that these things are normal, and it is only at times of crisis, when for some reason or other they fail to materialize, that we become aware that the world we live in does not just exist independently of us, but that we have also created parts of it. This is quite obvious if we think of a town or city, but it is important to remember that we have also created a sea that contains much more oil and far fewer whales, and a landscape in which trees have been removed, deserts created and forests planted. We have played a significant part in the distribution of the wild life of the world and, in addition, have created new animals of our own, such as 'toy' dogs, and cows that produce enormous quantities of milk. Without our active intervention and control the world would soon become a very different place, as all gardeners are painfully aware. As we go about our daily business we are in interaction with other people and with the material world around us; the people we meet affect and change us just as we affect and change them, while our burning of petrol or wasting of paper in turn means that oil has been extracted from the earth and that trees have been cut down. The world is a constantly changing place.

But what is it really like? Always we have before us the phenomena of the world – the objects that we can see, that we are conscious of – and the illusion that they are as they appear, that they could not be otherwise. But familiar objects seen in unfamiliar surroundings look strange to us – we see features of them that we never noticed before. And in fact we can often make familiar objects appear strange by looking at them critically, or by imagining how they might appear to someone else, and perhaps thereby gaining a fuller understanding of what they are really like – of what constitutes the phenomenon.

This is the project of the phenomenologist. For the phenomenologist society cannot be studied separately from the individuals who comprise it, neither can the individuals be understood without reference to society, for it is the interaction of people that produces both the group and the awareness of self in the individuals. In a rather similar way the phenomenologists argue that we can never perceive reality without first filtering it through our consciousness. Consciousness is always consciousness of something; we cannot separate the object from our awareness of it. What we can do is try to describe the various phenomena that make up the object; to reduce the object of consciousness to the phenomena out of which it is constituted.

For instance we are aware that there are rules which govern our behaviour, but many of them are hidden from our notice by virtue of the fact that they are so familiar to us. The problem for the sociologist is that if it is not always apparent to the people concerned what the rules are that govern their behaviour, how is it possible for the sociologist to discover them? We are now in the realm of the ethnomethodologist.

The ethnomethodologist is particularly interested in the unspoken rules which govern our day-to-day interactions – at home, on the bus or train, at work, in shops, in the street or even on the telephone. These unspoken rules are the unexamined, taken-for-granted bases of human action which the ethnomethodologist wishes to discover.

The term ethnomethodology was coined by Harold Garfinkel when he was investigating the work of a group of jurors by analysing tape recordings of their deliberations. He was particularly interested in 'how the jurors knew what they were doing in doing the work of jurors' (Garfinkel 1968 in Turner 1974). He concluded that they held certain assumptions, rules and methods in common. They were concerned with adequate accounts, adequate description, adequate evidence and with being legal. They had definite notions of evidence and of adequate demonstration, of relevance and of methodic procedure. Garfinkel wanted a term to label this phenomenon in a way that would remind him of its essential elements. Faced with a group of jurors who were 'doing methodology', 'ethno' seemed to refer to their common-sense knowledge and understandings of their society and situation. Thus the term referred originally to the methods of the subjects as they constructed their social world rather than to the methods of the sociologist observing subjects.

It is not easy to identify these methods and processes, so ethnomethodologists often disturb the normal, taken-for-granted ways of doing things and study the reaction of the people involved. For example, the researcher returns to her parents' home, but instead of behaving as usual on such visits she behaves as she does when lodging in a stranger's house. She then studies the reaction of her parents to her behaviour. From the point of view of the parents, initially at least, the situation is a familiar one, but it then gradually becomes one of crisis as their 'normal' rules of conduct in the familiar situation of 'child returning home' are found not to work. It is rather like an experienced cook preparing a familiar dish, the recipe for which was memorized long ago. It has always worked before, but now inexplicably it repeatedly fails. At first the cook ignores the failure expecting success next time, but as the expectations are repeatedly frustrated the cook will check the ingredients carefully, re-read the recipe, make sure the oven is operating correctly and so on. The things that before were done as a routine are now done consciously; what was previously assumed is now checked. Our researcher, herself the faulty ingredient, observes and records and tries to discover the rules previously assumed by her parents and, of course, by herself as well.

There are two rather different emphases that might be distinguished here. On the one hand there is the concern to understand how the social world became as it is – how it was created. How does it happen that parents have expectations that their children will behave in certain ways? How does it happen that in one society it is customary to queue and in others it is not? Clearly these customs change over time, they are built up with use, and so we may ask, 'How was the social world constructed?' 'By what processes do we sustain it?'

On the other hand we might choose to focus our attention more narrowly on the rules that govern our behaviour. We might ask, 'What are the rules that parents expect their children to observe?' 'How is queueing done in various societies?' This latter approach might be thought of as producing the perfect handbook for an undercover agent as it focuses on the everyday routines of social life, explaining how people greet each other, open telephone conversations, take their turn in shops and so on. It is often regarded as a distinct branch of sociology and, by some, as not sociology at all, but a quite separate enterprise.

In fact ethnomethodology is often regarded as a branch of symbolic interactionism and the two might be thought of as the 'micro' complement to functionalism because their emphasis on the small group and the interaction of individuals tends to ignore, and perhaps thereby take for granted, the wider social context in which the action takes place. Critics point to the fact that most of the writing in this tradition relates to minority, deviant, and relatively powerless people. The sociologist is seen as a spy from the dominant groups, who penetrates the world of the oppressed and brings back information about their habits, thoughts and organizations, and thus enables the oppressor to take appropriate action.

Perhaps phenomenological approaches are less susceptible to this criticism, in that their basic stance is to 'make problems' rather than to 'take problems', to locate that which is taken for granted and to explore the reasons why it is so. There is much in this perspective, therefore, to appeal to those who are dissatisfied with things as they are: to conflict theorists, for instance, who need to explain why the apparent injustices of society are not perceived more clearly by the individuals concerned but leave them in a state of 'false consciousness'.

However, having tried to draw some distinctions between interpretive approaches, it is important to stress again that there are many inter-relationships, with the perspectives being complementary rather than discrete.

Application of phenomenological perspectives

The early 1970s saw a distinct shift in emphasis in the sociology of education from the macro level of analysis to the micro, and with it an increasing emphasis on interpretive approaches. Indeed it has become customary to refer to the 'new sociology of education' when referring to the work of such people as M. F. D. Young, who edited the very influential book *Knowledge and Control* (1971), and this orientation is also reflected in the Open University course 'School and Society'. Schools, and particularly classrooms, provide excellent laboratories for the application of the techniques favoured by symbolic interactionists, and several such pieces of research have been reported in the last few years (see pages 260–2).

Whereas positivist researchers, and particularly those working within a functionalist perspective, have *taken* educators' problems as given, more recent researchers working within an interpretive framework have *made* their problems by questioning the categories which the positivists had begun to take for granted. So they question what we understand by 'under-achievement', 'failure', 'deprivation', etc. They ask, for example, 'What are pupils failing at? What counts as educational knowledge? What do we understand by schooling?'

When we ask questions like this it may lead to radical reappraisal of certain actions and policies. Bernstein has suggested, for example, that the concept of compensatory education and related ideas about working-class pupils' under-achievement is misleading because it focuses attention almost exclusively on what are claimed to be deficiencies in the child and his or her family. It 'serves to direct attention away from the internal organisation and the educational context of the school' (Bernstein 1971).

Howard Becker is an American sociologist who has not concerned himself directly with schools but has conducted research with medical students (1961). His work illustrates clearly how the phenomenon of medical school appears to the participants, the students and the tutors. The student group develops its own culture, which in this context is defined differently from the anthropological definition of 'life-style', which is used by macro theorists. Culture in this context is the set of shared understandings which emerge as the students face a common problem (of becoming doctors), and define their situation in a way which is meaningful to them rather than accepting their tutors' definitions. In effect this means that the students define their clinical work as most important and they arrange their priorities accordingly. Fred Davis used a similar phenomenological approach to study the socialization of nurses. He observed the subjective process whereby student nurses moved from their original definition of their role to a professionally approved definition (Davis 1972).

When this approach is applied to education, we might ask how pupils define their situation, what subjective meanings they bring to school with them and what meaning school has for them. In addition we might examine the assumption, so frequently taken for granted, that pupils and teachers share the same meanings. David Hargreaves's work at Lumley (1967), indicates that, for the 'delinquescent' or anti-school pupil sub-culture at least, pupils and teachers define the situation differently.

Once we start to question taken-for-granted assumptions we are led to a reconsideration of what counts as school knowledge, achievement, ability and failure. Cicourel and Kitsuse (1963) examined the way students came to be classified as 'college-going' or 'under-achieving', particularly by counsellors who had a significant effect on a student's career. Social class influenced the way teachers and counsellors processed and channelled students into particular courses. Middle- and upper-income students were more likely to be put into college-preparatory courses than lower-income students with similar academic records. In Britain, Nell Keddie's study, *Classroom Knowledge*, concludes that 'ability is an organising and unexamined concept for teachers whose categorisation of pupils on the grounds of ability derives largely from social class judgements of pupils' social, moral and intellectual behaviour' (Keddie 1971).

In this field, Hargreaves is one of the better-known figures and his work serves also to link education with the study of deviance in society, through labelling theory (Hargreaves 1975). Labelling theory has developed from the suggestion that the focus of study in deviance should 'shift from an exclusive concern with the deviant individual to a major concern with the process by which the deviant label is applied'. Hargreaves and his collaborators have used participant observation in the classroom to record and examine the sequence of events that culminates in the deviant label being applied to certain pupils and the acceptance by the pupils of that label. By examining the practices of teachers and pupils it is hoped that classroom behaviour will be better understood, and seen as the product of interaction rather than as the problem personality (see pages 261–2).

The application of this paradigm to the 'problem' of crime and delinquency leads researchers to ask quite different sorts of questions (see pages 324–9). More traditional researchers would ask:

Who is deviant?
How did they become deviant?
What areas or conditions produce most delinquents?
How can they be cured or controlled?

The phenomenologist would probably ask:

Under what circumstances do people become set apart and defined
  as deviants?
How are they cast in that role?
How do others respond to them when they are so defined?
How does the deviant respond to this definition?
How does such labelling affect his or her self-concept?

The functionalist approach viewed crime as deviance from established
norms (see pages 314–24). Crime was explained in terms of the individual's failure to internalize those norms during socialization. It is a
failure of socialization and leads to prescriptions of punishment and
'cure'. The conflict theorist might relate crime to deprivation and
alienation, resulting from factors like urban dereliction or neglect by the
'establishment', which chooses to spend money on new office blocks and
commercial ventures (or even minority interests like church-building).
The real vandals are seen as the investors, the planners and demolition
men who break up the old communities. As a result of such a situation,
Laurie Taylor has suggested that 'kids fall into trouble like ducklings
into water'.

By contrast, phenomenological perspectives examine the way situations appear to the delinquents themselves, that is the process by which
they define, interpret and put constructions on their situation. Clearly,
labelling and the definitions of others are significant here.

Applied to the family, the interpretive approach similarly involves
trying to achieve an understanding of process, how the members of the
family interact and the significance of their interactions for each other.
Peter Berger and Hansfield Kellner produced a paper 'Marriage and the
construction of reality' (1964), which illustrates this well and which also
indicates the need to interpret statistics, rather than to 'let the facts
speak for themselves'. They suggest that the commonly held assumption
that rising divorce rates indicate a decline in the importance of marriage
is wrong. Rather they claim that the fact that many of the divorced
remarry indicates that marriage is so important that couples have a lack
of tolerance 'for the less than completely successful marital arrangement
they have contracted with the particular individual in question . . . the
frequency of divorce simply reflects the difficulty and demanding
character of the whole undertaking' (see pages 235–37).

The practice of social work has been much affected by work in this
tradition, tending to deflect attention away from the individual and to

focus instead on the family as a unit, and increasingly to locate that family in the community of which it is a part.

Conclusion

What then are we to make of this variety of perspectives? Does one invalidate all the others? Is there one which is 'better' than the others? Not necessarily. We believe that each perspective offers insights which illuminate each 'problem' to some degree but, as yet, no one form of theorizing has overtaken all the others; nor is it likely to.

We need constantly to remind ourselves that all an approach like Marxism, or interactionism, or functionalism or ethno-methodology can do is to strike a more or less complex balance about the priority of individual or society. . . . It is possible to plump for one type or level or explanation as basic and to see the rest as derivative. But society's (and sociology's) existence depends upon there being reciprocal relationships between these levels. [Davies 1976]

So it is not a question of which one is 'best' or 'truest'. The great American sociologist, C. Wright Mills, reminds us of the need to be practical when he writes, 'the requirements of one's problem, rather than the limitations of any one rigid method, should be and have been the classic social analyst's paramount consideration' (1959).

The 'choice' of perspective will depend largely on the questions we ask.

Guide to further reading

The most readable book, by far, on sociological perspectives is Brown (1979), *Understanding Society*. He elaborates upon the perspectives outlined in this chapter. Cuff and Payne (1984), *Perspectives in Sociology*, provides a little more detail, but is probably more useful as a source of reference. For those who would like to pursue these issues in more detail, there are *Approaches to Sociology*, edited by John Rex (1975), or Lewis Coser's *Masters of Sociological Thought* (1977). Ronald Fletcher's work is always readable and his *Making of Sociology* (1971) is very detailed.

Editors' note Many of the examples given in this chapter are used again, usually at greater length, later in this book. This is deliberate, and is intended to help you grasp the ideas more easily by reading them more than once, when used in different contexts. You will find that many cross-references are given in this book, and you should always follow them up.

You should regard this chapter as your 'base', to which you will regularly return for revision.

3 Social research

Patrick McNeill

This chapter is not a guide to good research practice, nor an instruction manual on how to prepare a questionnaire or a random sample. If you do need practical guidance on these matters, you should refer to one or more of the texts referred to in *Guide to further reading* at the end of the chapter.

What this chapter will do is to discuss some of the important questions that lie behind the different methods, and demonstrate the relations between theory and method. In addition, we shall consider a number of other topics related to the whole question of social research.

But what is true of all the topics discussed throughout this book is most true of this chapter: there is no substitute for reading the original books. Obviously, some research reports are very long and some are very difficult to follow. But there are many which are very readable and very interesting. You will learn more about 'participant observation', for example, from reading Whyte (1955, 1981), especially the Appendix, than from reading any number of textbooks, including this one.

The basic questions

Sociologists start from the assumption that there are patterns and regularities in social life. In seeking to inquire into these regularities, they are faced with two basic questions: What shall I study? and How shall I study it? These questions are, clearly, interrelated, but we will consider them one at a time, and then draw them together.

Concealed within the first question is another – what is the purpose of my research? Is it simply to describe something in the way that, for example, Charles Booth described poverty in London at the end of the nineteenth century? Or is it to attempt to analyse and explain something, as Oscar Lewis (1961, 1966) set out to explain the causes of poverty? What I choose to study will be influenced, in part, by whether my primary purpose is simply to describe, or whether it is also to analyse and explain. In practice, of course, it is not possible to do one without the other. The choice will be further influenced by whether I am also hoping to get something changed.

The answer to this first question necessarily involves a judgement about what is interesting and/or worthwhile. Such a judgement is based on the values of the researcher, and also, incidentally, on the values of those who control research funds. It is likely to be easier to get financial support for an inquiry into ways of increasing workers' productivity than for an inquiry into how to negotiate higher pay rises. You may feel that these are the right priorities, but it is nevertheless a judgement, not a necessary or inevitable fact of life. All research, in all areas of knowledge, takes place within a framework of judgements about what is worthwhile.

Another important set of considerations concerning what is worthwhile is determined by the state of sociology at the time. Sociologists will have ideas about what is important, and which questions need to be answered if sociological knowledge is to advance (see the discussion of Kuhn's work, page 133). Closely related to this will be the researcher's ambition to do work in an area regarded as important by other sociologists, and therefore likely to improve career prospects. Again, these points are as true of natural science as they are of social science.

Having decided what to study, the researcher then has to decide what particular aspects of the chosen topic to concentrate on, and this too reflects prior assumptions. If you wish to study the occurrence and causes of marital breakdown, you are unlikely to start by recording the colour of divorced men's hair, or the day of the week on which divorced women were born. Having first decided exactly what 'marital breakdown' should mean, one type of researcher will tend to investigate housing conditions, or age at marriage, or income level, or numbers of children, etc. In other words, there will be from the start a half-formed theory about what is being investigated, which will guide the research in a certain direction.

This search for causes is typical of what you now know as the 'positivist' tradition in sociology. By contrast, a researcher in the 'interpretive' tradition, who is also interested in marital breakdown, will be less concerned with looking for causes. The research questions might be 'What is "marital breakdown"?' 'How is it that married couples, and their friends, and the divorce courts, come to regard a marriage as "broken down"?' This researcher will want to study very different aspects of marriage, and collecting statistics about this or that will not necessarily help very much.

This, then, raises the second major question of *how* to study social life, that is, what approach to adopt and what techniques to use.

This brings us back to the positivist/interpretive division in sociology. The positivist sociologist aims to follow the example of the natural scientist, for that perspective believes that the subject matter of the two fields of inquiry are essentially similar. There is an objective world 'out there', whether we know about it or not. It operates according to its own laws of cause and effect, to which we are subject, and which are waiting to be discovered. The problem is to devise techniques which are capable of making these discoveries. The task of the scientist, natural or social, is to seek out these laws by following a precise method which is itself objective and unbiased. The researcher must not allow emotion or opinion to affect logical judgement. The facts are simply there, like it or not. They can be measured, counted and otherwise expressed in quantitative terms, and it is in these terms that data should be collected and analysed. The hope is that, eventually, enough of these laws will be known to enable us to predict the future and, therefore, to exercise some kind of control over events. This is what the natural scientists have done, and they have been, in many ways, remarkably successful.

The phenomenological or interpretive sociologist, on the other hand, starts with different assumptions about social reality. This perspective stresses that society is not so much an objective reality as a subjective one, or rather an intersubjective one, that is, it exists in the shared world-view of the social actors who comprise it. A social situation is the outcome of the interaction and shared world-view of those participating in it. Social actions are the result not of external social pressures, but of people choosing to behave as they do. The choices they make are the result of their definition of the situation they are in. The patterns and regularities that are discernible are the consequence of definitions being shared among groups of people, who therefore behave in similar and largely predictable ways. It may be that others, including the researcher, disagree with the interpretation, even finding it offensive or dangerous, but this is irrelevant. The researcher's task is to investigate how the people under scrutiny view the world around them, and how they make sense of it *in their terms*.

Interpretive and positivist sociology, then, have different views of the nature of society, of individuals, and of the relationship between them. The positivist will tend to see society as the object of study, and the individual as a relatively passive product of it. The interpretive sociologist regards the individual as a conscious, active, choice-making being, and society as the outcome of all their collective action. The research methods of the former are aimed at discovering the objective and impersonal facts about society; the methods of the latter are devised to make it possible to get at the individual's consciousness and to spell out the shared world-view. The positivist will tend to regard the fact that, in social science, people study people, as a potential source of problems of bias, lack of objectivity, etc. Interpretive researchers exploit to the full the fact that their own social skills made it possible for them to 'get inside the head' of others, and to see the world as their subjects do. They will be objective in the sense that every attempt will be made to avoid introducing personal prejudice, but they will be subjective in the sense of making the most of their ability to think as their subject matter does. Where positivist sociologists will look for the causes of human behaviour in factors external to the people being studied, interpretive researchers ask, 'What is going on here?' 'How do these people define their situation?' and 'How do these definitions affect their actions?'

With these different assumptions and approaches, positivist and interpretive sociologists tend to use different research methods, and we will return to a more detailed consideration of these on pages 68–74.

But whatever method we are considering, we must always remember that the facts do not speak for themselves. All observation and measurement, however apparently objective and unbiased, involves making a selection from what is there, and this selection is made within a framework of prior knowledge and assumptions. Different people will therefore see different things. Consider two examples of this:

1　Four people are in a field full of cows grazing. They are a geologist, a botanist, a biologist, and the farmer. What does each one see?
2　Four people are walking down a crowded shopping street. They are a housewife, a police officer, a roadsweeper, and a pickpocket. What does each one see?

Given that each one will actually see something different, how far is it true to say that they are standing in the same field, or walking down the same street? Are there, in fact, 'multiple realities'? If they are walking down 'different' streets, whose street is the 'right' or 'real' one?

Theories, concepts and models

Sociologists are agreed that what they are trying to do is to produce knowledge which is superior to commonsense or conventional wisdom. In this limited sense, they are agreed that what they are doing is science, though there are disagreements about what this entails, as we shall see on pages 63–8.

Good sociology, it is claimed, is superior to commonsense because it is based on evidence derived from research, and it argues logically and systematically from that evidence. Though there is disagreement about what counts as good evidence, there is agreement that good evidence and logical arguments are what are needed. Such argument involves the use of theory, concepts and models.

A 'theory' is a general statement or set of statements about reality which is, as far as possible, established, tested, and supported by reference to evidence. A 'substantive theory' concerns an aspect of the behaviour of a particular society or group, for example, a theory about industrial conflict in Britain. 'Formal theory' aims to establish general statements about human social relationships, wherever they may be found, for example, a theory about why people accept the authority of others. Theory is built up through the assembling of facts and evidence, and ordering them into a systematic framework. It develops through the use of concepts and models.

'Concepts' are words that refer to abstract things or ideas. We use them to label the underlying quality or essence of what we are referring to, and to identify the quality held in common by a number of different objects or events. If I say 'That's not fair', I am using a concept, 'fair', and saying that some particular action or proposal does not fit in with it. You may disagree, either because you do not share my concept of fairness, or because, though sharing my concept, you think that the particular action *does* fit in with it.

Concepts should be used only in so far as they help to clarify thinking. They should be precise; their meaning should be agreed; they should refer to something that can be studied or analysed; we should be able to relate them to each other. Unfortunately, not many sociological concepts meet all these rigorous standards. Particularly, not all sociologists use the same concept in the same way, as you will see. Nevertheless, many sociological concepts have been developed which have proved to be important tools in the attempt to understand the social world.

Since concepts are abstract, they must be 'operationalized' for research purposes. For example, 'temperature' is a concept. To measure it, scientists have invented thermometers which give a quantitative measure of the temperature, usually based on the expansion rate of mercury. The concept is thus operationalized and quantified.

The same is true of a sociological concept like 'social class'. This is an abstract idea. What is needed is something more concrete which we can classify and count and which is a satisfactory 'indicator' of social class. In our society, we can often use occupation as this indicator (see page 158). 'Occupation' is not the same as social class, but we can say that the people in a particular occupational group (say, dentists) have in common many of the qualities that are wrapped up in the concept 'social class'. We thus operationalize the concept, and can conduct research on it. A common problem which arises when comparing one piece of research with another is that different sociologists have operationalized the same concept in different ways.

'Models' are the next stage in theory-building. These are tentative descriptions of the relations between the phenomena we are studying. They are not right or wrong, nor are they attempts to describe things as they really are. Rather, they aim to link concepts and evidence into a pattern which will throw light on reality. The model is a good one to the extent that it helps us to think more clearly about what we are studying, and opens up new possibilities for inquiry.

Figure 1 on page 45 of this book is a model of sociological theory. It is not saying that sociology is like this. It is saying, 'If you think about sociological theory like this, it will help you make sense of the immensely complex reality that you will be dealing with'. It is not to be assessed as right or wrong, but it should be evaluated in terms of whether it helps students to understand more about social theory, or whether it is either too difficult or positively misleading.

Good theory, then, is built up through the use of concepts, models, and research findings. It is superior to commonsense because it is based on evidence and on logical argument.

Sociology and science

'Science' and scientific knowledge have enormous status in our society. Sociology claims to be a 'social science', and, for many people, if it cannot show that this name is deserved, then sociological knowledge is devalued.

When we refer to 'science', we tend to mean 'natural science'. In the nineteenth century, where modern sociology has its roots, science and technology were having conspicuous success in enabling mankind to establish control over the natural world, and this is, broadly, still the case. Huge progress has been made in combating many diseases (though others have become more widespread); enormous increases in food production have been achieved (though its distribution around the world is not so successful); the limitations imposed by the cycle of night and day and of the seasons have been largely overcome in industrial societies. Western nations, particularly, have become absorbed in their attempt to control and dominate nature, and thus to become, as they see it, masters of their destiny. Science is seen to work. It produces the goods, both literally and metaphorically.

Nineteenth-century social science was caught up in this web of ideas. The purpose of social science was to reveal the laws of social life so as to predict and thereby control human behaviour, to the ultimate benefit of all.

During this century, the traditional view of science and technology has taken a considerable battering. We are much more aware of the destructive side of scientific 'progress', and of the abuse of nature that technology may involve. We know that scientists have often been wrong, or only half-right, and that much of what they do is not quite the same as what they claim to do (see pages 132-5).

However, despite this increasing scepticism, and the loss of status that has accompanied it, valid knowledge, in contrast to guesswork, superstition or commonsense, is still regarded as that which is developed through 'objective' investigation and analysis, based on rational argument derived from the 'facts'. It is therefore still important to consider the scientific status of sociology.

Whether or not sociology is a science depends on what is meant by

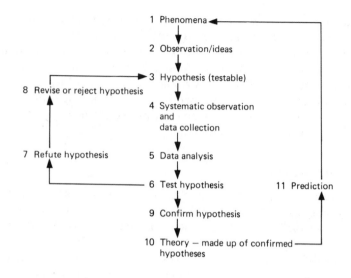

Figure 2   *The hypothetico-deductive model*

science, and the crucial point to appreciate here is that science is not a body of knowledge but a method of approaching and studying phenomena. It involves identifying a problem to study, collecting evidence about it and, eventually, offering an explanation for it. All this is done as systematically as possible.

The traditional way in which this is supposed to have been done in natural science is usually represented as the 'hypothetico-deductive model', as in Figure 2. You should look at it now, and follow the explanation through, using the numbered references.

Traditionally, again, the process was assumed to start with the phenomena (1), out there in the world, which could be objectively observed by scientists (2). As we have seen, it is now recognized that all observation occurs within a framework of previous assumptions, and we must be aware that the process is more of a cycle than a line with a beginning and an end.

However, the model in the diagram assumes that the phenomena are there, and that quite casual everyday observation (2) produces ideas about them (this process is known, technically, as induction). From these, the scientist develops an hypothesis (3). Let us take, as an example, the hypothesis that rising incomes lead to changing political attitudes. This hypothesis must be spelled out in a way that can be tested, using concepts that have been operationalized. Data relating to the hypothesis are then systematically collected (4), and analysed (5). The hypothesis is tested (6), that is, the data are analysed to see whether there is, in reality, a link between rising incomes (easily measured) and changed political attitudes (operationalized, perhaps, in terms of voting behaviour). If the hypothesis is not supported by the evidence (7), it may be repeated or revised (8), and a fresh hypothesis developed (3). If it is confirmed (9), then it contributes to the development of theory (10). If the theory becomes sufficiently elaborate, it becomes possible to think of it as a law, and to predict future phenomena from it (11). This latter stage is the 'deductive' phase of the process.

The problem with observation and data collection in the real world is that it is very difficult to isolate what is being studied from the mass of other phenomena around it. In natural science, this problem is met with the use of the experiment.

An experiment in natural science
Let us assume that a scientist wants to know what makes pigs grow fat. Their degree of fatness is a 'variable', in this instance the 'dependent' variable, that is, the scientist regards it as the *result* of which he/she wishes to know the *cause*. In the present experiment, however, possible causes, or independent variables, include heat, light, diet, exercise, heredity, etc. The scientist takes two groups of pigs that are absolutely alike in every possible way. One is the 'control group' and the other the 'experimental group'. The scientist will arrange identical environments for each group. The first step might then be to reduce the heating of the experimental group. If their weight goes up or down, the test is pursued in more detail. If it remains constant with that of the control group, heating can be ruled out as a cause of changing weight, and another independent variable will be systematically varied by the scientist. It is, of course, important not to assume a cause/effect relationship, where only coincidence is present, or where the cause is a separate independent variable, on which both known variables are dependent.

However, in the end, the scientist will arrive at a theory about how to fatten pigs, and the ultimate test will be whether the predictions about weight-gain in pigs are borne out by the evidence.

Experiments in social science
There are serious problems involved in conducting such experiments with people.

Firstly, there is a much larger number of variables to be taken into account. It is therefore much harder, or impossible, to control every one of them. Conducting the experiment in a laboratory is one solution, but such experiments are limited in both time and space, and there is no way of knowing if the results would also apply in a normal setting. This has encouraged some researchers to stay out of the laboratory, and to conduct 'field experiments' in the everyday world.

Secondly, people, unlike pigs, weather, chemicals or other matter, can and do know what is going on in an experiment, and this may affect their behaviour. This is true whether they are in a laboratory or 'in the field'. For example, in the Hawthorne experiment (see page 105), the presence and interest of the experimenters turned out to be the most important independent variable. One answer to this is to conduct experiments without the knowledge of the subjects, or to mislead them as to what the experiment is about. But is it ethically correct to lie to or deceive subjects in the interest of furthering our knowledge of human behaviour? Furthermore, those who have volunteered their services, or are being paid to participate, may not be representative of the population as a whole.

Thirdly, ethical considerations limit what aspects of human behaviour can be experimented on, whether the subjects are volunteers or not.

Despite these problems, social scientists, particularly those interested in the behaviour of small groups, have conducted experiments and have come up with some intriguing results. Eysenck and Nias (1978), for example, used the laboratory method in their study of the effects of sex and violence in the media, concluding that it produced the most clear-cut and reliable results.

Another example of a version of experimentation is that used by Garfinkel. Garfinkel, as an ethnomethodologist, wanted to uncover the taken-for-granted rules in social situations, and to show how they were 'constructed'. To do this, he arranged for his students deliberately to break normal social rules, and to observe how others coped with such behaviour, and repaired the break. Besides the example of the students acting as boarders in their own home (mentioned on page 52), students were told to engage friends in ordinary conversations and to pretend that they did not understand perfectly ordinary everyday expressions, for example, 'What do you mean, "you had a flat tyre"?' In this example, the researcher knows what is going on, but the subjects of the experiment do not.

Yet another example, in the symbolic-interactionist tradition this time, is described on page 324. Here, the experiment was to have some people admitted to a mental hospital by their feigning symptoms of 'insanity'. The idea was to observe how the medical staff treated people whom they considered to be 'insane', but who were, in fact, 'sane'.

The comparative method

An alternative to the experiment in social science is the comparative method, which rests on the same principles. It was widely used by the 'founding fathers' – indeed, Durkheim regarded it as *the* method of sociology – and is still much used today.

Instead of setting up an artificial experiment, the researcher assembles data about the real world. The researcher then compares one society or group with another in an attempt to identify the independent variable, or variables, which explain the presence of some particular phenomenon (the dependent variable) in one context and not another. In a sense, this method can be thought of as a 'natural experiment'.

Max Weber, for example, made extensive studies of different societies at various stages of development, and found that capitalism had developed in its mature form only in western Europe. He then noted that the other phenomenon peculiar to western Europe was Protestantism. He then argued that this religious belief could be shown to lead to the economic behaviour which created capitalism (Weber 1904). (For a fuller account of this, see page 136). In experimental terms, Protestantism is the independent variable and capitalism the dependent variable. What distinguishes Weber from the positivists is that the causal link he identified was the way in which Protestantism gave people a meaning to their world, in terms of which they acted. Their world-view, not some external social force, resulted in their behaviour. Weber thus bridges the positivist/interpretive divide, and is the best example of the danger of trying to put particular sociologists into particular slots in the model on page 45.

Durkheim's famous work on suicide (1897) is also based on the comparative method, and is often regarded as the clearest example of positivist methodology in sociology. Durkheim wished to show that the apparently highly individual act, suicide, was what he called a 'social fact' (see page 24). Firstly, he collected the official statistics on suicide for a number of European countries, and showed that the rates were were very stable over time. This could hardly be a coincidence, and was therefore evidence that a social fact was present. Durkheim then collected the statistics relating to a number of other variables, and, by statistical operations which involved holding one variable constant and observing the changes in the others, he established links between suicide rates and certain other rates. He showed that suicide rates were higher in areas where there were more Protestants, and lower where there were more Catholics. They were higher in cities than in the countryside. Within any one society, they were higher among the unmarried than the married, and among the childless than among those with children. By setting up one hypothesis after another, and testing each one rigorously, Durkheim built up a pattern of observed regularities in the world. The link he needed to bind all these regularities into a theory of the causes of suicide was the concept of 'social integration', the extent of a person's relationships with others in a group. Those who had fewer links (the unmarried, the childless, etc.) were more likely to commit 'egoistic' suicide. Similarly, the Protestant church provided a less supportive community for the individual to integrate with than did the Catholic church. Hence its members had higher suicide rates. Those who were so integrated that they regarded the group as more important than themselves, a circumstance found most often in tribal societies, were more likely to commit 'altruistic' suicide. Those in a situation which lacked norms within which to integrate were vulnerable to 'anomic' suicide.

Durkheim, then, set about developing a theory of suicide. By manipulating variables, a technique now known as 'multivariate analysis', he tested and confirmed a whole series of hypotheses until he had proved his case often enough for it to be regarded as a theory. His central concept of 'social integration' was operationalized in ways that meant he could measure and count it, and he believed that he had finally revealed a law about social reality.

Durkheim's work is a prime example of the hypothetico-deductive method in use. It was regarded, and in many ways still is regarded, as *the* method by which science should be done. We shall see, however, that interpretive sociologists, who stress meaning and consciousness in human social behaviour, argue that, while the hypothetico-deductive method may be appropriate to natural science, it is not appropriate to social science.

Methods of data collection

The distinction must first be made between primary data and secondary data. Quite simply, primary data are those which sociologists collect and then analyse. Secondary data are those which already exist, and which sociologists can analyse or re-analyse with their own concepts and models in mind.

Primary data collection

The data collection method most often associated with sociologists is the survey, and it is in fact the method most favoured by positivist methodology. The sociologist who conducts a survey wishes to find out the facts about something, which assumes that facts are there to be found. The survey may be descriptive, aiming simply at describing a state of affairs, or analytic, aiming to analyse or explain something. Surveys have to be very carefully planned if they are to obtain data which are valid, that is, which really represent what they claim to represent, and are reliable, that is, that whatever the survey finds would have been found by anyone else conducting the same survey. The task of the researcher is to assemble data about as many people as possible in as objective a way as possible.

Since this may involve huge numbers, it is usually possible to conduct the survey only on a representative sample of the population in question. If the sample is truly representative, we can assert that what is true of them is true of the population as a whole. The first requirement is a 'sampling frame', an accurate list of the whole population from which the sample is to be drawn. This is sometimes not easy to obtain.

'Random' sampling involves selection by chance, so that every individual has an equal chance of selection, for example, drawing names out
of a hat, or using random numbers generated by computer. 'Stratified'
sampling occurs where the population is divided into its known
groupings, and a random sample is taken from each category. This
reduces the chance of a highly unrepresentative sample, which is
always possible using a wholly random method. There are other
techniques of sampling, and all depend on knowing with some precision
the population to be surveyed.

Having identified the sample, the researcher may collect data through
the use of questionnaires, interviews, or perhaps attitude scales or other
more psychological measures.

Questionnaires are printed lists of questions calling for a written
response. They may be sent by post or administered in person. In a
questionnaire intended to collect data to be statistically processed, the
questions must be carefully worded to be as clear and unambiguous as
possible, and to provide answers which can be counted, for example,
yes/no/don't know. Some questionnaires ask much more 'open-ended'
questions, however. The advantages of questionnaires are that they are
cheap, and so a large number of people can be questioned. The results
can be easily recorded and, if quantitative, easily processed. The
disadvantages include the possibility that people do not answer truth-
fully, for whatever reason; that questions may be interpreted in a
different way from what the researcher intended; that the format of the
questions imposes strict and artificial limits on what kind of information
can be given or collected. Yes/no answers are futile for expressing
subtleties of attitude, belief or feeling.

Interviews overcome some of these problems. The highly structured
interview may be no more than a personally administered questionnaire,
in which the interviewer is trained to be as neutral as possible so as not
to influence the respondent's answers by seeming to approve or
disapprove of what is said. It is also important that each interviewer
should conduct every interview in the same way, and that one interviewer should interview in the same way as another. This is necessary to
ensure validity and reliability in the data. We may wonder, however,
how far this is possible. In an interview about racial attitudes, would you
give the same answers to a white as to a black interviewer? Or, indeed,
on any other topic? Would you be more truthful with someone of your
own age? What if you are a black person being interviewed by a white
person (see page 49)?

A more informal, open-ended or unstructured interview may seem like
no more than a guided conversation. This increases the interviewer's
intuitive understanding of the respondent, but produces data which
cannot easily be quantified. It is therefore more popular with interpretive
sociologists. The more researchers consider they are looking for the

'facts', the more concerned they will be to reduce or eliminate all bias introduced by the interviewer, the surroundings, etc. Positivist researchers assume that the facts are there, and that the problem is to devise instruments to get at them.

The more interpretive researchers do not, of course, share this assumption, and, accordingly, the methods of collecting primary data are rather different. Their task is, as we have seen, to get at the meanings that a social situation or activity has for those involved in it. The data collected are not quantitative but qualitative, and the questions asked are not 'How many?' but 'What kind?', not 'What is the cause of this?' but 'What is going on here?' Rather than starting with a theory or hypothesis and collecting data to test them, interpretive methods allow hypotheses and theories to develop from the data.

For symbolic interactionists, the main method is ethnographic, that is, providing descriptive accounts of the way of life of a group of people, much as social anthropologists have done, though with a different purpose, since the pioneering work of Malinowski (1884–1942). He stressed the importance of participant observation, arguing that it was necessary to live as a member of the primitive societies he studied, if a real understanding of their way of life was to be gained so that it could be written up for the information of others.

Such observation, in various forms, is the preferred technique for interpretive sociologists in our own society. Where pure observation is concerned, however, the techniques are more quantitative, and really belong more to positivist methodology. In this instance, the observer has a list or schedule of categories of interaction, and silently observes a group's activities. Every few seconds, the observer places a tick against whichever category of interaction is taking place at that moment. The observer can then quantify how much of each type of interaction has occurred. Flanders's account of life in school classrooms (1970) is a good example.

With the more participant versions of observation, the degree of involvement of the researcher can vary a great deal, as Gold (1958) outlines. He/she may be a complete participant, concealing his/her true identity and intentions from the group, and living entirely as they do. The participant-as-observer is actively involved in the group under observation, but they know the researcher is not really one of them. The observer-as-participant, a less common mode, usually involves a brief visit with limited participation.

Practical problems for the participant observer may be summarized as 'getting in, staying in, and getting out', that is, how to join a group and be accepted by them, how to remain a member of the group for as long as the research demands, and how to leave the group without doing damage to it or the friendships in it. The problems are both practical and ethical. The dilemma is to strike the right balance between becoming involved enough to gain a real understanding of the social processes in the group, and keeping detached enough to remain an observer and researcher. There is a very real danger of 'going native', that is, of coming to see the world only as those in the group do, and thereby losing the detached sociological perspective.

The best way to gain an understanding of participant observation is to read at least one of the books written by those who have used the technique. I recommend Whyte (1981), Gans (1967), Patrick (1973), Okely (1983) and Pryce (1979). All include descriptions of how the research was done, and the problems faced.

Qualitative data can also be gained through unstructured interviewing, or 'guided conversation', as we have seen.

The criticisms of these methods of data collection centre on whether they are 'scientific' or not, especially in terms of validity and reliability. How can we check that what the researcher reports is what was 'really' there, that is, that the researcher's account of what was going on is the same as that of the participants (validity). How can we know that, if the research had been carried out by someone else, or at another time, the same results would have emerged (reliability)? How can we know whether, even if the account is valid and reliable, the situation it describes is unique, or representative of a more widespread phenomenon? These accounts are certainly not objective, in that they rely on subjective intuition and interpretation, but that does not necessarily make them any more biased than more 'scientific' research. They are certainly limited to very small samples, even one-off case-studies or life histories, but what they lack in representativeness they make up for in providing far deeper insights into what they study. They do not attempt to be representative in the sense that a sample survey does, but rather they attempt to show how some general principle that the researcher has identified in social life actually operates in a particular instance. The long-term intention is to build up a whole series of studies, to create, as Becker (1966) has it, a more and more detailed mosaic of the reality of day-to-day social processes.

The symbolic interactionist style of interpretive research, then, attempts to give accounts of the way the social world appears to actors. The ethnomethodological style, on the other hand, inspired by a more phenomenological approach, gives accounts of how actors come to make the world look like that. The ethnomethodologist rejects the search for causes, and rejects the idea that there is some kind of higher-plane objective 'truth', available to sociologists when they explain the world, which is superior to that of the actors in that social world. Rather, ethnomethodologists aim to provide detailed descriptions of the way in which human beings construct a social world so that it appears objective and real to them, and which other sociologists have made the mistake of treating as though it *were* objectively real.

As an example, let us take Atkinson's work on suicide, written as a direct response to the positivist Durkheimian tradition (Atkinson 1978; Bell and Newby 1977). For Atkinson, suicides are not events out there in the world whose causes may be sought. Rather, suicides are deaths which are defined as suicides by those with the authority to define them so – coroners. The proper question for the sociologist to ask is, then, 'How do deaths get categorized as suicides?' This calls for research into, and a description of, the procedures followed by coroners in arriving at their verdicts. The research methods suited to this are interviewing of coroners, observation of inquests, and study of official records. Atkinson found that coroners have commonsense theories of the causes of suicide. When faced with a death without obvious natural causes (itself the result of a doctor's decision about what counts as a natural death), a coroner looks for facts about the dead person which support the commonsense theory, for example: Was he or she depressed? lonely? recently unemployed? If these factors are present, a suicide verdict is likely. The death *is* now suicide. It is the coroner's verdict which makes it so. It is entered in the official statistics.

The next stage is crucial. When positivist sociologists come to look at the official statistics of suicide, and to seek out, through multivariate or other analysis, the 'causes' of suicide in the backgrounds of the dead people, all they are in fact doing is rediscovering, in a very time-consuming way, the commonsense theories that coroners have of the causes of suicide. These findings are then published, are read by the coroner, who finds they confirm what he/she already 'knows', and then applies them at the next inquest, thereby perpetuating the cycle.

Atkinson is *not* saying that the official statistics are 'wrong', or that coroners are 'wrong' about the causes of suicide. He is saying that it is a mistake to regard suicides as facts out there in the real world, waiting to be counted if only we had the right techniques, and that it is therefore also a mistake to look for their causes. The sociologist must simply ask different kinds of questions.

It is worth noting, however, that, although Atkinson was interested in coroners' interpretations of death to produce 'suicides', and his first studies were in the interpretive tradition, the same topic can be studied using more positivistic (hypothetico-deductive) research methods, as follows.

Atkinson, Kessel and Dalgaard (1975) wrote up the evidence given at a number of real inquests in England and in Denmark, and invited English and Danish coroners to consider the evidence and to decide on a verdict. Their hypothesis was that Danish coroners would decide on a suicide verdict more often than English ones, because in England coroners have to find evidence of 'suicidal intention' for such a verdict, whereas Danish coroners only have to decide that 'on the balance of probability' it was a suicide. The experiment confirmed the hypothesis, and thus supported Atkinson's main hypothesis that suicide statistics reflect the behaviour of coroners rather than of the people now dead.

As well as being another good example of an experiment in social science, this shows how different research methods can be used on the same sociological problem, as we shall see in the next section.

You should also consider what questions this research raises for those who would argue that there is a higher suicide rate in one country than in another.

One method or several?

Two final and very important points about methods of data collection now remain to be made. Firstly, the distinctions between positivist methods and interpretive methods are no more clear-cut than the distinction between positivist and interpretive theory. It is more useful to regard the different methods as being placed on a continuum, as described by Worsley (1977). Here he shows how larger numbers are covered at the cost of deeper involvement, and vice versa. Broadly, the higher and further left the method comes on Figure 3, the more positivist it is.

The second point is that no piece of modern social research relies entirely on a single method of data collection, but rather uses the data from one method to complement that from another. Thus Newby (1977) in his study of farm-workers in East Anglia, states that 'The methodology was deliberately eclectic, involving the routine perusal of agricultural and population census statistics, a search of historical sources (both documentary and oral), participant observation and a

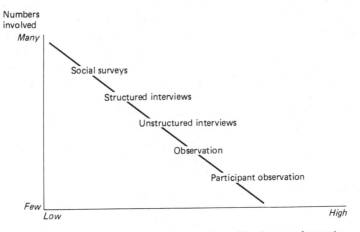

Figure 3   *Methods of data collection*

SOURCE: Worsley (1977).

survey investigation'. He selected a sample, and produced a questionnaire to guide his interviewing. 'In effect the survey and the period of
participant observation increasingly came to complement each other:
insights gained from participant observation could be checked against
survey data; on the other hand, much of this data could only become
meaningful through the experiences of living with a farm-worker and
his family in a tied cottage for six months and gaining first-hand
knowledge about the work and community situation.'

Secondary data

There is a vast mass of material already available for a sociological
researcher to analyse, both quantitative and qualitative, and historical
and contemporary.

Qualitative, that is, non-statistical, sources include newspapers,
novels, literature, art, letters, radio and TV programmes, parish registers
and other records. Such material may be historical or contemporary,
comprehensive or fragmentary. It is mostly used by interpretive
sociologists who use it to try to gain insights into the world-view and
ideologies of those who produced them, especially if the material is
historical. There are many problems inherent in this: the material is
usually unsystematic; written records tend to be left only by a small
group of the population, the literate, whose views cannot be assumed to
be typical; their purpose is seldom, if ever, sociological. Nevertheless, a
great deal of good work is done in this way, including Laslett's work on
the pre-industrial family (1977, 1983) or Johnson's on the early Victorian
educators (1970, 1976).

A more quantitative approach to secondary material is to make a
'content analysis' of it, that is, to sort out categories of data, and to go
through documents systematically, recording the number of occasions
on which items in each category occur. A recent example is the work of
the Glasgow University Media Group who video-recorded all TV news
bulletins over a fixed period, and made content analyses of how news
relating to industrial unrest was reported. They showed that it is
statistically the case that certain views on the causes of strikes, inflation
and so on were presented far more often, and at greater length, than
others. They then used this 'quantitative' data as part of their evidence
to show how the notion of 'bad news' is constructed by the media
(Glasgow University Media Group 1976, 1980).

Quantitative, statistical, secondary data include the mass of official
statistics produced by government through the census, and through
registration of births, marriages and deaths, as well as through the
social services, education, the police, etc. In addition, sociologists may
make use of statistics published by trade unions, other pressure groups,
in company reports and elsewhere.

What use can sociologists make of official statistics?

The problems presented by offical statistics are perceived differently by different sociologists.

If they are accepted at their face value, as they were by Durkheim, as a record of events in the world, the problems are concerned with presentation and with accuracy. For example, they are unlikely to have been collected and presented in the way the sociologist would have chosen. The categories and classification may be unsuitable. It may not be possible to make important correlations. Vital information may not be available. In addition, how can we be sure that the figures are correct? Perhaps some suicides go undetected, or are 'covered up' by relatives. We know perfectly well that many crimes, both minor and major, go unreported and so unrecorded. We may feel that the total of births recorded is likely to be as accurate as we need for all practical purpose, but can we say the same for the number of cases of 'battered babies'? For the quantitative, positivist researchers, the problem with official statistics is whether they can remedy their deficiencies enough to treat them as an accurate record.

The interpretive sociologists use official statistics in quite a different way. Rather than using them as a *resource* for their investigations, they treat them as a *topic* for investigation, by asking what it is that the statistics represent. Some may be relatively straightforward, for example, births and deaths are, surely, just a matter of accurate counting. Or are they? And why are they recorded in such detail anyway? (See Chapter 12, pages 364-5.) Other official statistics are even more qualitative. They are a record not of events in the world, but of interpretive decisions made by authoritative people. We have already looked at Atkinson's work on suicide statistics (see pages 72-3), so let us now consider crime statistics (which are discussed further in Chapter 11, pages 327-8).

A moment's thought shows that crime statistics are not a record of how many crimes have been committed. Quite apart from those actions which contravene the law but go unobserved or unreported, even the figures of 'crimes known to the police' are not what they appear to be. When the police witness an act which they define as law-breaking, or one is reported to them, they still have a choice as to how to respond. The act may be recorded, and thus become a statistic, or it may be treated more informally. If a crowd of lads are 'causing a breach of the peace', one police officer may make one arrest, but six of them may make six arrests. Does this mean that more crimes were being committed? It follows that an increase in the police force would result, at least in the short term, in an increase in the amount of recorded crime – exactly the opposite of what is intended by those who call for such an increase.

The sequence of social actions that produce a criminal statistic may be presented diagrammatically, as in Figure 4. At every stage, the police

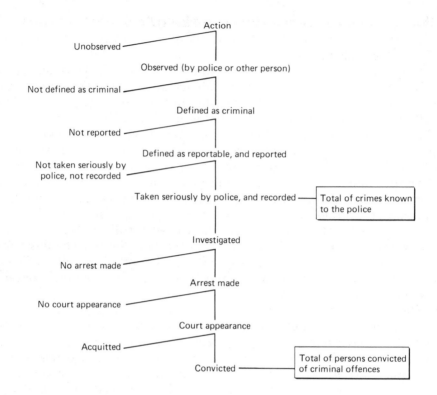

Figure 4   *The social construction of criminal statistics*

and other social actors are making decisions about what action to take, based on their definition of the situation. Decisions are made by reference to a combination of commonsense assumptions, experience, and professional expertise concerning crime and criminals, public opinion, expectations of fellow officers and superiors, the chance of securing a conviction, and other factors.

The crime statistics can tell us as much about the world-view of the police as they can about what crimes are committed. Thus interpretive, and particularly ethnomethodological, researchers will reject the notion that crime statistics are a record of events whose causes we should seek, and concentrate instead on how certain actions come to be defined as crimes. (See Cicourel 1976; Kitsuse and Cicourel 1963; and page 328 below, where this model is presented in a rather different form, to make an additional point about how crime is defined in a particular society.)

There is not the space here to develop other examples of this process, but you might try to construct a diagram, similar to Figure 4, to illustrate the social construction of divorce statistics, or strike statistics, or health statistics.

More Marxist sociologists take the argument a stage further. They stress that official statistics are produced by the state, which is active in protecting the interests of capitalism. Information is collected and presented in ways which protect the interests of the ruling class (Irvine *el al.* 1979). This influences which statistics are collected, or rather produced, by the state, the way in which they are perceived as objective and hence superior data, and how they are used. Thus, the Registrar General's social class scale (see page 158) ignores or conceals the very wealthy; women are largely concealed in many statistical records; the unemployment statistics systematically under-record the 'true' number of people who would work if work were available. (See also page 363–4.)

The choice of research method

It should be clear by now that the researcher's choice of what research methods to use is substantially influenced by theoretical assumptions. It is also influenced by choice of subject-matter, which in its turn is influenced by theoretical preferences. For example, symbolic interactionists will study face-to-face interaction, for which survey techniques are useless. But there are other factors involved, which can be summarized as time, labour, and money.

If the researcher has lots of all these available, an elaborate study can be set up which uses a variety of research methods, and lasts over a number of years. The results can be published as a series of articles in the learned journals, culminating in a major book. If the researcher is a lone student, working for a Ph.D on an Economic and Social Research Council grant, then both the choice of topic and the research method are going to be different. The former researchers, given an interest in the mass media, might set up an expensive and elaborate longitudinal study (that is, over a period of time) of the viewing habits of a representative sample of the population, together with more unstructured interviews with them and with influential media people, and a content analysis of programmes. The latter might, as did Tracey (1977), start with research in the library, and then get permission to sit in the newsroom of a major TV company, conducting an observer-as-participant study of how political television is produced.

These constraints exist also, of course, in natural science research, and throw even more doubt on the idea that science is a disinterested inquiry into the way the world operates. The allocation or refusal of research funds has an important effect on what research is done, and these funds are, by definition, controlled by powerful people in society.

Furthermore, research is more likely to be conducted into the lives of those who are not in a position to refuse to answer the questions put to them or to accept the participant observer in their midst. This is one important reason why we know much more about the poor than about the rich, about convicted criminals, about mental patients and, generally, about the weak than about the powerful. Questions about value-freedom in sociology become even more significant when these factors are considered.

Research in practice

As we have seen, science should be regarded as a method, and, when the scientific status of sociology is being considered, the test is whether its methods are as rigorous as those of the natural sciences. Concealed within this question is, however, the assumption that the *practice* of natural science research is in fact the same as is *claimed* to be the practice, that is, following the hypothetico-deductive model. Is natural science research really conducted logically, rationally and objectively? If it is not conducted like this, then social scientists are being asked to match up to an ideal that does not exist in practice. The ideal is revealed as no more than an occupational ideology of natural scientists, a view of their work that suits their interests. This question is taken up in more detail in Chapter 5, pages 132-4, where T. S. Kuhn's challenge to the orthodox view of natural science is explained. For the present, I draw to your attention Watson (1968). In this book, the author is a biochemist who describes how he and his co-workers discovered the DNA molecule, work for which they received the Nobel prize. The account shows how emotion, human relations, inspiration, dead ends, and sheer flair all played a part in the research, though it was finally presented as a logical sequence of hypotheses and experiments.

For sociology, Hammond (1964) and Bell and Newby (1977) give first-hand accounts of how research is really done. As Newby says, 'The outcome of that research, and even in some cases the substantive findings, were crucially affected by the nature of the personal and organizational relationships between the researchers themselves' (Bell and Newby 1977).

This bring us back to the questions: 'What is science?' and 'Is sociology a science?' If the ideal of natural science methods is in fact a myth and an ideology to which natural scientists do not themselves match up, what standards should social scientists aspire to?

And in any case, if there is this difference between what scientists do and what they say they do, is it important? It can be argued that what scientists should do is to provide a set of instructions which others can use to check their work and their results. So why should they include all the mistakes and the blind alleys? After all, if I made the mistake of going to Birmingham from London via Brighton, you would not thank me for giving you that route, rather than the shorter one I found later.

And if we dismiss the claims of the scientific method too readily, we are faced with the other question: In what way is a sociological account of the world superior to anybody else's? The answer must lie in these two points:

1 Sociological accounts and theories are based on evidence and argument, and the conclusions follow from the evidence. They are empirically based.
2 Sociological accounts are made public in a way that spells out the methods which could be used to check the results. This invites critical comment, checking, and, if appropriate, refutation by a community of scholars.

Commonsense accounts can seldom be right or wrong in the sense that scientific accounts can be, for they are rarely precisely stated, or operationalized, and the links in the argument are usually unclear. The methods by which the account was produced are rarely known. This is the important difference between commonsense and scientific work.

Sociology and social policy

There is no necessary link between what sociologists do and what policies governments pursue. One reason for this rests on the distinction between social problems and sociological problems, which is expressed most clearly by Worsley (1977): '. . . a problem, for sociology, is any pattern of relationships that calls for explanation; . . . A social problem is some piece of social behaviour that causes public friction and/or private misery and calls for collective action to solve it'. Thus divorce is both a social problem and a sociological problem. 'Successful' marriages are a sociological problem. The fact that some young people break the law is both a social and a sociological problem: the fact, perhaps more extraordinary, that most of them obey the law is a sociological problem. What is in practice regarded as a social problem is a highly political issue which is examined in more detail in Chapter 11, page 306. For the moment, let us simply recognize that much sociological work is not social problem-oriented at all.

A traditional view of social policy is that it is 'the policy of governments with regard to action having a direct impact on the welfare of the citizens, by providing them with services or income' (Marshall 1965). It includes national insurance, social security, health and welfare services, housing, education, and crime and its treatment. It is geared to the reduction of what are defined as potential or actual social problems.

A great deal of excellent social problem-oriented research has been done by sociologists who felt very strongly about the inequalities or injustices on which they were collecting evidence. This is true of the work on education and social class outlined in Chapter 9, pages 248–52, on poverty (see pages 81–6), and other work on housing, on crime, on health care, on discrimination on grounds of race or of gender, and so on.

Such an approach to social problems suggests that they can be alleviated by piecemeal social engineering, tackling one issue at a time. A more socialist view argues that these problems are all aspects of the central political conflict over access to scarce resources, a conflict based on class interests that can only be resolved by a fundamental reordering of society.

Whichever view is taken, research like this does not automatically produce the desired response from government, of whatever political persuasion. A sociologist may reveal some unwelcome fact about our society, and may even make very positive recommendations as to what should be done about it, but whether any action is taken is the result of a political decision which will take into account other factors such as spending priorities and election prospects. It is a grave error to believe that sociologists produce evidence about public misery for a benevolent government to act upon.

Even where there is, in fact, a direct link, it can be shown to rest on a mistake. Natural science research has had some dramatic and relatively quick success in solving problems of, for instance, illness and disease. A scientist discovers the cause of malaria, develops a method of preventing it, and governments invest in programmes that eliminate malaria in large areas of the world. The 'facts' about malaria have been revealed, a suitable policy followed, and the problem solved.

In social research this is not the case. The alleged 'facts' about, say, the causes of crime and delinquency have been revealed many times (see Chapter 11), and various policies of prevention and treatment have been implemented. The same is true of poverty. And yet crime and poverty persist. This may be because the theories of causation are wrong, but, in the light of earlier discussion, I would argue that it is because of an error about the nature of social reality. The 'facts' of delinquency are not the same kind of 'facts' as the 'facts' about malaria. Crime and poverty are social constructs, concerned with meaning and social action, and these change. It is a mistake to expect human social behaviour to respond to treatment in the way that we expect disease to respond. They are a different kind of phenomenon.

Finally, there is another and far more subtle way in which social science research affects social policy, and it is wholly indirect. Certain theories, of psychologists, economists, sociologists and others, are absorbed into the conventional wisdom of a society, and into its dominant culture. Why this is so, and how it happens, raise questions which we cannot pursue here. But, for example, Freud's theory of the interpretation of dreams, Darwin's theory of evolution, sociologists' ideas about the causes of educational failure, and others, are absorbed into the taken-for-granted commonsense of a society, and, in this way, will come to affect not only social policy, but the response to social policy. If everybody 'knows' that juvenile delinquents have been deprived of maternal affection (a fairly recent 'discovery'), then government policy to compensate for this is likely to meet with general approval. Equally, the suggestion that this explanation is rubbish is likely to meet with general scorn.

This is not, of course, a one-way process. Just as sociological ideas infiltrate 'commonsense', so commonsense and taken-for-granted assumptions tend to infiltrate social research – which is where this chapter came in (see page 58).

Poverty research

There is a long British tradition of research into poverty, and it raises most of the issues about social research that have been discussed in this chapter. For obvious reasons, the research has tended to be quantitative, and hence to follow a positivist methodology. The basic problems have been to define poverty, to operationalize the definition, to find the causes of poverty, and to suggest remedies for it. It has been regarded both as a sociological problem and as a social problem.

While the poor have been with us for centuries, they were for long regarded as a moral rather than a social problem, in the sense that their 'pauperism' was seen to be caused by their own laziness and fecklessness, rather than by social circumstances which called for social policy solutions.

The extent of poverty
Systematic study of the extent of poverty was first carried out from the mid nineteenth century onwards. Mayhew (1849), Chadwick (1840s–1860s), Engels (1844) and others shocked the Victorians with their revelations about the condition of the poor in their midst (see Keating 1976).

Charles Booth (1840–1916) opened the first phase of truly social scientific research in his seventeen-volume study, *Life and Labour of the People of London*, published between 1889 and 1903. Prompted by what he regarded as socialist writings, he determined to find out the facts about poverty, and carefully constructed the research tools to do this. To operationalize the concept of poverty, he established the first 'poverty line'. 'By the word "poor" I mean to describe those who have a sufficiently regular though bare income, such as eighteen shillings to twenty-one shillings per week for a moderate family, and by "very poor" those who from any cause fall much below this standard' (Booth 1889). He collected a mass of primary data from personal observation and interview, and also used secondary data available from the School Boards. From this he concluded that, of the 900,000 East Enders he initially studied, 12 per cent were very poor, and another 22 per cent were poor. They made up the four lowest classes of the eight into which he divided his population. For London as a whole, some 30 per cent were poor or very poor.

In addition to this quantitative material, Booth produced vivid accounts of the experience of poverty, revealing his admiration for the toughness and stoicism of the poor, and a sympathy for them. The more he became aware of the facts, the more humanitarian his commitment became.

Booth showed that poverty was largely caused by circumstances outside the control of the poor, mainly low and irregular wages. Whether prompted by genuinely humanitarian feelings, or by a fear of revolutionary upheaval, the policy-makers responded by constructing, in the period 1905–14, the foundations of the modern Welfare State.

Seebohm Rowntree (1871–1954) was a wealthy Quaker businessman who lived in York. He read Booth's study, and conducted his own research into whether poverty in York was equally extensive. In *Poverty: a Study of Town Life* (1901), he identified 28 per cent of the population as in poverty, caused by low wages, sickness and unemployment. He gathered his data by direct inquiry from almost every working-class family in York, and further refined Booth's 'poverty line' by consulting nutritionists and other experts for advice on what food, etc., was required to maintain 'merely physical efficiency'. He listed these requirements, costed them, and concluded that, for example, a worker with three dependent children who earned less than 21s. 8d. per month was in poverty. Those whose income fell below this line (10 per cent) were in 'primary poverty'. Those whose income was above this line, but who spent their money in such a way that they went without what Rowntree defined as bare necessities (18 per cent) were in 'secondary poverty'.

He also identified the 'cycle of poverty', which refers to the way that a man can move into and out of poverty at different stages in his life. As a child, he will be poor, as a young single wage-earner, he rises above the line; as a young parent, he falls again; when his children are earning, he rises above the line; and in old age, he sinks finally into poverty.

Rowntree developed the notion, implied in Booth's work, that what counts as poverty changes as average living standards rise. Though he never used the phrase 'relative poverty', it is implied in much of his writing.

The second, less dramatic, phase in British poverty research is marked by Rowntree's second study of York, done in 1936 and published in 1941. Here he identified 18 per cent of the population as in poverty, most of this being caused by high unemployment.

In 1951 he published (with Lavers) a third study, in which he found only 1.5 per cent in poverty, caused mostly by old age and ill health. This research, together with the increase in general affluence in the 1950s, and the associated idea that class inequalities were disappearing in Britain (see page 173), all encouraged the complacent belief that poverty in Britain had been largely abolished by the twin policies of full employment and the Welfare State.

Towards the end of the 1950s and through the 1960s, poverty was both redefined and rediscovered. As early as 1954, Townsend had challenged the idea that poverty had been abolished. Harrington (1963) showed extensive poverty in the USA, and Titmuss (1962) argued that income redistribution, through taxation and welfare, had been far less than was imagined. Wedderburn (1962) found 12 per cent of the population living at subsistence level, and Coates and Silburn (1970, 1983) made a detailed study of the crushing multiple deprivation of the people living in the St Ann's area of Nottingham. The most important study is that of Abel-Smith and Townsend (1965), which is discussed below.

All these studies rejected the absolute or fixed definition of poverty, and redefined it as a relative phenomenon. People are poor in relation to the standards of the society around them and with which they compare themselves (subjective poverty), or with which the researcher compares them (objective poverty). Furthermore, what is needed for physical survival varies according to age, sex, occupation, place of residence and climate. And, crucially, acceptable minimum standards rise as national prosperity increases.

Poverty thus becomes a relationship rather than a condition. The poor are defined in relation to the non-poor. In this way, the concepts of poverty and equality become related, and the debate about poverty becomes a part of the more obviously ideological debate about social inequality.

This new view of poverty also stressed the powerlessness of the poor, and their inability to help themselves or to exercise influence in a society which is organized in such a way that some people will always be poor. Poverty thus becomes a political rather than a moral or humanitarian problem.

By operationalizing the concept of the poverty line in this new way, researchers, as well as changing the underlying value-commitment of their research, began to 'discover' more poverty than was 'there' before.

Abel-Smith and Townsend (1965) took as their poverty line the current level of National Assistance Board payments, plus 40 per cent. These are linked by government policy to a notion of an acceptable minimum standard of living. They conducted a re-analysis of the secondary data to be found in the official statistics produced by the Ministry of Labour in 1953 and 1960, and produced the figures in Table 1, of those below the poverty line, in Britain in 1960. This total constituted 14 per cent of the population, and one-third of them were children.

Table 1   *Numbers of people in Britain living below the poverty line,*
1960

Cause of poverty	Individuals in millions	Percentage of poor
Fatherless families	$^{3}/_{4}$	10
Incapacity of wage-earner		
age	$2^{1}/_{2}$	33
ill health	$^{3}/_{4}$	10
Unemployment	$^{1}/_{2}$	7
Low wages, related to size of family	3	40
Total	$7^{1}/_{2}$	100

They also stressed the importance of the cycle of poverty first
identified by Rowntree, and showed that, though 14 per cent of the
population might be in poverty at any one time, many more would
experience poverty at some time in their lives.

With research like this, the myth that poverty had been abolished was
exploded. In addition, it was shown that the major cause of poverty was
low wages, closely followed by old age, which exploded the further myth
that the poor were idle or feckless.

In 1979, Townsend published his massive study *Poverty in the United
Kingdom*, based on research carried out in 1969 on 10,000 individuals in
3250 households. In it, he provided a new definition of poverty:

Individuals, families and groups in the population can be said to be in poverty
when they lack the resources to obtain the types of diet, participate in the
activities and have the living conditions and amenities which are customary, or
are at least widely encouraged or approved, in the societies to which they belong.
Their resources are so seriously below those commanded by the average
individual or family that they are, in effect, excluded from ordinary living
patterns, customs and activities

He found that, according to the official poverty line (supplementary
benefit level), 6.1 per cent of his households were poor. By his own
definition, the figure was 22.9 per cent. Broadly, the same groups are in
poverty as were identified in Abel-Smith and Townsend (1965). Because
of the cycle of poverty, 'Well over half of the people in Britain are likely to
experience poverty for a substantial period of their lives'.

During the 1980s, the number of people living below 140 per cent of
Supplementary Benefit level has risen rapidly, until it now stands at
some 13 to 14 million, about 25 per cent of the population at any one time.
All the groups identified by Abel-Smith and Townsend in Table 1 have
increased in size. The proportion of each group in the total has changed,
with the unemployed (three-quarters of whom live below the poverty
line) forming a larger proportion. The number of children in poverty has

doubled in this period. Two-thirds of those over pensionable age and living alone are in poverty. In the 1980s, poverty is with us again.

The causes of poverty

Having established the extent of poverty in Britain in the post-war period, researchers have drawn different conclusions about its causes, and hence the appropriate remedies. All the research has been done as a result of some commitment by the researcher, and the findings are usually intended to exercise some influence on social policy.

One major type of explanation is known as the 'culture of poverty' thesis. Derived from the work of Lewis (1961) (described in greater detail in Chapter 11, page 322), this thesis emphasizes how poverty is passed on and perpetuated through families, socialization and community attitudes. It tends to stress the negative aspects of the way the poor live, their defeatism, and apparent lack of organization. The deprivation and inadequacy of one generation is passed on to the next.

This thesis has been vigorously attacked by, for example, Valentine (1968) who argues that, though some of the poor may be resigned to their situation, there is little evidence that the attitudes and life-style that Lewis identifies exist on a large scale. Rather, it is a matter of the middle-class researcher assessing their life-style in terms of his or her own values, finding it objectionable, and rejecting it.

Coates and Silburn (1970, 1983) developed a variant on the 'culture of poverty' thesis, with its stress on the attitudes of the poor, by emphasizing the circumstances in which the poor are trapped. These circumstances combine to form a mesh from which, regardless of attitude or ability, there is little chance of escape. In order to survive on a day-to-day basis, poor people have to spend money in ways which are, strictly speaking, uneconomic, but which are the only ones possible at the time. The poor pay more for many goods and services than do the better off (Williams 1977).

In so far as the original culture of poverty thesis places the responsibility for their poverty on the poor themselves, it can be regarded as supportive of the basic structure of the society in which the poverty occurs, even if only by ignoring that structure. In practice, it has given rise to such policies as the American government's 'War on Poverty' in the 1960s, which was entirely geared to changing the life-styles of poor people and remedying their perceived social and educational weaknesses. It thus implied that the fault lay with them, but that they could, with help, escape. It in no way challenged the system which produced the situation in the first place.

These policies illustrated the basic weakness of the 'culture of poverty' thesis in the first place – it explains the continuation of poverty rather than its original causes. Coates and Silburn similarly have more to say about the persistence of poverty than about its causes, but their analysis did throw more light on the relationship between poverty and the wider social structure.

It is this relationship that has been stressed in more recent studies, which have regarded poverty as an aspect of the structure of social inequality in society, which is itself analysed from a conflict perspective. Thus Townsend (1979) argues that the key to poverty is the unequal distribution of wealth, income and power. The rich can take action 'to preserve and enhance their wealth and to deny it to others'. Certain sections of the population are denied access to their share of resources (not just income, but education, housing, health care, etc.), and have to adopt ways of living that cut them off even more from the rest of society.

A competitive economy of the capitalist type means that there must be losers, just as much as winners. While the Welfare State may compensate the losers to some extent, it cannot fully do so because that would threaten the foundation on which the whole political and economic system is constructed. 'People become poor in this country because either they work for a poverty wage or, unable to work and lacking capital assets to produce an unearned income, they become dependent on inadequate state benefits' (CPAG 1979b). Poverty has positive functions in supporting the competitive social order (Gans 1971), and 'any serious attempt to abolish poverty endangers the whole structure of inequality in society' (Kincaid 1973).

Being old or sick is not in itself always a cause of poverty. Single parents and the unemployed do not have to be poor: it is a matter of government policy that their benefit payments are set at the level they are. Whether age, sickness or unemployment strike at all, and whether they result in poverty, is partly a matter of the social and economic position of the individual concerned (see Chapter 6, pages 156-62). It is being old and working-class that produces poverty, or being young and black that increases the chance of unemployment.

A theory of poverty that rests on a conflict model of social stratification calls for a very different policy response, for poverty will not be abolished without a radical restructuring of our society. Kincaid (1973) calls for a full socialist reform of society. Townsend (1979) advocates the abolition of excessive wealth and income, the end of unemployment, the reorganization of employment and professional practice to reduce hierarchies at work, and the reorganization of community services.

It is safe to assume that such radical solutions are not going to be welcomed by governments, and are not therefore likely to be put into practice. However 'scientific' the research may be, what use is made of it remains a matter of political decision.

Guide to further reading

For a more detailed, but still introductory, account of research methods and the issues involved, try *Research Methods* by Patrick McNeill (Tavistock 1985), and the section 'Finding out' in Meighan, Shelton and Marks (1979), *Perspectives on Society*. Shipman (1981), *The Limitations of Social Research*, provides a guide to how to assess the reliability of research, and is refreshingly honest. Bell and Newby (1977), *Doing Sociological Research*, as we have seen, is a set of accounts of how research was really done. The Introduction is difficult, and should be left to the end of an A-level course.

For practical guidance in research techniques, try, in ascending order of difficulty, Stacey (1969), *Methods of Social Research*, Madge (1953), *The Tools of Social Science*, and Krausz and Miller (1974), *Social Research Methods*. All tend to stress quantitative methods.

Gomm and McNeill (1982), *A Handbook for Sociology Teachers*, has many ideas for research exercises, as does McNeill (1985), mentioned above.

But the best way to learn about social research is to read the original studies and their descriptions of how the work was done. For studies that emphasize the survey technique, try Schofield (1965), *The Sexual Behaviour of Young People*, and Goldthorpe (1980), *Social Mobility and Class Structure in Modern Britain*. Several participant observation studies are suggested on page 71. Good community studies include Stacey (1960), *Tradition and Change: a Study of Banbury*, and Gans (1967), *The Levittowners*. Bell and Newby (1971), *Community Studies*, discusses this kind of research very thoroughly in Chapter 3. (See also page 226.)

Burgess (1982), *Field Research*, includes selections from ethnographic and interpretive studies. For some short interactionist accounts, try Rose (1962), *Human Behaviour and Social Processes*, and, for discussion of the issues involved, Becker (1971), *Sociological Work*.

Of the many studies that use several techniques, try Young and Willmott (1957), *Family and Kinship in East London*, and Barker (1984), *The Making of a Moonie*, as well as Newby (1977), *The Deferential Worker*.

On poverty, Keating (1976), *Into Unknown England* is an excellent collection from the Victorian social explorers, and Coates and Silburn (1983), *Poverty: the Forgotten Englishmen*, has a good summary of research up to that date, as well as a vivid account of life in inner-city Nottingham. Townsend (1979), *Poverty in the United Kingdom* is a massive study that you can only use selectively, but it too has an excellent summary of poverty theory to date, and has a mass of important evidence. The publications of the Child Poverty Action Group are always thoroughly supported with evidence.

4 Social order, social change and socialization

Mike O'Donnell

Taken together, the three concepts that make up the title of this chapter cover the basic links between the individual and society. 'Socialization' describes how the individual learns to participate in society, although the way a person is socialized varies from one society to another. For instance, much of what is taught in modern societies is not acceptable in primitive cultures, and vice versa. In the former, eating without cutlery is considered 'uncivilized', whereas in many primitive societies it is normal. These differences extend to fundamental matters such as sexual behaviour and the treatment of older kin. For example, letting old people live alone, a common occurrence in 'advanced' Western countries, would not be acceptable in most primitive cultures.

The notion of 'what is acceptable' provides the link between socialization and 'social order'. For social order to continue, it is necessary that individuals conform to generally accepted patterns of behaviour, *at least to some extent*: without a measure of conformity, chaos would overtake order. Thus, if all the members of a school – teaching staff, pupils and others – arrived one morning and did exactly what they wanted instead of carrying out their normal roles, order would quickly disappear. Social order largely depends on people fulfilling the 'roles' (or parts) they have learnt to play in a given situation. Pupils are expected to behave as pupils, teachers as teachers, and so on. Let us take a more realistic example to illustrate the relationship between social order and socialization. When groups socialized into different cultures (ways of life) have to live together, social order and stability can come under *strain* simply because members of the groups have different values, customs and attitudes. This often happens as a result of large-scale immigration. Specifically, adult West Indian immigrants to Britain have often been genuinely upset at the 'liberal' (or 'lax', as they might see it) way in which parents and teachers treat children here. More traditional discipline is usually employed in the West Indies. Differences of this kind can create tension and misunderstanding between immigrant and host communities.

The relationship between social order and social change does not lend itself to simple generalization. Change can undermine social order but it can also strengthen it. Really, it is necessary to examine specific instances of change to know its effect. Thus, the growth in power and wealth of commercial men in the sixteenth and seventeenth centuries did lead to a challenge to the old order and temporary social breakdown in the form of civil war. Similarly, the technological advance of the nineteenth and twentieth centuries has had divisive effects but has also provided a basis of affluence that seems to have partially stilled social discontent. In our own time, we wait to see the social change that will undoubtedly follow upon the 'silicon-chip revolution'.

Socialization
Self and society
From the moment of birth, the individual or *self* is part of society. He or she cannot survive without others. Society is, of course, made up of people and it is only by interacting with others that a child can develop into a full member of society. Socialization is about how the individual learns to behave in a socially acceptable way. Most of what we think of as manners and correct behaviour, as well as more important matters of morality, are learnt through socialization. Much early socialization consists of the child being encouraged to imitate certain patterns of behaviour and being discouraged from others. Thus, adults require children to wear clothes and to eat in a certain way, and even exercise close control over their leisure activity, though precisely what is expected varies from culture to culture. Rules about how people should greet each other and express friendship vary considerably. In some societies men may hold hands, or kiss each other, in a way that would not imply the relationship that it would imply in Britain. All definitions of socialization emphasize the effect of society on the individual, but some sociologists also stress the active participation of the individual in the socialization process. We return to this point later; for the moment let us further examine how society forms the individual.

Functionalists, such as Talcott Parsons, describe socialization in terms of the learning of values, norms and roles. These are usually first learned within the family. Values concern what is considered good or bad or desirable or undesirable in a society. They provide general guides to conduct. For instance, respect for human life is virtually a universal value today, although many cultures have practised ritualized killing, including human sacrifice and cannibalism, thus showing a profoundly different evaluation of life from that held in modern society. Most, if not all, societies set a high value on loyalty to the tribe or nation. Some values are more characteristic of some societies than others. For example, Americans are often considered competitive and aggressive, and the type of hard, physical games they play, such as baseball and American football, certainly develop these values and attitudes.

Norms are the conventions or rules that govern behaviour. Thus, you do not play football in classrooms; you do not drive on the right-hand side of the road in Britain. There is a close relationship between values and norms: norms are frequently the observable behaviours that represent particular values. Thus, the norm of standing up when an important person enters the room suggests the value of respect for authority.

A role is the pattern of behaviour appropriate to a given situation. The appropriate roles for the classroom are teacher and pupil; for the surgery, doctor and patient. Watch a small child run around the doctor's surgery and you will appreciate that even behavioural roles that we take for granted have to be learned. As we shall see shortly, interactionists, more than functionalists, stress that roles can involve an active, even creative element. The symbolic interactionist George Mead (1863–1931) expresses rather well both the active and the passive aspects of socialization in the following extract:

The self . . . is essentially a social structure and it arises in social experience. After a self has arisen, it in a certain sense provides for itself its social experiences, and so we can conceive of an absolutely solitary self. But it is impossible to conceive of a self arising outside of social experience. [Mead 1934]

Primary socialization

Charles Cooley (1864–1929) suggested that socialization can be analysed in terms of primary and secondary socialization. Primary socialization refers mainly to early socialization within the family, but can be extended to describe the influence on behaviour of any intimate relationship, such as that with a close neighbour or friend. Secondary socialization refers to the influence of more impersonal organizations, such as schools, place of work and the media. Peer groups, that is friends and acquaintances of equal status (social standing), are usually also regarded as secondary socializing influences, but it is worth noting that intense personal friendships within peer groups can acquire the character of primary socialization. What this character is we must now discuss in more detail.

Primary socialization is less formal than secondary socialization. It occurs 'naturally', in face-to-face relationships. Its influence is all the more effective because it occurs in this informal manner. A young baby or child is psychologically very open and, in that sense, is exposed to the ideas, feelings and moods of its parents. It has no formal defences against the influence of its parents, whether that influence is for good or ill. Often it is only in adulthood that we realize just how powerful the effect of our parents has been on us. It is in childhood that we 'internalize' fundamental values and norms. Most psychologists would agree with Freud that the basis of character is laid down in the first few years of life, even though, unlike him, many would stress the possibility of later change.

Secondary socialization

Secondary socialization refers to the formative effect on behaviour of relatively large and formal organizations and groups. A formal organization is one that is based on set rules and procedures. A child's first experience of organizations of this kind usually occurs when he or she goes to school or nursery. Nurseries and infant schools, however, can be regarded as 'half-way houses' between the all-embracing security and protection of the family and the more impersonal outside world in which the child must gradually learn to survive and, one hopes, to flourish. In nurseries and infant schools the responsible adult combines the role of parent or guardian with that of teacher. At this level, teaching is often relatively informal, though not quite so informal as the parental role. The personal side of the relationship between infant and teacher is further strengthened by the fact that all or most teaching is done by one individual. This is in marked contrast to what happens at secondary school and beyond.

As the child gets older, the schools he or she attends become larger and their organization more complex. For schools to run smoothly, it is necessary that pupils and teachers understand and observe the various procedures and arrangements relating to the timetables, teaching rooms and other organizational matters. In addition, pupils usually have to observe certain school rules, just as teachers must fulfil their contracts and, generally, behave in an acceptably professional manner. 'Sanctions', or punishments, can be used against those who do not conform. Thus, a teacher could be suspended or even lose his or her job through misconduct. Learning to participate in relatively large organizations like schools, and learning how to respond to the hierarchy of authority within them, is a very important part of education in modern societies, even though it is not, of course, part of the official timetable. Most pupils eventually go on to work in equally large, if not larger, organizations, whether these be factories or offices. Because many of us are used to such organizations, we tend to under-estimate the amount of self-control and adjustment required to function in them. Organizations of this kind do not exist in primitive societies and a person from such a society would have no idea of how to cope with one if suddenly required to do so. It is no wonder that some people and, perhaps particularly, some older citizens are genuinely intimidated by large, complex organizations such as the various departmental offices of central and local government. By contrast, a modern child educated in a large secondary school is, by the very nature of that experience, better equipped to deal with these institutions.

Sociological perspectives on socialization

What has so far been said about socialization would be acceptable to most sociologists. We now briefly discuss the emphases and insights particularly associated with given perspectives.

First, let us analyse the functionalist perspective. Following Emile Durkheim, functionalists have tended to stress the influence of social structure on forming and controlling individual behaviour. In particular, Talcott Parsons has described individual social action largely in terms of performance of *roles* determined by the needs of society. The functioning of the social system requires that people perform such roles as industrial worker, clerk, teacher or company director. Parsons pays little or no attention to what it *feels* like to fulfil these roles. Similarly, he sees social norms as rules and conventions that it is socially *necessary* for people to observe. Thus, he makes norms seem somewhat rigid and constraining (limiting).

It is largely on the matter of rules and norms that interactionists disagree with Parsons. They consider these to be much more flexible than do functionalists. They point out that different people fulfil the same roles very differently and argue that it is important to understand and interpret precisely what a given role means to the individual performing it. The role of teacher may be fulfilled in many contrasting ways. One teacher may be strict and traditional, another permissive and progressive. No doubt their different philosophy and behaviour greatly affect what they actually achieve as educationalists. Yet they are both performing the same role! Quite reasonably, interactionists insist that sociology must take into account such differences in actual role performance. In the same way, interactionists tend to regard norms as open to considerable individual interpretation. Indeed, some interactionists and ethnomethodologists avoid the concept of norm altogether, preferring to use the broader term 'typification'. A typification is most easily understood as what is typical, for example, a typical teacher, or a typical way of behaving in certain circumstances, such as at dinner or at a discotheque. Interactionists consider that people belonging to the same society or group tend to share the same typifications. But they recognize that typifications can be interpreted very differently. What, for instance, is normal behaviour in a disco? The fact that there are only general, rather than precise, answers to that sort of question persuades most interactionists that, just as normal behaviour must be broadly defined, so the distinction between normal and deviant (abnormal) behaviour must also be considered vague.

It will be clear that emphasis on the ability of the individual to exercise some control and choice in his or her own life is a feature of interactionism. George Mead, an early interactionist, defined the human self in such a way as to allow for this. He divided the self into two parts, the 'me' and the 'I'. The 'me' refers to the part of the self acted upon and formed by society (the part prominently noticed by functionalists). The 'I' is the active and creative part of the self which 'enters into' society and, to however small an extent, changes it. Later interactionists have tended to emphasize the active 'I' just as much as the passive 'me' of Mead's model. This has partly redressed the balance struck by functionalists in the opposite direction. Mead presented the process of socialization in terms of the active participation of the self.

In the earliest stages of babyhood, the baby imitates the actions of others, but the actions remain meaningless to the baby. They may, of course, be given meaning by a fond parent – for example, when a baby waves its arm.

In the next stage, the 'play stage', the child, with the help of simple language, learns about the social world by playing at it. He or she plays at nurses, or shopkeepers, or mothers and fathers. In this way, they begin to learn to 'take the attitude of the other', that is, to put themselves in another person's shoes (or 'inside their head' – see Chapter 2, page 47.) However, at this play stage, the child is limited to taking account of one role at a time, one after the other, and behaviour is much influenced by particular 'significant others', for example, parents, brothers and sisters, perhaps teachers.

In the 'game stage', which follows, the child begins to orient its behaviour to that of the whole group, all at once. As in a football game when a player passes the ball after summing up the whole situation, so in social action the individual comes to take account of the 'generalized other' rather than of just one person at a time. However, the 'generalized other' refers not to actual people, but to the shared perspective of a whole group or community of people. Thus, to belong to a club is to share a common identity with others, even though individuals play different roles in the club. The individual's behaviour is regulated in terms of the opinions and attitudes that the individual assumes others hold. In this way, self-control and social control become aspects of the same process. However, Mead never forgot that individuals can help to change the 'rules' of the organizations or communities of which they are a part.

Marxists, like functionalists, tend to see socialization as a process that 'happens to' the individual. In this, as in other cases, the emphasis of the two perspectives is structural rather than interactional. For instance, they stress the function the family plays in passing on the main ideas and values of a society to the individual. Characteristically, however, Marxists question whether what a child learns is always in his or her own interest. Thus, in a slave family, a child may be brought up to accept a position as a slave. In other words the slave-child comes to take as normal a social position in which, Marxists consider, he or she is exploited. Similarly, according to this perspective, working-class people may be socialized to conform to a society which exploits them and this conformity may be passed on through the generations. Marxists consider that, to some extent, the family, the church, the educational system and other *agencies* of socialization do this (see page 256). Thus, a priest who tells the poor and deprived to 'accept their lot' is seen as socializing them to come to terms with exploitation. A teacher who merely seeks to 'keep control' of, say, tough and disillusioned inner-city children, without trying to understand and explain the reasons for their behaviour, is similarly regarded. Marxists do, however, stress the limits of control and conformity. The everyday experience of people *at work* and *in their neighbourhoods and communities* can provide an alternative basis of ideas, values and behaviour. This is especially so in enclosed communities such as mining or docking areas. Shared experience of work, including industrial conflict, and/or leisure can create a strong sense of 'solidarity' (togetherness) and of conflicting interest with more privileged classes. Some members of the working class (Marx anticipated a majority) might go so far as to take the political step of rejecting a society which seems to give the middle and upper classes much more than it gives them. Class experience, at work and in the community, can provide sources of socialization which *conflict* with the message of conformity from elsewhere. So Marx did consider that people can make choices within the limits of their consciousness (understanding) and social circumstances.

Social order

Commonsense seems to tell us that order is necessary if society is to exist at all. Order appears to require that rules and regulations, customs and conventions, should govern and guide human behaviour: without them, each day would be a fresh start to chaos. There is, of course, much truth in this. But sociology requires that we take a second look at commonsense. We must ask if what we take for granted is entirely as it seems. There are, after all, few societies which are completely orderly. Nearly all the advanced industrial nations have experienced severe conflict in recent history, either with other nations, or internally, or, more usually, both. Much of this conflict has taken place outside the framework and control of international or national law. Wars are the major example of the former. In Spain, internal differences have resulted in civil war, and several other nations have experienced periods in which law and order has virtually broken down. Even Britain, which has been relatively peaceful internally, has experienced disorderly civil conflict. The suffragette movement, demonstrations, clashes between police and union pickets, and racial violence are all examples. The 'troubles' in Northern Ireland are the most violent example. Further, all societies are characterized by a certain amount of criminal disorder, in addition to that generated by political and social conflict. Disorder and conflict have been so general a feature of history that they cannot be regarded as abnormal. Marx went further in arguing that one kind of conflict, class conflict, is the major driving force of history – a point we can more appropriately consider in a later section of this chapter (see pages 116–18).

Despite the conflict-ridden history of our species, it is probably true to say that most people hope for a peaceful and orderly society. What they disagree about is the sort of society that should exist in the first place. Hitler's Germany was relatively orderly, but most would consider that conflict and disorder were worth risking to overthrow him because of the kind of society the Nazis created. Other societies have attempted to allow for a considerable measure of conflicting opinions to be expressed but within a regulated context, that is, without resort to violence. Any genuine democracy must do this, but there is debate about whether all those countries that claim to be democratic actually achieve the conditions in which fair debate can take place. Marxists consider that British and American democracy is fundamentally flawed because the wealthy have more power to make their voices heard than the less well-off and poor (see Chapter 7, pages 214–15).

Social order and social control

We now briefly describe the basic means of social control used to keep order. The broadest way of examining this problem is to divide the means of social control into the formal and the informal. Thus, the government, judiciary, police and armed forces are the major formal means, whereas informal means are mainly concerned with socializing people to conform through, for instance, the family, educational system and mass media (see Chapter 5, pages 140–5). We examined this process in the previous section. Here, we prefer a slightly more complex way of categorizing the means of social control. These categories are: the physical; the moral; the material.

First, the physical means, of which the armed forces and the police are the major examples. In general, they are only used as a last resort to prevent order breaking down or when it has already broken down. Second, come moral means. When people agree about basic values and behaviour they conform to society's norms almost automatically. Socialization, especially early socialization, is the means to achieve this moral agreement or, to use functionalist terminology, 'consensus'. Marx fully recognized that this process occurs, but he argued that the poor and exploited are often socialized to accept a social order that is against their true interests. This brings us to the third means. Social order is more secure when people have a material interest in its maintenance. Those with property and wealth usually want the social order in which they have prospered to continue. Marx pointed out that the less well-off might favour change. This provides a basis for social conflict.

Finally, before examining the various perspectives on social order it needs to be pointed out that order and conflict are as much a part of small group as of large group life, or, put otherwise, they are a 'micro-level' as well as a 'macro-level' phenomenon. Even relationships involving only two people, or 'dyads' as Simmel called them, typically involve both agreement and disagreement – though the proportion of each varies immensely in given cases. Tension as well as harmony exists in most families. Sometimes conflict centres on very real, if often unadmitted, or even unrecognized power-struggles between, for instance, child and parent, or husband and wife. These can end in the child leaving home or in the couple becoming separated or divorced. More typically, however, families try to 'get along together', despite such difficulties. Larger institutions, such as the school, factory or office-complex, are also characterized by order, control and conflict and, again, the balance between them varies. To an extent, organizations can be usefully thought of as 'mini' societies. Essentially the same means of control – physical, moral and material – which operate in society also operate in organizations. Thus, you may obey school rules to avoid the cane, because you believe you should, or because you expect to be rewarded for doing so. Modern societies are 'organization' societies. Much of our lives, particularly our working lives, is spent contributing to and being controlled by formal organizations. Formal organizations seem to be a condition of the orderly functioning of modern societies and we will consider them in detail (on pages 104–11) after first discussing some major theories of social order.

Functionalism and social order – Durkheim (1858-1917)

Durkheim was profoundly aware of the changes that *industrialization* and *urbanization* were bringing about. Though determined to be scientific in his investigation of these developments, he was motivated by deep concern about their effect on the quality of social and moral life. Despite material progress, he considered that some of these effects were negative. It would not be too much to say that he thought he saw the beginnings of widespread moral disease in industrial, urban society (see pages 112–5).

Durkheim produced a model to distinguish the nature of order, or 'solidarity' as he called it, in pre-industrial or traditional societies from that in industrial ones. He referred to order in traditional societies as 'mechanical' solidarity and in industrial societies as 'organic' solidarity. Mechanical solidarity depends on the fact that members of society share common values, beliefs and patterns of life. Thus, a genuinely primitive tribe of Indians all believe in the same gods, practise the same rituals and, allowing for differences of age and sex, otherwise live very similarly. This similarity extends to work. All braves do the same basic things – namely, hunting, fishing and defending the tribal territory. In the same way all squaws tend to lead domestically oriented lives (though this is not true of women in all societies). Individuality is not usually of great importance in 'mechanical' societies. People gain their fulfilment and sense of meaning by identifying with society as a whole. Because so much is experienced in common, there is little separate, private life. The family is part of the wider network of relations and these in turn spill over into community life. Communal religious worship is seen as the highest expression of both personal and collective identity.

Durkheim argued that the nature of social solidarity changes from mechanical to organic *as societies become more complex*. In his view, complexity occurs as a result of the development and extension of the 'division of labour'. This term must be explained before organic solidarity can be understood. As Durkheim referred to it, the division of labour is the process by which work becomes more specialized. As society develops, more and more jobs appear. Once a family would grow their own food, build their own house and make their own clothes, whereas now we have specialist farmers, builders and cloth manufac-turers to do that work. More complex still, particular jobs have also become increasingly divided into different parts. We have seen the culmination of this process in our own time with the introduction of assembly-line production. Durkheim observed that population increase accompanies the growth in the division of labour. More people doing more jobs paves the way to a more *individualistic* society. How could such a varied society hold together in an orderly way? The answer, for Durkheim, was that role variety in work makes for *interdependence*. Mechanics, engineers, butchers, grocers, refuse-collectors, teachers and doctors do very different jobs but they all depend on each other. Take any one group away and the rest would be, at the least, inconvenienced. Indeed, some jobs are so important that society could not function without them. This interdependence is the basis of organic solidarity. Though the division of labour makes individuals more dependent on the services offered by society as a whole, in giving people specialized roles it also promotes individuality. If we can use a phrase not at all familiar to Durkheim, people 'do their own thing' and this *differentiates* them from others and gives them a more specific identity. This is the paradox of organic solidarity, and Durkheim himself describes it well:

In fact, on the one hand, every individual depends more directly on society as labour becomes more divided; and, on the other, the activity of every individual becomes more personalised to the degree that it is more specialised. [Durkheim 1893]

Morality is a key concept in Durkheim's model of society, and this is true of societies characterized by organic as well as by mechanical solidarity. He believed that social unity and order are only possible because people share and act upon *a consciousness of common moral values (conscience collective)*. These values underlie custom, convention and criminal law and provide the ultimate justification for punishing those who misbehave. Fundamental values vary from society to society, though similarities do exist. Murder and treason, for instance, are almost universally condemned. On the other hand, sexual values and those governing relations between family and kin vary enormously. In many primitive societies, for instance, pre-marital sex carries no social stigma, but it often does in economically advanced societies.

Durkheim contrasted collective moral consciousness in mechanical and organic societies. In the former he saw it as all-embracing. All aspects of life are governed by accepted beliefs and moral sentiments. If society's rules are seriously broken, retribution follows. Durkheim called this 'repressive justice'. There is no room for fundamental moral disagreement in mechanical societies: offenders are punished as guilty, and rarely, if ever, accepted as merely different. In organic societies, shared moral consciousness is not quite so all-inclusive. People begin to acquire more varied identities as the number and variety of jobs increase. Individuality increases because far more roles exist to be performed than in a primitive society. At the same time, home and family life slowly become more detached from the immediate community. Part of the individual's life becomes somewhat distanced from that of others. To a degree, the individual has more opportunity to think, feel and act independently. Nevertheless, Durkheim was quite insistent that in organic, as in mechanical society, the individual is still part of society and subject to its laws.

Durkheim clearly found it difficult and uncomfortable to imagine a society which ran entirely on practical lines and in which shared values played little part. He believed that individuals needed to be part of, or *integrated* into, a wider moral community. He described the situation in which norms and values break down as 'anomie'. A society characterized by anomie loses its cohesion and *ceases to be a community*. Anomie, for Durkheim, refers to a situation where norms are absent, or at least unclear. Durkheim's analysis of the cause and effects of anomie are of considerable interest. He argued that it was in times of great change, particularly economic change, that anomie is likely to occur. When the basic conditions of social life change, existing moral beliefs and norms governing conduct become less relevant. For instance, in our own time, the belief that work is the major source of personal identity and fulfilment is being undermined by the impact of the new micro-chip technology which reduces the need for human labour. Until adequate new means of self-identification can be found, this change is likely to produce anomie in society. There are no clear rules for the new social situation. This affects the way people behave. Uncertain of what to think and do, individuals can become depressed, morally insecure and destructive or aimless in their behaviour. These are signs that 'society is sick' or of 'social pathology' to use Durkheim's own term. This concept is fundamental to Durkheim's analysis of deviance (for example, crime, suicide) which is analysed in Chapter 11, pages 317–18.

Functionalist perspectives on social order since Durkheim

We can distinguish five major points about social order as stated by Durkheim with which more recent functionalists would agree. In particular these points have greatly influenced the theoretical work of the major modern functionalist, Talcott Parsons. The points are:

1 Values are the basis of social solidarity (or order).
2 Social solidarity changes from mechanical to organic as society itself becomes more complex.
3 Social order is more *natural* and *normal* than disorder.
4 Disorder does occur in society and it is likened to pathology (or disease).
5 These assumptions about social order and disorder powerfully reflect the biological or organic analogy.

In many ways Parsons's work is a continuation of Durkheim's, although it also reflects that of Weber, as well as containing some original elements. Parsons was less concerned than Durkheim and Radcliffe-Brown (see Chaper 2, pages 26–8) to develop sociology by drawing parallels between biological and social life. Rather, he wanted to describe in detail how society works *as a system*. The result is his 'social systems theory', which has already been described in Chapter 2, page 26. All that is necessary here is to bring out the central importance of order in Parsons's systems model. Indeed, the very basis of his model is that order has to be maintained so that society can meet human needs and so that individuals can contribute to society. The Parsonian-based model given here illustrates this. In this case, the economic sub-system has been developed, but you may like to 'fill in' the boxes for another of the sub-systems, for example, the political, or the educational.

Figure 5 shows how the individual is 'fitted in' to the functional requirements of the economic sub-system. For this to be so, he or she must share the values and norms of a worker and, of course, fulfil the relevant role, in this case, that of assembly-line worker. Various roles, including those performed by the line workers, make up the institution of the factory. In turn, factories and all other economic institutions make up the economic sub-system. The latter is one of the sub-systems that resolve the functional problem of society that Parsons calls 'adaptation' (see Chapter 2, pages 26–8).

Orderly functioning is a result of the mutual interdependence of the individual and society. However, the integration of the individual into society (that is, making individuals feel that they are a part of the society) requires the involvement of other sub-systems, notably kinship

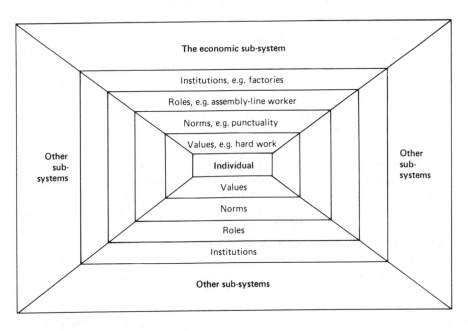

Figure 5 *The social system*

and cultural and community organizations. Thus, the local minister may exhort workers to work hard and to take a pride in their work. So, not only is each sub-system full of complex and mutually supportive connections, but the sub-systems themselves are interdependent, and overlap in a way that contributes to the creation of an orderly society.

Robert Merton has done more than anyone to build the concepts of disorder and conflict into functionalist thought. It has been mentioned (in Chapter 2) that he introduced the notion of dysfunction as a necessary balance to that of function. Here, his development of Durkheim's concept of anomie may be briefly mentioned, before a more detailed treatment in Chapter 11, page 317. Merton, revising Durkheim somewhat, considered that anomie occurs when the goals of society, for example, a good standard of living, are not matched by provision of the means to attain them, for example, there may not be enough well-paid jobs. Those excluded from the legitimate opportunity structure may turn to non-conformist or deviant means to achieve what they want. In this case, theft would be a way of obtaining a higher standard of living. Merton's work does introduce greater elements of disorder and conflict into functionalism, but it is to Marxist sociology that we must turn in order to find a much fuller treatment of these issues.

Marxist perspectives on social order

The starting-point of Marxist sociology is not social order, but the clash of interests which is considered to characterize all societies except the most primitive and the, as yet unachieved, fully communist society. The clash of interests is the basis of class formation and conflict; because of class conflict order is seen as subject to permanent stress (see Chapter 2, pages 31–2).

Marxists see the purpose of social order differently from functionalists. They want to know who benefits from social order and who does not. Social order is not something to be taken for granted, a mere matter of commonsense. It is *imposed* by the ruling class and operates primarily *in their interest.* Thus, in feudal society, the ruling class, that is, the class that owned the means of production, was the landed nobility. Undoubtedly, the feudal system enabled them to live far better than the average peasant. Marxists, however, mean rather more than this when they argue that, in a given type of society, the system works for the powerful at the expense of the weak. They mean that the law itself and the way it is enforced is biased in favour of the ruling class. In feudal society, for instance, the serfs, the lowest group of peasants, were legally required to give up much of their own produce to their lord or were required to work, often several days a week, on their lord's land in return for which they were guaranteed in law very little indeed. In any case, the lord was in a better position than the peasant to ignore the law if he so chose. Indeed, it was largely up to the lord and his men to enforce the law. For their part, the peasants had to hope for the best protection they might receive from their lord.

How do the same Marxist principles of analysis apply to capitalist society? At an obvious but important level, it can be pointed out that extreme inequalities in wealth persist (see Chapter 2, page 40; Chapter 6, page 152. It is less easy to show that the law and its enforcement favour the bourgeoisie, considered by Marxists to be the ruling class in capitalist society (see Chapter 11, page 332). Two points, however, may be made here to illustrate this view. First, the law is often an extremely expensive business. The legal costs of solicitors and barristers can run into hundreds of thousands of pounds. As a result, people on low and middle incomes are disadvantaged compared to the rich. Thus, an individual may decide he cannot afford either the time or money to, say, sue somebody for damages resulting from a motor accident. Or, if he does, he may have to settle for inferior legal advice and representation. The law is a commercial business and the maxim 'you get what you pay for' applies. A second point argued by Marxists is that more manpower, money, time and effort is put into apprehending working-class than middle- and upper-class criminals. In their view, this is not merely because there may actually be more working-class crime, but because the crimes of the 'respectable' and higher status are more easily condoned and overlooked than those of others.

The issue of law and order enforcement is important in the Marxist perspective. They see physical coercion not so much as the 'last resort' of capitalist society, as funtionalists do, but as a permanent threat to any militant challenge to the existing order. The powerful presence of the police and armed forces serves as a very visible deterrent to such plans. Marxists agree with functionalists, however, that another effective way of achieving conformity and consensus among all groups in society is through ideological persuasion, that is, to persuade people to think and feel that they *should* conform to and believe in the system – even if they are getting very little out of it (see Chapter 2, page 35; Chapter 7, page 191). Much as they dislike it, Marxists fully recognize that this happens. Consensus is generated through the various agencies of socialization. As indicated in the last section, however, Marxists consider that alternative sources of socialization, such as the experience of poverty, unemployment or exploitation, which can lead to conflict, do exist. As we shall see later, conflict is regarded not merely as a challenge to order but as a means of change.

Interactionist perspectives on social order

Social order is a large-scale or 'macro' concept. Interactionists tend to be more at home at the level of small-group behaviour. Nevertheless, they have contributed some interesting insights on social order, even though together these do not make up a complete theory.

Interactionists successfully manage to bring the concept of order down to a level meaningful to the individual. Two ideas help to achieve this. These are 'negotiated order' and 'impression management'. Interactionists do not see symbolic communication as rigidly pre-programmed. What people say and do is far from being wholly predictable. We will deal with the concept of negotiated order first.

Interactionists regard power relations between people as continually open to change. From day to day, week to week, the relationship between employer and employee, teacher and pupil, parent and child, can vary and develop. One of the major elements in this flux is that individuals in a shared social situation can negotiate or bargain about the on-going terms of the relationship. Thus, a teacher may tacitly 'strike a bargain' with a class that a particular lesson is going to be fairly free and easy as long as a given minimum of work is done. If the pupils break their side of the 'contract' the teacher may feel free to ignore his or her own side, and if the teacher suddenly changes the mood and direction of the lesson the pupils may, in their turn, feel aggrieved. Different teachers negotiate different general relationships with classes, though these are, of course, open to variation.

The concept of impression management was first introduced by Erving Goffman. He drew on Mead and Cooley to argue that people present themselves so as to affect others' impression of them. Although Goffman intended to stress individual choice, he is sometimes seen as presenting people as manipulative. More, perhaps, than they like to admit, most people manage their relationships with their friends with some care. For example, this can be done by subtle use of language. Thus an acquaintance who is told to 'drop round sometime' may well be intended to interpret this as 'you seem to be quite pleasant; I might invite you to my home in the future'. Thus, self keeps more control of matters than the actual words indicate.

Underlying these ideas is a quite different perspective on norms and roles from that adopted by functionalists. We examined this on page 93. We can add here that institutions such as schools, families and factories are also analysed from the point of view of the personal experience and creative efforts of their members, rather than in terms of their functions and goals. The example of pupil–teacher negotiation given above illustrates the point. In contrast, functionalists and Marxists are primarily concerned about structural matters, such as the relationship between school and work and between school and social class.

Let us take a further example of an interactionist perspective on organizational analysis. A typical interactionist approach to industrial sociology would examine 'factory life' (informal as well as formal) in a *single* factory rather than, say, develop a large-scale theory of, for example, the relationship between the economic sub-system and the political sub-system, which is the sort of thing a functionalist might try to do. Thus, Jason Ditton did a participant-observation study on how workers coped with boredom in a bakery. Appropriately, his article was titled 'Absent at work: or how to manage monotony'. Contrast this with our previous description of how functionalists see the worker as fitting into the economic sub-system (Ditton 1972).

For all the emphasis placed by interactionists on the personally meaningful nature of social existence, they recognize that society is a *shared* experience. Shared meanings and assumptions are necessary if life is to continue in an orderly way – though ethnomethodologists stress that these can be subject to continuous renegotiation. Quite simply, 'people know how to behave' in given situations, say, at a disco or in school. These shared assumptions are a form of 'typification', a typical idea of how to behave. This gives a measure of structure and order to existence. Within this framework the unpredictable as well as the predictable can be made to happen, and what happens can change the framework itself.

Social order and organizations

A preliminary definition of organizations is that they are bodies of persons existing over time to achieve the goals of specific groups. Thus, schools are organizations which exist to achieve the educational goals of various groups, including pupils, parents, industrialists and the government. Sociologists of the various perspectives stress different aspects of organizations, some emphasizing the power of organizational structures to control people, and others pointing out that it is, after all, people who originally create organizational structures and that, in the last analysis, organizations are people. We deal with these differences below.

Organizations, particularly large ones, are part of modern social order. Some feel that business and governmental organizations are too big and too powerful, but nobody would argue that we can do without organizations altogether. The extent and power of organizations is a very good reason for being interested in them. You and I are very likely to spend our working lives within large organizations and, in any case, we cannot avoid involvement with them. Paying taxes and rates, settling household bills, drawing social security and even shopping bring us 'up against' large organizations. It is, therefore, surely prudent to try to understand how and in whose interests organizations operate. Those who find organizations 'too boring' to merit serious study will probably be less able to deal with them than those who take the trouble to understand them.

The broadest distinction between types of organizations is that between formal and informal organizations. Formal organization is one in which activity is planned and regulated to achieve certain goals. Thus a factory is formally organized to achieve a given output, and a school is formally organized to obtain various educational aims. Informal organization is created and usually controlled by people working within formal organizations, but is not the direct result of formal planning. For instance, informal organizations exist within factories and schools. Indeed, it is difficult to imagine any kind of large organization, however rigidly organized, in which people do not manage to organize for their own purposes. Even in concentration camps and prisons, 'underground' communication systems emerge.

Given its obvious importance, it is surprising how long it took social scientists to stumble on the existence of informal organization. We use the words 'stumble on' advisedly, because it correctly describes how researchers first discovered this pattern of interaction. The occasion on which they did so is worth recounting.

In 1927 a team of researchers headed by Elton Mayo began to examine the variables, such as light and heat, which affected production in the Hawthorne plant of the Western Electricity Company in Chicago. They assumed that organizations did actually operate according to the formally pre-determined blueprints of bosses or managers. To their surprise even quite substantial variations in environmental factors like heat and light had remarkably little effect on production. What finally emerged as the most important independent variable was the presence of the researchers themselves! The workers they observed seemed to react positively to their interest and, when they were present, production tended to increase almost regardless of variations in environmental factors. They concluded that *social* as well as environmental factors are important in motivating workers. This conclusion was confirmed in further experiments carried out by the team, and particularly by an experiment known as the Bank Wiring Room Experiment. Again, they wanted to establish what variables affected production, but this time they concentrated on the interaction of the workers themselves rather than on environmental factors. They observed that the team of fourteen workers established their own production norms, and that these operated to a large extent independently of production incentive schemes introduced by management. Individual workers were expected to fit in with group norms and were 'made to feel it' if they did not. A clearer example of the operation of an informal social group could hardly be found.

It is worth giving a further example of how informal groups operate within formal structures and affect the functioning of formal organization. Let us take the familiar situation of the classroom. The teachers who ignore informal groups do so at their peril. Friendship groups or personal antagonism grow up within a class and influence the classroom 'atmosphere' in a positive or negative way. The teacher needs to be able to recognize and, to some extent, control such relationships in the cause of education. Earlier in this chapter we noted that in infant and primary education the role of the informal peer group is very important. For a teacher to divert informal peer group interaction in the direction of constructive learning is quite an art. Thus, peer group rivalry can be used to bring out children's best efforts, and friendship can provide a basis for co-operative projects. (You may wish to consider what moral questions are raised by such a use of superior knowledge by the teacher to manipulate the group.)

The important preliminary distinction between formal and informal organizations will help us in understanding some of the more specific theories of organizations to which we now turn. The first of these is Max Weber's famous theory of bureaucracy. Bureaucratic, or 'mechanistic', organizations are highly formal in structure. They are divided into specialist roles, some of which carry more power and status than others (that is, they are hierarchically ordered). Further, in bureaucratic organizations, employees are qualified and trained to perform the duties officially allocated to them. This definiton is derived from Weber's own ideal type description of bureaucracy, and it would be a mistake to expect all bureaucracies to conform precisely to it. The purpose of an ideal type, rather like a model, is to describe certain central, but not invariable, characteristics of a phenomenon. Most factories are organized in a typically bureaucratic way. At the top of the hierarchy is the managing director and the board of directors. Beneath them are specialist managers, such as the production and marketing managers. Beneath them are assistant managers, and so on down to the tea-lady. Weber was convinced that the bureaucracy is the most scientifically rational and efficient form of organization possible. He imagined that management would take decisions and that lower-level employees would faithfully execute their prescribed functions. In practice bureaucratic functioning is rarely quite so simple, but before we describe the dysfunctions of bureaucracy it will be helpful to introduce an organizational form that contrasts with bureaucracy: the 'organic'.

Organic organizations are loosely divided into specialist roles, which can overlap and be adjusted as necessary. Instead of a rigidly hierarchical (top-downwards) system of authority, control and communication, a 'network' structure exists which involves a broader spread of responsibility and participation in the work process and even in policy-making. Burns and Stalker (1961) first popularized the distinction between mechanistic/bureaucratic and organic organizational systems. They found that organizations, or parts of organizations, which are concerned with research and development, such as electronics companies, often adopt aspects of the organic organizational approach because this better enables them to collate (bring together) and develop knowledge. Like Weber's brureaucratic model, the organic model is an ideal type construct, and very often given organizations reflect aspects of both approaches.

We can now appropriately consider the dysfunctions of bureaucratic organizations. Weber has been criticized by a number of more recent writers for too readily assuming that, in organizational terms, bureaucracy is best. We have already seen that Burns and Stalker have argued that, in certain circumstances, organic organizational structures are more effective than bureaucratic ones. Thus, when it is necessary to pool knowledge in order to develop and achieve goals, rigid, bureaucratic structures may be dysfunctional.

Robert Merton (1968) offers additional criticism of bureaucracy. He points out that absolute obedience to bureaucratic rules and procedure may prevent an official from improvising a response to an unusual situation. At worst, such an attitude might even lead to what Merton calls 'goal displacement'. By this he means that the bureaucrat might come to attach more importance to observing the rules than achieving the purposes for which the rules exist. Thus, a ticket-collector who insists on collecting *every* ticket during a rush-hour is certainly doing his job but at the expense of the free-flow of busy people. With such examples in mind Merton is sensitive to the way in which bureaucracy can reduce people almost to the status of things or, more precisely, to that of parts in bureaucratic machines. He considered that the typical 'bureaucratic character' is excessively conformist, over-mindful of authority and afraid to act off his or her own initiative. Further, the clients as well as the officials of bureaucratic organizations can be belittled by the bureaucratic process. The hours of waiting often required to sign on for social security may or may not be necessary, but many find such a long and semi-public procedure humiliating. In fairness to Weber, he fully recognized that bureaucracy can sometimes seem to depersonalize both bureaucrats and those whom they deal with. Whilst he considered bureaucracy to be the most efficient form of organization, he also appreciated its capacity to dehumanize. However, Weber does not follow through the logic of his own insight. As Merton understood, dehumanizing organizational structures are likely to be dysfunctional because they are almost bound to smother commitment and fully efficient involvement.

Peter Blau (1963) offers an interesting piece of research into how two groups of officials working in separate departments of a state employment agency operated. For various reasons, one group operated on the basis of bureaucratic and competitive norms, and the other adopted a more co-operative and personal approach both to each other and to clients. Blau found that, on balance, the second group was more efficient when assessed in terms of official goal achievement because it succeeded in placing more clients in jobs. However, this is to over-simplify his findings. Sometimes officials in the non-bureaucratically operated department reacted too personally to clients and effectively discriminated in favour of some at the expense of others. Bureaucratic rules cannot always ensure fairer administration. Blau suggests that what is necessary for efficiency is a balanced operation, involving bureaucratic and less formal procedures. What is 'balanced' may, of course, vary with circumstances. On the whole, the administration of an army is better weighted towards the bureaucratic; that of a primary school towards the informal.

Finally, a study by Alvin Gouldner (1954) illustrates the importance of understanding organizational functioning and dysfunctioning within the context of existing traditions of management–employee relations and of what is appropriate in particular situations. Gouldner's case-study was of a gypsum mine and plant. He analysed the effect on the work-force of an attempt by a new manager to impose a bureaucratic regime on both the plant and the mine. This worked in the plant but was strongly resisted by the miners, who had been used to running 'their side' of the operation with a great deal of freedom and responsibility. This suited their work-situation which was, in any case, difficult to supervise closely. Gouldner concludes that bureaucracy is not equally appropriate to all work-contexts and that to impose it regardless of established traditions of management–employee relations can cause unrest.

It is not, however, necessary to cite sociological studies to show that bureaucracy can be dysfunctional. 'Working to rule' is a well-known form of industrial action, and it is based on the observation that if the rules of an organization are obeyed to the letter so much time will be wasted that efficiency will be greatly impaired. You can witness this for yourself next time your local bus or railway employees 'work to rule'. The conclusion is that for organizations to function efficiently not only rules are necessary but also commonsense and good-will in interpreting them.

Given the above criticisms of the classical, bureaucratic model of organizational analysis, it is not surprising that alternative models have been developed. We have already examined one radically different model from the bureaucratic, namely the organic systems model suggested by Burns and Stalker. A model of analysis that is closer to Weber's own is the systems theory of Talcott Parsons. The latter sees organizations as naturally evolving systems which have a primary interest in their own survival as well as in achieving prescribed goals. The approach is still functionalist but somewhat more subtle than Weber's. Peter Selznick adopts a systems perspective in a piece of empirical work on the Tennessee Valley Authority which was set up by President Roosevelt during the 1930s depression in order to develop the area. Selznick (1966) contrasts the ideals and the reality of the Authority. Theoretically, it was to serve the people of the area by providing jobs and by generating wealth. Local people were to be involved in policy-making. In practice, the policies of the Authority tended to be made in consultation with the powerful farming interests in the area and not with people more genuinely representative of the majority of the population. Predictably, it was the farming elite rather than the masses that primarily benefited from the development. Selznick's explanation of this is that in order for the Authority to survive, its officials had to compromise with those who had real power in the region, that is, leading farmers. By doing so the officials sacrificed the democratic aspirations that had been part of the original inspiration of the development.

Systems-based theory of various kinds remains popular, but another approach to organizational analysis, the social action perspective, has also been widely employed in recent years. The social action and interactionist perspectives are generally compatible with the organic systems approach of Burns and Stalker. They all conceive of organizations primarily in terms of human interaction rather than institutional goals. David Silverman (1970) stresses that it is the meanings individuals attach to organizations that define the action approach. Organizations are founded, developed and changed as a result of the actions of people. If this seems obvious, it must be remembered that the opposite, positivist emphasis on the effect of social institutions on individual behaviour has historically been much more dominant in sociology.

Whereas social action theory has been mainly influential in Europe, symbolic interactionism is an American 'product', and until recently was almost exclusively developed there. The major application of interactionist analysis to the understanding of organizations is Erving Goffman's now famous study, *Asylums* (1961). This work is much broader than its title suggests, though Goffman does draw extensively upon his own observational research in a Washington mental hospital. He is really attempting to define the essential characteristics not merely of asylums but of 'total institutions' in general. A total institution is an organization which is substantially cut off from society, and in which a large group of individuals is required to submit to a formally administered regime. In addition to closed asylums, we may cite monasteries, prisons, concentration camps and army barracks as examples of total institutions.

Goffman examines how the individual responds to the attempts by the officials of total institutions to break down the 'old' self and remould or 'force' it into the desired pattern, whether as monk, soldier or 'normal' person. He assumes, rather than fully demonstrates, that similar processes to those he describes in the asylum also occur in other total institutions. Various 'rituals' imposed on the new inmate symbolize his or her loss of independence and the stripping off of the old self. Literally, the inmate or recruit is often stripped of personal clothes and possessions and issued with a standard uniform which may carry an identifying number. Various attributes, such as height and weight, might be measured and noted. The individual will be allocated a bed and locker or, at best, a cubicle or cell – almost certainly identical with those of other inmates. Life then becomes institutionally regularized with little scope for independent and private action. Any personal freedom would challenge the institution's power to control and 'reform' the individual.

Despite Goffman's awareness of the power of total institutions to, as it were, 'melt down and remould' the self, he still stresses the various ways in which individuals 'fight back'. Indeed, this emphasis is generally typical of post-war interactionist writings. Goffman categorizes five modes of adaptation or adjustment: withdrawal; intransigence (refusal to co-operate); colonization; conversion; 'playing it cool'. Understanding the first two of these should pose no problem, but the other three require explanation. Colonization involves an identification by the individual with the institution so extreme that it comes to seem preferable to the world outside. For some persistent petty offenders and long-term or recurrent mental patients, total institutions may well provide a refuge from a world with which they cannot cope. Conversion occurs when the inmate accepts the official view of himself as, say, 'sick and in need of help' or 'criminal and in need of reform'. In Goffman's view, the mode of adjustment most frequently adopted is 'playing it cool'. The inmate more or less conforms to make life as easy as possible in relation to authority and in the hope of being released early and fully intact. Various incentives such as day-release (from mental hospitals) and parole and sentence remission (from prisons) encourages inmates to conform, although authorities generally hope that 'conversion' is genuine rather than just a 'cover'.

Goffman has been criticized for interpreting interaction within too narrow a context. In order to understand why people act as they do within given organizations it helps to know both something of their previous social experience and of the relationship of the organizations to society. It is to the latter issue that Marxists address themselves. Marx himself saw commercial and industrial organizations as the immediate means by which capitalists control the economic life of society in their own interests. Recently, Samuel Bowles and Herbert Gintis (1976) have developed and extended Marx's analysis. They consider that the hierarchical and highly fragmented division of labour in capitalist society prevents the working class from understanding the productive process as a whole, and therefore helps to prevent them from organizing to change it. It is difficult to change a system you do not fully understand. As Graeme Salaman puts it, Marxist analysis of organizations 're-politicizes those aspects of organization which much organizational analysis regards as the working out of some neutral law of market, technology or organizational purposes – the design of work and organizational structure itself'.

Social change

It is a cliché that we live in a world of change. To state that the speed of change has intensified in the modern era is only to say what everybody knows. More thought-provoking, perhaps, is the observation that before the modern period people were hardly aware of change and did not expect it. In the middle ages, the power and position of the church, monarchy and aristocracy were regarded as part of the unchanging, natural order of things. Individuals might quarrel, wars might be fought about who should occupy a given position in the social hierarchy, but the feudal system itself was the accepted *framework* with which these conflicts took place.

It is not too fanciful to suggest that the common medieval attitude to disturbances in nature as fearful 'portents' (signs) of future 'happenings' was an attempt to understand change. Freak bad weather, 'monstrous' births (for which we now have biological explanations), 'strange bodies in the heavens' (modern astronomy has cleared up this misunderstanding), were often regarded as indications that divinely or satanically inspired events were about to happen. After all, if God was responsible for the order of existence, only He, or his arch-antagonist, the Devil, could tamper with it. Of course, change did take place and, ultimately a whole way of life passed away. Even so, for decade after decade, even century after century, the tempo and quality of life varied little, as did the social order within which it took place.

It is helpful to set the concept of change in the above historical context. To do so suggests more probing and interesting questions about change. We can divide these questions into two categories: the first considers the causes of change and, to some extent, the means by which change is brought about – we discuss these issues in the section 'models of change'; the second briefly examines the experience and effects of change.

Models of change

Functionalist: from rural community to urban society

The functionalist model of social change, like Darwin's model of biological change, is based on the theory that societies evolve (gradually develop). When we discussed Durkheim's model of mechanical and organic solidarity, we stressed its application in the concept of order. Here we can see it as a way of understanding social change. As societies develop, their basis of solidarity becomes more complex. The way modern American society 'holds together' is immensely more involved and intricate than the way a primitive society does. Yet, less than five hundred years ago, America itself was peopled only by American Indians. A contemporary of Durkheim's, Ferdinand Tönnies (1855–1936), also sought to analyse the change from pre-industrial to modern society.

Tönnies and Durkheim particularly wanted to understand and explain the social effects of indstrial change. They described these effects largely in terms of the break-up of rural society, in which community and moral consensus existed, and the emergence of an individualistic urban society characterized by a great variety of moral attitudes and beliefs. They saw these developments largely in terms of a 'loss of community' – though the phrase is Tönnies's rather than Durkheim's. The change they perceived was a very general one, but it penetrated deeply the personal lives of individuals. This is because the framework of everyday life, including family and neighbourhood relations, was radically affected by industrialization, population movement and the need to adjust to urban living conditions. So loss of community has both a broad and a narrow application; it can affect society as a whole and it may also touch individuals in their immediate social context. For instance, a major economic depression may both undermine a nation's solidarity – as in inter-war Germany – and upset the lives of many individuals and communities.

Tönnies, in *Gemeinschaft und Gesellschaft* (1887), and Durkheim, in *The Division of Labour* (1893), repeatedly contrast the social life of traditional rural communities with that of rapidly developing urban areas. On the one hand, they stressed the family, neighbourhood and community as sources of personal identity and support and, on the other, the relative weakness of these institutions and the emergence of a more individualistic and impersonal way of life. Tönnies's terms, *Gemeinschaft* and *Gesellschaft*, describe this broad sweep of social change. *Gemeinschaft* means community and *Gesellschaft* can be translated either as society or association. He considered *Gemeinschaft* relationships to involve the whole person and to be typical of rural community life. *Gesellschaft* relationships are seen as associations for practical purposes, with little emotional content. He regarded associational activities as typical of urban life. Thus, a shopkeeper in a rural village could also very well be a friend and, on relevant matters, an adviser. Today's large-scale supermarkets on the other hand, are staffed by shop assistants who often change from week to week and to whom shoppers relate in a very specific and limited way. You might tarry for a chat at the corner shop but not at the supermarket cash-register!

We will first examine the change in the moral quality of life that Durkheim and Tönnies considered to have taken place as a result of industrialization and, then, the change in the quality of human behaviour.

Durkheim believed that evolution from a society with a *universally accepted moral system* to one in which *moral pluralism* (difference and variety) prevailed was fraught with difficulty for the individual. Undermining of previously unquestioned norms and values could leave a person in a moral vacuum. As we have seen, Durkheim referred to this state of normlessness as one of 'anomie' and he associated it particularly with times of rapid social change, such as that produced by industrialization and urbanization. Both Tönnies and Durkheim also noted that, in societies characterized by organic solidarity, people joined organizations and associations which, as well as meeting specific purposes, could also provide a measure of guidance and personal identity. Examples are trade unions and business associations. Tönnies, however, did not believe that these could provide the sense of belonging he regarded as characteristic of rural community: they were essentially concerned with associational activity. Durkheim held out a rather greater possibility that trades, business and professional associations might help to cement the insecure foundations of organic solidarity.

We now turn to the change in human relations which Durkheim and Tönnies supposed to have occurred as a result of industrialization. A key factor in the loss of community was the relative *impersonality* of urban life. We need to consider this point further. Durkheim considered impersonality to be the inevitable result of sheer numbers. It would drive the urban dweller mad to try to relate to all the people he could theoretically relate to in a given day. Simply in order to cope he must 'cut himself off' from the majority of 'passers by'. To do so is a matter of psychological survival. Incidentally, in professions such as teaching and medicine, where, in order to provide the required service, it is not possible to 'cut off' from people in this way, severe mental strain can result. Where interaction does take place between two 'urbanites' it is often for a specific purpose, such as buying or selling something. As likely as not, the people involved will not know each other and will confine their exchange to polite practicalities. The possibility of being lonely in the city crowd is obvious. In contrast, members of a small village population are more likely to mix 'business' with friendly chat. In a village, even to ignore someone is usually meant to convey some deliberate exclusion.

A further factor mentioned as contributing to impersonality in urban life is the growth in the division of labour. Increase in job specialization, particularly in respect of the provision of services, affects not only individual work satisfaction but also *relationships between people*. Let us take a couple of modern examples. The job of punching holes in a train ticket, or, say, serving potatoes and cabbage in a meal queue, are so completely structured to the achievement of their function that the possibility of personal exchange between worker and customer is very limited. Perhaps modern-day lorry drivers regret the passing of the 'trannie cafe' in favour of the large-scale, 'assembly-line' restaurant as much for the loss of the personal touch as for any decline in the quality of the food.

The type of social interaction referred to above, that is, one engaged in for a specific and limited purpose, is sometimes referred to as 'segmental'. Segmental relationships usually involve little emotional interchange or satisfaction. For example, relationships with receptionists, salesmen, shop assistants, ticket-sellers and administrators of various kinds are likely to be segmental. It may be added that the cash-nexus is often the major motivation underlying such interactions. It is partly because Durkheim and Tönnies saw an increase in this category of relationships and a decline in 'holistic' (personally as well as practically meaningful) relationships that they felt there had been a breakdown of community. The relationship of all this to theories of bureaucracy and of formal organizations is clear.

Two important continuing strands of influence can be traced to the Tönnes–Durkheim model. First, the concept of social breakdown in central urban areas, and the accompanying notion of anomie, are still used. Indeed they have been employed in the 1980s to interpret parasuicide amongst the mobile young (Sussex University, recent research). (Parasuicide is attempted or apparently attempted suicide, with the possibility that the attempt was not serious.) Ironically, considering Durkheim's preference for 'pure' sociology, his contribution here is really in the area of social psychology rather than in that of sociology narrowly defined. However, to explain the development and decay of urban areas, an analysis more fully reflecting inequalities of power and resources than Durkheim's is required. Secondly, community, used as a macro-level concept, has been very influential within American sociology. Several traditions of social scientific thought are apparent in the work of Talcott Parsons, one of which is a tendency to focus on those values and patterns of social action that keep society together rather than on those which divide it. This is an emphasis which clearly owes something to Durkheim.

Tönnies and Durkheim wrote of a 'loss of community' in industrial societies at a time when the socially disruptive effects of industrialization were highly conspicuous and before welfare state policies had been widely introduced to improve matters. Their observations are perceptive and relevant as a comparison between their own and pre-industrial times, but they clearly cannot be regarded as a final statement on the nature of modern society. A telling criticism of the 'loss of community' thesis is that it pessimistically under-estimates the ability of human beings to express their needs and feelings in new ways by developing or adapting institutions. Thus, for the young in modern society, the peer group is often more important for expressive purposes than neighbourhood, friends and kin, excluding immediate kin. In any case, working-class communities did strongly re-emerge in most industrial towns. Further, it is arguable that the modern nuclear family provides emotional support just as readily as the extended family, albeit for fewer people, and that the modern home is well equipped to enable family members to express many of their interests and feelings.

It can be argued that both Tönnies and Durkheim tend to emphasize the negative elements of the emerging individualism. No doubt isolation, loneliness and anomie did result from the breakdown of community but, for many, escape from the cloister of family and community meant the prospect of personal opportunity and self-expression. There is little appreciation of this in the work of either Tönnies or Durkheim.

Durkheim and Tönnies are also open to criticism from a Marxist perspective. Marx used the concept of class rather than community as the basis for his sociological analysis. He considered sentimental any concern for the supposed wholesomeness of pastoral community. In his view, the industrial revolution had simply changed society from a system of exploitation based on the ownership and control of land to one based on the ownership and control of industry. Ownership or lack of ownership of the means of production determined class position. What interested Marx was class conflict, not speculation about loss of community. We shall examine Marx's views on social change in greater detail on page 116. Next, we examine the work of a group of American sociologists, the Chicago school, who were substantially influenced by Tönnies and, particularly, Durkheim.

Louis Wirth, perhaps the most influential of the Chicago school of urban sociologists, described what he considered to be the essential features of city life in an essay first published in 1938. His starting point was that urban populations are *larger*, more *dense*, and contain a greater *variety* of people than rural populations – relative to the same space. His comments on the impersonal, practical, functional nature of urban life echo those of Durkheim. In a given day, an individual may have dealings with ticket-collectors, shop-assistants, clerks, assorted bureaucrats, and – at a distance – telephone operators. As Wirth well understood, this impersonality was the price we pay for an economy based on a complex division of labour in which many people do small and specific tasks for others.

In addition to Wirth's observations on population and its immediately obvious social effects, other Chicago sociologists concentrated on the relationship between rural–urban migration, population movement within the city and the physical environment of the city itself. In particular, Burgess (1925) closely analysed social life in what he termed the 'zone of transition' or 'zone of deterioration' which was located as an inner city ring around the city centre business district. He regarded the zone of deterioration and, for that matter, other urban zones, as the 'natural' product of human activity, rather as various pond habitats are the natural product of pond life. Because of this comparison, the Chicago school of urban sociologists are known as urban 'ecologists'. Their comparison of social to biological processes is highly functionalist. Most sociologists now agree, however, that the ecological approach cannot fully explain urban processes. It ignores class and power in the city. We turn now to Marxist perspectives on change, which give much greater stress to these factors in accounting for all kinds of change.

Change and conflict

Marxists consider that fundamental change is produced through conflict. Class conflict is the dynamo or engine that drives history forward: revolution is regarded as the ultimate logic of class conflict. Traditional Marxists consider that it is only through revolution that fundamental change can be achieved, although some contemporary Marxists argue that parliamentary institutions can be used for this purpose. It is important to be clear, however, that Marx saw revolution only as the culmination of a complex series of developments. This will become clear shortly.

In order to explain the revolutionary aspect of Marxist theory, it is necessary to recall Marx's analysis of the link between the economy and social relations. He argued that, apart, perhaps, from early history, there has always been a producing class and a class that has controlled the means of production and enjoyed the profit from what has been produced. During the ancient mode of production, classes were polarized into slaves and slave-owners; under feudalism, into land-owners and serfs; under capitalism, into capitalists and wage labourers. According to Marx, the economic relationship of these classes determined their social relations. The class that owns the means of production is always of higher social status and has more power than the class that works the means of production.

Marx argued that class relations change primarily because *new* means of production are introduced (see Chapter 6, pages 152-4). New productive means affect social relations. Groups that introduce the new means of production challenge the existing dominant group, who may resist innovation. Thus, capitalists, who wanted to borrow large sums of money as a *means* of financing investment in commerce and industry, challenged the social, political and legal dominance of the feudal land-owning class. It was legally and practically difficult for ordinary individuals and small groups to raise money by borrowing in this way. If they did, and made great wealth out of it, they would threaten the position of the feudal nobility, which, not surprisingly, the latter did not want. Marx saw the turbulence of the seventeenth century in England, including the civil war, largely in terms of the conflict between the rising capitalist class and the landed aristocracy. The former wanted less taxation and changes in financial and commercial law and practice. Eventually, they got what they wanted and became the ruling class themselves. With the example of the transformation of feudalism into capitalism in mind, the following quotation from Marx is worth a careful reading:

At a certain stage of their development, the material forces of production in society come in conflict with the existing relations of production. . . . From forms of development of the forces of production these relations turn into their fetters. Then occurs a period of social revolution. [Marx 1859]

Applied to our example, this means that once the capitalist class had gained economic control, it was in a position to take over power in other areas as well. Marx believed that, in his own time, economic developments were taking place which would result in the capitalist class, in turn, being replaced by the working class as the dominant group in society. After this, he anticipated that a classless society would be established. We now analyse these points.

It is hardly possible to exaggerate the importance and influence of Marx's analysis of the conflict between the bourgeois (capitalist class) and the proletariat (working class). Marx considered that capitalist production tended to move from small to very large scale. This process of centralization also brought the working class together in larger numbers and enabled them to organize. Marx anticipated that the working class would use its collective strength to take over the centralized capitalist system of production. In other words, he believed that they would *socialize* the economy. He puts his analysis plainly enough himself:

Centralisation of the means of production and socialisation of labour at last reach a point where they become incompatible with their capitalist integument (skin). This integument is burst asunder. The knell of capitalist private property sounds. The expropriators are expropriated. [Marx 1867]

The fact is that nowhere has a socialist revolution occurred in quite the way that Marx anticipated. Socialist revolutions have, typically, taken place in agricultural rather than industrial societies. The Chinese and Cuban revolutions are relevant examples. This has been for a variety of reasons, most of which Marx could not have been expected to foresee.

Marx may have suffered from being too ready to play the prophet, but this should not be allowed to obscure his immense contribution as a sociologist. Much of his analysis of the contribution of class conflict to change remains invaluable. He provided a model of conflict structuralism that has inspired generations of subsequent sociologists. Further than this, his major contribution to explaining historical change lies in his awareness that economic reality provides the structural framework which limits and influences change. It is only within this framework that the role of the individual or group in bringing about change – which others have rightly emphasized – can operate.

As a useful balance to the previous section on functionalism and rural–urban change, I will briefly describe how Marxist concepts have been applied to understanding the same problem.

Although Marx was as much concerned as Durkheim and Tönnies to analyse the effect of industrialization on social life, he regarded the work situation, which produced the class situation, as the correct starting point for doing so. For him, community depends on class. Indeed, he preferred to use the concept of 'class culture' to that of community to describe particular class life-styles and modes of thought. The separate leisure and cultural lives of the working class and middle class reflected their separate and antagonistic position in the work-place. It is hardly surprising that, before the mines were nationalized, miners sought their own company rather than that of the owner-bosses! Engels, too, who made a close study of the living conditions of the English working class, did so within a strictly class-conflict perspective (Engels 1844). He stressed the exploitation of one class by another and the social crisis he thought this would eventually produce, whereas Durkheim sought to find and describe the processes by which society recovered equilibrium and adjusted to economic and social change.

It is certainly true, as far as modern societies are concerned, that for the concept of community to have any theoretical usefulness or practical applicability, it must be used in conjunction with that of class. The major formative influence on modern communities is the class system. Differences in wealth, norms and values are major class variables that influence the nature of communities. Members of middle-class communities relate to each other differently, and form a different local culture, from members of working-class communities – which is not to deny, of course, that there can be considerable variation within the two types. Traditional working-class culture is, for instance, typically closely knit and often involves a 'them and us' attitude to life, whereas middle-class social networks are more widely dispersed and there is less immediately local community life. As is made clear on pages 173–80 these patterns are changing, but the immediate point is to grasp through a concrete example that class greatly affects community.

Recent Marxist urban sociology, such as the work of Manuel Castells (1977), has tended to stress that the wealth and power of capital and particularly of big corporations gives capitalists great control and influence in urban and, for that matter, rural affairs. The power of a company to invest in or to withdraw investment from a given area can fundamentally affect the lives of thousands of people. Thus, social problems such as poverty and demoralization among unemployed youth are related to economic realities, and particularly to the power of those who take the major economic decisions. In Castells's opinion, government in advanced Western society rarely attempts to control industry. What the welfare state does is to 'mop up' the main problems caused by private enterprise but not to deal with their root cause. While Castells and other Marxists applaud the emergence of community groups to defend their territory against unwelcome redevelopment, they consider that what they regard as the irresponsibility of capitalism can only be completely stopped by a socialist party in power.

Marxists and other conflict theorists have paid particular attention to the decline of the inner city in the post-war period. As well as the power of capital, they also stress that planners, building society managers and others who control valuable resources such as public housing or mortgages can make or break the lives of ordinary people by their decisions. Ray Pahl (1970) refers to these powerful individuals as 'gate keepers' and their role must be considered in any analysis of power in the city.

Conscious of inequality and poverty in the city, David Harvey (1977) has attempted to put forward a set of principles for resolving conflicting claims about how collectively produced wealth should be distributed on a 'territorial' basis, that is, which areas should get what resources. From many possible criteria for a 'just distribution', Harvey selects three which he considers most important – need, contribution to the common good, and merit. Harvey makes a strong case that 'need' is currently the most neglected of this trinity. Yet, Harvey's attempt at rational evaluation and measurement notwithstanding, these matters of value and policy have always been and will remain a matter for disagreement. Of course, sociology is helpful in understanding the nature, dimension, location and causes of urban problems – all of which need to be known if the problems are to be solved. But sociology does not prescribe the solution itself.

Functionalist and Marxist perspectives on world development and underdevelopment

The same argument reviewed above about how best to conceive of change – whether through evolution or conflict – recurs in a world context. Functionalists stress that traditional societies 'normally' go through certain 'stages of growth' before reaching modernity. They tend to consider that if these societies remain open to Western investment, expertise and technology, their development will occur almost naturally. Marxists, by contrast, argue that to rely on the capitalist West is a form of dependency, a neo-colonial relationship. They urge Third World countries to develop independently and socialistically, relying on each other for help. Thus, the functionalist/Marxist debate about change is global.

As the previous paragraph implied, the 'bias' of functionalists and Marxists is especially obvious in respect to the issue of development. When functionalist and Marxist arguments are viewed in an international perspective, the same potential weakness in both of them becomes very apparent. Both theories of change tend to appear determinist (to claim the knowledge to predict the future) when taken to extremes. Perhaps this is because the organic (functionalist) and dialectical (Marxist conflict) models both have an impersonal, almost mechanical aspect to them. In fact, both gradual and revolutionary change occur. In part, people themselves decide which course to take. Weber was aware of the importance of human motive as indeed, are many less dogmatic functionalists and Marxists. (See also Chapter 14.)

Conclusion

This brief section is to serve as a reminder that, for good or ill, change affects the lives and happiness of human beings. It would be comforting to think that change is synonymous with progress. That illusion was perhaps sustainable in the nineteenth century, but in this century of wars and international tension it is not.

Change usually requires social adjustment. A major argument in favour of evolutionary rather than revolutionary change is that it gives people time to adjust. This is a conservative position inspired by some feeling of humanity. Others argue that sometimes revolution is necessary to get rid of rich, selfish and exploitative elites. Whether people like it or not, in the modern period change has, in fact, occurred at great speed and sometimes through revolution. The word 'revolution' has been freely applied to a variety of events and developments of the past two hundred years. Some of these have been political, such as the French, American and Russian revolutions, but we also speak of the technological, industrial, urban, and, more recently, of the computer revolutions.

It would be impossible to try to work out a balance sheet of the positive and negative effects of such widespread change, but some assessments may be attempted. If improvement in the material standard of life (at least in the West) is the most obvious benefit, it is also difficult not to be struck by the great human cost of change. The urban squalor of mid nineteenth century has been well documented, by Frederick Engels (1844), and Charles Booth (1889) among others. The price of socialism and modernization in Russia was the loss of many millions of lives. Fascism in Germany, which was in part an attempt to give leadership and direction to change, ended in severe cruelty and repression.

Pursuing this pessimistic theme further, it is remarkable how often scientific invention produces mixed benefits. Few would wish to deny the positive effects of medical advance but, in combination with better methods of birth control, it has produced a population with imbalanced age-groups. In Britain one person in six is over retirement age, and the problem of having so large an unproductive and, inevitably, relatively unhealthy proportion of the population is well known. Let us take another example of science's double-edged blade: today we readily hail the 'silicon-chip marvel'; but how 'marvellous' it will be for those millions who may be put out of work as a result of its use remains to be seen.

Contemplation of the sociology of change tends to drift into speculation about the future. The history of social prediction is littered with failures. Study of the present and past does not produce the blueprint of the future. What sociologists and historians can hope for is to discern certain structural influences and social trends which, at best, offer clues to the direction in which things might move. There is, however, no pure science of society which can produce reliable predictions. People make history though some make it more than others. The challenge is to make your own contribution. There now exist the material means to help fashion a world of rich humanistic vision, or equally to destroy it.

Guide to further reading

Major topics merely touched on here, such as education and deviance, are given a bibliography at the end of their specific chapters (Chapters 9 and 11). The clearest presentation of the interactionist perspective on socialization is chs. 3 to 5 in Peter and Brigitte Berger (1976), *Sociology: A Biographical Approach*. From the point of view of A-level syllabus coverage, the book suffers through inadequate treatment of perspectives other than symbolic interactionism. A useful and enjoyable read, somewhat later in the course, is Stanley Cohen and Laurie Taylor (1976), *Escape Attempts: The Theory and Practice of Resistance to Everyday Life*. This is partly inspired by the work of the American symbolic interactionist, Erving Goffman (1961). Goffman's own book, *Asylums*, also available as a Penguin paperback (1970), is a clear and influential example of interactionist analysis of order and organization. A good account of functionalist analysis of social order is in Chris Brown (1979), *Understanding Society: An Introduction to Sociological Theory*, Chapter 2, although the scope of the chapter extends to a full account of functionality. The best basis for understanding theories of social change is a knowledge, at least rudimentary, of modern history. A helpful book as far as Britain is concerned is Judith Ryder and Harold Silver (1977), *Modern English Society*. A sociological account of change, global in scope, is Anthony Smith (1976), *Social Change*. It might be attempted much later in the course. My *New Introductory Reader in Sociology* (Harrap-Nelson, 1983) contains readings on the main topics covered in this chapter.

5 Culture

Patrick McNeill

The concept of culture is one of the most straightforward and at the same time one of the most complex ideas in sociology. Part of the difficulty is that the word is used in various ways. In everyday life, we use it to refer to the arts, painting and music, whereas in sociology it is used to refer to whole lifestyles and group perspectives.

Imagine, if you can, a new-born infant which has been separated from its mother and all human contact at birth. It is, at this stage, a wholly biological being; that is, all its activities are based on the physical bodily functions. It does not know its own identity, and is probably not even aware of its own existence. Imagine, too, that this being is kept separate from all human contact for, say, twenty years. Its physical life is sustained by machines, but it never sees any other human being, and receives no other stimulus or experience of any kind.

Assuming that this being lived for the full twenty years, what would it be at the end of that time? A vegetable? Would it be human? It would certainly not be social. It would still not be aware of itself as a being . It would be incomplete, or partial. When compared with the typical 20-year-old, it would lack a vast amount of experience which, in normally socialized people, has become organized and stored in a way that makes it possible for them to participate in social life (see Chapter 4, pages 90–5). It has, in fact, had no contact with culture.

Looked at in this way, we may regard culture as everything that a person is, thinks, or does that has been learned through contact and interaction with others.

It is only through socialization into a culture that people become social at all. By learning and acquiring culture, a person can make sense of his or her day-to-day experience in a way that is similar to that of other members of society, and can thus come to participate in social life. Social life would be impossible if people did not, by and large, interpret situations, objects, gestures and signs in similar ways and, broadly, share opinions about them. You can test this proposition simply by pretending not to understand what somebody is saying to you, however much they explain it, or by behaving in a doctor's waiting-room as though it were a public house, or even vice versa. Ordinary social relationships become impossible, and pressure is soon brought to bear to 'bring you back into line'.

But culture is not confined to interpersonal actions, thinking and feeling. It includes the way we think about and make sense of the material world. For example, a drainpipe is a drainpipe because that is the way in which our culture makes sense of that particular arrangement and position of a tubular object made of iron or plastic. A tree is a botanical object, but where it is planted, how it is trimmed, whether it is considered beautiful, and what value is placed on its timber content – all these are cultural. Taking in nourishment is a biological need. Where it is done, how, when, with whom, what is eaten and how it is prepared, are all cultural, and vary from society to society and group to group.

Think about a typical three-bedroomed semi-detached house in a suburban street. How does its design, structure and location express and symbolize the cultural norms and values about family life, work, leisure and life-style of its occupants? How does the house influence and constrain the life-style? Like all culture, the house simultaneously expresses and makes possible a certain way of life, and at the same time makes other ways impossible or, at least, very unlikely.

Primary socialization (Chapter 4, page 91) is the process whereby the growing child learns the culture of the society into which he or she is born. It is learned so thoroughly that it becomes what we call 'second nature' but is, of course, not natural at all. It is not until we pause to reflect on how much we take for granted, or until we have to explain something to a child or perhaps a foreigner, that we become aware of the complexity of culture.

Some definitions

There are many definitions of culture, and four are reproduced here for you to consider in detail.

1 'Culture refers to the organization of experience shared by members of a community, a process which includes the standards and values for judging and perceiving, for predicting and acting.' (Walton 1979)
2 'Culture . . . the accumulated experience, meanings, rule-systems and forms of understanding of groups and societies'. (Davies 1976)
3 'Culture . . . that complex whole which includes knowledge, belief, art, morals, law, custom, and any other capabilities and habits acquired by man as a member of society'. (Tylor 1871)
4 'Culture consists of models or patterns of thinking, feeling and behaviour which have been socially learned.' (Giner 1972)

While there is clearly some overlap among these definitions, they vary in the way in which they present culture as 'out there', waiting to be learned and absorbed by new members of a society, or as being 'in here', that is, in the consciousness of members of society, and being created and recreated by them in their day-to-day lives. Whenever a group of people meet and interact in a new context, they create a culture, or subculture (see below). This may be the temporarily shared perspective of, say, a bus queue, or the more long-lasting culture developed by a group of students following a course of study. 'We see group perspectives as arising when people see themselves as being in the same boat and when they have an opportunity to interact with reference to their problems' (Becker 1961).

It is important to see that while it is obviously true that without social beings there would be no culture, it is equally true that without culture there would be no social beings. While culture exists in people's consciousness, that consciousness is shared. Though we sustain and reinforce our culture through our actions, we tend to think of it and experience it as external to us and influencing and controlling those same actions.

Subculture and counter-culture

Not all members of a society share the same culture. In one sense, of course, they do: to be a member of a society is to share in its culture. But there are sub-groups in society whose culture may vary so much from those of other sub-groups that they must be regarded as subcultures, or even counter-cultures (where the sub-group's values are opposed to those considered acceptable in the wider society). But even the most hostile counter-culture must share some cultural traits with the wider society if it is possible to identify it as part of that society at all.

Sociologists have claimed to identify subcultures among the poor, among criminals, in social classes, in ethnic minorities, in occupations, in residential institutions, in schools, among young people, and in different parts of the country. So many such subcultures have been identified that we must ask the question of whether there is a mainstream culture at all. Some sociologists argue that a society is made up of a plurality of subcultures, while others maintain that what counts as 'normal' is in fact the culture of the dominant group in society. (See below, and also pages 318–323.)

Summary

Culture is relatively integrated and relatively stable over time. It can be identified in the structure of a society or group, in its institutions, and in the actions of its members. It is socially learned, socially accumulated, socially shared and socially reinforced. It involves what we know, what we believe, and what we think is right or wrong. Our day-to-day behaviour is guided by the cultural framework in which we live. We recognize social situations, and react appropriately.

At the interpersonal level, culture provides us with ways of responding to everyday experience and serves as a guide to action. At a societal level, it promotes social order.

Language

The use of language is one of the most important ways in which human beings differ from other animals. Most animal species can, of course, communicate with each other, and some can transmit quite complex messages. But when an animal communicates with its fellows it selects a signal or signals from a finite range available to it. What a human being can do, and we are unique in this, is to assemble a group of signals (words) in a way that no one has ever done before, transmit them, and, provided that we observe basic rules, make ourselves understood. We can say things that no one has ever said before, and be understood.

Furthermore, human language can deal in abstractions, and so discussion can take place. Human beings can discuss possibilities, and can reflect on and choose between alternative views or courses of action. We can make plans. It is this ability to reflect, to be consciously aware of ourselves and our relationship with our environment, that distinguishes human beings from other animals. And it is language that is the key to this ability.

We have seen that social interaction is only possible between people who share some cultural background, however limited. Their interaction is conducted through a shared language. If they have no words in common, they can interact to a limited degree by interpreting each other's gestures. But they cannot get beyond the basic level until they share language. Culture is the basis of social interaction, and language is the vehicle of culture. The study of language is therefore fundamentally important in the study of human social behaviour.

To be a member of a group or society is to share in its culture, and thus to see the world as other group-members do. We feel at ease with those who, broadly speaking, share our world-view. You may have heard or used the everyday expression, 'Yes, I like him – he speaks my language'. This does not mean, literally, that he speaks English, but that he thinks as I do, responds as I do, and shares my assumptions. Language, therefore, binds a group together. This is especially obvious in the case of some subcultural groups, whose private slang and vocabulary enable them to identify each other and to exclude others, especially authority, from the group.

This great importance of language has been increasingly recognized by philosophers and sociologists during this century. Phenomenologists, particularly, have given language a central role in their theory of social life. As we have seen, their basic theme is that the individual socially constructs his or her reality, and they regard society as an immensely elaborate construct of shared meanings, continually created and recreated in interaction (see Chapter 2, page 50). Since language is the tool used to create and sustain this shared reality, reality to an extent depends on and exists in language. Indeed, what is 'really' so may be changeable by using different words to refer to it. If we think of 'old age pensioners' as 'senior citizens', does this change our attitude to them, and their own self-image? If it does change our attitude, then our behaviour towards them will change. In that case, they will *really* be a different phenomenon from that which they were originally. By referring to someone as a 'terrorist' or as a 'freedom-fighter', we are not only making our attitude clear, but also implying what action should be taken towards him or her. Whether we refer to the 'foetus' or the 'unborn child' has crucial implications for our views on the morality of 'terminating' it, or 'killing' it.

Ethnomethodologists take this argument further and may argue that the world is ultimately no more than talk. Some therefore confine their sociological analysis to the study of conversations and verbal exchanges. They try to show how such verbal exchanges create the social reality in which the participants share, and which they have continuously to 'accomplish' (Chapter 2, pages 52-3).

Language, then, gives meaning to our experience by organizing it. When a young child first sees a furry four-legged animal with a tail, his parent may say 'dog', and the child will learn the word, and hence share the experience. Then next time he sees a furry quadruped with a tail, he may say 'dog' and be told 'No - cat'. After a number of similar experiences, the child learns that animals as varied as a chihuahua and an alsatian are all dogs and that cats, some of which may look very similar in appearance to some dogs, are a separate species - or, rather, that they are defined as a separate species in our culture. The child learns too that, whereas Mummy is a woman, not all women are Mummies, and still less are they all his Mummy. But it is only through his use of the word 'Mummy' that he can learn that, to the little girl next door, another woman is Mummy. He can learn that her relationship to her Mummy is of the same order as his relationship to his Mummy. He can thus learn to abstract the concept of Mummy from his experience, and apply it in other contexts.

Language also enables us to share experiences which we have not had first-hand. I have never seen an angry African elephant charging through the undergrowth at me, but I have read accounts of it in books. I thus have some idea of what it is like, I have an attitude towards it as an experience, and I think I know how I would react. Indeed we know most of what we know only because others have told us about it, in language. Most of our experience, and hence our knowledge, is second-hand, and is filtered to us by others, through language. We will return to this point when considering the mass media.

Language, then, enables us to make sense of and share our experience.

But how far does it limit our experience, by organizing it in one particular way to the exclusion of others? Initially, language may be thought of simply as labels applied to an objective 'out-there' reality. But, if language is understood as giving meaning to reality, it follows that a different language may give a different meaning to experience. Experience, and so reality, may vary according to which language is used to give it meaning. The question is: can we experience something for which we have no word? Or, more sociologically, can we share an experience with others if we cannot express it in language?

The philosopher Wittgenstein maintained that the world in English is different from the world in French, that is, that English speakers actually perceive a different reality from French-speakers. Bernstein (see Chapter 9, pages 251) has argued that children whose language-code is different from that used in schools may under-achieve because their use of language and thus their perception of experience is different from that of their teachers.

This view of language lies behind the efforts of some feminist writers, and of people concerned with race relations, to change the very language we use when discussing these issues:

Language is . . . our means of manipulating reality. . . . One semantic rule which we can see in operation in the language is that of the male-as-norm. . . . those who are plus male and those who are minus male. . . . By arranging the objects and events of the world according to these rules we set up the rationale, and the vindication, for male supremacy. [Spender 1980]

It follows that, to begin to change this situation, we must change how we view the world, by changing the language we use to make sense of that world. (See also page 354.)

Language is essential for us both to interpret our experience and to become social, and at the same time it limits what we are able to experience. It is, therefore, a social institution like any other, created by human beings and yet exercising control over us, regulating our patterns of thought and our relations with others, making many things possible and many others impossible.

The sociology of knowledge

The central theme of the sociology of knowledge is that all knowledge can be accounted for in terms of the social context in which it is known. This is the principle of 'relativism', which contrasts with 'absolutism'. Relativism maintains that, since ideas about what is factual truth vary from one society and social group to another, such ideas are relative. It is not that some societies are right and others are wrong, in an absolute sense that applies in all places and at all times. Rather, there is no final 'right' or 'wrong', either of fact or of morality.

What is knowledge?

Knowledge can be regarded as being divided into two main categories.

1 Specialist knowledge, known to relatively few people, and divided into separate disciplines, such as physics, philosophy, biochemistry, sociology.
2 Commonsense, everyday, taken-for-granted knowledge, which includes everything which people think of as true, whether they can 'prove' it or not, and which they usually never question.

Until quite recently, the sociology of knowledge concentrated on the study of specialist knowledge. It asked how and why particular ideas appeared when and where they did, why they had particular appeal at that time and in that place, and what effect they had on social action. Weber's work on the Protestant ethic and the rise of capitalism is an example of this tradition, as is R. K. Merton's study of the part played by Puritanism in the early development of the natural sciences (Merton 1957).

This kind of work, however, has always drawn a distinction between science (including mathematics) and non-science subjects. The natural sciences (physics, chemistry, biology, etc.) have been regarded as different from the arts, humanities and social sciences (history, literature, aesthetics, philosophy, sociology). Where the latter subjects have been regarded as, to a greater or lesser extent, the outcome of their social and historical context, the laws of natural science have been seen as independent of their context. It is, of course, recognized that time and place influence what kind of research is done and thus what discoveries are made but, once a law of nature is identified, it is considered to be true at all times and in all places. It is seen as a realm of objective, value-free knowledge which exists independently of the observer, and accurately reflects an 'out-there' objective reality, which is waiting to be discovered.

This view of natural science, which is broadly known as 'positivism', has become part of the commonsense knowledge of our society, and is shared by most natural scientists. Though most of us know very little about the natural world, we assume that the scientists do and that, when they say something is the case, it is foolish to argue. Advertisers use this blind faith extensively, especially when marketing branded medicines. This view has, however, been challenged by philosophers in recent years and also, to some extent, at a commonsense level, and we shall return to this point later.

With the rise of phenomenological sociology, the sociology of knowledge has been extended to include commonsense knowledge. This development is largely a result of the work of Peter Berger and Thomas Luckmann (1966), which derives from the earlier work of Alfred Schutz. They point out that commonsense taken-for-granted knowledge varies from one society to another and, indeed, within any one society. What is seen as reality therefore also varies between and within societies. Since commonsense and reality are relative in this way, the sociology of knowledge must be concerned with the processes whereby different realities are created in different social groupings, that is, with the 'social construction of reality'. Realities are socially constructed (subjective) but, once constructed, take on a solidity and apparent concreteness (objective). Rather than confining itself to the history of ideas, sociology of knowledge must be concerned with 'whatever passes for knowledge in a society'. Whether the knowledge is right or wrong is irrelevant. The sociologist should study how it comes to be seen as right, indeed obvious – in fact 'commonsense'.

Seen in this way, sociology of knowledge becomes the centrepiece of sociological analysis. Indeed there is no great difference between knowledge and what has, earlier in this chapter, been called culture.

Marxist influences

In the last ten years or so, the renewal of Marxism has contributed substantially to the sociology of knowledge. Questions are asked about the relationship between what is regarded as knowledge in a society and the interests of the dominant group in that society. In terms of specialist knowledge, studies have shown how dominant scientific ideas have been used to promote the interests of the ruling class (for example, the Darwinian theory of natural selection and the survival of the fittest is used to justify the ethic of competition, and to show that top people are there because they are best fitted to that position – social Darwinism). Also, as we shall see in Chapter 9, page 264, it has been argued that specialist knowledge is used as a commodity which can be owned, bought and sold. It gives power to those who possess it, and is passed on by them only to the favoured few. The professions, too, may usefully be seen as an occupational group with a monopoly of a particular kind of knowledge (see page 280).

In terms of everyday knowledge, the emphasis has been on showing how the dominant ideology (a conception of reality that promotes the interests of the ruling class and thus helps maintain the *status quo*) so saturates everyday commonsense that we are not even aware of it. Ideology, in this sense, operates beneath the level of consciousness. Commonsense knowledge legitimates the social structure.

The development of the sociology of knowledge

Karl Marx developed the fundamental notion that human knowledge and consciousness is the outcome of social context. You may recall from Chapter 2, page 34, the quotation: 'The ideas of the ruling class are in every age the ruling ideas.' For Marx, human thought originates in activity (labour) and the social relationships resulting from that activity. 'Being determines consciousness, rather than consciousness determining being' (Marx 1859). The economic substructure generates a superstructure which includes knowledge, culture and ideology. Those who control the substructure will control the superstructure. There is debate among Marxists as to whether the superstructure has any great independence from the substructure, but it is probably best to think of them exchanging influence, with the economic base being, in the end, the more influential.

Marx's conception of ideology is that it represents ideas that promote the interests of a particular class. The dominant ideology in capitalist society distorts the true reality and obscures the real facts of exploitation, oppression and ultimate self-destruction. Even the ruling class are subject to its mystifications, as is apparent from their failure to cope with the repeated crises of capitalist economies. This inability to see the real situation, and therefore to understand one's true class position, is called 'false consciousness'.

However, Marx argues, it is possible to get at the truth and establish a scientific understanding of events. He claims to have achieved this insight, drawing a contrast between 'science' (truth) and 'ideology' (class-based mystification). He suggests that a proletarian class-consciousness also has access to the truth, an idea adopted by Lukacs in the twentieth century.

Emile Durkheim also argued that the culture of a society reflected its social structure. He pointed out that we have to learn to perceive our surroundings as others do, and to categorize and to classify experience and objects in the way that others around us do. How things are classified varies between societies, and he maintained that a society's systems of classification reflect the basis on which it is organized. Thus simple societies with mechanical solidarity (see page 97) only have the most rudimentary classification schemes. More complex societies, with organic solidarity, have more sophisticated systems of classification. Modern science is the reflection of the most elaborate system of social organization, and of the division of labour, yet developed. Durkheim linked these ideas with his views on religion, which is founded on the most basic of all classificatory distinctions, that between the sacred and the profane (see page 136).

Karl Mannheim laid the foundations of modern sociology of knowledge in the 1930s. In *Ideology and Utopia* (1929) he picked up the threads of the Marxian thesis and argued that all human thought (except for mathematics and natural sciences) is ideological in that it is inescapably tied to its social context. All knowledge is known from a particular viewpoint which is located in time, place, and social position. Its ideological content is invisible, and the task of the sociologist of knowledge is to try to overcome the distortions and to transcend class-based knowledge. Mannheim believed that the intellectuals, whom he thought of as relatively classless and free-floating in relation to the economic structure, were in the best position to do this.

Mannheim distinguished between ideology and utopia. Ideologies are outmoded world-views that distort reality in ways that tend to justify it, and are thus basically conservative. Utopias are also ways of thought that distort reality, but they are critical of it, and thus justify radical change. Both are incapable of seeing the truth of any existing social condition.

Recent developments

Recent work in the sociology of knowledge and of culture owes a great deal to phenomenology and to Marxism. As soon as we recognize the phenomenological view that knowledge and world-views are relative and are socially constructed, the question must arise, 'Why this version of reality and not some other?' The answer provided by Marxism is that this version is the outcome of the distribution of economic power. It is sustained through what Gramsci called ideological hegemony, that is, the overbearing influence that the ruling class has over what counts as knowledge. Gramsci argued that domination in capitalist society is most successful when it is least apparent to all concerned that it is happening. Where a consensus theorist talks of a central value system, and a phenomenologist of a shared meaning system, the Gramsci-influenced writers (for example, CCCS 1977) talk of dominant ideology and hegemony, which operate at an entirely unconscious level. Commonsense thus appears to be spontaneous, natural and obvious. As CCCS (1977) argues, commonsense *explains* nothing: it simply makes experience *fit* into the already dominant world-view. Hegemony is exercised, as Althusser describes, through the cultural institutions: education, the media, etc. We are all subject to it and all unaware of it. However,

despite the foregoing, we are not witnessing a conspiracy. The bourgeoisie is not permanently in conclave plotting how to exploit and repress the masses. Exploitation is the essence of the capitalist mode of production – nobody has to work at it: it works itself. The ideology of freedom and equality, the deeply held beliefs about the individual and competition are not deliberately perpetrated by a group of sinister men. They are simply generated historically by the mode of production through the agency of the dominant class. [Brown 1979]

The argument is that once something is regarded as a fact, as truth or as commonsense, it is at the same time regarded as inevitable and therefore unchangeable. It is obviously foolish to question the inevitable and to suggest that things could be different. In this way, 'facts' and commonsense serve to justify the *status quo*.

Science

Increasingly in the last 150 years, these 'facts' have been supplied by natural science.

As we have seen, natural science has long been regarded as different from other kinds of knowledge. The facts of natural science, and the process by which they are discovered, have been assumed to be objective, neutral and value-free. The natural world is objectively real, and natural law can be discovered through unbiased observation and logical deduction (see Chapter 3, page 63).

In recent years theorists have questioned (a) this account of how scientific research is done; (b) the kind of knowledge that emerges from the research; (c) the uses to which this knowledge is put. Obviously, these three points are closely interrelated.

The most sophisticated account, in the traditional mode, of how science progresses is that by Karl Popper. He argues that science progresses by accumulation, and a continuous process of 'conjecture and refutation'. Scientists, in a spirit of open-minded inquiry, make observations of the natural world, develop logical hypotheses for them, test these by attempting to prove them wrong and revise them in the light of further observations and experiments. Popper stresses that no amount of evidence in support of an hypothesis can ever finally confirm that hypothesis. On the other hand, a single item of evidence that contradicts the hypothesis proves it conclusively wrong. We can be conclusively wrong, but never conclusively right. All knowledge is therefore provisional.

This account of the logical progress of science sounds convincing, but it has been challenged. Kaplan (1964) argues that the logic only emerges after the research is complete. A final published account reconstructs the research process to make it appear logical, but omits all the blind alleys, false starts, strokes of luck and inspired guesses that are, in practice, part and parcel of the everyday work of natural scientists.

Kuhn (1970) has presented a comprehensive alternative account of scientific work. He argues that, at any particular time, scientists operate within a set of assumptions about what the natural world is like. They are not permanently on the alert to disprove these basic 'facts', but assume them to be correct. Kuhn calls this set of assumptions a 'paradigm' and says that 'normal science' operates within paradigms which guide the selection and evaluation of evidence. The orthodox approach is to accept the paradigm unquestioningly and not, as Popper would claim, to be permanently sceptical of it. Indeed, the very language of scientific discourse structures and limits scientific ways of thinking (see page 126). However, as time passes, so more and more evidence appears that does not fit the paradigm. Kuhn calls these 'anomalies'. For a while they can be rejected, ignored or explained away, but eventually they become so numerous that the paradigm is overthrown in a 'scientific revolution' such as those inspired by Copernicus or Einstein. A new paradigm is established, and a new period of normal science begins.

Kuhn is therefore arguing that scientific knowledge, like all knowledge, is socially constructed within a framework of assumptions which come between the scientist and the data, and in terms of which observations are interpreted. Natural science is not therefore a special case of knowledge. In this way, Kuhn therefore challenges both the accepted accounts of how scientific knowledge is produced and the status of the scientific knowledge so produced.

The third challenge concerns the use to which scientific knowledge is put. 'Radical science' (Rose and Rose 1980) argues that both the production and the use of science is inevitably related to the processes of economic production and of profit, and its development is thus profoundly ideological. Science is used by the state to ensure social control. This is done in obvious ways through the development of surveillance techniques, anti-riot equipment, and interrogation techniques. The scientific and technological research that goes into the development of weapons systems, or of alternative systems of energy supply, are not ideologically neutral (see page 200). The medical research carried out by drugs companies is done in the pursuit of profit, not the disinterested pursuit of knowledge.

Science permeates our culture, mechanizing and dehumanizing our view of human beings in ways that blind us to the importance of feeling and emotion (Roszak 1971) and encourage us to accept that many things cannot be changed. Above all, social inequality of all kinds (racial, gender, economic, intellectual) is explained in terms of biological facts. Arguments like this, therefore, 'shift the problem from the social to the biological sphere where nothing can be done about it' (Cotgrove 1974).

Summary

Debates about the sociology of knowledge are of crucial importance to sociology, for it is itself a form of knowledge. The sociology of sociology has become an area of controversy in the last decade.

We cannot consider the question of whether sociology is a science until we have clarified what we mean by 'science'. We cannot decide whether sociology is ideological until we have a clear notion of ideology. If *all* knowledge is ideological then sociology is too. If it is possible to produce some non-ideological knowledge, can sociology be non-ideological? If all knowledge is socially constructed and therefore relative, then our knowledge that this is the case is itself socially constructed, and we must accept our own relative status. Is there then no fixed standard of truth? or objectivity?

We can rescue ourselves from this despair by making two important points:

1 Knowledge that claims to be scientific must bear some relation to empirical reality; it is not a matter of individual choice.

2 The fact that I can show that some item of knowledge is a product of its social context, and indeed may serve the interests of some people more than others, does not, in itself, tell me anything about whether it is true or false.

Religion

The second point is especially important in considering the sociology of religion. For many religious people, the sociological approach to religion is offensive as it seems to question their deeply held beliefs. Sociologically, however, the truth or falsity of religious belief is irrelevant. What concerns us is the part religion plays in social life. On the other hand, when we realize the huge variety of religious belief in the world, the sociology of knowledge makes us ask why any one set of beliefs should be regarded as superior to any other.

Religion involves beliefs that explain experiences by claiming that there is a superhuman or supernatural agency of some kind, often a god or gods. It also involves rituals to express these beliefs in public and private ceremonies of worship. It provides a moral code to guide our everyday behaviour. All primitive societies have some kind of religious belief, but the position of religion in advanced societies is more complex and will be discussed later.

The classical tradition

The classical sociologists all attached importance to the role of religion in society.

Marx never made a detailed study of religion, but his views are clear and follow from his broad themes of dominant ideology, alienation and false consciousness. Religion is central to these, especially alienation. For Marx, religion is an illusion. It originated among primitive people as a response to their fear of the unknown, and would disappear as people came to a rational understanding of the world. However, rather than being eliminated with the rise of industrial capitalism, religion was taken over by the bourgeoisie and built into the ruling ideology. It is there used, like all dominant ideology, to justify the *status quo*. In his famous phrase, 'Religion is the opiate of the people', Marx (1844) implied two things: that the content of religion diverts the attention of the proletariat away from present miseries towards a (mythical) future salvation; and that religious belief is crucial in the process of alienation, whereby humans fail to see that they can take control of their own destiny.

Marx was a thoroughgoing atheist. He denied the existence of a superhuman being, and argued that religion must be abolished before oppression and alienation could disappear. People invented God, and had now been taken over by their own invention. People must reclaim control of their own fate.

In *The Elementary Forms of the Religious Life* (1912), Durkheim studied the role of religion in the simplest society he knew of, the Australian aborigines, in order to reveal it in its simplest form. He identified a basic distinction between the 'sacred' and the 'profane'. Anything which people regard as sacred (for example, a totem, an altar, a cow, a person) inspires respect, love and awe. Anything else is ordinary or profane. Sacredness is not built into anything, but is a quality bestowed by human beings. Durkheim argues that people recognize that the social group is greater than the individual and that they rely utterly upon it. The sacred is the symbol of the group or society. When people worship, they worship the moral unity of society, and at the same time, as individuals they reinforce that unity. The moral unity of society must be repeatedly affirmed and this is the function that religious ritual performs. The existence of religion is thus explained in terms of its social function. Indeed any unifying ritual would be regarded as religious in Durkheimian terms.

We may note, in passing, that Parsons's theory of religion owes a great deal to Durkheim. He too regards society as a moral grouping, and religion contributes to the continuing integration of that grouping. Religious belief expresses basic social values, and the ritual that goes with it serves to unite the society.

Weber, in his studies of religion, was, as usual, concerned with the problem of meaning, and he argued that religious beliefs provide the ultimate answers to the basic questions of human existence. In his continuing 'debate with the ghost of Marx', Weber tried to show how religious ideas, rather than being the result of economic activity, could actually cause changes in it. He made wide-ranging studies of the relations between world religions and economic life, but his best-known work is *The Protestant Ethic and the Spirit of Capitalism* (1904).

The thesis of this work is that the Calvinist version of seventeenth- and eighteenth-century Protestantism in Europe resulted in behaviour that, together with other factors, produced modern capitalism. The Calvinists believed that their fate after death is predestined by God, and that their conduct in this life cannot affect that destiny. However, rather than treating this as an excuse to behave just as they chose, the Calvinists looked for reassurance that they were among the elect, and they believed that success in work was an indicator of elect status. Hard work is a form of worship, and glorifies God. Combined with a rational rather than a traditional approach to business activity, hard work results in financial success. However, since Calvinists must lead a puritan ascetic life, they cannot spend money on good living. All they can do is reinvest it in the business, which will produce more wealth. Thus the systematic and rational self-discipline of Calvinism is echoed in the systematic and rational business discipline of capitalism.

More recently, the Weberian emphasis on meaning has been developed in the phenomenological approach to religion. Berger and Luckmann (1963) argue that religion has become a fringe interest in sociology and that it should be restored to a central position as a key element in the sociology of knowledge. Religion plays a central legitimating role in the social construction of reality. By giving ultimate meaning to experience it provides a 'shield against the terror of anomie' (Berger 1973).

Religious organizations

As well as the variety of religious belief in societies, there is a variety of religious organizations.

Weber's student, Troeltsch (1912) distinguished between models of church and of sect. A 'church' is conservative and supports the established social order; it attempts to influence the entire lives of its members, and to integrate with and influence the institutions of the wider society; it is intolerant of other religious groups; its leaders are wealthy and powerful; its membership is all-inclusive; it is bureaucratically organized. A 'sect' is radical and rejects the wider society; it is comparatively small, highly integrated, and dominates the whole lives of its members; it is intolerant of other religious groups; its membership is exclusive and members regard themselves as the elect, the saved minority; it is often connected with the lower classes; it often has a charismatic leader and may last for only a short time.

Later writers have added to Troeltsch's original models, and several include the 'denomination'. This falls somewhere between a church and a sect: it does not claim a monopoly of religious truth; it is tolerant of other religious groups; it is bureaucratically organized; it compromises with the wider society; membership is voluntary.

As with all models, these are not descriptions of the real world. Rather they are useful models with which to compare real-world examples, which may have characteristics from more than one model. They are particularly useful when looking at how religious groupings change over time. Thus Christianity started as a small sect with a highly charismatic leader, developed over the centuries into the church of the Holy Roman Empire, and is now represented by many denominations. Some of these, like the Church of England, retain the title of church.

A typical, though not universal, pattern for the appearance of new religious groupings in complex societies is for a sect to emerge within a church-type organization. This is a continuing problem for any religious grouping in complex societies; how can it come to terms with the wider society without losing its religious purity? If a group within a group feels that this purity is being lost, it may form a break-away sect, for example, the Quakers or the Methodists. Such a sect may fade away when its charismatic leadership is lost, or develop into a denomination. This is not, however, inevitable, and the term 'established sect' is used to refer to those groups which have neither faded away nor compromised, for example, the Mormons, or the Salvation Army.

It may be argued that there is no church-type organization in Britain today, and that there never has been in the USA. There are only sects and denominations.

Religion and social inequality

There is often a close relationship between the religious teachings of a church, denomination or sect and the social conditions of its members. Indeed the change from sect to denomination or church may be linked with the changing status of members. An example of this is the change from eighteenth-century Methodism, a break-away sect which appealed mainly to the urban working class, to twentieth-century Methodism, a highly respectable denomination seriously considering a union with the Anglican Church.

Churches tend to be related to the established order and encourage social stability. The classic example is the verse from the well-known hymn:

> The rich man in his castle,
> The poor man at his gate,
> God made them high and lowly,
> And ordered their estate.

That is, God ordained social inequality, and it is anti-religious to question it. The fact that this verse is no longer included in modern hymn books reflects a change in *expressed* attitudes though the basic values may remain the same. Sects, on the other hand, embody protest against the established order. They compensate for members' feelings of social and economic inferiority with feelings of religious superiority. Thus Hill (1970) points to the popularity of Pentecostalist sects among West Indian immigrants in Britain. More recently, the growth of Rastafarianism among West Indian youths in Britain is an example of the same process, as are the Jehovah's Witnesses in the USA.

Wilson (1961) develops this theme by pointing out that some sects, like the Christian Scientists, appeal to the comfortably-off by stressing human control over the world and the importance of those who exercise this control. The Elim and Christadelphian sects, on the other hand, appeal to the deprived by promising them their reward in heaven.

An alternative appeal to the deprived is offered by the various 'millenarian' or 'messianic' religions. These promise success in *this* world, with the overthrow of the oppressors and power being given to the dispossessed. Perhaps the best-known example is the Jewish belief in the coming of the Messiah. Many writers regard such beliefs, which occur over and over again in history, as weakening the political will needed to bring about genuine revolution.

Worsley (1957), however, argues that the 'Cargo Cults' of Melanesia are an elementary form of political protest and a real threat to the established order. In these cults, the islanders enact rituals which, they believe, encourage their ancestors to send a boat or an aeroplane loaded with cargo, consisting of Western goods, food, clothing and equipment, possibly including guns. In expectation of this, the islanders refuse to work, and throw their own goods away, leaving themselves destitute. The Western colonialists then have to help the islanders as they need them to continue to work. The cult leader is likely to be arrested as a threat to the stability of the islands.

Religion in industrial society

The term 'secularization' refers to 'the process whereby religious thinking, practice and institutions lose social significance' (Wilson 1966). Commonly, this process is assumed to have occurred in industrial society. As sociologists, our task is to examine the concept and the evidence for and against the proposition.

As far as religious practice goes, there has certainly been a decline in England and Wales in church attendance, baptisms, confirmations, church weddings and Sunday school attendance. However, it is difficult to collect accurate figures, and there are wide variations by region, by type of community, by age, sex, class and religious grouping (Wilson 1977). However, in alleging a decline we must specify our point of comparison, and there is little evidence that the ordinary British person was ever an active practitioner of religious ritual.

In institutional terms, the influence of the church in England and Wales has declined in politics, the law, economic affairs, family life and especially in education. Though churchleaders comment more freely on earthly matters such as nuclear weapons, race relations or secondary picketing, their influence is markedly less. The status and the pay of the clergy has declined. Churches are maintained or demolished for architectural reasons, not religious ones.

How is one to measure whether religious *belief* has declined? Some writers point to the way that science now provides rational answers to questions traditionally answered by religion, and to changing attitudes to sexual morality, divorce and abortion. Others (Martin 1967) argue that ordinary people have a strongly religious element in their moral attitudes and their world-view. The huge majority still believe in something they call God. Bare statistics can reveal nothing about feeling or depth of commitment.

In a pluralistic society like ours we should not expect any one set of religious beliefs to dominate. Thus, while we see a decline in the position of the universal church, there is a vigorous growth of sect-type religions. Indeed, much recent sociology of religion has involved studies of religious sects and cults, such as Barker (1984) and Wallis (1984).

Religion provides private guidance and meaning rather than public unity. There is much evidence of people's continuing belief in the supernatural, both in sect-type religions and in interest in the occult and in witchcraft.

The argument about what secularization is and whether it has occurred has become so confusing, and the evidence so contradictory, that Martin (1967) has said that it should be abandoned. Where Wilson (1977) claims that 'in society at large religion is becoming so much an optional extra', Martin (1967) says that 'far from being secular, our culture wobbles between a partially absorbed Christianity, biased towards comfort and the need for confidence, and beliefs in fate, luck, and moral governance incongruously joined together'. (See also Martin (1978).)

The debate is made more complicated if we look at the situation in other industrial societies. Church attendance has been increasing in the USA in recent years, and events in Northern Ireland in the last seventeen years show that religion is clearly not an 'optional extra' there. This is an important reminder to us that not all industrial societies follow the same pattern.

Sociologists of religion have usually stressed how religion contributes to the stability and continuity of society. However, if we think of recent events in Northern Ireland, in Iran, and of the storming of the Sikh Golden Temple in India, it is clear that religion is often involved in instability and conflict. The key to explaining this lies in the concept of legitimacy. Religious beliefs can be seen to be capable of legitimating, that is justifying, or providing more or less rational arguments in favour of a very wide range of activity, whether for or against the *status quo*.

The mass media

A 'medium' is a means or channel of communication, such as speech, writing, the telephone, or even music and painting. The mass media are so called because they involve very large numbers of people in the communication process. We must always remember, however, that though the audience (the receivers) may be large, the number of senders (transmitters) may be very small; and that the communication is almost entirely one-way. Whether we are talking of television and newspapers (the most commonly studied mass media) or of radio, films, advertising, or mass popular fiction, there is very little feedback from receiver to transmitter. This lack of access that the public has to the media puts those who control the media into a very strong position.

The transmitters operate within complex formal organizations (see Chapter 4, page 104), such as newspaper companies or the TV companies, which are run as business enterprises. Using advanced technology, they transmit publicly to large, scattered, varied and unorganized audiences.

Table 2   *Estimated average hours spent by British adults per week with major media in 1982*

	Primary activity	Primary and secondary activity	Primary secondary and tertiary activity
Television	18	21	35
Radio	2	23	30
Newspaper and magazines	5	6	10
Total per week	25	50	75

SOURCE: Tunstall (1983)

In measuring how much use people make of the media, Tunstall (1983) identifies three kinds of use. 'Primary activity' involves paying concentrated attention to the medium in question. 'Secondary activity' means having part of your attention on something else. 'Tertiary activity' can mean many things, but essentially refers to having the medium switched on or lying about but only paying scant attention to it. Using these measures, Tunstall produced Table 2 (adapted).

Daily sales of newspapers have declined steadily over the last twenty-five years, though the morning dailies have just about held their own. Total daily sales are now around 23 million. As with TV viewing, there are many variations within these totals, according to age, gender and social class. Thus, 55 per cent of copies of *The Times* are read by managerial or professional people (who are 16 per cent of the population), compared with 6 per cent of copies of the *Sun*. Manual workers are 61 per cent of the population, but read 75 per cent of copies of the *Mirror*, and 19 per cent of the *Guardian* (Tunstall 1983).

The effects of mass communication

Early researchers (1930s and 1940s) were influenced by studies of war-time propaganda and, later, by interest in the effects of advertising. They studied the effect that the media had on people's behaviour. With a highly positivistic approach, this research tended to assume that individuals responded passively to media output, and were moulded by it. This assumption is still found among those who argue that 'TV violence causes juvenile delinquency' or that TV is the cause of a decline in moral standards. There is a tendency to see TV as external to society and exerting influence on it, rather than as an integral part of social structure and culture, both reflecting and creating.

While some versions of this view saw the media as causing a decline in standards, others stressed the power of the media as the instrument of a ruling elite seeking totalitarian control.

In general, such research produced no definite results, but found that the direct influence of TV was greatly exaggerated. Instead researchers began to stress the way in which people respond actively to media content, and developed the 'Uses and Gratifications' model of media use. Writers like Katz and Lazarsfeld (1955), Klapper (1960) and Halloran (1964), stressed (a) that there is great variety in media output; and (b) that people actively select what they see, hear, and read, interpret it, and selectively remember it. As Halloran says, 'We must get away from the habit of thinking in terms of what television does to people, and substitute for it the idea of what people do with television.' People come to the media with a set of pre-existing attitudes and they respond to the media in terms of these attitudes. While the media may help to form opinion in entirely new areas, they will merely reinforce views that are already held.

Katz and Lazarsfeld also introduced the 'Two-step Flow' hypothesis. They argue that it is wrong to assume that the media are directly experienced by each individual. Rather, people are influenced by 'opinion leaders' in their social group, who interpret media content. Other group members then respond to the versions of media output passed on by these opinion leaders.

Recent media sociology

Since the early 1970s, the development of the sociology of knowledge and of conflict theory has led to different questions being asked about the media. At first, the emphasis shifted away from the effects of the media towards their content. As these studies have become more sophisticated, so interest has again reverted to the effects, though in a much more subtle way then before. There has been an emphasis on studies of the news, particularly TV news.

While it is certainly true that people today know a great deal about the world around them, especially the social world, we learn most of this at second-hand, through the media. Most people have never been on a picket-line, or worked in a factory, or been mugged, or met the royal family or the Greenham women; but we all feel that we know something of what they are like. The media filter events into our experience, we build this into our world-view, and we act according to this world-view. The media provide 'the guiding myths which shape our interpretation of the world' (Cohen and Young 1981). Their effects are cultural and ideological, rather than immediate or direct.

This raises important questions: What are the 'guiding myths'? Why are they as they are? What effect do they have on our attitudes and our world-view, and so, ultimately, on our actions?

The first question is answered with the help of detailed content analysis of the media, especially news bulletins. The work of the Glasgow University Media Group (1982, 1985) and Chibnall (1977) suggests that the media present a fundamentally conservative image of society. A basic consensus is assumed, and conflict is seen as regrettable and caused by a temporary problem or a difficult individual, rather than as integral to our political and economic system. Conflict, where it occurs, is to be resolved within a set of rules which all 'reasonable people' would accept. The justice of the system of parliamentary democracy is not questioned. The image presented legitimates our political and economic system, and thus helps to maintain it in being.

Other studies have tried to show how images of women in the media have served the interests of men and of patriarchy by stereotyping women as domesticated, feeble, dependent, or sex-objects. Similarly, the portrayal of ethnic minorities as 'immigrants' and as a source of trouble has been seen as racist, and as legitimating and worsening the harassing of black people by racist individuals and organizations.

The analysis of media content has, more recently still, been influenced by semiology. Semiology is the study of signs and of symbols, including language, dress, gesture, and any other medium through which messages are transmitted, whether consciously or unconsciously. Groups of signs are organized into codes, and TV news has developed a wealth of codes through which a deeper connotation is transmitted to the viewer, thereby cancelling out any supposed 'objectivity' in the surface presentation. This kind of analysis draws our attention to the way in which, however 'balanced' or 'objective' a news bulletin may appear to be, its connotations still encourage us to view what is reported in a particular way.

The question of why these images and myths are as they are is answered partly through studies of media organization, and partly in terms of a more or less Marxist-based theory of dominant value-systems.

Many studies stress how journalists select and present news (Chibnall 1977). It is not a simple matter of news happening and journalists reporting it. The facts do not speak for themselves. News is news because journalists make it news. They define some events as newsworthy, fit them into categories and put them into context. Journalists manufacture news from the raw material of events (Cohen and Young 1981). The sociologist studies how this process occurs, and how it is affected by a professional 'nose for news', by the ethics of journalists, by their taken-for-granted assumptions, and by their notions of what is reportable and what is not. It is also affected by organizational factors such as publication deadlines, the amount of time available in a bulletin or space in a front page, the need for illustration, and so on. The journalist is anything but the passive and impartial transmitter of self-evident news.

The question of a dominant ideology is relatively clear-cut to a Marxist sociologist such as Miliband (1973). For him, the so-called 'free expression of ideas and opinions mainly means the free expression of ideas which are helpful to the prevailing system of power and privilege'. The important influences are the ownership and control of the 'means of mental production', the power of advertisers, and the role of the state, which, while seldom using direct censorship, exerts pressure in various ways, as was seen during the Falklands War and over the 'Real Lives' affair in 1985. Enzensberger (1976) writes of the 'mind-making industry' and that 'the few cannot go on accumulating wealth unless they accumulate the power to manipulate the minds of the many'. Hall (1978) explains the moral panic surrounding 'mugging', in the creation of which the media played a crucial part, as helping to legitimate the strengthening of the police force at a time when the stability of capitalism was under threat.

Many sociologists who do not necessarily accept a Marxist view nevertheless draw attention to the ownership of media companies. While this is a fast-changing picture, the fact is that companies which own newspapers, magazines and TV companies are, typically, huge conglomerates, with business interests stretching far beyond the media. Ownership and control of media production companies is highly concentrated. In the late 1970s, three companies controlled well over half of all national newspaper circulation. Five companies control about three quarters of each media market, such as TV, records, the press, commercial radio, and books (Curran and Seaton 1981). Such figures, however, omit the BBC and IBA, an omission noted by those who maintain that, while it is certainly true that a few major companies dominate the field, there are nevertheless many smaller and more specialist ones involved. In the early 1980s, it has also been interesting to observe the re-emergence of figures reminiscent of the old-style press 'barons', such as Murdoch and Maxwell.

Glover (1984) describes contemporary media sociology as using a 'cultural effects' model, i.e. its emphasis is on the way the media influence the overall culture of society, rather than on any immediate or short-term effects. The extent of such influences is very hard to assess and to research. The public certainly exercises choice in media use, actively interpreting and selectively remembering. However, this selection is made from a narrow range of options previously established by the 'gatekeepers' of the media, who 'set the agenda' of public discussion. It is important, too, to study how the same programme or article is interpreted by audiences from different social backgrounds (Morley 1980).

It is important to note that, while much recent media sociology has studied the news, for many people TV means light entertainment. The gender, class and racial stereotypes in such programmes play an important part in forming people's everyday assumptions, as has been shown by feminist sociologists (Adams and Laurikietis 1976).

An exception to this 'cultural effects' work has been the continuing research into whether TV violence causes real violence. The experimental work of Eysenck and Nias (1978) suggested that there is a link between media violence and violent behaviour, and Belson's (1978) survey of 1500 London adolescents reached a similar conclusion. The problem with both these studies is, however, their validity. How do we know that what Eysenck and Nias found in their laboratory has any relevance to the real world? And how do we know that what Belson's adolescents told him authentically reflects their viewing habits and their actual behaviour, quite apart from the problem of measuring the degree of 'violence' of a programme or an action? On the other hand, it seems inconsistent to assert the power of the media to reinforce racist and sexist stereotypes, and to deny its influence when it comes to violence.

Youth culture

The 'problem' of the young has existed, in the minds of their elders, throughout our history. The young have often been regarded unfavourably, and even seen as a major threat to social order.

However, the concept of 'youth culture' has only been developed in the last thirty years. The result is that sociologists have written about groups such as teds, punks and mods at the same time as these groups feature in the mass media, and sociological theories about youth culture come and go in large numbers and at great speed.

Firstly, we must recognize that 'youth' is itself a social category, which emerges in connection with a particular way of life. Very young children are, obviously, dependent on adults for their survival. They are not expected, in any society, to take responsibility for themselves or to be fully competent social beings. By contrast, an adult is expected to be self-reliant, responsible and mature. There is great variety among societies as to where the child/adult borderline lies, and how precise it is. In some societies it is marked by initiation ceremonies; in others it is much more vague. But only in advanced industrial societies is there an extended period *between* childhood and adulthood, which is called 'adolescence' or 'youth'. It is a consequence of industrialization in that the separation of family life from working life, and the emergence of full-time schooling in the space between them, creates a particular set of experiences for those in that space.

As we have seen, culture and social action are best regarded as a collective response to everyday experience. In our kind of society, people aged between, say, twelve and twenty are faced with the problems of being neither children nor adults, not quite dependent and yet not independent, not incompetent and yet not given full responsibility, lacking the status of full-time workers and yet being expected to behave as adults. Youth culture is a cultural response to these contradictions.

These problems are not the same for all young people. The

contradictions are experienced differently by boys and girls, by blacks and whites and by the different social classes.

A second basic point is that society contains many sub-groups, each of which develops its own ways of thinking and acting in response to the way it perceives its surroundings. While these sub-groups must share some culture with each other (for example, language), some develop such distinctive styles that they are regarded as subcultures. Some subcultures are more isolated than others and provide a more comprehensive way of life, for example, that of gypsies. Others overlap and interweave with each other in much more complex ways.

In terms of this section, we must consider how useful the concept of subculture is in aiding our understanding of youth, and how far youth culture is cross-cut by class and by ethnic subcultures. In addition, most of the sociology of youth has ignored girls – a remarkable omission of 50 per cent of the age-group in question.

The third point is that stratification by age is an important feature of our society. Both young and old people have lower status and less power than adults of working age, and have a different economic position (see Chapter 6, page 166). This generates a response from the young, but the response varies according to their varying class position. Also it is apparent that youthful rebellion is age-related and that most people 'grow out of it'. The stratification position of the young is one that is solved, at the individual level, by the passing of time.

Post-war youth cultures

It is not easy to decide where 'normal' or acceptable youth culture ends and deviant subculture begins. Most young people in our society live at home, go to school and/or college, get on reasonably well with their parents, obey the law in all important respects, buy records, go to parties and discos, and, before long, marry for life and raise a family. All this is part of the mainstream culture of our society, and cannot be regarded as subcultural. It is in no way deviant, though it may sometimes disturb adults and other authorities.

On the other hand, a minority of young people develop group responses to their situation which result in 'moral panics' (Cohen 1972). It is these groups which have particularly attracted the attention of sociologists. 'Folk devils' (Cohen 1972), from teddyboys to punk rockers, fascinate and horrify us, via the media, and their exotic and rebellious image has exerted equal fascination on sociologists.

In the 1950s and early 1960s, writers like Eisenstadt (in 1956) developed the concept of adolescence as a transitional phase in the life-cycle. In this phase, young people lack a stable identity and respond by seeking to create such an identity through their peer groups. Albert Cohen (1955) in the USA argued that gangs were the working-class teenagers' way of gaining the prestige that they were denied in school and at work. The adolescent peer group replaces the family as the dominant socializing influence, and so functions to bridge the child/ adult, home/work gaps. As we have seen, this gap had existed for decades. What was new in the post-war era was free compulsory secondary education for all; mass teenage affluence in the late 1950s and the 1960s; the explosive growth of mass entertainment and the leisure industry. Abrams (1961) showed how teenagers had become major consumers of goods like clothes, records and motorbikes. This mass market was exploited by manufacturers who both responded to and created a particularly teenage leisure industry, focused on certain styles of music and dress.

In the 1960s, a continuing period of affluence and full employment, the hippies and the student revolutionaries were hailed by some neo-Marxist writers as the new revolutionary class (Lenski 1966; Roszak 1971). The students were detached from the means of production, and were therefore neither capitalist nor proletariat. As a new revolutionary class, they were, it was argued, generating a world-view which rejected capitalism, materialism, rationality and the work ethic. They would carry out the historical task which Marx had assigned to the proletariat.

This view has been heavily criticized for over-estimating both the extent and the unity of the youth movement of the period. The bohemian life-style attracted, largely, the privileged and middle-class young, mostly in the universities. No united revolutionary consciousness emerged outside a small group among this minority. Furthermore, and vitally, it was never shown that the young had class interests opposed to those of their elders.

In the 1970s, the question of class divisions within youth cultures was examined more closely. These studies (for example, Hall *et al.* 1976) have regarded particular youth groups (teds, mods, skinheads, punks) as working-class responses to the experience of social class in post-war Britain. This view builds on that of Cohen (1955) but in the British context, and with a much closer look at aspects of style in music and dress (Hebdige 1979). They examine the phenomenon from the 'kids' ' point of view, and try to make sense of it all rather than explain it away. Brake (1980) says: 'Subcultures arise as attempts to resolve collectively experienced problems arising from contradictions in the social structure.'

These problems vary from one group to another. It is absurd to imagine that the experience of the white upper- or middle-class public schoolboy would generate a cultural response similar to that of the black working-class factory girl. Hall (1976) and others (Cohen 1972) argue that we should regard each major group as a subculture deriving from a particular parent culture. Thus beatniks and hippies are the response of middle-class youth to the materialism of the 1960s and 1970s; the mod style is a reflection of the existence of the socially mobile white-collar worker; skinheads reflect the experience of the working class by reasserting its traditional puritanism and chauvinism. Rastafarianism is the response of British-born West Indians to their experience of racism, unemployment and deprivation. Conflicts between the groups (greasers v. skinheads, mods v. rockers) replace what would be intolerable generational conflicts within the family.

The emphasis in recent studies of subcultures of working-class youth and of black youth has been on the concepts of 'resistance' and 'style'. With the help of semiology (see page 143), the clothing, music, ritual and style of these groups has been interpreted as a symbolic rejection and a resistance to the class-based domination to which they are subject. Such resistance is, however, 'magical', in the sense that it does not directly tackle the problem, while nevertheless enabling the oppressed to express their feelings.

As mentioned above, most of this work concentrates on young males. McRobbie (1978) is one of the few studies of the culture of working-class adolescent girls. She found their lives to be dominated by pressures towards domesticity and a traditionally female role, but also that this role was an effective response to the situation in which they found themselves as working-class and female. They seemed to cooperate in the restrictions imposed on them. Here as elsewhere, ideology works best when those who are its victims feel they are choosing to do what, in fact, they have to do: 'They are both saved by and locked within the culture of femininity'.

The impact of high levels of unemployment on young people, and their subcultural response to it, is not yet apparent. Some writers have suggested that 'youth culture', as known in the 1950s and 1960s, may be over. The transition from school to work and adulthood may not happen when there are no jobs. A style which depends on having spare cash cannot flourish where there is no cash. Some may respond by working even harder at school and college; others may reject, possibly with violence, a social system which they feel has rejected them.

Guide to further reading

Language is a very difficult field of study, but Berger and Berger (1976), Chapter 4, develops the important points. The same comment applies to the sociology of knowledge, but Glover and Strawbridge (1985), *The Sociology of Knowledge*, is written for A-level readers, as is Trowler (1985), *Further Topics in Sociology*.

Budd (1973), *Sociologists and Religion*, remains an excellent introduction to the sociology of religion, and Berger (1973), *The Social Reality of Religion*, Martin (1967), *A Sociology of English Religion*, and Wilson (1961, 1966 and 1977) are worthwhile. Recent books have been more specific in their focus, though Wilson (1982) is worth a try.

Cohen and Young (1981), *The Manufacture of News*, is invaluable reading, as is Tunstall (1983), *The Media in Britain*. Shorter but more general texts include Glover (1984), Trowler (1984) and Barrat (1986). For semiology and TV, consult Fiske and Hartley (1978).

There has been a wealth of recent material on youth culture, but Hall and Jefferson (1976), *Resistance through Rituals*, Brake (1980), *The Sociology of Youth Culture and Youth Sub-cultures*, and Hebdige (1979), *Subculture: the Meaning of Style*, are important. You might also look at Frith (1984), O'Donnell (1985) and Trowler (1984), all written for the A-level student.

6 Differentiation and stratification

Ian Shelton

This chapter is concerned with one of the most important characteristics of societies: *social stratification*. Wherever there is a social stratification system we will be able to identify *social inequality*. In our society social inequality is so central that it pervades all aspects of social life. As you might expect, then, social stratification is a theme which runs throughout this book.

It has been usual for sociologists to compare social stratification with geological stratification, that is, comparing ranking in society with the layering of rocks on the earth's surface. Many of you will have seen the exposed layers of rock on eroded coastal cliff faces, or the sides of gorges and canyons worn by rivers. The Grand Canyon in the South-West of the USA is the best, and best-documented example. The principle of layering, however, can be seen in the more humble context of constructing a *gâteau* with layers of sponge, cream and fruit filling, sponge and icing. It is enough that you have an image of society being similarly layered or ranked, albeit layered or ranked in an uneven or inconsistent manner. The purpose of this chapter is to enable you to analyse those layers or ranks both in your own and in other societies. The concepts which you meet in this chapter can be used to study any stratification system.

'Stratification' means different things to different people. The most common synonym is 'social class'. Be careful! I shall try to show you that social class is only one type of stratification, and that there are others. For the moment, however, let us disregard this complexity. Ask yourself the following question: of what differences between people are you aware? If that question does not make sense, try another: if you compare yourself with others, how do you distinguish yourself from them? No doubt, between all the readers of this chapter, you would cover a vast range of answers. You yourself might be noticing physical features, like male or female, or relative attractiveness; you might notice hair colour, figure, strength, patience, quietness, helpfulness, age, clothing, type of house, job, income, parental strictness, skin colour and club membership. All of these characteristics can be the basis for differentiation. However, we usually reserve the term 'social differentiation' for those differences which are commonly held to be important in a society and which can be attributed to a position which a person fills. Such positions might include 'youth', 'student', 'factory worker', 'sister', 'investor', 'Christian' and many others. We can distinguish between people according to the positions, like these, which they fill, but some positions carry substantially greater benefits within society. Wherever some positions carry greater or lesser benefits, be they in money, gifts, prestige, even the power to control others, we have the basis for 'social stratification'. A social rank, or 'stratum', comprises all those who fill the same position or similar positions.

Many differences between people, such as quietness, hair colour or attractiveness, may attract comment from acquaintances, but they do not result in advantages and disadvantages in the wider society. It is the essence of social stratification that advantages and disadvantages are distributed *systematically* according to a particular characteristic. The stratification system is *structured* around possession of the characteristic. In South Africa, for example, skin colour and ethnic group have massive implications for income, education, housing and political power. For the time being, then, try to remember that all stratification must involve some differentiation between positions, and the people who fill them, but that not all differentiation necessarily leads to ranking, that is, to stratification. In the remainder of this chapter, I shall try to accomplish two tasks: first, to show the different ways in which societies are ranked; and second, to try to explain why there is ranking in society.

Economic ranking

I mentioned above that people often differentiate between others in terms of job or income. In conversation we might mention that so-and-so is well-off or 'poor'. Economic ranking refers to the differential rewards attached to positions within the economy. (The economy is the institution or sub-system in society which is devoted to the production of goods and services. Of course, in less developed societies economic activity typically takes place within family units, and it is thus less easy to discern 'economic institutions' as such.) Some people have greater rewards because of their economic position; others have lesser rewards. In many circumstances 'economic position' refers to a person's 'job' or occupation, to the work accomplished between more or less regular starting and finishing times. However, there are other forms of economic activity, such as investment in companies, which are not always recognized as 'jobs' although they certainly produce rewards. In the following discussion I shall use the term 'social class' to refer to all those who share roughly the same economic position (and rewards entailed by that position).

In due course I shall analyse economic ranking – *social class* – in terms of occupations and occupational rewards. It would be a mistake, however, to regard social class only in this way. Indeed, one of the most influential of all analyses of social class – that of Karl Marx (1818–93) – concentrates upon property-ownership. I doubt if any short account can do justice to the complexities of Marx's work, because he was not only analysing social class but was also using the notion of social class to explain how societies change. Nonetheless, there are some basic principles within his work that you must try to understand.

Marx's theory of social class

Marx said that societies develop through a series of stages or 'epochs'. Each epoch is distinguishable by virtue of its 'mode of production', that is, its dominant way of producing goods to satisfy people's needs. The mode of production comprises two elements:

forces of production – tools and techniques, or 'technology';
relations of production – relationships arising from productive activity,
    for example, owner and non-owner.

This is the kernel of Marx's theory. First, he argued that societies change when the forces of production develop too quickly for the existing relations of production to cope. Second, the relations of production are the basis of social class. Let me try to illustrate the latter.

Marx divided all history into epochs. These were *antiquity* (or Ancient Society) in which the major economic relationship was between master and slave; *feudal society* in which the major economic relationship was between lord and serf; and the epoch in which Marx was most interested, *capitalism*. 'Capitalism' refers to an economic system based upon the private ownership of industrial property, that is, factories, the land upon which factories are built, the wealth created by factories, and so on. Capitalism is thus an industrial rather than an agricultural mode of production. It is debatable whether some of Marx's critical arguments were stimulated by the general features of industrialization and industrialism, or specifically by capitalism.

Nonetheless Marx saw capitalism as an evil system. He identified the significant differentials in economic power and economic reward between capitalist and wage-labourer, and the consequences for their life-styles and access to political power. Of course private ownership involves a little more than might at first be apparent. It certainly does involve possession of a factory, its land and its machinery. In addition, however, private ownership involves temporary possession of *labour*. To wage-labourers, their labour has a value (represented by the wage paid at the end of the day or week). That same labour, however, has greater value to capitalists. By efficiently sub-dividing the work process into simple stages, and by introducing machinery, they can secure greater value from wage-labour than they pay in wages. This excess value is called 'surplus value'. It is the property of the capitalists. Once their running expenses have been deducted, it is the basis of their profit. This led Marx to conclude that capitalism is an exploitative mode of production because, by its very nature, it generates inequalities of reward and power.

In the early stages of capitalism – the early nineteenth century in Britain – Marx had identified two major social classes: the 'bourgeoisie' (capitalists) and the 'proletariat' (wage-labourers). In addition, he recognized that there were a number of major land-owners (whose land formed large agricultural, rather than industrial, estates) who constituted the third major social class. However, these three social classes did not account for everyone; there were, in addition, groups of professional workers, such as doctors and teachers, plus many shopkeepers and clerks, none of whom fitted easily into the scheme of three major social classes. These people constituted the 'intermediate strata'.

It was Marx's view that capitalism as an economic system would become increasingly difficult to sustain, that it would generate increasing numbers of crises (not least because capitalists' profits would decline as each had to buy more and more new machinery, factories and the like to try to gain a greater share of the available markets). These crises, which would have adverse consequences for wage levels and the standard of living of wage-labourers, would create the conditions under which wage-labourers would become aware of their condition. In other words, they would become aware that they were being exploited for surplus value, and that working conditions did not have to be so unpleasant. At this critical point the proletariat are being transformed from a 'class-in-itself' to a 'class-for-itself', that is, from a social class defined by the objective criterion of non-ownership of property, to a social class defined by both the objective criterion *and* a subjective awareness of that same objective position. It is at this point that we can say that 'class consciousness' has developed, that is, subjective awareness of 'true' economic position.

The development of class consciousness in both bourgeoisie and proletariat signals the *polarization* of the two classes and, as the two move further apart in terms of common interests, so does each 'camp' become more unified, that is, 'homogeneous'. Furthermore, the original intermediate strata would, Marx forecast, join with whichever of the two polar camps they felt most compatible. The final steps of Marx's analysis are more pertinent to a study of social change: he anticipated increasing industrial and political strife, with every strike or lock-out, and every political demonstration, being an indication of the increasing conflict between bourgeoisie and proletariat. Eventually this increasing conflict would produce a revolution (see Chapter 4, pages 116–8).

On the one hand Marx provides a subtle, objective analysis of social

structure and social change, stressing the key role of economic relationships. On the other hand Marx incorporates his views about what *ought*
to happen in society to eradicate faults. Criticism of Marx's work, then,
might be addressed to his analysis of structure and change, or to his
promotion of 'revolutionary' or 'communist' views, or to both. The reader
should be sensitive to whether others are criticizing Marx as social
scientist or Marx as political ideologist. The best thing for us to do is to
examine the nature of the ownership of industrial property in contemporary Britain, and to relate it to Marx's analysis. In so doing we shall
have started to build up a picture of economic ranking in the late
twentieth century.

The distribution of wealth

In the early nineteenth century, ownership of private firms was a very
risky matter. If firms 'went bust', owners could be declared bankrupt
and their personal possessions, and those of their immediate family,
seized to pay off debts. The introduction in 1855 of appropriate
legislation limited the liability of investors. They could, in subsequent
years, only run the risk of losing what they had invested. If a person
invested £1000, the maximum loss could not exceed that amount.
Limited liability was thus an incentive for investment, and it should
have followed that the numbers of small investors would increase
substantially. Certainly the principle of limited liability encouraged the
separation of ownership and control of firms. Originally the capitalist
had both owned and managed firms. After the introduction of limited
liability, investors simply sought the investment likely to produce the
greatest return; day-to-day control of the firm could be left in the hands
of a manager who received a salary. Limited liability also created the
possibility of firms having multiple ownership: these are 'joint-stock'
companies, that is, the stock of the company is held jointly by a number
of people or institutions. Nowadays, insurance companies and pension
funds own a great deal of the stock of private companies.

All this would seem to indicate that capital (in the sense of ownership
of companies, their finances, land and machinery) had been dissipated
into many hands, and that the small homogeneous group which Marx
called the 'bourgeoisie' would become far more numerous and heterogeneous (or internally varied). Throughout the twentieth century,
however, the distribution of wealth has changed, but not massively so.

Westergaard and Resler (1975) have attempted to estimate how much
of the available personal wealth is owned by what proportion of the
population. Using data obtained from Revell (1965), they demonstrate in
(my) Table 3 the unequal distribution of private property. Data from the
Royal Commission on the Distribution of Income and Wealth (1979)
confirms the same basic pattern of inequality (see Table 4). Compared
with 1960 and earlier, it is clear that there has been something of a

Table 3 *Distribution of private property, 1911–60*

Groups in adult population owning stated proportions of personal wealth	1911–36 (%)	1936–54 (%)	1954–60 (%)	1960 (%)
Richest 1%* owned	69	56	43	42
Richest 5% owned	87	79	71	75
Richest 10% owned	92	88	79	83
Remaining 90% owned	8	12	21	17

*Percentages in Tables 3–6 are cumulative, that is, the richest 5 per cent includes the richest 1 per cent etc.

Table 4 *Distribution of private property, 1974 and 1976*

Groups in adult population owning stated proportions of personal wealth	1974 (%)	1976 (%)
Richest 1% owned	22	25
Richest 5% owned	(not known)	
Richest 10% owned	57.5	60.6
Remaining 90% owned	42.5	39.4

redistribution of wealth within the population, but such redistribution has not substantially altered the basic inequalities. Indeed, the Royal Commission demonstrated that, between 1974 and 1976, inequalities widened. More recently, Inland Revenue data, published in their 1984 review, shows how the wealth owned by the top 25 per cent of people increased from 77 per cent to 81 per cent between 1979 and 1982. The share owned by the top 1 per cent had fallen, but by only 1 per cent (to 21 per cent). This reversal in the redistribution process is attributable to rises in share prices, and a slowdown in the real increase in house prices.

Westergaard and Resler examine one particular year, 1954, in terms of ownership of particular types of property and wealth. These include not only stocks and shares, but also bank deposits, land and business assets, and various kinds of securities. Again, it is clear that ownership is concentrated in few hands, and nowhere is this concentration more marked than in the ownership of stocks and shares (see Table 5).

You might be tempted to point out that the data in Table 5 refers to a quarter of a century ago. All the evidence relating to the 1970s, however, suggests that there has been limited change from the 1950s. Only about 7–8 per cent of the population own stocks and shares, and many of those have only small or moderately-sized holdings. We can reasonably estimate that no more than 2 per cent of the population own some 90 per cent of the privately-owned stocks and shares. We might conclude then that ownership of industrial property has widened since Marx's day, but that there is still a strong tendency for a small number of people to own

Table 5 *Concentration of main types of private property, 1954*

Groups within adult population owning stated proportions of the aggregate value of property of the kind indicated (%)	All net private capital (%)	Cash and bank deposits (%)	Land, buildings, trade assets (%)	Government and municipal securities (%)	Company stocks and shares (%)
Richest 1% owned	43	23	28	42	81
Richest 5% owned	68	48	58	71	96
Richest 10% owned	79	64	74	83	98

SOURCE: Lydall and Tipping (1961)

the vast majority of industrial property. Objectively, the bourgeoisie have not broken up.

From Marx to Weber

The German sociologist Max Weber (1864–1920) agreed with Marx that economic power and economic rewards were major bases for ranking in society. Weber did not dispute that property-ownership was itself a major criterion for the formation of social classes. However, he widened Marx's notion of economic ranking: he said that people's 'market situation' was critical. Broadly, this refers to a person's position in the economic system. More precisely, it refers to a person's opportunity to sell goods and services (including his own labour power). A social class thus refers to the objective characteristics of the market situation of individuals who share the same 'life-chances'. The latter term, in Weber's words, denotes the 'typical chance for a supply of goods, external living conditions, and personal life experiences, in so far as this change is determined by the amount and kind of power ... in a given economic order' (reprinted in Gerth and Mills 1948). Apart from the ownership of wealth and property, then, we need to consider other rewards and benefits which befall people in specific economic postions. One of the most obvious of these rewards is income.

The distribution of income

'Income' means a profit or gain from economic activity. Conventionally we would interpret income as the weekly wage or monthly salary payable in return for certain services, the performance of which we call 'work' or an 'occupation'. Such income might not necessarily be monetary, but include fringe benefits (such as expense accounts, sickness benefits, pensions and concessionary travel). In addition, income can be unearned, that is, not the direct reward for performing an occupation or 'going to work'. Rather, it might be continuing interest from deposits placed in banks, or dividends from investments in stocks and shares.

Table 6 *Distribution of personal allocated income after direct taxation, 1938-67*

Groups of 'income units'	Estimated percentage share of total value of all personal allocated income received by the groups of 'income units' (couples and individuals) shown on left					
	1938 (%)	1949 (%)	1954 (%)	1957 (%)	1963 (%)	1967 (%)
Richest 1% received	11½	6½	5½	5	5	5
Richest 5% received	24	17	15½	14½	15½	15
Richest 10% received	33½	27	25	24	25	24½
Richest 40% received	*	64	65½	63	64½	64
Poorest 30% received	*	14½	11	13	12	11½

SOURCE: adapted from Westergaard and Resler (1975)

Irrespective of the type of income, there is a clear pattern underlying its distribution. Westergaard and Resler (1975) extract data from a wide range of sources to enable them to estimate the distribution of personal income in recent years (see Table 6). The data in Table 6 reflect a redistribution of income: it is noticeable how the share of the richest 1 per cent, 5 per cent and 10 per cent have all fallen between 1938 and 1967. However, the richest 40 per cent have retained a virtually constant share, suggesting that any redistribution has been from the richest to the next most rich, and not to the poorest. Indeed, the share received by the poorest 30 per cent decreased between 1949 and 1967!

The most recent evidence is contained in the *Report of the Royal Commission on the Distribution of Income and Wealth* (1979). The Commission reports that 'if the decline in the share of the top 1 per cent is ignored, the shape of the distribution is not greatly different in 1976-77 from what it was in 1949'. The income share of the top 1 per cent had fallen to 3½ per cent in 1976-77; the share of the top 10 per cent had fallen to 22.4 per cent. The top 50 per cent of the population receive 72.6 per cent of all income, the poorest 50 per cent receive 27.6 per cent. The basic pattern of income inequality remains (see *Social Science Teacher* 1979a).

In an 'income' sense, there is stratification. However, this does not imply that all those people with common or similar incomes *perceive* themselves as similar or as a group, nor that they are conscious of themselves as a distinctive rank placed in a hierarchy by virtue of income. Indeed, there is evidence to suggest that people receiving similar incomes often are quite dissimilar in other respects. Research by Lockwood (1958) on clerical workers revealed their status consciousness, that is, an awareness on the part of clerical workers of their superiority over manual workers even though their incomes might be identical (see below, page 177). Later research by Goldthorpe and colleagues (1968a) has shown that manual workers receiving relatively high incomes do not necessarily identify with non-manual workers, nor develop social relationships with them (see below, pages 173–4).

Occupation and life-chances

As we saw in Chapter 3, pages 59–61, the problem of putting such an abstract and complex concept as social class into practice is very great. And yet, if empirical research is to be carried out, it must be done. Reid (1977) provides an excellent discussion of the problems involved.

Most researchers use occupation as the indicator of social class. For example, the Registrar-General, who is responsible for the Census, has developed the following scale:

Class I   Professional and managerial, e.g. doctors, lawyers, clergy
Class II   Intermediate occupations, e.g. sales managers, authors, MPs, farmers, nurses
Class III Routine non-manual, e.g. typists, shop assistants; Skilled, e.g. cooks, bricklayers, foremen
Class IV   Partly skilled, e.g. bar staff, telephone-operators, bus conductors
Class V   Unskilled, e.g. cleaners, stevedores, labourers

In Britain in 1971, the economically active and the retired population was made up as follows:

Class I   4 per cent
Class II   18 per cent
Class III 21 per cent + 28 per cent
Class IV   21 per cent
Class V   8 per cent

Another example is the Hall–Jones scale, devised for the social mobility study edited by Glass (1954):

Class 1   Professional and higher administrative
Class 2   Managerial and executive
Class 3   Inspectorial, supervisory and other non-manual, higher grade
Class 4   Inspectorial, supervisory and other non-manual, lower grade
Class 5   Skilled manual and routine non-manual
Class 6   Semi-skilled manual
Class 7   Unskilled manual

There are many other scales like this, and many are given in detail in Reid (1977). For example, the Registrar-General has another scale, the seventeen-point 'socio-economic groups' scale. These are supposed to share similar social, cultural and recreational standards.

All such scales tend to reflect assumptions about the superiority of white-collar work, the importance of the professions, etc. Young and Willmott (1956), on the other hand, showed that a number of their sample of London East End manual workers used quite different criteria to evaluate occupations, based mainly on what they saw as their contribution to society. They produced a very different order of ranking for thirty given occupations than did the Hall–Jones scale.

In the end, of course, it is a contradiction to try to produce a social class scale, based on occupation, on which everyone can agree. By recognizing class differences in the first place, we recognize that there will be differences in attitudes and life-styles. We should not, then, expect to find agreement on the evaluation and ranking of occupations. It is those who occupy the dominant positions in society who can impose their system of social evaluation, and it is they who have produced the scales for use in sociological research. Despite these problems, many pieces of official and private research have examined the relationship between occupation and aspects of people's lives, that is, their life-chances. The latter include fertility, infant mortality, health, education, work and housing.

Fertility

We know that in the last quarter of the nineteenth century the so-called 'middle class' started to limit the size of their family. No doubt this had something to do with their wish to maintain, or even improve, their living standards at a time when trade was becoming increasingly competitive, and domestic costs greater. Manual workers' families did not follow a similar trend. For a hundred years or so the same pattern has been in evidence; the lower down the social scale, the larger the family.

The special Family Census of 1947 and the 1961 national census both showed that salaried employees were likely to produce only half the number of children produced by manual labourers. The most advantaged in society, including employers and professionals, did have a fertility rate slightly in excess of salaried employees, although nowhere near so great as that of unskilled manual workers. (See also pages 365–6.)

Infant mortality

There has been research upon both general mortality, that is, the number of deaths of people in certain social classes (irrespective of their age), and infant mortality, that is, the numbers of deaths of infants per social class group. In both cases there is a clear relationship between social class and mortality. Research by Douglas (1958), Spicer and Lipworth (1966), and Gough (1970) has shown that the incidence of infant mortality increases from the Registrar-General's Class I to Class V. Different sources often cite different figures, but since the Second World War the infant mortality rate for R-G Classes IV and V seems to have been between one-and-a-half and twice that of Class I. Furthermore, the gap is, if anything, widening. And this gap is wider in the United Kingdom than in the rest of Europe (see also page 380).

Health

During 1961–2, a government department studied how often people were unable to work because of sickness. Atkinson (1973) has reported the findings of this study, pointing out that 'the rate of sickness absence was considerably higher for unskilled workers than the average for all workers. . . .' The General Household Survey (1973) has also shown that people in Registrar-General Classes IV and V are more likely to 'lose time' through illness than are people in Classes I and II. This latter survey revealed that all illnesses such as bronchitis, injuries, mental disorders, ear and digestive problems (but not eye diseases) were found increasingly as one moves from Class I to Class V. Of course, we do not know whether these illnesses are attributable to factors operating in home, community or work.

The increasing amount of sickness absence in 'lower' social classes does not mean that they use the health service more frequently. Research suggests that they are less likely to have ante-natal maternity examinations, and less likely to use clinics either for examination or for subsidized food and vitamins or for immunization (see pages 382–3).

There is contradictory evidence regarding the use of the family doctor service. For example, people in R-G Classes IV and V in the 45–64 age-group consult their doctor more frequently than others, whereas people in Class I in the 65+ age-group consult more frequently. In any case, great care must be taken with this sort of evidence because there is a greater frequency of ill-health amongst classes IV and V, which would lead us to expect a higher incidence of doctor consultation. The final piece of evidence worth mentioning refers to the use of the dental services. These are used more frequently by people in Class I than by people in Class V.

Education

The relationship between social class and educational opportunity is one of the most well-documented areas in sociological research. In Chapter 9 you will find a discussion of the effects of social class upon admission to grammar, technical and secondary modern schools. In addition to this you should be aware that studies by Jackson (1964) and Barker Lunn (1972) have demonstrated a clear relationship between social class and allocation to streams in the primary school. In Table 7 below you can see how it is more likely that children in Class I will be in the A stream, and that children in Class V will be in the C stream.

At the secondary level, Ford (1969) has shown that very able children in 'lower' social class groups are less likely to find their way into higher

Table 7 *Eleven-year-old children – father's occupation in 252 three-stream schools*

Social class indicated by father's occupation (Registrar-General's scale)	A stream (%)	B stream (%)	C stream (%)	total (%)
I Professional and managerial	58	28	14	100
II Clerical	47	32	21	100
III Skilled manual	41	35	24	100
IV Semi-skilled manual	29	41	30	100
V Unskilled manual	20	34	46	100

SOURCE: adapted from Jackson (1964)

streams in comprehensive schools than similarly able children in Classes I and II. And this pattern of class inequality persists into higher education. Data from Westergaard and Resler (1975) demonstrates how young people in Classes I and II are more than four times more likely to obtain a university education; the gap between Class I and Class V is, of course, even wider.

Work

Some very detailed research has been undertaken on the contrasting work situations of manual and non-manual workers. Implicit in the two main researches, by Wedderburn (1970) and Moonman (1973), is a comparison between R-G Classes I and II, on the one hand, and Classes III, IV and V, on the other. A clear pattern emerges: manual workers are more likely to work longer hours; to undertake shift work; to have to 'clock in'; to have automatic deductions made from their pay if they are late to work; to have fewer days' holiday per year; to have pay docked for absences from work for compassionate reasons, such as family funerals or ill-health; to have accidents at work; to receive less sick pay (if any); to be unemployed; to receive poorer redundancy pay in the event of a company running down its work-force; to receive less favourable pensions (if any) from their firms.

Housing

Most of us are aware that many people live in sub-standard accommodation. 'Sub-standard' includes numerous factors, including shortage of rooms, lack of inside toilet, lack of a bathroom, lack of a permanent source of heating. In general terms, people living in houses which they have bought or are buying are far less likely to experience these conditions. The majority of sub-standard accommodation is in the privately rented, furnished and unfurnished houses and flats. Although there is some excellent quality, expensive accommodation within this category, that which is sub-standard tends to be occupied by families and individuals in R-G Classes III, IV and V.

All the above evidence is related directly or indirectly to people's position in the economy. The advantages they receive, be it in the form of good health, plenty of money, share certificates tucked away, or a fair chance of their children going to higher education, are related to economic power (or lack of it!). This, then, is *social class* – indicated by property-ownership, income or occupation.

Status ranking

In sociology, the term 'status' has various meanings. It might be used to refer to any social position which a person fills, for example, mother, friend or vicar. Some of these positions are *achieved*. Achieved status, however, should not be taken to imply that it takes hard work (such as passing examinations) before the position is filled (although coincidentally that might be the case with some such positions, such as solicitor or doctor). Rather, achieved status denotes that the position has been filled as a result of a course of action (or even failing to take action). Thus 'husband' is an achieved status, as is 'friend'.

Alternatively, some positions are automatically bestowed upon an individual who has virtually no choice about whether to fill the position. Examples include 'male', 'teenager', 'sister', 'Hindu' and 'negro'. As you can see from these examples, there are different categories of ascribed status: age, sex, kinship, religion and ethnicity (see below). Of course, these categories are not necessarily inflexible. People move through different age-stages, for example, from infant to child, right through to ancestor; and it is medically possible to change one's sex. In South Africa there have been many examples of people having their racial group reclassified. Many people are at liberty to change their religion. However, there are many societies, and circumstances within our own society, where such status positions are bestowed without people having any choice.

The critical point here is that many status positions are not merely differentiated from each other (in terms of social expectations, values and the like), but also that they carry different amounts of social prestige – amounts of social prestige accepted and recognized by other members of society – and therefore of power and authority. Wherever prestige is accorded in greater or lesser amounts to specific social positions we have an alternative system of ranking to social class. The two are often related in practice, but more of that later.

I shall use the term 'status group' to refer to a group of people who are hierarchically ranked according to their possession of one or more status characteristics. Status groups have distinctive life-styles which are accorded greater or lesser prestige. By 'life-style' I mean that they have distinctive norms, values and beliefs which are recognized as 'superior' or 'inferior' by others. These may include people's attitude to marriage, how they spend their income (irrespective of the source and size of that income), what and how they eat, and where they live. All these aspects of life-style may well be in your mind when you think of 'social class' differences. However, sociologists usually follow the approach of Weber who was the first to separate class from status for the purpose of analysis and discussion, not because the two are in practice unrelated in our society, but because in some societies one or other is far more important and influential. This would be true for societies as diverse as traditional Aboriginal societies (where age status is most significant) and contemporary South Africa (where racial category determines life-chances).

South Africa could be regarded as an example of a 'caste' system of stratification, although this term is usually associated with the ranking in traditional Hindu areas of India. Caste is a good example of status ranking. It is true that many ranks and groups in the Indian caste system are distinguishable by virtue of typical occupations pursued by members, but it is more important to realize that individuals are born into positions within the hierarchy – their positions are ascribed. There are rules which ensure the separation of one group from another, rules which are underpinned by the basic value of 'purity'. This value is rooted in the Hindu religion. Not surprisingly, the highest rank is that of the Brahmins or priests, and the lowest the 'untouchables'; the ranks in between are accorded differential amounts of prestige. Higher ranks or castes try to ensure separation from those below; intermarriage is normally forbidden; there are complex arrangements relating to the receiving of drinking water, the consumption and preparation of food and inter-caste social relationships.

In reality the Indian caste system is infinitely more complex than this rough picture can portray. However, you should appreciate that ranking is ascribed, that the hierarchy is fixed and clearly defined and that it is rooted in religious faith. Religion does in fact legitimate social stratification; caste members see their current position as the result of their actions in a previous life – and therefore indisputably just – and they recognize that caste position in the life to come is determined by their qualities in this life. I have suggested above that contemporary South Africa could be regarded as a caste system; but whereas traditional caste arrangements in India are rooted in religious faith, in South Africa ethnic or racial group – indicated by skin colour – is the basis for ranking.

Ethnicity

Many of you may have been disturbed by the violence and deaths in South Africa in 1976 (in Soweto), in 1980 and in 1985/6. As you probably know, South African society is based upon the principle of 'apartheid', or racial segregation. The whites constitute one status group, the coloureds (or people of mixed race) the second, and the blacks the third. Ethnicity is thus the determining status characteristic. It would not matter how rich coloureds or blacks became (even if there were sufficient opportunities) – they could not enter the white status group. Of course, in South Africa the consequences of status-group membership are considerable: income, health services, housing and the like are all substantially worse for coloureds and blacks. The expenditure per head on education for blacks, for example, is but a fraction of that for whites. It would be true to say that there has been a marginal improvement in working and living conditions of urban blacks in recent years, but the inequalities are still present.

South Africa highlights status stratification, but it is by no means the only example. Slavery in the USA was associated with race, and the experience of negro slaves is well documented. It is a moot point whether the USA has 'lost' this form of status stratification. Although a city like Los Angeles has a remarkably varied ethnic mix, still there are considerable differences in life-style between ethnic groups. Elsewhere, in large cities like New York, there is clear evidence of the low status accorded to negroes and other ethnic groups. This shows itself in job opportunities, housing, education and so on (see, for example, Worsley 1977, ch. 5, and Banks 1976). One of the most powerful indicators of the strength of status stratification is the absence of intermarriage between members of status groups. There is no evidence of substantial racial intermarriage in the USA.

I mention the USA only because there has been a good deal of research on ethnic groups. Our own society provides equally compelling evidence of discrimination in job opportunities and housing, and there is a similarly low rate of intermarriage. For example, research by the independent research group, PEP (see Smith 1977), has shown that immigrants are allocated fewer council houses than whites, and that the council houses which *are* allocated are of a poorer standard. This confirms the pattern identified by the Runnymede Trust (1975) which also showed that certain immigrants are allocated housing in less favourable areas. The PEP research demonstrated how much more difficult it is for immigrants to secure jobs, and that the jobs they do secure are less favourable in terms of pay, security and prospects for promotion. This confirms the pattern identified by Ballard and Holden (1975), which showed that coloured college graduates were disadvantaged compared with equivalent white students. A 1985 government committee of enquiry (chaired by Lord Swann) demonstrated how West Indian and Bangladeshi children were seriously under-achieving in schools. This under-achievement is not attributable to lower intelligence, but to low socio-economic status and prejudice and discrimination (Swann, 1985) (see also page 269).

The low prestige of some ethnic groups is reflected in the perennial jokes about Pakistanis, Irishmen and Jews (jokes based upon some stereotypical characteristics of life-style, or of individual character). Once inferiority is assumed, of course, people not in the group feel at liberty to invent aspects of life-style which reinforce the justice of the inferiority, which 'prove' that the ethnic group is both different and inferior. Justifications of superiority and inferiority are an integral part of the dominant ideology of a society (see Chapter 5, page 131). Dominant ideologies legitimize the position of groups in the status hierarchy.

Gender

Societies impose different meanings upon the physical characteristics of sex, and therefore have different expectations of males and females. These cultural meanings we call 'gender'. It is a commonplace of cross-cultural studies to display how women are dominant, aggressive and forceful in their relationships with men in some societies. Margaret Mead (1950) illustrates how women amongst the Mundugumor of New Guinea are assertive and forceful, and detest child-bearing and child-rearing, and how Tchambuli women in New Guinea get on with tasks such as fishing and going to market while their husbands decorate themselves, carve, paint and practise dancing. However, in the vast majority of societies, be they past or present, there has been a remarkably consistent tendency for females to be dominated. As a result of this male domination, women experience fewer privileges and rewards than men. These privileges and rewards include freedom and autonomy, the ability to make decisions, as well as lower wages. Commentators have argued that, in pre-industrial societies, women had higher prestige because they were an integral element of the productive system (which was centred around the home and family). In industrial societies, however, production has become divorced from the home and based in factories, which means that the child-bearing role of women becomes more difficult to sustain without damage to economic activities. Some of the disadvantages experienced by females in the education system are described on pages 268 and 342. Let me simply point out here one or two patterns: girls are far less likely to enter degree courses – less so in the arts and humanities, but markedly so in the medical, physical and technological sciences. In all types of postgraduate research, women are seriously under-represented. They are also a tiny minority in such occupations as university teaching, engineering, the law, accountancy, medicine and architecture. In all these, under 10 per cent are female. The picture is not uniform, however, for in occupations such as teaching and social work women are predominant. These latter occupations are not very highly ranked in prestige; you might like to consider whether the low prestige attached to such occupations is a result of predominantly female recruitment, or whether females are recruited to such occupations because the latter are low in prestige.

It is also true to say that, in the field of productive industry, women are more likely to be in semi-skilled and unskilled (rather than skilled) jobs, and to receive lower average wages. Because of the skill level of their jobs, women are likely to receive lower average wages than men. Recent legislation designed to promote equality of incomes can never be fully successful while women continue to be recruited mainly to those jobs which carry less pay. (See also pages 347–8.)

This sort of discussion should start to indicate to you the pervasive nature of gender as a basis for status ranking. Although the physical characteristics of male and female do not, in our society, carry the same inflexibility as some ethnic characteristics, they are, nonetheless, extremely influential, and there is no doubt that gender status positions do carry connotations of superiority and inferiority. It matters little whether alleged female inferiority is supported by evidence; in actual fact the evidence is to the contrary. There is little reason why menstruation, pregnancy, childbirth and lactation should more than marginally affect daily activities. Physical prowess is significant in few occupations. What does matter is whether societies attach conceptions of superiority and inferiority to this particular status category. (See also Chapter 12.)

Age

I suppose that for centuries parents have told their offspring that they are 'too old' to do one thing, yet chided them the next moment for claiming a privilege when too young; for example, 'act your age', followed by 'you're not stopping out all night at your age'. Implicit in this is a measure of superiority and inferiority, linked to some extent to age. Thus, our values include at least partial respect for the elderly and experienced. For this reason we accord a few privileges to old people; we reward people for advancing age and experience in some occupations, and there is a tendency for certain key positions and occupations, such as in political life, to be filled by people of mature years. However, it would be difficult to sustain the view that in our society age is the basis for hierarchical organization. The reward system is not clearly and consistently developed, and it is possible for relatively young people to gain access to positions of economic and political power, and to the associated rewards.

In some societies, however, the old – even ancestors – are revered. In pre-communist China this was the case; in parts of rural Afghanistan the old have traditionally exercised great power to settle disputes and exert social control. There, the ultimate definitions of social rules and conventions, and the reinforcement of shared values, rested with the elderly. Since all the older men carried this power and responsibility we can see that the two ascribed statuses – age and gender – were the basis for the hierarchical organization of society. Many traditional Aboriginal societies displayed the same characteristics: males moved from one age-stage to another – childhood to early manhood to husband to elder. The transitions from age-stage to age-stage were accompanied by major rituals. These rituals – rites of passage – involved physical markings on the body which signalled to the rest of the community the change in age-status. Within each group there are no differences. Increases in prestige are guaranteed by virtue of advancing years. The rewards attached to age-status include ownership of land, political control and leadership, participation in rituals and ceremonies and the like.

Life-style

Although I have argued that status inequalities might be based upon such ascribed categories as age, gender and ethnicity, the widest use of the notion of status inequality refers to the allocation of prestige according to life-styles. Many people, I suspect, allocate prestige according to occupation. In such cases, an occupation is accorded prestige not simply because of economic rewards – if this were the case we would be talking about social class – but in terms of the perceived superiority/inferiority of the incumbent of the occupational position. It is often thought that the clergy carried high status even though their economic rewards have not been high. Similarly, a factory worker in a mass production industry might earn, with over-time and bonuses, a high weekly wage without ever attracting much social prestige. For this same reason, many people who rapidly acquire or earn large fortunes are not accepted by high-status groups such as the aristocracy and landed gentry (who may themselves lack such wealth). 'Life-style' is not something which is easily purchasable, even though finance must help! Occupation may ultimately be a major determinant of status, but this in turn may be related to educational experience and qualifications, levels of responsibility and authority over others.

In Western societies, family line and titles, such as 'Lord' or 'Duchess', do convey status; so also do accents and clothing (or the place from which clothing is purchased!). Status is assigned too to certain patterns of consumption of goods; in short, it matters less what you earn, and more what you purchase with what you do earn. Types of house (or the fact of ownership), car, furniture, food and diet, location of holidays may all generate differential social status. There is no doubt too that in Britain and, I suspect, in other societies, great prestige is attached to attendance at private schools and at (in our case) Oxford and Cambridge universities. We noted in Chapter 2 that there is a strong link between private school education and access to high political office (page 40; see also page 267).

You may also have gained some impressions through the mass media of status inequalities. Sporting events at Royal Ascot and the Henley Regatta contrast with speedway racing in Manchester and greyhounds in Sheffield; compare members' enclosures with public terracing at cricket matches; compare grouse shooting and polo with darts and soccer. In these instances, and indeed many others, you will notice life-styles which include not only leisure pursuits but also accents, clothing and food. Such patterns of consumption are *status* characteristics which are taken for granted in British social life.

Political ranking

You will recall that Max Weber distinguished between 'class' and 'status'. In addition to these, however, he also identified a third, analytically separate, dimension of social stratification. This latter is sometimes referred to as the 'power' dimension. Strictly speaking, however, Weber used the term 'party'. In a sense both class and status involve forms of power: the power that comes from economic rewards and advantages, and the power that comes from having a prestigious style of life or social attribute which other people desire. In Weber's use, 'party' denotes political power. This sort of power rests with those who are the key decision-makers in society or who wish to influence those decision-makers. Political decision-makers in our society include the government, parliament, the civil service and the judiciary. Such groups (or parties) devise and implement policies regarding the distribution of national resources, international relationships and the like.

In the general sense of 'leadership' and 'decision-making', it can be easily recognized that there is some form of political ranking in many societies. The existence of a single informal ruler or adviser in a pre-industrial society does not by itself constitute evidence that there is social stratification. Weber's use of 'party', however, denotes the desire by some group(s) to maintain or achieve control; in many societies there will be a permanent group of decision-makers who can be replaced or withstand attempts to replace them.

We might be inclined to associate 'party' with political parties. Certainly political parties such as the British Conservative and the American Democratic parties constitute 'parties' in the Weberian sense. So also do parliament and the civil service. There are a number of groups which we call 'pressure groups' which rarely have economic or social power, but which unmistakably try to influence key decision-makers in society either by promoting a cause or protecting an interest. There is an enormous variety of such groups: you might have heard of the Wildlife Trust, Greenpeace and ASH (the anti-smoking association). Such groups try to influence government policy, advising on the passing or withholding of legislation relevant to their interests. They correspond with members of parliament, and debate with them in the lobbies of the House of Commons. Any consideration of political ranking must take account of these politically influential groups (see Chapter 7, pages 210–11).

The most significant pressure groups in contemporary times are undoubtedly the trade unions, but it is difficult to assess the extent of their political power. Throughout their more than century-long history trade unions have, in varying ways, and to varying extents, fought for the improvement of their members' wages and working conditions. In some cases, disputes have been between trade union members at local level and an individual owner or manager of a firm. In other cases, the disputes have been between the government (as employer) and national union officials. It is particularly with the latter sort of case that it appears that trade unions have political power and are therefore part of the political ranking system. The reason for this is clear, if the employer is the government, then the willingness of the latter to accede to wage demands is determined by its overall policy (or lack of policy) on the funding of the public sector of the economy. Trade unions are thus inevitably brought into the political arena. A recent example occurred in 1974 when the then Conservative government suffered an electoral defeat which was directly related to their handling of a confrontation with miners over pay (see Chapter 10, pages 296-7).

The extent to which governments involve trade unions actively in helping to formulate policy is variable. The 1974-79 Labour government, on the one hand, negotiated a 'social contract' with the unions whereby the latter exercised restraint over pay claims in return for improvements in the 'social wage', that is, benefits received through social services and the taxation system. On the other hand, the Conservative government from 1979 to the present day has sought to place legal limitations on the power of unions.

It should also be noted that some disputes between workers and the management of private firms involve the police as peace-keepers. The police are agents of the state. It is therefore not unusual for union action outside factory gates to assume the character of a political demonstration, with hostility addressed to the police who are, by the nature of their role, bound to defend the *status quo*.

So far I have briefly sketched the sorts of individuals and groups who have political power in Britain. To conclude this section I would like to consider in a little more detail the nature of parliament. Specifically, we should consider the educational and occupational background of members of parliament. This may provide some useful background information about those in high political office; more pertinently, however, we should be able to see some connections between political rank and both class and status. Table 8 summarizes the educational background of members of the House of Commons over a half-century. You should be able to see strong connections between membership of the House of Commons and high status educational experience, notably at public schools and certain universities. Of the 1980 Conservative government inner cabinet, twenty out of twenty-two were educated at public schools, six of those twenty at Eton. Seventeen out of the twenty-

Table 8 *The educational background of average House of Commons members, 1918–35 and 1951–70*

Education	1918–35		1951–70	
	Con.	Lab.	Con.	Lab.
Elementary school only	2.5	75.5	1.2	28.3
Grammar school	19.0	15.5	23.2	52.1
Eton	27.5	1.5 ⎫	75.5	19.6
Other public schools	51.0	7.5 ⎭		
Oxford University	22.3	3.4	30.6	13.7
Cambridge university	17.0	4.3	22.0	6.4
Other universities	10.5	10.8	11.0	24.6

SOURCE: Guttsman in Stanworth and Giddens (1974)

two attended Oxford or Cambridge University. A high-status education thus clearly has some relationship to high political office (*Social Science Teacher* 1979b).

Table 9 summarizes the occupational background of members of parliament over a twenty-year period. You should note that MPs are being drawn increasingly from professional occupations, and far less from manual occupations and non-professional white-collar fields. The number of MPs with a background in the ownership and management of firms has not changed dramatically over the twenty-year period.

The political ranking system implicit in the above is not a clear one. There is no neat single hierarchy, just as there is no such single hierarchy in class and status ranking. As with the last two, we can only say that within the political ranking system there is a range of competing groups which have differential, and not always constant, power.

Ranking systems do in fact change, and it is to the changes in the British ranking system that we must now turn.

Changes in the British class structure

You may remember that Marx's theory of social class was an integral element of his theory of social change (see Chapter 4, page 116). He tried to explain all history as the history of conflict between social classes. He analysed in detail the transition from feudal society to capitalism and, in addition, he predicted the course of the change from his contemporary epoch, capitalism, to socialism and communism. Although Marx's predictions were necessarily based upon his understanding of the nature of early capitalism, and therefore not always applicable to contemporary stratification and social change, they do provide a neat baseline with which to compare recent changes in the stratification system.

I mentioned above (page 153) that Marx predicted that the bourgeoisie

Table 9 *The occupational background of members of parliament, 1951-70*

	1951		1955		1959		1964		1966		1970	
	Con.	*Lab.*	*Con.*	*Lab.*	*Con.*	*Lab.*	*Con.*	*Lab.*	*Con.*	*Lab.*	*Con.*	*Lab.*
Armed forces	10.0	0.7	13.7	1.0	9.9	1.2	9.2	0.6	7.5	0.8	7.2	00.0
Farmers	4.6	0.7	9.0	1.7	10.5	1.2	11.5	0.6	10.7	0.5	9.4	00.3
Professions	30.5	30.8	29.3	34.2	33.1	35.6	36.2	38.2	36.4	40.8	36.1	45.6
Commerce/Industry	37.0	12.8	32.6	13.3	33.5	11.2	28.3	12.3	32.0	10.2	32.4	11.8
Politicians and journalists	7.8	13.2	10.5	12.2	10.2	12.4	10.2	10.7	7.5	10.5	12.1	13.2
Workers and white-collars	1.5	40.6	1.4	36.7	1.4	37.2	2.3	36.0	3.6	36.1	0.9	27.5
Private means	8.4	—	3.2	—	1.1	—	1.3	—	2.0	—	—	—

SOURCE: Guttsman, in Stanworth and Giddens (1974).

and proletariat would each become more homogeneous; furthermore he suggested that the intermediate strata would gradually become assimilated into whichever of the polar classes they felt they were most compatible with. Under inspired leadership, each of the two classes become increasingly aware of their common interests, and of the fact that their common interests differ from those of the other class. Progressively, each industrial dispute, each strike and lock-out, and each political demonstration take on a greater significance, and reflect the deep-seated conflicts of interest between the classes. This conflict ultimately culminates in widespread and dramatic social change – a revolution – with a complete upheaval in all social institutions, (including, of course, government). The hiatus caused by the overturning of the former distribution of power is filled by a dictatorship of the proletariat, with state ownership of the means of production, before the 'true' classless society (with power-sharing, and the equal distribution of resources) is ushered in.

We will now examine how far certain of these predictions have been borne out in practice.

The managerial revolution

You will remember that early capitalism was characterized by private individual ownership of factories, but that multiple ownership and widespread investment was encouraged by the introduction of the principle of limited liability. Firms which are jointly owned by a number of people, however, must commission the services of managers to control the day-to-day running of the firm on their behalf.

In theory, then, the separation of ownership and control cuts across Marx's prediction that the bourgeoisie were becoming more homogeneous. Ownership was spreading; capital was 'decomposing'. The evidence on pages 154–6 does suggest, however, that the decomposition of capital has not been so widespread; indeed, direct ownership of industrial stock has remained in the hands of a small proportion of the population. (Many more people are indirect owners through insurance schemes and pensions funds.)

Nonetheless, although ownership is still concentrated, the role of owners as shareholders and/or boards of directors is very different from what it was. Even the extent to which owners actually determine anything other than very broad policy may be very limited. Of great interest to us is the nature of the managers who now exercise considerable control over firms. Dahrendorf (1959) argues that, whilst the gap between the controllers and labour might be narrower, the gap between ownership (or capital) and labour has widened precisely because owners have nearly all disappeared from their direct involvement with production. What do you think? Are managers completely different from the traditional capitalists? Or do you think that the interests of managers are very similar to those of the owners because both seek maximum profit? Does the manager simply act in pursuit of profit on behalf of the owners?

Irrespective of whether they are owners, managers have considerable economic power: to impose decisions upon others, to terminate labour, to secure fringe benefits and other rewards. In this sense, managers constitute one further complexity in economic ranking (or social class). In early joint-stock companies, many managers 'worked their way up' through various occupational grades; they were socially mobile in an economic sense. More recently, however, there has been a marked tendency for managers to be recruited on the basis of specialized education, not least at university. This opens up the possibility that managers are recruited from a relatively distinct status group by virtue of their possession of the important status characteristic – education. Indeed, Dahrendorf suggests that there are considerable ties socially and politically between owners and managers – certainly more ties than between managers and labour (see also page 283).

Changes in the working class
Dahrendorf has suggested that Marx took too little account of the changes taking place within the industrial work-force. It may not do justice to Marx's analysis, but the prevailing image of the work-force of the mid-nineteeth century is one in which the majority were relatively unskilled and impoverished. In practice, what has happened is that the industrial work-force – the proletariat – has become increasingly heterogeneous in terms of skill level. There are complex grades of skilled, semi-skilled and unskilled workers, with the last of these declining in number. Some current industrial disputes are not just about the size of wage increases, but about 'differentials', that is, wage differences as reflections of differences in skill. The contemporary 'proletariat' will often compete with each other to restore these differentials, rather than join other manual workers in dispute with the owners and managers (see page 283).

It may be thought that developments in technology would generate a uniform manual work-force. Marx could hardly have anticipated the developments in mass production and continuous technology which have affected the nature of job satisfaction and financial rewards. Mass production workers have attracted a great deal of attention: first, because they are potentially the most alienated of workers (see Chapter 10, pages 277 and 293), and second, because their earnings are above average. The latter is of particular significance here.

Embourgeoisement
One of the most debated theories of stratification is the embourgeoisement theory. This theory suggests that, as certain types of manual

worker, particularly in mass production industries, attain high wages, they are gradually being assimilated into the middle class (see Zweig 1961). A research team led by Goldthorpe and Lockwood attempted to assess the extent to which this process had taken place (see Goldthorpe *et al.* 1968a, 1968b, 1969). They showed that, logically, the process of assimilation into the middle class was complex and occurs by stages. A traditional manual worker, living in a working-class community, with working-class norms and values, would have to:

1 first become privatized, that is, become separated from membership of working-class communities, without relinquishing working-class cultural norms;
2 then reject working-class norms and values in favour of ones which are middle-class, without yet entering into social relationships with middle-class individuals and groups;
3 and finally accept middle-class norms and values, and enter into social relationships with middle-class individuals and groups.

Only with the last of these stages has true assimilation occurred.

Implicit in the above sequence of events are two issues: what kinds of norms and values are those of manual workers, and into what kinds of relationships, and with whom, do they enter? Consequently, there is a need for two types of evidence, which Goldthorpe and Lockwood called 'normative' and 'relational'. In addition, of course, we would need to assess the precise nature of the *economic* advantage of these affluent manual workers under consideration.

Goldthorpe and Lockwood's research did confirm that affluent manual workers received higher than average weekly wages. These wages, however, were at the 'cost' of overtime and shift working, conditions rarely experienced by non-manual workers. In addition, these manual workers did not receive other benefits as did non-manual workers receiving comparable incomes – benefits such as pensions, sick-pay schemes, paid holidays and the like. So the *economic* element of embourgeoisement has not taken place to the extent originally envisaged.

There is no firm evidence that these manual workers have adopted middle-class cultural standards. They certainly have become more home- and family-centred; they certainly have a continuing concern for their children, particularly their children's education. They certainly have adopted some apparently middle-class consumption patterns, purchasing material goods such as cars, freezers and washing machines from their high earnings. There is no evidence, however, that these purchases reflect a desire to join the middle class: such material goods are valued only for their intrinsic usefulness. In one respect, however, there is evidence that these manual workers are different normatively from traditional manual workers who live in tightly-knit communities centred around primary and productive industry. The latter, including miners, iron and steel workers, and fishermen (see Dennis *et al.* 1956 and Tunstall 1962, for example) typically join together to achieve goals which benefit their whole community. In other words, they use collective means in pursuit of collective ends. By contrast, the traditional middle class would pursue individual ends using individual means: for example, believing that you only benefit yourself (and your family) in terms of rewards and prestige by your own efforts (see page 39).

Affluent manual workers represent a different pattern: as we noted above, they are very home- and family-centred. These are their ends or goals. However, they do still use collective means in pursuit of these individual ends. The collective means, which include trade union membership and Labour party voting, are employed as part-and-parcel of such workers' instrumental orientation to work. In sum, this 'instrumental collectivism' of affluent manual workers is like neither the traditional working class nor the traditional middle class. They represent a 'new' class – the 'new working class'. It may be that, in the Conservative general election victories of 1979 and 1984, considerable numbers of manual workers shifted their allegiance away from the Labour Party. Such a shift, however, could still be consistent with a calculative, instrumental orientation to voting, and not reflect middle-class aspirations. Instrumentalists will vote for the party which they think will 'deliver the goods' at a particular moment in time.

Finally, there is no evidence of affluent manual workers being accepted in social relationships by those in the traditional middle class. They do not reside in close proximity: there is no marked intermarriage; there is no marked home-visiting; there is no significant membership of middle-class associations and clubs.

I mentioned above that these workers may represent a 'new working class'. 'Class', here, can mean a number of things. In one sense, by virtue of *size* of income, such workers could be said to be more highly ranked economically than other workers. By virtue of the *source* of income, however (including shift work, overtime, and performing alienating tasks), such workers might still be as 'proletarian' as the wage-labourers of Marx's time. Their experience of work is very much akin to the powerlessness and meaninglessness implicit in Marx's analysis of labour. It is significant, however, that such workers do not necessarily perceive themselves as underprivileged economically: Goldthorpe and Lockwood did in fact find evidence that their affluent manual workers positively selected this type of work because of the high rewards which could be devoted to personal and family ends.

I have also mentioned that these workers show a pattern of consumption not typical of the working class, and one more associated with the middle class; and I suggested that such consumption of material goods does not take place with the intention of 'becoming middle class'. Furthermore, their instrumental collectivism is characteristic of neither the traditional working class nor the traditional middle class. These factors thus raise the possibility of the 'new working class' being a variation not much in the social class system as in the *status* system. As a status group it would carry no great prestige because of its occupational base. Yet their material possessions, and normative commitment, suggest an alternative life-style. One solution would be to regard the new working class as a social class because economic position is the determining factor; yet you could still retort that economic position is chosen precisely because of prior commitments to a certain type of life-style. What do *you* think?

The new middle class

Marx identified intermediate strata existing alongside the proletariat and the bourgeoisie. I pointed out earlier that these intermediate strata, in Marx's view, would be assimilated into one of the two polar camps. Since the middle of the nineteenth century, however, the nature of industry has changed a great deal. The primary sector, which includes the production of raw materials such as coal, and both forestry and agriculture, has declined in terms of manpower requirements. The secondary sector, which is that associated with manufacturing industry, has slightly declined in the same way. The most dramatic change has taken place within the tertiary sector. The latter, sometimes called the service sector, includes such service industries as catering, insurance, administration, transport and retailing. Such services did exist a century or more ago, but their growth in the last forty years has been enormous.

Potentially, then, we see the growth of strata in society which might act as a 'cushion' between the two polar classes, bourgeoisie and proletariat. Potentially, the existence of these new groups 'in the middle' might create a stratification system shaped more like a diamond than a pyramid. Unfortunately it is not quite so simple, in the main because these intermediate strata are themselves so differentiated and heterogeneous. This is easy to see when you think that they include such varied occupations as administrators in local and central government, scientists and technicians, teachers and social workers, caterers, secretaries, bank tellers and clerks. This list is hardly exhaustive. I think it is reasonable to follow Dahrendorf (see Chapter 2, page 38) and distinguish between those occupations which involve the exercise of authority and those which do not. A senior civil servant must necessarily advise governmental ministers about possible courses of action; such a person must necessarily implement governmental and parliamentary policies. In both these respects the position is powerful. Similarly the departmental head of research in a drug company is powerful because such a person frames guidelines for directions of research, and provides technical expertise to help others. Such a person may be able to hire and fire people, or at least provide the information which allows others to do so. By contrast, copy typists may simply and routinely follow the instructions of their supervisors, as might, indeed junior clerks (see pages 290–3).

David Lockwood studied the 'black-coated worker', or clerk, some years ago (Lockwood 1958). He started from the proposition that clerical workers were property-less, and thus apparently proletarian in Marx's terms. Yet clearly such workers do not perceive themselves as 'proletarian', with interests similar to those of manual workers. This might seem surprising given that the *market situation* of clerical workers is very similar to that of many manual workers. The size of clerical workers' incomes is probably only equivalent to many manual workers' incomes. The *work situation* of clerks, however, is quite different. Lockwood found that clerks enjoyed more favourable working conditions (including pensions and other benefits), and their relationships with employers and managers were more 'particularistic'; that is, they were known as individuals, and were treated according to their individual qualities and personal circumstances. It is hardly surprising, then, that clerks identify more with managers than with manual workers. Clerks work in the same offices as their managers; collectively they are often physically as well as socially segregated from the manual work-force. It is hardly surprising too that clerks share the same sort of values and attitudes to managerial groups, and perceive status differences between themselves and manual workers. Lockwood considered that the marginal position of the clerk (in terms of income), plus the relatively close contact with employers, generated an 'exaggerated status consciousness', that is, an awareness of their superiority to manual workers. This status consciousness derives from their work situation and preferred life-style. It thus seems that clerks, whom Lockwood thought might be 'falsely conscious', that is, unaware of their 'true' class position, are highly status conscious. Their relatively low class position is balanced by a higher status position.

However, Lockwood did anticipate the changes taking place in the nature of clerical work. Some such work still takes place in relatively small offices, where relationships remain much more personal, and a sense of worth and value develops. During the past three decades, however, the size of industrial and commercial enterprises has increased considerably in the search for efficiency and effectiveness. In such organizations, the clerk might be one of thousands; his or her relationships with the employer depersonalized; the advantages of work situation non-existent. In such circumstances it is much more likely that clerical workers will identify with manual workers, and become aware of their common dilemmas. What *has* happened is that many such white-collar workers, typically those with less authority, have started to use collective means in pursuit of their individual ends. They join white-collar unions such as NALGO (the National Association of Local Government Officers) and ASTMS (the Association of Scientific, Technical and Managerial Staffs), and some vote Labour – in both cases because they think that these are the best means for improving their personal standards of living. Given this developing instrumental collectivism, it is easy to see why some people have talked about the 'proletarianization' of the white-collar worker. This proletarianization is most likely to occur where the white-collar worker works in large, impersonal offices, estranged from management, and performing menial and repetitive tasks which have little intrinsic satisfaction to compensate for moderate earnings.

You should have recognized here a similarity between this development and the tendency of some affluent manual workers to use similar means to achieve similar ends. It has certainly been argued that the new middle class and the new working class have *converged*, but there is no evidence whatsoever that they have recognized common interests. Are there still status differences between the new middle class and the new working class? Or has the 'de-skilling' of routine clerical work been so great as to remove the divide between non-manual and manual workers? (See pages 292–3.)

Social mobility

'Social mobility' refers to the movement of individuals or groups up and down the social scale. While this could, and perhaps should, include the mobility of all kinds of group (including, for example, women and ethnic minorities) in terms of class, status and political power, in practice most research has compared the class position of sons with that of their fathers. Taking occupation as the indicator of class, researchers have distinguished between long-range and short-range mobility, and between inter-generational (father to son) and intra-generational (within an individual's life-time) mobility. The major interest has been the question of whether Britain is or is not becoming a more 'open' society, that is, one with more equal opportunity and less inherited privilege, and what the consequences of any change might be.

The first major study, Glass (1954), was based on data collected in 1949, and used the Hall–Jones scale (see page 158) to show that, while there was a good deal of inter-generational mobility in Britain, most of it was short range. Thus, around 30 per cent of the sons of manual workers became non-manual workers, and about 30 per cent made the opposite move. One-third of all sons remained in the same class as their fathers, but this figure was higher in Class 2 and much higher in Class 1. There was thus high 'elite self-recruitment', that is, top class people could help to ensure their son's future class-position through such means as private education, the 'old boy network', etc. This latter finding was confirmed by many other studies, for example, Kelsall

(1955). Conversely, Glass showed that those in Class 7 found it harder to rise out of their class. Glass concluded that the patterns of social mobility in Britain had long remained constant.

The next major study of social mobility in Britain is that of the Oxford Mobility Studies Group. This is a deliberate repeat of the Glass research, based on data collected in 1972. Findings have been published at intervals since 1972, but Bourne (1979) is a useful summary, and Goldthorpe (1980) is the major report. The study concludes that there has been a considerable increase in the amount of upward social mobility in Britain, but that the relative chances of mobility are distributed through the classes much as they have always been. Elite self-recruitment has declined as educational qualifications have become more important and as competition has become keener. However, there is still limited mobility into the positions of real power in society.

The major reason for this net upward mobility is the change in the structure of the work-force, with substantially more white-collar, and a declining proportion of manual, occupations. The occupational structure is swelling in the middle as the middle class expands. To fill these new jobs, some sons of working-class fathers have to be upwardly mobile. When this is coupled with the fact that fertility rates (see Chapter 12, page 368) are such that the middle class do not replace themselves in the same numbers in the next generation, and that fertility rates increase the lower down the Hall–Jones scale you go, a good deal of upward mobility is inevitable.

The role of education is also, of course, of central importance. Turner (1960) identified two models of social mobility, each reflected in an educational system. The 'sponsored' model involves the current elite selecting those who are to do well in the educational system, and thus reach elite status themselves, by weeding out the rest at regular intervals throughout the educational process. The 'contest' model involves as many people as possible being kept in the educational process to the end, with selection being delayed to the last possible moment. Turner argued that the first model was closer to that of Britain at that time, and the second was closer to that of the USA. Since Turner wrote, the British system has appeared to move towards a contest model, with greater opportunity for climbing up the social ladder via education. The Oxford Study supports this suggestion to some extent, but also points out that there is a penalty. Educational opportunity can and does lead to high upward mobility, but, if educational qualifications are not obtained early, the lack of them can totally close off promotion and thus reduce intra-generational mobility. As we shall see in Chapter 9 (page 249) educational success itself depends to a great extent on family attitudes and support, and on early socialization for 'achievement motivation'.

In terms of the wider class structure, the Oxford Studies conclude that all these changes are producing a 'growing but increasingly hetero-geneous middle class underpinned by an increasingly tight, self-recruited working class' (Bourne 1979).

So what are the consequences of all this? A functionalist sociologist would stress increasing upward mobility as evidence of greater opportunity in Britain today, and thus of the greater efficiency of society in selecting those needed to fill the top positions (see Chapter 2, page 30, and page 181). Greater opportunity reduces class tensions and class conflict, social justice is seen to be done, and thus the continued stability of society is assured. Dysfunctions might include some social isolation of the upwardly mobile, as they leave their familiar surround-ings and class subculture and may find it difficult to integrate into their new class. There might also be some frustration among those left behind in the race.

A more conflict-oriented sociologist, especially a Marxian one, would argue that social mobility in fact reinforces the *status quo*. Upwardly mobile working-class people have found an individual solution to the collective problem of exploitation, and this weakens class solidarity. Mobility acts as a safety-valve, releasing tensions and grievances that would otherwise lead to social conflict and radical social change. Conversely, the downwardly mobile tend to try to hold on to their lost life-style, rather than rejecting the system that has rejected them. Potential leaders of the working class are creamed off and absorbed into the middle class, where they take on that class's world-view and political outlook, rather than staying in the working class and attempting to improve its situation.

The possibility of moving up and down the social scale reaffirms the notion that it is an open ladder, whereas the fact of the matter is that, if it is a ladder, it is one entirely controlled by those on the top rungs.

Summary

What, then, might we conclude about the current state of social stratification in Britain? I have no neat answer. Not only are there economic, social and political ranking systems in operation, and inter-locked, but also the most recent changes have produced considerable heterogeneity in the majority of cases, with just an indication of some unforeseen homogeneity in lower ranks. Britain has many more subtle and complex strata than Marx could have anticipated.

There remains one further teasing question which needs answering: why should there be stratification in the first place? What creates it? What sustains it? And does your answer to these questions depend upon the type of sociology you are using?

Theoretical explanations of stratification

As you have read in Chapter 2, and elsewhere no doubt, functionalist sociologists assume that there are certain basic conditions which must be fulfilled if society is to survive, and avoid breakdown. These conditions are called 'functional prerequisites'. One of these prerequisites in 'role differentiation and allocation'. This simply means that it must be determined what tasks must be done to enable society to survive, and it must be ensured that people are allocated to perform these tasks.

Davis and Moore (1945) argued that social stratification ensures that this prerequisite is fulfilled. They argued that some positions in society are more significant than others for the maintenance of society; in other words, some tasks are functionally more important. Not everyone has the talents appropriate for the fulfilment of functionally important tasks. To convert their talents into skills requires a period of training. The incumbents of these positions, then, need rewards to compensate for the sacrifices endured during training, and for the demands of the positions themselves. By such rewards, society ensures that important tasks are undertaken, and the stability of society is ensured. The actual rewards may include income and other material benefits, opportunities to express personal qualities at work, self-development and intrinsic job satisfaction. In sum, inequality is the 'unconsciously evolved device by which societies ensure that the most important positions are conscientiously filled by the most qualified persons' (Davis and Moore 1945) (see also Chapter 2, page 30).

This theory has not gone unchallenged, however, even among functionalists. Tumin pointed out potential dysfunctional characteristics of social stratification, that is, consequences which might lessen the maintenance of the system (Tumin 1953). He argued that it is very difficult to identify the relative functional importance of specific positions and tasks. We all know from personal experience that considerable problems arise when steelworkers, or refuse and sewage-workers go on strike; yet these are not the most highly rewarded of occupations. You might like to consider whether all white-collar occupations in receipt of high salaries or other benefits are indispensable for the wellbeing of society. Remember, too, Young and Willmott's (1956) findings (page 159). Tumin also points out that the alleged sacrifices borne during training might not be so sacrificial as they appear. Training, such as that undertaken at university or college, might actually be pleasurable, involving the postponement of adult responsibilities, together with a rare measure of freedom and autonomy. No doubt grants are not equivalent to full-time earnings, but the loss of earnings during training is quickly made up in the first few years of work after which time considerable advantages accrue.

Perhaps the most telling part of Tumin's critique is his questioning of the assumption that there are no barriers to the full use of talent. Society will never fully utilize people's talents because there are unequal opportunities in recruitment for training. Even more significantly, people have access to unequal motivation in the first place. Quite simply, people's hopes and aspirations are a product of socialization; young people internalize the aspirations of parents. It is easy to see how the young, through adult role-models, come to view the powerful and advantaged as legitimately so. The rewards of the latter constitute 'proof' of their functional importance.

In addition, there is considerable evidence that there are barriers to social mobility. The barriers may be less than they were thirty years ago, but mobility is now critically centred around the possession of educational qualifications. And we know that children whose parents are professional and managerial workers are much more likely than the children of unskilled manual workers to be selected for higher streams both in primary and secondary schools. We know that such children have always been more likely to find their way into selective secondary schools and higher education. Even when we compare high ability R-G Class I children with high ability R-G Class V children, the former have greater 'success' (even within comprehensive schools). The reasons for this are not our concern here, but such evidence does support Tumin's view that there is marked wastage of ability (see pages 248–51).

Tumin also suggests that powerful groups find it to their liking to try to maintain such advantages; advantages are easier to maintain when there is a formal inheritance system whereby wealth can be transmitted from one generation to the next, thus ensuring that the second generation has a head-start. Those who are powerful may also develop ideologies which appear to justify their position 'in the interests of society', thus placing a high value on the kind of roles they perform, and upon the talents they possess. It is unlikely that all people accept such an ideology, but Lockwood (1966), in his analysis of working-class images of society, suggested that the traditional deferential workers (who are more often found in smaller, family-based firms, where relationships with employers are more personal) have a hierarchical model or image of society. They see society as ranked like a step-ladder, with movement up and down the ladder a product of people's hard work and efforts. They see those at the top as legitimately so, and those lower down as either lazy or content (in which case they cannot grumble!). This view of society seems compatible with Davis and Moore's assumption that there is consensus within society on the criteria for ranking.

Tumin's critique focused upon the *dysfunctions* of stratification, and is still located within the functionalist framework. Yet clearly Tumin's work does raise the possibility that the distribution of rewards can lead to the formation of powerful groups which are in a position to pursue their own interests under the guise of 'the good of society'. Furthermore,

Tumin raises the possibility that the social stratification which ensues is inflexible, with barriers to social mobility. It may well have occurred to you, then, that we are on the verge of what is usually referred to as 'conflict theory'.

In a manner not at all dissimilar to that of Tumin, conflict theorists might accept that the fulfilment of functional prerequisites helps to maintain society; they are more likely to claim, however, that the fulfilment of these prerequisites will systematically benefit some more than others. Nowhere is this more clear than in social stratification. And whereas functionalists tend to assume that underlying society there is basic agreement on core values, conflict theorists contrastingly assume that the basis of society rests upon conflicts of interest. Consequently some have power, and command, and others have little power and are subordinate. More often than not, conflict theorists argue that power is strongly tied to economic organization. You will recall that Marx defined social classes in terms of the ownership and non-ownership of property which, in the capitalist epoch, meant the ownership of industrial property: factories, the land upon which factories were built, the machinery within factories, and the consequent profit generated. For Marx, then, it is clear that the capitalist and the wage-labourers have quite different and irreconcilable interests. The interests of the former centre around the maximization of surplus value, which is the basis for the acquisition of profit. The interests of the wage-labourers centre around securing and retaining at least a subsistence wage.

Of course, Marx did point out that wage-labourers were *falsely conscious* of their true economic position, and their true interests. He showed how bourgeois ideology helped to maintain the system by convincing the wage-labourers that their true rewards would come in heaven and not on earth. Religion was one mechanism which served as a palliative for pauperization, making current troubles acceptable, and current inequalities 'God's will' (see Chapter 5, page 138). Even within a conflict model of society, then, it is quite conceivable that the dis-advantaged accept their lot in life. There might, therefore, be an appearance of consensus. For Marx this would be false consciousness (see page 135).

Weber's work, on which I based our analysis of class, status and political power earlier in this chapter, is usually regarded as a logical development from Marx. As we indicated above, however, Weber did not accept that the ownership of property was the only basis for social stratification. He argued that there were different forms of power which determined which groups would be dominant. There might be a close relationship in some societies between these different forms of power, but they *are* both logically and empirically separable into the economic, the social and the political.

Although we might usually associate Marx with a conflict model of society there are elements of other sociological perspectives within his work. He argued, for example, that both religion and crime were functional for society. The kind of society which is being maintained, however, is one in which some groups have power and others do not, and in which the former have mechanisms at their disposal to maintain that power. You will remember too that Marx made a critical distinction between class-in-itself and class-for-itself. A class-in-itself is one which shares the same objective economic position (for example, property-ownership). A class-for-itself, however, is one whose members are *subjectively aware* of their common position and their common interests. This issue of subjective perceptions of class and stratification – which was implicit in our discussion of the new working class and the new middle class – is one which we might normally associate with an interactionist perspective.

Both functionalist and conflict perspectives tend to emphasize the structural – that is, macro – features of society. In this respect the two perspectives are in agreement. Interactionist sociologists ask different questions about social order. They do not assume that society is an objective reality – a 'thing' or entity which necessarily exercises constraint over individual members. Rather they assume that society is actively constructed through face-to-face interaction. Actors interpret the situations they encounter; they make sense of the behaviour of others; they have commonsense understandings of the way in which society is organized. Interactionists are therefore likely to ask: what subjective perceptions do actors have of the way in which society is ranked? and what subjective perceptions do they have of their place within the perceived ranking system?

I mentioned above that Lockwood (1966) identified differences between manual workers. I doubt whether he would thank me for incorporating his argument within the 'interactionist' section of this chapter, but there is a sense in which his work relates to our concern here. He identified three types of manual worker: traditional deferential, traditional proletarian, and privatized. I outlined the first of these above (page 182), and pointed out that they have a hierarchical model or image of the way society is ranked. By contrast the traditional proletarian worker has a 'power' model of society, seeing society as divided into two polar camps, 'them' and 'us'. The third type of manual worker, the privatized worker, typically works in mass production industries, and has become partially or wholly separated from traditional working-class (proletarian) communities such as the miners. The privatized workers – the same workers who were regarded as the most likely to have passed through the process of embourgeoisement – have a pecuniary image of society: that is, they see society as ranked according to the acquisition of material goods and possessions – the trappings of conspicuous consumption. Clearly these different types of manual worker share the same economic position in terms of non-ownership of property. Yet they perceive power in society in quite different ways. Although we have here contrasting *images* of ranking, it is quite possible that these images may be generated by prevailing patterns of community relationships, by factory relationships, and by technology. In which case we still have a structural analysis of stratification.

Various pieces of research, however, have attempted to look explicitly at how people identify themselves within a stratification system. For example, various studies in the 1940s in the USA pinpointed people's varying perceptions of their own positions. When asked whether they were *upper, middle* or *lower* (class), about 80 per cent said that they were middle. When others were asked whether they were *upper, middle* or *working* (class), considerably more identified with the latter category of 'working class'. People assign different *meanings* to categories of stratification. Similarly, Gross (1953) simply asked people to which class they belonged. One-third could not answer, suggesting that the category 'social class' itself had no objective meaning.

By contrast, Martin (see Glass 1954) asked people to identify those social classes which existed in England; unlike Gross's respondents, Martin's had no trouble in answering, and they found it possible to assign themselves to one or other of their nominated categories. What emerges from all this is that some non-manual workers identify themselves as 'working class', and some manual workers identify themselves as 'middle class'. Runciman (1966) found exactly the same apparent inconsistencies between objective rank based upon occupation on the one hand and subjective perception of rank on the other. Some sociologists would regard this inconsistency as a problem, upsetting a neat classification. We should regard it as a rich indication that members of society attach different meanings to those everyday (and sociological) labels applying to ranking, and have quite distinctive and varied definitions of their economic, social and political situations.

Both Runciman and Martin encourage us to consider whether everyday labels such as 'working class' and 'middle class' might reflect different types of meaning: one category might refer to occupational characteristics whilst the other denotes life-style (including norms and values, attitudes to work, property-ownership and the like). In addition, Runciman's work is important because we are directed to consider with whom people compare themselves when determining their rank, and whether they are 'well-off' or 'poorly off'. For example, when comparing non-manual and manual workers earning the same income, he found that the non-manual workers feel more deprived relative to others. Clearly this sense of relative deprivation hinges upon with whom these non-manual workers compare themselves. Our understanding of the organization of the work-place, and of patterns of residence, would suggest that non-manual workers are more likely to use other non-manual workers (earning more) as a reference group.

Manual workers labelling themselves as 'middle class' constitute another interesting group. Runciman found that they did not feel relatively deprived in economic terms, but that they did feel relatively deprived in status terms: they wanted a 'better' education and a more prestigious occupation for their sons.

There is not a great deal more to say here. For an interactionist, these considerations of self-assigned class are merely examples of the everyday process of differentiation, categorization, labelling and definition of situations. You must have observed how people use racial categories to denote the superiority or inferiority of a given group. Such categories are used frequently in face-to-face interaction. It follows then that a wide range of stratification-related categories can be, and are, used in interaction.

Finally, I suggest that you try to apply Goffman's dramaturgical analogy (see Goffman 1961) to ranking. Goffman analysed everyday behaviour as a series of performances taking place on a stage before an audience. Obviously there is far more to Goffman's analysis than this statement reveals; however, it opens up the possibility of investigating how social actors put on performances consistent with their perceived social rank. What skills in impression-management do people use to create the 'right impression' for others? The best china on the table? More serious and intellectual magazines on the table? Foreign travel brochures in the magazine rack? A prestigious car in the drive, to be ostentatiously washed on Sundays? The 'right' furniture, food, clothing and accent orchestrated for a work colleague, or to impress your fiancé(e)'s parents? And if this smacks too much of aspiration towards upper strata, do you think that some people want to create the impression of lower rank?

Guide to further reading

The majority of general introductory texts – for example, Haralambos (1980), O'Donnell (1981) – include chapters on social stratification. Many other books have been written on the subject, but frequently the depth of their theoretical arguments, and the extent of their details, makes them inappropriate for your purposes. Your teacher will summarize the most important for you. However, you might find that Bottomore (1965), *Classes in Modern Society* is a manageable analysis of 'social class'. Both Littlejohn (1972), *Social Stratification*, and Kelsall and Kelsall (1974), *Stratification*, review theoretical approaches and empirical material. Perhaps the most useful collections of readings are Beteille (1969), *Social Inequality*, which has a strong comparative emphasis, and O'Donnell (1983). Other books are, as I have said, not for beginners. Yet, although Westergaard and Resler (1975), *Class in Capitalist* Society, is an extraordinarily well-documented review of evidence within a conflict perspective, it can still profitably serve as a reference book.

Remember that many other useful books will be filed under 'political power', 'age', 'gender', 'ethnicity', 'race' and 'poverty'.

7 Power and democracy

Chris Brown

The central focus of this chapter is power. We experience power in many ways. For most of us the experience is one of doing what we are told. However, as we shall see, power is an almost invisible force which both guides and limits not only our actions but also our wants and expectations.

In this chapter our concern will be primarily with how power is used in relation to government. To some extent this is what politics is about, but we shall be looking not so much at the everyday conflicts between political parties but at the processes which structure the political system as a whole.

Conceptions of power

Power has fascinated people for centuries. As far back as ancient Greece we can find lengthy and sophisticated writings on power, as in Plato and Aristotle. In this chapter we shall be concerned with a small fraction of the literature on power, dealing with democracy and elites. However, during our discussion, it should be constantly remembered that, though we shall be referring to power in conceptual terms, power is manifested directly in people's lives. There is, of course, the common experience of a brush with authority, whether parent, teacher, managing director or the police. Still more fundamental than these experiences is the way power has shaped the societies we live in.

In most Western countries it hardly ever crosses people's minds that power is real in this sense. In the political systems of democracy power has become invisible. We *see* no tanks and no secret police, we are *aware* of no apparent censorship and there is no direction of labour. So, we think, power is only something which less civilized nations experience. But democracies are systems of power also. Sometimes democratic systems collapse and then we are able to see the operation of power more clearly. And the consequences for human beings in these circumstances can be fearful. Whether it is the bitter fratricidal strife of civil war or the sudden terror of revolution, ordinary people find themselves caught up in forces which reach down to them and kill, maim or humiliate.

On the other hand, power is also at work in stable societies. Even peaceful, democratic societies have been shaped by the operation of power, and their future development likewise reflects the way power is operating 'behind the scenes'. And even political stability may only be bought at the cost of the suffering of sections of the population, regardless of whether the system is called democratic or not. Thus our discussions in this chapter are not just academic, they concern the forces which touch all of us in our daily experiences.

Weber's definition

At this point some readers will hope for a neat definition of power. However, like many another concept in sociology 'power' is not easy to define in the way, for instance, that 'energy' might be defined in physics. It is not that the word power has no meaning, still less that it is meaningless; it is rather that its meaning cannot be summed up in a single succinct statement. It is both the frustration and the richness of sociology that its concepts are capable of almost endless discussion and interpretation.

Actually there is one quite famous definition of power in sociology but it is possibly the source of more confusion than a whole book would be. The definition in question was formulated by Max Weber (1864–1920) who, as a German, naturally wrote it in his own language. The problem arises with its translation into English. A recent paper (Walliman *et al.* 1980) identifies eight different translations involving such varying meanings that one translation might say something quite different from another. For the record, Walliman *et al.* offer the following translation but whether it is any more authoritative than the others is beyond my competence to judge. Here is their version:

Within a social relationship, power means any chance (no matter whereon this chance is based) to carry through one's* own will (even against resistance).
 *[individual or collective]

However, rather than look for simple definitions of power, I would rather suggest that there are two broad conceptions of power. Both of these regard power as a property of a social system rather than as a capacity of an actor in a social situation. It is just this point at which many critics have taken issue with Weber, or rather with the most common of the translations of Weber's definition of power. Weber appears to be saying that 'power is the probability that one actor in a social relationship will be in a position to carry out his own will even against resistance'. This suggests that power is basically what A does to B. Walliman *et al.* attempt to build into their translation what they consider to be Weber's intention; they remove reference to 'an actor' and, by use of the asterisk, indicate that the 'one' in 'one's own will' could be an individual or a collectivity. Thus power can be exercised as a group phenomenon in which actors are little more than agents.

Power and social structure

This is a more useful way of understanding power in sociological terms but it may not go far enough. Power, even with this view, is still only what group A does to group B. This is still to regard power as a deliberate act, something which happens in human behaviour. A more sociological way of understanding power is to see it as being structured into social relationships. Thus power does not simply emerge in the actions or intentions of actors or groups but is a force which shapes those actions and intentions. It is a lurking presence in social relationships rather than just a behavioural outcome of them (Giddens 1979).

If we examine a concept like 'hierarchy', this structuring of power may become clearer. The essence of a hierarchy is that each level has power over lower levels but is subordinate to higher ones. Individuals at each level act in relation to each other in terms of this difference of power. They have no real choice in the matter, so it would be misleading to attribute acts involving power to the deliberate intentions of the actors. Power is built into the social fabric of which they are all a part. The only sense in which acts of power can be said to be intentional is that actors may have the choice of leaving the hierarchy.

Without necessarily regarding a society as a hierarchy, power in society can be seen in a similar way. Social and political power is essentially a property of the social fabric. Individuals and groups who operate within this framework will utilize the power available to them but that power is not 'theirs'; rather it is an element in the structure of society itself.

Power as a circulatory medium

Now, if power is an aspect of social structure it is not surprising that conceptions of how power actually works depend very much on what model is used to explain the structure of society. If society is seen as a structure of coercion in which minorities have domination over majorities, then power will be seen to be located with the dominant groups and it will be used mainly to prevent change. But if society is seen as an interdependent community of equals, then power will be seen to be evenly distributed. It will be seen as a resource for maintaining equilibrium by adjusting relations between groups. In this sense it can be seen as a way of effecting change.

This latter view of power is put forward by Talcott Parsons (1902–79) and fits a structural–functional model of society.

Power is here conceived as a circulating medium, analogous to money, within what is called the political system but notably over its boundaries into all three of the other neighbouring subsystems of a society (as I conceive them): the economic, integrative and pattern-maintenance systems. [Parsons 1969]

The nature of power as a structural phenomenon is clear in this definition. Like money, power is a resource for getting things done. More specifically, it is a 'mechanism operating to bring about changes in the action of other units, individual or collective, in the processes of social interaction' (Parsons 1969). Like money, power is a freely circulating medium, not something locked up in only one sector of society. If some individuals have more power than others, this is a reflection of their own capacities and contribution to society rather than an intrinsic aspect of the social system.

What is particularly significant about Parsons's approach to power is that all 'resistance' has disappeared. In Walliman's translation of Weber, as well as most of the other translations, it is clearly indicated that the action of power might engender resistance. Parsons, however, is using a consensus model of society, in which power is not challenged but is regarded as 'authority', a concept we shall discuss shortly. For Parsons there seems to be no possibility of non-legitimate power. Force, coercion and violence are simply not aspects of power in his theory.

Power as ideology

Alternatively we might adopt a conflict model of society in which power has an altogether different nature. Ferrarotti (1979) indicates something of this nature – 'Power, power . . . where is power? One of the most insidious powers of power is the power to act indiscreetly, without exposing itself'. In this approach, power is assumed to be a means by which some social groups exercise domination over others and ensure that social arrangements continue to benefit the dominant groups. Sometimes domination is maintained by force, but, while this may be an aspect of power in a conflict model, long-term stability is only achieved when the use of power is not obvious. A critical view of those political systems calling themselves 'liberal democracies' is that they are precisely those regimes which most successfully disguise the operation of power behind a façade of freedom and open government. The trick is done by persuading people that what is not really in their interests, is.

Obviously, this view rests on the assertion that it is possible to say that what an individual believes to be in his interests, is not. Nevertheless, it is precisely this ability to present reality in ways that distort its real functioning that is the mark of power. The power of A to command B is as nothing against the power of a structure of domination to construct such definitions of social reality as it wishes. And from this perspective, of course, the belief in power as a 'freely circulating medium' is one of those constructs.

Authority and legitimacy

An attempt at some more definitions

So far we have been discussing power as if it were one single concept, but

if our understanding of it is to be extended we now need to break it up
into several component concepts:

a *Power* is force, coercion and repression; it is the gun, the fist or the
fine; it is the police officer's hand on your arm or the bullet hole in
your head.
b *Authority* exists where power is used by superiors with the consent of
the subordinates; in these circumstances force will not be necessary
although it will continue to exist as an ultimate sanction.
c *Legitimacy* is the process by which power becomes authority; but
whether legitimacy is freely given or whether it is actively elicited by
rulers is a crucial issue which will keep recurring in this chapter.

Again, it is Max Weber to whom we are indebted for this way of
analysing power.

Traditional authority

Weber proposes three forms of legitimacy – traditional, legal–rational
and charismatic. These give rise to three types of authority. Traditional
authority derives its legitimacy from the sanctity of custom. If something
is 'the done thing' or 'has always been done this way' then those doing it
are likely to have the consent of those to whom it is done. Societies where
traditional authority predominates are usually small and pre-industrial.
Rituals and ceremonies keep alive custom and tradition, and social life
is ordered in terms of norms and rules which may often be complex but
which are passed on to successive generations through the family,
through village life and through religious observance.

Although traditional authority is typical of pre-industrial societies, it
is not altogether absent in advanced societies. Perhaps Britain, particularly, displays a strong attachment to tradition. Compared with the
Americans, for example, who are often thought to welcome anything
new on principle, the British cling to their traditions, and a political
appeal to custom may generate considerable support.

Legal authority

Legal authority is the system of authority with which most readers of
this book will be familiar. It is based on law, rules and regulations. These
have been formulated and sanctioned after a due process of debate.
Their fundamental quality is their rationality in so far as they are
means designed to meet specified ends. Under traditional authority
customs become outdated and anomalous but nevertheless retain their
force, thus becoming inappropriate or irrational. Under legal authority,
if a regulation ceases to serve a purpose it can, in principle, be replaced.
This may not always be done, however, and even in a rational age some
laws may acquire a degree of authority through sheer antiquity.

Charismatic authority

The third type of authority is of a quite different order to the other two and is somewhat novel, not to say bizarre. Weber called it 'charismatic authority', by which he meant a situation where a ruler is so personally liked that people will do whatever he says without question. Such legitimacy will extend to anyone acting in the name of, or on the orders of, the ruler. Many great leaders have attained this sort of stature – Napoleon, Lenin, Stalin, etc. A more recent example of a highly charismatic leader is the late President Tito of Yugoslavia.

Charismatic leaders usually arise in situations where one of the other two types of authority has broken down. Likewise, with the death of the leader his 'charisma' will become routinized into either one of the other types of authority. Thus charismatic authority is unstable and short-lived.

Any actual society will probably display elements of all three types of authority, though one type will predominate. For instance, advanced societies will be primarily legal–rational but may contain areas where authority is based on tradition (the monarchy? the House of Lords?, that is, the hereditary principle). Then again, leadership, even in a legal authority, even in a democracy, may give rise to a certain amount of charisma. A president of the United States who achieves a high level of popularity may have greater authority on that account.

Authority or domination?

Much more important than the type of legitimacy is the question of how legitimacy is achieved. It is quite clear that legitimacy in some way smoothes the path of power; it facilitates the exercise of power by reducing resistance. But does it give rise to a situation of *authority* or of *domination*?

Thus far in the discussion we have used the term 'authority' but, as we saw in looking at Parsons's definition of power, this term has certain connotations. It suggests not only that consent has been given to those exercising power but that their commands are in keeping with some notion of natural law. To exercise authority is to claim unrestricted rights within the framework of legitimacy. It is further implied in using the term authority that the consent which transforms power into authority is freely given, that it is an act of voluntary choice, a representation of the will of the people. Authority, then, is a way of thinking about power that fits with a consensus model of society.

The problem here is that in most other respects Weber cannot be understood as a consensus theorist. We have already seen that his definition of power recognizes the possibility of resistance, while the concept of authority seems to deny this possibility. Thus Weber's use of the term authority strikes a false note.

Some secondary works on Weber choose not to translate him as having used the term authority. What others translate as authority, they give as 'domination'. The difference between the two terms is basically related to how each one thinks of the process of legitimacy. 'Authority' suggests that rulers acquire their legitimacy because the ruled voluntarily bestow it on them; 'domination' suggests that rulers secure the co-operation of the ruled through various peaceful means. Legitimation does not occur by force, that much is clear, but it may come about as a result of manipulation through ideology, through persuasion, through material rewards and through symbolic punishment. Domination also implies that resistance is to be expected, and thus social and political conflict is a 'natural' aspect of society.

In considering whether Weber meant authority or domination, it can be argued that he was not consistent (Brown 1979). Another recent discussion of the problem takes the view that it is once again a difficulty arising from translation (Lukes 1979). This time the offending word is *Herrschaft*. In the definition of power by Weber discussed earlier, Weber's word for power is *Macht*. But when he goes on to refer to power in its more controlled and legitimate form he uses *Herrschaft*. Now, it is the case that the first accessible translation of Weber, and therefore the most influential, was done by none other than Talcott Parsons (Weber 1947) and when he came to *Herrschaft* he translated it as authority. We have already seen that Parsons employs a consensus-equilibrium model of society, and elsewhere in this book there is a longer explanation of Parsons's position (see Chapter 2, pages 26–8). Thus it comes as no surprise to us that Parsons should want to interpret Weber's analysis here as emphasizing the 'integration of the collectivity' rather than the leader's power over his followers.

Other sociologists, however, have rendered *Herrschaft* as 'domination'. Perhaps the best known of these is Bendix in his extended essay on Weber's sociology (Bendix 1966). Lukes believes that Bendix is right. He says:

Parsons is therefore quite mistaken in translating *Herrschaft* as 'authority'. Rather, the celebrated 'three pure types of authority' single out prevailing rationales for obedience to authority *within* structures of domination. [Lukes 1979]

This is not just a debate about terminology or even emphasis. To a conflict theorist, power is the ability of groups to ensure the compliance of other groups over whatever issues they choose to exercise that power. If it can only be done by force, so be it. But far better to get people to obey without having to use force. It does not matter whether they obey out of sheer habit or through a rational calculation of advantage, or through an internalization of the dominant values. All that matters is their obedience.

To gain that obedience regimes will go to any lengths. Through persuasion, public argument, appeal to law, appeal to national interest, custom and tradition, all these means will be employed to ensure compliance. Legitimacy then is not simply conferred on regimes, it is worked for. As Weber says:

. . . in no instance does domination voluntarily limit itself to the appeal to material or affectual or ideal motives as a basis for its continuance. In addition every such system attempts to establish and to cultivate the belief in its legitimacy. [quoted in Lukes 1979]

Democracy

The organization of power known to us as a democracy is the form most typical of modern industrial states. Following from our preceding discussions it is perhaps best to understand the term 'democracy' as having two functions. The first function is as a description of an actual state of affairs. In this context, democracy is a political system in which the will of the people determines government policy. In such a system power is distributed fairly evenly. Moreover, since such a system is so clearly based on principles which treat all citizens alike and offer all an opportunity to be involved in their own governance, there are few grounds for resisting those whose authority stems from the rational-legal principles underlying the democratic state. This is a political system based on consensus and the voluntary bestowal of legitimacy.

In the second case, however, the word 'democracy', with all its associations, functions as a legitimating device. If rulers can successfully convince their subjects that they live within a democratic system, they have already achieved a substantial amount of legitimacy. Few people in the modern world would deny a claim to legitimacy founded on democratic principles, though some might want to contest that what was being offered was democratic.

So, then, we have two conceptions of democracy. One in which democratic institutions are really thought to exist; another in which processes described as democratic are at best only marginal approximations to democratic principles and, at worst, devices for concealing inequality and exploitation. The choice is between democracy as truth and democracy as illusion. The parallel is with power as money and power as ideology and also with the two different interpretations of *Herrschaft*.

Classical democracy

Classical democracy lies at the root of what we think of as the nature of democracy and what we understand to be the case when we describe a society as democratic. The most famous and the most influential version of democracy, which we can call 'classical democracy', is Abraham

Lincoln's – 'government of the people, for the people, by the people'. The essence of this formula is that government shall be 'by the people' – not by some of the people or by the top people, whether aristocracy, oligarchy or elite. Neither wealth, nor breeding, nor even achievement, entitle a group to wield power over others. True democracy is the participation of all in decision-making.

Lincoln's authority for his summary of the democratic principle is the American Declaration of Independence:

We hold these truths to be self-evident, that all men are created equal, that they are endowed by their Creator with certain inalienable rights, that among these are Life, Liberty and the pursuit of Happiness – That to secure these Rights, Governments are instituted among Men, deriving their just powers from the consent of the governed.

It is inconceivable that the slightest objection should be raised to the sentiments expressed in this statement. It is surely the most fundamental article of faith about the control of power in the modern world and lies at the root of virtually everyone's thinking about democracy, at least in the advanced societies.

The origins of this notion of democracy lie in ancient Greece and particularly the city–state of Athens. Finley (1973) describes the mechanics of Athenian democracy:

... attendance in the sovereign Assembly was open to every citizen, and there was no bureaucracy or civil service, save for a few clerks, slaves owned by the state itself, who kept such records as were unavoidable, copies of treaties and laws, lists of defaulting taxpayers, and the like. Government was thus 'by the people' in the most literal sense. The Assembly, which had the final decision on war and peace, treaties, finance, legislation, public works, in short, on the whole gamut of governmental activity, was an outdoor mass meeting of as many thousand citizens, over the age of eighteen, as chose to attend on any given day. It met frequently throughout the year, forty times at a minimum, and it normally reached a decision on the business before it in a single day's debate in which, in principle, everyone present had the right to participate by taking the floor. *Isegoria*, the universal right to speak in the Assembly, was sometimes employed by Greek writers as a synonym for 'democracy'. And the decision was by a simple majority vote of those present.

It is frequently objected that this was not government by all the people because many of them, such as slaves, did not count as citizens. Finley attempts to modify the force of this argument, and in any case it does not detract from the fact that Athenian democracy was very 'advanced' for its time. But, of course, it is impracticable in a society with a large population (though some arguments now propose the use of some sort of feedback mechanism on televison sets to recreate the essence of the Athenian assembly). When democracy was rediscovered in the eighteenth century it was in relation to states very much larger than Athens.

The consequence was the emergence of a theory of representative, or indirect, democracy.

Representative democracy

Schumpeter (1943) defines the representative version of classical democracy as:

> . . . that institutional arrangement for arriving at political decisions which realises the common good by making the people itself decide issues through the election of individuals who are to assemble in order to carry out its will.

Representative democracy requires a process which was definitely absent from Athens – elections. Elections are a system whereby individuals offer themselves as candidates to undertake government on behalf of the people and are then chosen by the people. Thus the people cease to have any direct part in decision-making, but they can influence decision-making through their ability to withhold their votes at the next election.

Although representation seems to constitute a fair compromise between direct participation and the problems of a large population, it is in reality a very different form of democracy compared with direct democracy. One sort of problem arises over the relationship between representatives and their electors. Are the representatives merely spokesmen or must they act according to their own consciences? How can representatives 'represent' conflicting opinions amongst their electors? However, from a sociological point of view there is another class of problem arising from representation. This has to do with the nature of the electors rather than the difficulties of the representative.

In representative democracies, voters are supposed to possess a number of characteristics:

a they should be fully informed on all the issues which might affect them;
b they should discuss politics seriously amongst themselves;
c they should participate in public debate, such as writing letters to newspapers and contributing to phone-ins;
d they should read party manifestos at election times and never fail to vote.

In other words, the vote is considered, in theory, to be a rational decision based on systematic and coherent principles.

Imagine the horror then when, at about the beginning of this century, social scientists began to study elections and quickly discovered that very few electors conformed to the theoretical model. Most people's response to politics is a mixture of boredom and cynicism. Even when they have strong views they are irrational and inconsistent. Michael Margolis has produced a summary of recent research findings relating

Table 10 *Participation in political activity*

United States	percentage of the population	United Kingdom	percentage of the population
1 Follow presidential campaign on television (1964)	89	1 Follow general elections in media or personal conversation (1964)	92
2 Pay much or a little attention to political campaigns (1960)	87	2 Pay much or a little attention to political campaigns (1959)	71
3 Report voting regularly in presidential elections (1967)	72	3 Report voting in 1964 general election (1970)	77 (72)
4 Report always voting in local elections (1967)	47	4 Report voting in local elections where contested (1964)	43
5 Active in at least one organization involved in community affairs (1967)	32	5 Nominal members of political party (including trade-union membership) (1964)	25
6 Member of organization active in political affairs (1960)	24	6 Member of organization active in politcal affairs (1959)	19
7 Ever contacted local government official about some issue or problem at least once (1967)	20	7 Ever contacted local official or county office (1970)	18 26
8 Ever contacted state or national official about some issue or problem at least once (1967)	18	8 Ever contacted MP about any issue or problem at least once (1970)	8
9 (not available)		9 Ever complained to public or private corporation (at least 26% to public corporations)	40
10 Ever formed a group to attempt to solve community problem	14	10 (not available)	
11 Ever given money to candidate or party (1967)	13	11 Subscribed to local party (1964)	14
12 Attended a meeting during election campaign (1952-68)	Varies 7-14	12 Attended political campaign meeting during 1964 general election	8
13 Worked actively for a political candidate (1952-68)	3-5	13 Have a 'political attitude' (1972)	7
14 Held public or party office	less than 1	14 Held public or party office (1964)	less than 1

SOURCE: Margolis (1979)

Table 11 *Earliest party preferences by parents' Conservative or Labour preference, 1963*

Parents' partisanship

Respondents' own first preference	Percentage of both parents Conservative	Percentage of parents divided Con./Lab.	Percentage of both parents Labour
Conservative	89	48	6
Labour	9	52	92
Liberal	2	—	2
Total	100	100	100

SOURCE: Butler and Stokes (1974)

to some aspects of voter behaviour in both the UK and the US. The obvious conclusion to be drawn from these findings is that relatively few electors do more than cast a vote and that the electorates in Western democracies are largely indifferent to, and ignorant of, political issues (see Table 10).

Even when voters do cast a vote, it is usually on the basis of various irrational factors; 'irrational' in the sense that their vote is determined not by a careful, reasoned decision but on the basis of various non-political factors. For example, research suggests that the first vote cast by a new voter is strongly influenced by parents: and this pattern is only marginally affected by the passage of time (see Table 11).

Likewise, there is a consistent relationship between social class and voting preference throughout the Western democracies, though perhaps the relationship is clearest in the UK. In the UK this relationship appears to be weakening slightly. Table 12 shows the changes since October 1974. It also shows that voting patterns are still significantly linked to social class, especially if account is taken of the increase in Liberal/Alliance support as well as the decline in the Labour vote in all social groups.

The relationship between class and voting makes good sense, of course. It is entirely reasonable that people sharing a similar position in the class structure should discover a common interest at the polls. In

Table 12 *Voting allegiance by social class, Oct. 1974–83*

	All (%)			Managerial (AB) (%)			Junior non-manual (C1) (%)			Skilled manual (C2) (%)			Other manual (D) (%)		
	'74	'79	'83	'74	'79	'83	'74	'79	'83	'74	'79	'83	'74	'79	'83
Conservative	36	44	42	65	67	54	53	58	57	27	44	37	23	32	33
Labour	39	37	27	12	18	11	25	21	17	52	45	36	60	55	43
Liberal/ Alliance	18	14	25	23	15	35	22	20	27	21	10	27	17	13	24

SOURCE: adapted from Drucker *et al.* (1984)

fact, the party system in the twentieth century has developed along class lines. Socialist and other parties of the Left attract support mainly from working-class groups, while parties of the Centre and Right tend to represent middle-class interests. Nevertheless, social class is not a part of the classical theory of democracy, in which the individual is thought to be independent of external influences.

Even if it is accepted that there is a rational link between politcial parties and voting behaviour, it can be seen from Table 12 that a substantial proportion of the working class support the Conservatives. The link between class and party is even better illustrated by Table 13. This demonstrates that nearly half of all those who vote Conservative are from the manual working class, and here it is hard to argue that there is a connection between economic self-interest and voting preference.

How are we to explain working-class Tories? McKenzie and Silver (1968) suggest two types of 'working-class Conservative'. One they call 'deferential'. 'Deferentials tend, on the basis of certain *a priori* assumptions, to invest the Conservative leaders with an innate and transcendent superiority over all possible political rivals which borders on the magical.' One working-class Conservative summarizes this position: 'They are businessmen who know what they are doing. They have been brought up to rule, to take over leadership. They have been educated to a certain extent to take over. They have no axe to grind for themselves. They look out for other people . . . all types and the country as a whole really.'

The second type is called 'secular'. These are likely to be younger than deferentials and have a higher than average wage packet. They believe in Conservatism because of its emphasis on private enterprise and its encouragement of the strong and the confident. Seculars support the Conservatives on an assessment of their performances and policies in

Table 13　*The social basis of major party support, 1964–74*

Party and occupational class	Party's support base from each occupational class (%)				
	1964	1966	1970	Feb 1974	Oct 1974
Conservative					
Non-manual	57	59	54	63	58
Manual	43	41	46	37	42
Labour					
Non-manual	17	19	22	25	27
Manual	83	81	78	75	73

SOURCE: Crewe *et al.* (1977)

office. They say things like: 'I would say that the Conservatives have done well as regards housing, labour and schools. There is more of a headway as regards work – if you start a business, there is more opportunity.' In many ways, secular working-class Conservatives represent almost the ideal voter in terms of classical democratic theory, since their support for the party is based on something like a rational assessment.

Although there is a small, but growing, group of 'middle-class radicals' who consistently fail to support the Conservative party, it is the disunity of the working class in its voting behaviour which is the most significant feature of political behaviour in Britain and Western societies generally. If the Western working class was united in support of parties of the Left it is difficult to see how the present forms of economy and democracy could exist. Alternatively, it seems unlikely that electoral systems as we know them would ever have evolved.

The combination of apathy and irrationalism amongst democratic voters is quite enough to destroy any belief in the theory of representative democracy as a description of reality. In the face of this evidence we can take two courses of action. Either we abandon our claims to be running a democratic system or we redefine the meaning of democracy. In the next section we shall look at some of those who have taken the first course of action (though they did not need empirical studies of voting behaviour to inspire them) and then examine an attempt to redefine the meaning of democracy.

Elite theory

The general thesis of the elite theorists is that any system of government, indeed any organization, is necessarily dominated by elites. However, there are significant differences between them. The classical elite theorists, Mosca, Pareto and Michels, were reacting against the impact of Marxism on European thought and politics, and believed that the inevitability of elites was simply a scientific fact. A later group of elite theorists, appalled by the excesses of both communism and fascism, argued for the necessity of cultural and intellectual elites to maintain civilized values. Finally, some writers have pointed to the way in which the existence of elites undermines democratic principles.

Classical elite theory

Classical elite theory is stated most clearly by Gaetano Mosca (1858–1941). Mosca taught constitutional law and political theory in several Italian universities. From 1908 to 1919 he was a Conservative member of the Italian Chamber of Deputies and later a Senator throughout the period of fascism.

In all societies – from societies that are very meagrely developed and have barely attained the dawnings of civilisation, down to the most advanced and powerful societies – two classes of people appear – a class that rules and a class that is ruled. The first class, always the less numerous, performs all political functions, monopolises power and enjoys the advantages which power brings, whereas the second, the more numerous class, is directed and controlled by the first, in a manner that is now more or less legal, now more or less arbitrary and violent.... [quoted in Jack 1974]

Another way of putting this is to say that power will always be distributed amongst a privileged few, leaving the masses relatively powerless. Elite theory at this level is frequently regarded as either obvious or trivial. Yet elite theorists made no exception of any particular society. They regarded democratic systems as being just as much dominated by elites as any other system. For them, democratic claims were an illusion. As Parry (1969) puts it, 'No mechanism for ensuring the accountability of the leaders to the public, no ideology which enshrines the principle of majority, will or can prevent the elite from imposing its supremacy over the rest of society.'

Elites develop what one writer has called the 'three Cs' – group consciousness, coherence and conspiracy. The elite know who they are and are conscious of their distinction from the masses. This consciousness gives them unity or coherence as a group and enables them to act in such a way as to maintain their exclusiveness. Special education systems for the young, and the privileges of wealth for the adults, are both a reason for the unity of the elite and factors impelling them to stick together.

The elite maintain their rule over the majority because they already control the apparatus of power. A more interesting issue is how elites acquire power in the first place. To this there are two sorts of answers, one psychological, the other organizational.

Pareto and the psychological basis of elites

The Italian sociologist Vilfredo Pareto (1848–1923) began his career as a railway engineer but turned to economics and became Professor of Political Economy at the University of Lausanne. He based his theory on the premises that elites were simply those people who occupied the top in any field. So in aspects of government such as political parties, trade unions, the military, etc. the top people constituted a 'governing elite'. In areas of life not related to government, that is, occupations, entertainment, sport and leisure, the top people formed non-governing elites.

The governing elite is of two sorts, who differ in terms of their psychological make-up. Pareto believed that human beings are characterized by two basic psychological types which are constant through history. Some people reflect an 'instinct of combinations'. This is a tendency towards theorizing and hypothesizing; an ability to bring

ideas together and see relationships in apparently unconnected phenomena. The instinct of combinations gives rise to change and innovation
and encourages a pragmatic approach to principles. Governing elites
based on the instinct of combinations will tend to be made up of
sophisticated ideologists and political 'wheeler-dealers' who govern by
cunning and guile and to whom Pareto gave the delightful name of
'foxes'.

The other basic instinct is called the 'persistence of aggregates'. This
instinct leads to a tendency to want to conserve whatever forms of
organization or relationships have developed. In other words, a
resistance to change. Such resistance will be manifested not with the
intrigue and plotting of the foxes but by force and the suppression of new
ideas. This elite are known as the 'lions' and while foxes attempt to
govern by consent, lions seek to impose their will without compunction.

The lions and the foxes vie with each other for power, and a
'circulation of elites' occurs. The rule of the foxes is gradually undermined
as their intrigues and manoeuvring eventually wear everyone out and
alienate increasing sections of the ruled. Then the lions take over. They
in their turn eventually find their strength exhausted, helped by the
activities of the foxes, who then regain power. In Pareto's view, ruling
groups, whatever their nature or political complexion, could be understood in these terms. It could be a military junta (lions) giving way to
politicians (foxes) and then getting fed up with them, as happens in
many countries. Or it could be conservative politicians (lions) circulating
with radical or social democrat politicians (foxes).

Whatever else can be said about this theory of elites it does have the
great merit of being fun. You can have a happy time applying it to
contemporary political history, trying to identify the lions and the foxes.
Moreover, however absurd it all may sound, it is what a lot of people
believe to be the reality of power, even within so-called democracies.
Western democracies are typically thought to display a certain shuttling
back and forth between governments dedicated to change and others
determined to preserve the *status quo*. What is more, many people hold
the view that, whatever sort of government is in power, the ordinary
people, the non-elites, have little influence on the game going on 'above
their heads'.

Michels and the organizational basis of elites

If psychological theories of elites are widespread, how much more so are
those elites which are based on organization. That is, the view that
organizations of any sort always give rise to the dominance of those who
run them. In its most common form this view is expressed by the
committee members of tennis clubs, constituency parties, playgroups,
etc.; in short, any voluntary organization not big enough to give those
who work for it any status. They complain that it is always the few who

do all the work. But when the organization is a large one, like a national political party or the British Olympic Committee, the power and prestige accruing to those who run it may be worth the hard work and it may also become a full-time job

Robert Michels (1876–1936) was a German sociologist whose academic career was spent mainly in Italy, where he was a close personal friend of both Mosca and Pareto. He is known today mainly for his book *Political Parties*. This book is a study of the German Social Democratic Party (SPD) in the early years of this century. Michels had been a member of the SPD but he became increasingly critical of its loss of revolutionary fervour. Then, shortly after going to Italy in 1907, he rejected his socialist beliefs entirely and became a leading spokesman for academic elite theory. Eventually this led him to provide a theoretical rationale for the emerging Italian fascist movement.

Michels chose to subject the SPD to analysis partly because of his earlier associations with it, and partly because he wanted to show how an organization devoted to the establishment of social democracy was itself a wholly undemocratic structure. The same paradox applies to virtually any modern mass party, simply because no party could be successful today without appealing to mass support and any such appeal must logically be based on acceptance of democratic principles. However, *Political Parties* can serve as a study of any organization; its relevance goes well beyond just the organization of political parties.

Michels's argument is that, if an organization is to be effective, its leaders need to be free to act quickly, as they see fit, without constant reference to the members. In the case of a political party, bargaining and compromise with other parties may be necessary, while policy must be formulated in the light of political realities which are known in their fullest extent only to party leaders. The tension between the leaders' need for freedom to manoeuvre and the democratic demands of party members is exemplified perfectly in the persistent antagonism between the parliamentary leadership of the British Labour party and the party's conference.

Those who run organizations acquire a great deal of technical knowledge and experience in the course of their work which is not available to ordinary members. The outcome of all this is that the leaders become a distinct professional elite separated from party members. So, in the case of the early socialist parties, where the leaders retained for some time their outside identities and trades as workers, they eventually came to work for the SPD full-time in return for a salary.

Having attained this position, the leaders are further set apart from members. Not only do they now have a vested interest in the organization as such, as distinct from its goals, but they now control party finances and the means of internal communication. In addition to these organizational factors impelling leaders to constitute an elite, Michels believed that party members in the mass also have a psychological need to be led. For all these reasons, then, when it comes to elections, the mark of the party's democratic structure, candidates running against incumbent leaders are at a considerable disadvantage since few people know them and they do not have access to the means which would enable them to compete on more favourable terms.

Thus, for Michels: 'Who says organization – says oligarchy'; the so-called 'iron law of oligarchy'. And while this 'law' applies to parties and tennis clubs, how much bigger is the organization of the state? Oligarchy is just as inevitable at the level of the state, perhaps even more so. In an article written several years prior to *Political Parties* Michels said:

> History appears to teach us that no popular movement, however powerful and energetic, can effect any lasting changes in the organic structure of social life. The reason is that the most outstanding elements of such movements, the men who originally led them and set them alight, always become gradually detached from the masses and assimilated by the 'political class', to whom they contribute few new ideas, maybe, but all the more youthful energy and practical intelligence, and thus through a process of repeated rejuvenation serve to perpetuate their supremacy. . . . History also teaches us that the government – or, if you like, the state – can only be the organization of the minority, whose purpose is to impose on the rest of society a legal order appropriate to the requirements of its own control and exploitation of the masses; it can never be the product of a majority, let alone represent their interests. The majority of mankind will never have the possibility, nor even the capacity, to govern themselves. A cruel fate of history has pre-destined them to suffer passively the domination of a small minority risen from their midst, and to serve merely as the pedestal for the greatness of their rulers. [quoted in Beetham 1977]

Mosca, Pareto and Michels aspired to provide a scientific analysis of power in modern societies and rejected both the Marxist tenets of socialism and the prevailing claims of liberal democracy. Their writings and personal careers are inextricably bound up with the monumental political upheavals of Europe in the early twentieth century. Nevertheless, their ideas are still discussed today in academic terms, perhaps because at the level of everyday thought they are still very strong. There are some who would go further and say that elites are not merely inevitable but that they are very necessary.

The elite and the average person

Although in a democratic and egalitarian age it is difficult to say so, there are many who still believe that elites are vital to ensure that standards of civilization are maintained. Such people regard modern democracy as threatening the destruction of traditional values and perhaps leading to chaos and anarchy. Two world wars and the rise of fascism and communism seem to them to be ample evidence that the process of destruction is well under way.

One such thinker was a Spanish philosopher Ortega y Gasset (1883–1955). Writing in 1930 Ortega opens his book thus:

There is one fact which, whether for good or ill, is of utmost importance in the public life of Europe at the present moment. This fact is the accession of the masses to complete social power. As the masses, by definition, neither should nor can direct their own personal existence, and still less rule society in general, this fact means that actually Europe is suffering from the greatest crisis that can afflict peoples, nations and civilisation. [Ortega y Gasset 1932]

A more restrained and moderate advocate for the persistence of elites was the sociologist Karl Mannheim (1894–1947). Born in Germany, Mannheim made his home in England in 1933. For him, the political history of the twentieth century clearly pointed to the need to qualify the claims of democracy in such a way as to contain the drift towards control by the mass. As he puts it:

In a society in which the masses tend to dominate, irrationalities which have not been integrated into the social structure may force their way into political life. This situation is dangerous because the selective apparatus of mass democracy opens the door to irrationalities in those places where rational direction is indispensable. Thus, democracy itself produces its own antithesis and even provides its enemies with their weapons. [Mannheim 1940]

Both Ortega and Mannheim fear the 'irrationality' of the average person, which they see as the cause of war and social unrest. On the other hand, the superior culture and rational behaviour of the elites or higher social classes encourage stability. In Mannheim's case it is not so much that he is against democracy, as that he wants to see democracy tempered by the existence of elites. Ortega, on the other hand, is less willing to accept modern domocracy. he appeals to a model of democracy which he sees as characteristic of the nineteenth century. In this model the extent of egalitarianism was limited and elites continued to enjoy special privileges in such a way that they could direct society on a peaceful course. But now this limited form of democracy is disappearing:

In almost all (countries) a homogeneous mass weighs on public authority and crushes down, annihilates every opposing group. The mass – who would credit it as one sees its compact, multitudinous appearance? – does not wish to share life with those who are not of it. It has a deadly hatred of all that is not itself. [Ortega y Gasset 1932]

Mannheim's concept of 'negative democratization' parallels Ortega's nightmare of the masses crushing all opposition and insisting on uniformity. He says:

The crisis of culture in liberal-democratic society is due, in the first place, to the fact that the social processes, which previously favoured the development of the creative elites, now have the opposite effect, i.e. have become obstacles to the forming of elites because wider sections of the population still under unfavourable social conditions take an active part in cultural activities. [Mannheim 1940]

As a postscript to this discussion of Mannheim, readers of this present volume will be interested to know that he regards social science as an essential training for the elite.

Instead of a new interpretation of the classics, social science instruction may well become the core of a curriculum destined to integrate a new ruling elite. Why approach the study of man and of his contemporary problems in a roundabout fashion? Historical studies will broaden one's horizon, but it should be the horizon of contemporary life and its problems. How can new leaders lead without an adequately informed understanding of contemporary society and its problems and without a social philosophy to fit an evolutionary democratic society? [Mannheim 1951]

The power elite

Elite theorists who believe that elites are necessary and desirable tend to be worried that they are under threat. Conversely, elite theorists who regard elites as undesirable and as a deliberate thwarting of democratic processes, tend to believe that elites are strong and getting stronger. Thus C. Wright Mills (1916–62), an American sociologist with a strong inclination towards Marxism, identified in America the existence of a power elite.

Mills saw power as being attached to the top positions in major societal institutions. The occupants of these positions were members of the power elite. The main institutions which Mills singled out were government, business corporations and the military. The top people in these areas were in a position to make fundamental and far-reaching decisions and they acted as a unified and relatively coherent group. This coherence arose from the penetration of each elite area by individuals from other areas. Thus generals became presidents of the United States, business leaders became members of the administration, and business and military interests were closely related through defence contracts.

In Mills's view, the activities of the power elite frustrated the operation of democracy in the first modern nation to implement such a system. The last paragraph of Mills's book (1956) makes this clear:

The men of the higher circles are not representative men; their high position is not a result of moral virtue; their fabulous success is not firmly connected with meritorious ability. Those who sit in the seats of the high and the mighty are selected and formed by the means of power, the sources of wealth, the mechanics of celebrity, which prevail in their society. They are not men selected and formed by a civil service that is linked with the world of knowledge and sensibility. They are not men shaped by nationally responsible parties that debate openly and clearly the issues this nation now so unintelligently confronts. They are not men held in responsible check by a plurality of voluntary associations which connect debating publics with the pinnacles of decision. Commanders of power unequalled in human history, they have succeeded within the American system of organised irresponsibility.

It is clear from Mills's description that this is not the elite which Mannheim had in mind. Mannheim's elite were intellectuals; Mills's elite are ruthless power seekers. In Mills's view, civilization is not under attack from the ignorant mass but rather democracy is under threat from an immoral and uncultured elite.

Pluralism

The revised theory of democracy

In the 1950s and 1960s there arose another theory of democracy, which sought to defend the concept against its dismissal by elitists. The new theory defended the political systems of the West as authentic democracies. It denied that power was so concentrated in the hands of a few that the masses were effectively powerless. At the same time, the existence of elites is recognized, but these are claimed to be compatible with democracy. What we have, in effect, is a new definition of democracy. One of its proponents, Robert Dahl, has called it 'polyarchy', but its opponents tend to call it 'democratic elitism', thus highlighting the contradiction.

Mannheim (1940) foreshadowed this new approach to democracy:

... the great strength of the liberal system and of democracy consists in the fact that they can bear criticism, and as long as they are vigorous, they are elastic enough to find ways and means of bringing about reform. The source of our criticism consists neither in the snobbish condemnation of the masses which is so widespread nowadays, nor in cheap grumbling about the principles of liberalism and democracy. The ultimate drive is rather the wish to make an appeal to those to whom freedom and justice are still ultimate values, to think about the proper means to secure them under the changed technical and social conditions of the present world; and this in the first instance means keeping a watchful eye on the deteriorative tendencies in liberalism and democracy which are emerging in this era of mass societies and the growth of monopolies.

However, the basic formulation of the new theory is again to be found in Schumpeter (1943):

The democratic method is that institutional arrangement for arriving at political decisions in which individuals acquire the power to decide by means of a competitive struggle for the people's vote.

In this revised theory of democracy, the democratic principle is not now that the people decide issues through their representatives, still less that they do so directly. Democracy has now simply become a procedure, in which the people vote every so often and, inbetween-times relinquish all control over their leaders. The reason that the procedure can be called 'democratic elitism' is because it allows for the existence of elites who offer themselves for election. What makes these elites democratic is that they compete with each other for popular support. The guarantee of freedom is to be found not in the participation of the people in their own government but in the toleration of different viewpoints necessitated by the existence of elites vying with each other for the vote of the people.

Political participation

The emphasis in this new theory of democracy is on the system rather than the qualities of the people. Indeed, it strongly supports the view that, when electors are not voting, they should keep quiet. The classical theory of democracy assumed that the people would take a full and active part in politics. The finding that, on the whole, the people were not very active prompted the new theory of democracy. So now democracy may be said to work more efficiently, and political stability be better assured, if the level of participation in political life is low. Far from being a sign of the imperfect nature of democratic systems, political apathy is a sign of their health!

One argument is that low participation in politics and perhaps even a low turn-out in elections is evidence of satisfaction with the prevailing system. Another argument is that high turn-outs in elections may actually indicate an impending breakdown of a democratic order, such as happened in Germany where, in the series of elections preceding the Nazi seizure of power, there were exceedingly high turn-outs. Note, however, that in the Australian democratic system electoral voting is compulsory! It can also be argued that people may have other things to do than be constantly engaged in politics and that this is a good thing for society as a whole, and therefore indirectly for the political system (Lipset 1960).

Even so, it is a slightly odd definition of democracy that can justify the withdrawal of the people from the political system whose literal meaning is 'the rule of the people'.

Democratic elitism

While on the one hand the revised theory of democracy allows for a low level of political participation, on the other it recognizes the place of elites within a democratic framework. In what way is this different from elite theorists such as Pareto or Mannheim? Only really in matters of definition. The elite theorists do not, on the whole, see elites as compatible with democracy in its classical sense. The new theory simply says they are compatible; indeed, necessary.

The model of society used by Dahl and other exponents of 'polyarchy' is generally called 'pluralist', and within this model democratic elitism can be given some plausibility. A pluralist society is one which contains a range of distinct social groups into which individuals are integrated. These groups might be broad social classes or ethnic groups, or groups based on gender. They might be occupational groups, or groups like trade unions which are related to work. They could be more formally organized groups, such as political parties, or groups involved in institutionalized religion. An individual could be part of more than one group.

The variety of groups provides a richness for the total society and offers individuals a social 'home'. Pluralism differs from models of society in which an elite confronts a mass in so far as individuals are integrated into their several groups and are not a rootless and irrational mass. At the same time the leaders of the various groups constitute a series of elites and, where an elite is a governing elite, to use Pareto's term, it will be in competition with other groups for power.

Pressure groups

Pluralism is the background against which pressure groups have been accepted. This is particularly true in Britain where parliament, composed of the elected representatives of the people, was thought to be uncontaminated by the influence of 'sectional interests'. Here again, a number of empirical studies, this time of how policy is formulated, showed how much of it in Britain originated within the bureaucracy and how there was a close relationship between the civil service and a great host of pressure groups all wanting to promote or defend their own interests. Pressure groups are an established part of American politics, but even in contemporary Britain there is some feeling that they ought not to take precedence over the political parties and parliament in determining legislation.

Duverger (1972) makes the following distinction between pressure groups and political parties:

Political parties strive to acquire power and to exercise it – by electing town councillors, local officials, mayors, senators, and deputies, and by choosing cabinet ministers and the head of state. Pressure groups, on the contrary, do not participate directly in the acquisition of power or in its exercise: they act to influence power while remaining apart from it; they exert 'pressure' on it. . . . Pressure groups seek to influence the men who wield power, not to place their own men in power, at least not officially. However, certain powerful groups actually have their own representatives in governments and legislative bodies, but the relationship between these individuals and the groups they represent remains secret or circumspect.

Several attempts have been made to classify types of pressure group. Perhaps the most common is the distinction between 'sectional' groups, which are concerned to advance or defend the general interests of their members, and 'promotional' groups which are organized to advance a cause or policy. Examples of sectional groups would be the CBI, the TUC and individual trade unions, and organizations such as the Claimants Union which was formed to support those who apply for state benefits.

Promotional groups are those which people join because they believe that 'something should be done' about whatever the group is concerned with. A good example is the National Viewers and Listeners Association which aims to influence government policy over the public presentation of sex and violence. Again, when abortion became the subject of parliamentary discussion and eventually legislation, various pro- and anti-abortion lobbies developed.

It must be remembered that not all pressure groups are pressure groups only, or all the time. For instance, pro-abortion groups may advise individual mothers who want an abortion. Moreover, any organized group may become a pressure group if its interests are threatened; every tennis club in the country would become a pressure group overnight if the government proposed to levy a tax on tennis. Nor do you have to be organized to bring pressure to bear, at least at local level; a group of mothers who hold up traffic in support of a campaign for a zebra crossing are effectively a pressure group.

In terms of a pluralist theory of democracy, pressure groups have become a key mechanism.

... by acting to check one another's power; by channelling citizen demands to political officials; by protecting their members' rights against encroachments of overzealous officials, demagogues, or aspiring dictators;interest groups actualise democracy.... In a democracy there is a struggle for power among a multiplicity of interest groups in which no single interest, majority or minority, emerges as a clear-cut winner on all issues of concern. That means an interest group that dominates one area of policy will fail to dominate other areas. *Minorities* – plural – will rule. [Margolis 1979]

The mobilization of bias

Dahl's own empirical work is based on an examination of decision-making. In his major study of New Haven, Connecticut (Dahl 1961), he examined a series of concrete cases where key decisions were made; decisions such as taxation and expenditure, subsidies, welfare programmes, etc. It may come as no surprise to know that Dahl found a series of competing elites in New Haven.

However, Dahl's critics have pointed to his somewhat naive notion of power. 'Power, power... where is power?' says Ferrarotti. Does it lie in the ability to secure the right decision? Or rather does it lie in the ability to ensure that some issues never become ones over which decisions have to be made? If the latter is true, then it is no use looking at decision-making to locate the distribution of power, because some issues are organized into politics while others are organized out. The power to achieve this sort of organization is of considerably more significance than the power to win decisions in those issues which do become political.

Matters do not just become issues at random; the structure of power in bureaucracies and governmental hierarchies 'allows' some issues into the arena of public debate and not others. So what really matters is not so much decisions as 'non-decisions'. If, for instance, it can be success-fully established in a given political system that poverty is a consequence of individual inadequacy, then no serious decisions are ever likely to be made pertaining to social policies designed to eradicate poverty. The political system is in a constant process of creating a bias against the serious consideration of poverty as an outcome of basic economic policies. Thus the only decisions which are made tend to be ones where the outcome is of only marginal interest to the real elite.

In support of these views the critics of democratic elitism have pointed to the actual workings of the system. In the words of Margolis (1979):

If the political system were as democratic as proclaimed, then every significant interest in society ought to have a fair chance to present its case to the ruling elite, or to compete for positions of power within that elite. Yet if every interest really had a fair chance, then why did systematic patterns of discrimination persist against minority racial and religious groups, women, the poor, and others in such diverse areas as housing, educational opportunity, health care, and employment.

Thus, large numbers of people may be excluded from the benefits of pluralistic democracy because they do not join in any groups, or because groups of which they are a part do not have access to public debate or are consistently unsuccessful. Then again, those who are active in public affairs are likely to be drawn from the more affluent and articulate classes and, even where they are not, like the leaders of trade unions, they may come to form a separate group on the basis of the 'iron law of oligarchy'. In all these ways, then, the much vaunted processes of polyarchy may end up as very little different from oligarchy, or perhaps even Mills's power elite.

Class and state

This last section brings us back to the question of social class. So far democracy and power have been discussed almost as if they operated within a political world quite divorced from social and economic forces. The 'political' has been presented in virtual isolation from other aspects of society. And yet democracy, if it means anything, has been the opening up of political life to the working class. Indeed, in the first instance, it was an opening up of political life to the middle classes. Through the democratic system, different class interests can, in theory, be represented.

The development of democracy has been the progressive extension of 'citizenship' to the masses. But, as we have just seen, in the way that democracy is currently working, large numbers of 'citizens' appear to be outside the system. What is more, the current orthodox definition of democracy appears to endorse this exclusion in the name of efficiency and stability. How can we explain the paradox that greater democracy has not led to any significant redistribution of power? A Marxist explanation offers a solution.

A summary of the Marxist view of capitalism might be as follows:

> Bourgeois democracy performs the function ... of securing and maintaining the consent of the masses to their own exploitation and subordination. This point should not be oversimplified but nor can it be evaded. ... It throws up a screen (which is not just a fiction, however, but a real structure with real effects) of elections, parliamentary legislation and debate, equal democratic rights, etc. behind which the central, executive apparatuses of the state and their points of contact/access to the capitalist class are obscured. It thus creates the illusion in the masses that they control this democratic state at least as much as anybody else. [Geras 1976]

In order to understand the Marxist position we need to discuss the concept of the state. The state consists of those procedures and institutions concerned with the government of a society. Some very small-scale societies may not have a 'state', being perhaps ruled by hereditary chiefs through custom and norm. But beyond a certain size, some administration of custom and law is required in the form of courts and civil service. Perhaps a body to determine law comes into existence and then some system for enforcing law. Problems of external defence require centralized military control. All these are aspects of the state. Once a state exists it is usual for it to become the only proper agent for the use of force and violence.

In political systems which are not thought to be democracies, power to use the apparatus of the state is enjoyed by a small clique or a single ruler. The point about democracies is that this power is supposed to be widely dispersed and it is therefore easy to miss the significance of the state in liberal democracies. Nevertheless, few democrats would deny that democracies require a state for their efficient management. Marxists, however, go further. As Marx and Engels said in the *Communist Manifesto* (1848), 'The executive of the modern State is but a committee for managing the common affairs of the whole bourgeoisie.' Control of the state is in the hands of the ruling class. The system of law and law enforcement effectively protects the institution of property, while the legislature and administration manage the system of private enterprise. There may be conflicts as to how best to manage it, but there are no conflicts over its essential rightness. From this base the state 'mobilizes' bias against fundamental attacks on the central values of capitalism.

Capitalism and democracy

For a Marxist, capitalism and democracy belong together intrinsically. Any political system is a reflection of the dominant mode of production. Politics is an activity carried on within the superstructure, like religion or leisure. Its basic shape will therefore be determined by the nature of the mode of production (see Chapter 2, page 33). Liberal democracy is the political system most suited to a capitalist social formation.

We can see this most clearly by consulting history. When the capitalist system emerged out of feudalism a new political order was needed. The capitalist market system of production was characterized by individual mobility, contract, and impersonal market allocation of work and rewards. It was based on the principle of free labour and individualism. A new political system was needed for this new type of society. It must embrace the concepts of 'freedom' and individuality, and be able to create the political conditions in which free enterprise would work. 'Freedom' in this context was freedom from old feudal relationships so that an individual's sole obligation was shaped by his position in the market. The individualistic creed of democracy was then an appropriate political arrangement as it would not have been under feudal, absolutist regimes.

However, there is a very difficult contradiction between an economic system based on inequality and a political system based on equality. As Macpherson (1966) puts it:

This society based on individual choices had of course some drawbacks. There was, necessarily, great inequality, for you cannot have a capitalist market society unless some people have got accumulated capital and a great many others have none, or have so little that they cannot work on their own but have to offer their labour to others. This involves inequality in freedom of choice: all are free but some are freer than others.

The problem, then, in a nutshell, is how to justify an unequal distribution of rewards in a society where the central political values were based on the equality and freedom of all citizens. As the capitalist mode of production matured, demands for more open access to the political system also developed and could not be denied. As some of the great wealth of capitalism seeped out of the capitalist class and changed the economic existence of the workers, there was no way in which the political system could remain closed to them. The history of the struggle to extend the franchise is, on this interpretation, just a reflection of the steadily widening effects of the industrial revolution fired by private capital. (For the history of franchise reform, see any standard history source.)

Thus the new bourgeois state is faced with a legitimation crisis. The political system constantly promises more than it can ever deliver without a fundamental change in the structure of class relationships. Of course, part of the work of legitimation is done by the production system itself. Capitalism is so effective in developing production that it generally ensures a steady raising of the standard of living with the result that disadvantaged groups are little inclined to complain. But occasionally there are short-term interruptions in economic growth which can lead to political instability, for example, the depression of the 1930s. More important is the question of whether capitalism can go on promoting growth for ever. At a point where it can no longer do this, the political system will need to take on the whole burden of legitimating capitalist power relations.

For a Marxist, it is at this point that the full significance of the revised theory of democracy becomes apparent. If it can be successfully put about that democracy is not 'government by the people' but 'government by competing elites', the people's expectations of the system can be lowered. Provided a system of elite control can be passed off as 'democracy', political apathy can be encouraged and the full revelation of the inherent contradictions postponed.

The cloak of democracy is, of course, only one means by which a 'false consciousness' is created amongst the masses. The long-term effects of schooling and the short-term influence of the media are also very important in maintaining the hegemony of dominant values (see page 143 and page 265). These are all processes by which rulers in capitalist societies actively seek legitimation for their power and it is in this sense that democracy is a legitimating device rather than a description of reality.

Conclusion

The system of government known as liberal democracy is enjoyed by large numbers of people throughout the Western world. It allows more genuine freedom to more people than most other political systems. Nevertheless, its 'enjoyment' is greater by some than by others, and if some people are more free than they were, others are freer still. Whether its benefits can be spread further than they are now in the advanced democracies, without a fundamental alteration in the social relationships which it legitimates, is the essence of the sociological debate surrounding power and democracy.

Guide to further reading

For a fuller discussion of nearly all the issues raised in this chapter, there is a choice from three excellent, short and readable books. Tom Bottomore's old favourite (1966) has a gentle critical interrogation – *Elites and Society*. Peter Bachrach (1969), *The Theory of Democratic Elitism*, is written from the perspective of a critique of the revised theory

of democracy. The most bloodless discussion is *Political Elites* by
Geraint Parry (1969), A recent and rather more catholic discussion is
Viable Democracy by Michael Margolis (1979). It has a lively style but
concludes with a somewhat tired proposal for giving democracy another
go. The classic Marxist account is, of course, Ralph Miliband (1973), *The
State in Capitalist Society*, but for a short and succinct Marxist-based
critique of democracy, *The Real World of Democracy* by C.B. Macpherson
(1966) is a little gem.

8 The family

Adrian Wilson

Family life is something that many people take for granted. It is seen as part of the natural, biological world, rather than as a social institution which is a human creation. Sociology itself has experienced some difficulty in the analysis of the family, and many sociologists still see the family as a weak spot in the development of the discipline.

The study of the family creates a number of problems for the sociologist. In the first place, it is a very private area of our social lives. Many people will not want this sphere of their lives opened to academic scrutiny, for it is within family relationships that many of us are most insecure. It is difficult to gain sociological insight into such a sensitive area. Secondly, the family takes many forms according to differences in culture and history. A historical perspective shows that the family is a constantly evolving institution. Even if we attempt to study an individual family, we will find that it has its own life-cycle. Each individual starts his or her family life as a child, passes through a period that we call adolescence, and then as a young adult establishes his or her own family through courtship and marriage. This new family starts with the young couple, grows with the arrival of children, and then eventually declines as the children grow into adulthood and start the family life-cycle again. The sociologist studying the family is faced with an immensely complex institution.

The family is also one of our ideological blindspots. We become used to what was normal in our own upbringing, in our own home. All of us notice the little differences when we visit another person's family. It is hard to avoid feeling that our family was the more normal one. How much greater then are the difficulties of sociologists who study family structures which show clear structural and cultural differences from their own.

Anthropology has given us many examples of family structures which are in sharp contrast to the British experience. The Nayar people of southern India, in the period before British colonial rule, are a good case to consider. The family group was composed of brothers and sisters, together with the children of the sisters, and their daughters' children.

They formed one economic group, who lived in one household under the legal guardianship of the eldest male. However, the most notable feature of the Nayar family was in the marriage relationship.

Nayar girls went through a ritual marriage before they reached puberty. But once the ceremonies were over, the ritual husband left and had no further obligation to his bride. The bride had only one obligation to her ritual husband. At his death, she and her children had to mourn his passing. The ritual marriage brought the girl full social maturity. She was now a woman.

Women were able to have a number of visiting husbands, perhaps four to eight in number, who rewarded her for her sexual services. Some of these men would be expected to acknowledge that they might be the fathers of her children, so legitimizing those children in the eyes of the community. But a Nayar man did not have to maintain his wife. Food, clothing and all other needs were met by her matrilineal group. The same family took care of the children. The biological father had no rights over his children or obligations to them. In the Nayar, we have a family structure which contrasts strongly with the nuclear family of the modern western world.

The fieldwork of anthropologists has also shown us that sex roles within the family can vary tremendously. The work of Mead (1950) in New Guinea provides many interesting comparisons. The Mundugumor had been cannibals, and the men had been fierce fighters and hunters. The Mundugumor women were as assertive and active as the men. They provided most of the food by collecting sago and coconuts, and by fishing. We tend to assume the continuity of childbirth as inevitable because of its biological origin. But both male and female Mundugumor hated childbearing, and pregnancy was avoided if possible. Such an attitude contrasts greatly with the gentle Mountain Arapesh where both sexes share and emphasize the parental role. The Tchambuli show yet another pattern of roles. It is the women who are the confident, industrious breadwinners. The 'weaker' men decorate themselves with ornaments, carve, paint and practise their dance steps.

There are also examples of different family forms in our western experience. The Oneida community was one such case. It was founded in 1848 in New York State, by a charismatic preacher, John Humphrey Noyes. He taught that it was possible to achieve a perfect Christian life on earth if people loved each other and shared their worldly possessions. The life of Oneida was designed to promote common bonds, while closing the community off from the corrupting influence of the outside world.

Group marriage was practised. Any adult could have sexual relations with any other adult. Sexual approaches were made through a third party, often an older woman, and such an advance could be declined without fuss. A strong distinction was drawn between sexual activity as recreation and sexual activity for reproduction. Oneida also developed a eugenically based programme of controlled breeding, with only selected adults being chosen as suitable for parenthood.

The children who were born into the community were brought up in a nursery run by the women. Parents did see their children, but there was a deliberate effort to play down these strong bonds of affection. All adults were encouraged to treat all children as if they were their own.

These examples show us as sociologists that we cannot take the structure of the family for granted. The family will vary its form according to any number of social, cultural, economic and demographic factors. It is essential for sociologists to step outside the experience of personal attributes to their own family life, and look at the family from a number of perspectives.

Theoretical approaches to the sociology of the family

The various theoretical perspectives within sociology have resulted in markedly different approaches to the study of the family. However, one perspective, that of functionalism, has clearly been predominant, and only recently have more critical approaches come to the fore.

The functionalist perspective

The functionalist perspective has seen the family as one of the corner-stones of the social structure, a universal institution which serves the same basic functions in all societies. The crucial functions of the family are the reproduction and socialization of the young into the roles and culture of society (see Chapter 4, page 91–2), and the stabilization of adult personalities. The family is seen as having a crucial role in maintaining stability in society, and so functionalist studies have often been concerned with the pathology of the family, for instance, the increase in divorce rates, and the problems of single-parent families.

The family is obviously formed by the social and economic structure which surrounds it, and as society changes, so the functions of the family will alter. For example, the family before the industrial revolution was often a productive unit where the members of the family were involved in agricultural or craft manufacture within what was essentially a domestic framework. The introduction of the factory system took away the productive role and sent the individual members of the family out of the home to work. The economic function of the family is now essentially reduced to being the basic unit of consumption within our economic system.

The functionalist concern with the way that the family has adapted to the forces of industrialization and urbanization can be clearly seen in the British and American tradition of community studies. The findings produced by these studies have led some functionalists to claim that the nuclear family is inevitable as it is perfectly suited to the modern world. But underlying the whole functionalist approach is the assumption that the family has an essential and positive role to play in society. This is reflected in the overwhelming support given to the family by all the major institutions of our society. The churches have consistently championed the family as a bulwark against changing values in a more secular society. Local authority social workers try to give support to families under stress. Schools look to the family to give the necessary encouragement to the good pupil, while teachers blame the family when such support is lacking. Advertisements show the nuclear family shopping happily amidst all the benefits of a consumer society. The Labour government of the late 1970s even considered giving a government minister responsibility for family matters.

The interactionist perspective

The interactionist approach to the family is also centrally concerned with the socialization process. It is through interaction within the family that the child develops its personality and its awareness of 'self' (see Chapter 4, pages 90–1). The adult members of the family, particularly the parents, consciously and unconsciously structure the social world of the child, giving order and meaning to the chaotic jumble of things around them. The interactionist is interested in the way the developing child comes to understand the actions and attitudes of others, and with how the child learns to adjust its behaviour to fit the pattern of family life, and of the social world which surrounds it.

This approach to the study of the family is essentially concerned with the internal workings of the family, and could be termed a micro-approach. Interactionists are interested in such processes as courting, the selection of a marriage partner, marital adjustment, and parent–child relationships. In particular, the study of changing roles within the family can help to reveal the basic social norms which guide our behaviour both as individuals and in groups. In order to help this analysis, many sociologists are turning to historical data as a means of throwing light on the assumptions we have made about roles within the family. The weakness of the interactionist approach, in this context as in others you have studied, is in the under-emphasis on those forces working at the broader macro-level of society.

Critical perspectives

The development of a critical approach to the sociology of the family has been slow and uneven. Engels (1884) published his classic critical study over a hundred years ago, but it was not until the 1960s and 1970s that his ideas were picked up and developed in a more coherent form. The critical approach can be roughly divided into three main branches. These are the Marxist approach, the work of the radical psychiatrists and, perhaps more interestingly, the critical feminist view.

The analysis of the family has been seen by many Marxists as of secondary importance to their concern with the political issues of the class struggle in the capitalist industrial world. Nevertheless, the work of Engels is crucial in showing that the family is an institution which changes in response to developments in the economic substructure of society. Marxists see the family as being culturally determined, a reflection of the dominant values of society. Engels argued that the nuclear family of today evolved through a series of stages that coincide with the emergence of private property. Relationships within the family are the outcome of property ownership, just as wider class relations are. In the family, men gained control of private property and the power that went with it. The power that accompanied this ownership of property has been crucial in the economic and political domination of women by the men of their family. The recent interest in the writings of Marx and Engels on the family has come not so much from traditional Marxist writers, but rather from the new generation of feminists. Marxist sociologists have still to develop their ideas on what is happening to the family at this time, particularly in socialist societies, and have yet to clarify their thoughts on the future of the family if capitalism does collapse.

The radical psychiatrists and the feminists both attack the modern nuclear family for the way that it prevents the individual from achieving personal freedom. Laing (1964) and Cooper (1971) see the family smothering individuality in a cocoon of love and security. Love becomes an emotional weapon used to keep an individual's behaviour within acceptable limits. These psychiatrists wish to see the family broken up precisely because it is too strong for the individual to fight (see also Chapter 11, pages 330–1).

The development of the feminist perspective has had a most interesting impact on the sociology of the family over the last two decades. The feminists have paid particular attention to the link between the biological and social worlds in an attempt to understand how women have come to occupy an inferior position in society as a whole, and in the family in particular. The sociologists working within this perspective have taken their studies back through social history in order to explain the development of women's roles, and to attempt an explanation of family life from a woman's point of view (see, for example, Oakley 1974a and 1974b).

The sociologist coming to the study of the sociology of the family for the first time needs to become familiar with all these approaches. No one perspective by itself seems to give a satisfactory explanation. Each perspective poses certain problems, but also contributes in part to our overall understanding of the sociology of the family.

The changing British family

It is easy to make the mistake of assuming that there is only one type of family structure in Britain. However, this clearly changes over time, and varies according to social class. The family is inevitably affected by changes in the economic and social structure of society. Urbanization and industrialization have left their mark.

A historical view of the changing British family

There is an assumption that the family has evolved from an extended form to the small, democratically managed family of today. The work of Laslett (1983) has cast doubt on this supposedly straightforward progression. As mentioned earlier (see Chapter 3, page 74), social historians are faced with great methodological difficulties in using historical material. They need to be wary of interpreting historical processes with the attitudes of the present day. Historical evidence may be biased by undue emphasis on the public activities of the rich and educated, that is, those literate members of the community able to record the details of their own lives. Our knowledge of ordinary people may be dependent on the judgement of the parish priest, or the anecdotal material in the diaries and letters of the upper class. However, there is enough evidence to give us some indication of family structure before the industrial revolution.

Laslett (1977), using records of sixty parishes in England, and another twenty communities in Europe, suggests that there was a family pattern in the seventeenth century which was common to England, the Low Countries (Holland and Belgium) and to northern France. This western European family can be clearly distinguished from the extended family found in southern and eastern Europe. Laslett suggests that it had four features. It was nuclear in form. Women had children relatively late in their lives. The age gap between the partners was relatively small. Many families included non-kin in their households, for example, domestic servants.

Late marriage, a high infant mortality rate, a low level of fertility, and a much later age of sexual maturity, are all likely to produce a small, two-generation family. The evidence of parish records between 1650 and 1750 suggests a mean age of marriage for women in England of 27 years. Children would therefore be born to mature women in their late twenties or early thirties. The age gap between husband and wife was quite small; the records for Ealing suggest three and a half years. In Yugoslavia, it was about ten years. Indeed, over one-fifth of English wives seem to have been older than their husbands.

A key difference from the modern family was the presence of non-kin who worked within the household. In the rich families they were domestic servants; in more ordinary families they were farm-workers who lived in. Laslett suggests that some 40 per cent of all children became servants in their late teens; it was part of their normal life-cycle. Service was a means of exploiting the earning power of a child, and of getting some form of training for that child. However, by the turn of the twentieth century, service was largely a domestic matter for the wealthy.

It would be wrong to suggest that there was only one form of pre-industrial family. The family of the rural farm-worker was likely to be vastly different from that of the upper-class land-owner or the urban businessman. The majority of ordinary families were units of production in the sense that all members helped to earn their living. Young and Willmott (1973) call this the Stage 1 family, where survival depended on the economic partnership of all the members of the family, regardless of their age or sex. A wife, in particular, was an economic necessity as she could supervise the dairy work, the cheese-making and help with the harvest, while still cooking, baking and brewing. Children were also made to earn their keep on the land or in cottage industry.

Industrialization in the latter half of the eighteenth century brought major changes to social and family life. Steam power brought the growth of large-scale factory production in those towns near to a coalfield. The Industrial Revolution was not a sudden event, but a process that lasted over fifty years. It killed the family industry, and forced family members into the factories and the mills as wage-earners. Young and Willmott suggest that this period of disruption created the Stage 2 family.

Anderson (1971) studied the cotton town of Preston and suggested that industrialization may have increased the proportion of married couples living with their parents. Old age had often meant poverty, and a reliance on the harsh regime of the Poor Law. But in the cotton towns, family income could be increased by getting the parents or other elderly relatives to care for the children, freeing the wife to work in the mill. Anderson's work is important in showing that industrialization could have increased links between kin, rather than weakening them as so often supposed.

Economic necessity made it essential that as many members of the family as possible went out to work. Social conditions in the towns were poor, though not necessarily worse than in the country. Poverty, ill health and unreliable employment affected many families. However, in the latter half of the nineteenth century, there was the growth of a 'child-saving movement' which obtained legislation to take children out of the worst industrial work, and place them within the 'civilizing' influence of the new school system.

The middle- and upper-class family was very different. Fletcher (1966) claims that the ideal type Victorian middle-class family was based on the subservience of women and the hard work of domestic servants. The 'home' was seen as a moral sanctuary from the chaos of urban life. The male head of the family, like the country squire, protected his dependants. He alone risked contact with the wider society. The mother–wife was an important symbol who, by her virtue, acted as an example to save men from their base selves. The women of the family were carefully cosseted, and did not go into public places unescorted. Davidoff (1973) has shown how a complex set of rules of etiquette grew up which allowed orderly but limited mixing between the new urban middle class and the old gentry. However, the whole edifice of middle-class respectability rested on double standards of sexual morality. Women's sexuality was denied, while male sexual licence was met by prostitution on a scale that sharply contradicted the public morality of the day.

The changes in family structure should be set alongside the demographic patterns that accompanied urbanization. The population grew rapidly from 8.9 million in 1801 to 36 million in 1911. Infant mortality, a sensitive indicator of community health, actually increased in the second half of the century (see Chapter 12 for a full discussion). The figures show the impact of bad housing, poor sanitation, a restricted diet and low standards of hygiene. The death of a child was a normal feature of family life.

The latter part of the nineteenth century also saw a fall in the number of married women working. In 1851 24 per cent of married women worked, but in 1911 it was only 13 per cent. It has been suggested that this change reflects the increase in male earning power, together with the growth of the male-dominated engineering industry. There was a high proportion of working wives in textile and pottery towns, but much lower levels in mining areas, in the country, and in London. Towards the end of the nineteenth century there was a growth in hostility to wives working, backed by widespread concern over the effect on young children of mothers working. This was part of the wider concern with the 'health' of the family, that would eventually lead to the first elements of the welfare state.

Urban development has continued to have a major influence on family life in the twentieth century. The growth of suburbs and programmes of slum clearance have reshaped our towns and cities. The introduction of council housing in the early 1920s altered the pattern of working-class life. War-time bombing and consequent reconstruction increased the number of large council estates on the edges of our cities. The post-war housing shortage brought high-rise blocks of flats, resulting in social isolation for both the young family and the old person imprisoned several storeys above the ground. The social problems of high-rise living were compounded by technical problems with lifts, with condensation, and even structural collapse. Local authorities have now turned to low-rise, high-density developments in the hope that they will prove to be more cost-effective, and at the same time may restore some kind of community structure to local neighbourhoods. Inner-city areas are still blighted by 'multiple deprivation', that is, high unemployment, poor housing, low wages, overcrowding, etc. This hits young single people, the elderly and ethnic minorities particularly hard. The housing shortage meant that it was no surprise to observe the reappearance of squatting in the 1970s.

Housing is likely to remain a major social problem. The cost of home-ownership has soared, while at the same time government expenditure cuts have forced local authority house building programmes to a post-war low. Sociologists should perhaps give more attention to housing. What is the impact of housing policy on family formation and on the structure of family life? What is the likely future significance of the growing gap between the house-owner and the tenant of the local authority.

Demographic changes within the family

Major demographic changes have resulted from improvements in diet, sanitation, housing and from the expansion of our medical knowledge. This can be seen in two main areas: the decline in the rate of infant mortality, and the increase in life expectancy.

The latter part of the nineteenth century saw a continued decline in infant mortality and a marked increase in family size. The increase in life expectancy resulted in many more three- and four-generation families. Such demographic change is the result of a complex interplay between biological and social factors, such as the age of marriage. The complexity of such processes can be seen in the fluctuation in the birth rate in England since 1950. The sharp drop in the birth rate from 1964 onwards can perhaps be linked to economic problems, the availability of contraception and abortion, and the fundamental changes within society in our attitudes to both women and children.

Religion, social class and ethnic background also play a major part in influencing the size of families. The birth rate of minority ethnic groups has become a political issue in itself. However, the age structure of the Asian community is radically different from that of the English host community, and so it is unrealistic to compare birth rates. What is clear is that we live in a predominantly pronatalist culture, that is, a culture where adult sex roles and personality traits are closely linked to the dominant role that parenthood plays in our gender definitions.

Changes in kinship patterns

As we have seen, the commonly held view is that there has been a movement from some form of extended family to the smaller and more closely knit nuclear family. The study by Young and Willmot (1957) of Bethnal Green is perhaps the best known. Their work was designed to explore the impact of redevelopment on family life, and involved a comparison of the old working-class community in the East End of London with life on the new council estates in the suburbs. They found that kinship ties in Bethnal Green were still crucial in finding work, in housing and in the rearing of a family. The relationship between mother and daughter was especially strong, based as it was on the exchange of services at the crucial periods of life, that is, marriage, childbirth, illness and old age. When the young families moved out to Greenleigh, these close ties of kinship were partially severed, forcing the family to turn inwards on itself.

The Bethnal Green study was typical of a number of community studies that took a sympathetic view of working-class life. Kerr (1958) found another female-oriented family structure in her study of dockland Liverpool. Dennis, Henriques and Slaughter (1956) noted the strong communal ties amongst the miners of Ashton. Tunstall (1962) was able to show how changing housing patterns and a declining industry were affecting the long-established fishing community of Hull. Rosser and Harris (1965) confirmed the role of the extended family in Swansea in giving social identification, and the demise of that family in the face of its dispersal throughout the new estates of the city.

Not all these studies have been of working-class communities. Young and Willmott's study of Woodford (1960) showed that the middle class maintained family ties, albeit from a slightly greater distance. Bell's (1968) study of the middle-class family in Swansea showed a strong flow of male-mediated financial aid from fathers to sons or sons-in-law. He suggested that there were two forms of middle-class family: that of the burgess with strong roots in the local community, and that of the spiralist who is both socially and physically mobile.

Studies of the family in farming communities show the crucial economic function of kinship. Arensberg and Kimball's classic study (1940) of County Clare showed how marriage was arranged to build up the family holding. In the studies of Llanfihangel (Rees 1950) and Gosforth (Williams 1956), it was found that marriage was delayed in order to maintain the succession of the eldest son to the family farm.

The theme emerging from all these studies is that the modern British family is increasingly influenced by national rather than local factors. Stacey's (1975) follow-up to her classic study of Banbury in the immediate post-war period (Stacey 1960) shows that by the 1960s the community was much more open to national influences. Her study showed that the network of kinship was of far less importance, although the study concludes that the elementary family, as in 1950, was still of crucial significance.

Changing roles within the family
The family is a major source of our identity and social roles. Most sociological attention has been focused on the changing role relationship

of husband and wife. The early studies of working-class family life show clear examples of role segregation according to sex. The husband was the bread-winner, while the wife was primarily concerned with the domestic and maternal roles. But the changing position of women in society, and alterations to the family structure, may have created a new balance of authority within the family. Bott (1957) argues that the decline in extended relationships has weakened the segregation of the roles of husband and wife. She suggests that there is more equality within the family than ever before, and this can be seen in the growth of shared or joint conjugal role relationships. Other sociologists, particularly feminists, suggest that the degree of equality has been overstated and that the family has remained essentially patriarchal in form.

The roles of children have also changed. Aries's pioneering study (1960) showed that, in the past, children were treated as young adults from a very early age, and played a crucial economic role within the family. This did not end until the introduction of compulsory full-time education. A historical view of childhood, showing it to be a relatively brief period, contrasts vividly with the modern family in which childhood has been considerably extended. Teenagers now form one of the most important 'leisure classes' in our consumer society (see Chapter 5, pages 145-6, for a discussion of youth culture).

Young couples who have managed to secure relatively well-paid jobs may be able to settle into independent married life much earlier than previous generations. Their position contrasts vividly with the experience of the growing number of elderly who are isolated from their families, and who as pensioners are forced to rely on the welfare state. Retirement from work removes a major source of social identity and signifies a major change in status. However, many people, either as individuals or as members of pressure groups such as Age Concern, are campaigning for a more active and socially significant role for old people in modern society.

A typical British family?

Sociologists have asked if some form of family can now be said to be the norm in Britain. Fletcher (1966) sketches an ideal type in his important work, *The Family and Marriage in Britain*. He says it is of long duration since it is founded at an early age. It is small in size because of birth control, and is separately housed in an improved material environment. The family is economically self-supporting and is therefore independent of relatives. The couple who founded the family are of equal status and enjoy a marriage relationship based increasingly on mutual respect and consideration. Family decisions are democratic and take into account the interests of husband, wife and children. The family is built round the care of children, and the family is aided in achieving health and stability by a wide range of public provision, both statutory and voluntary.

Young and Willmott (1973) talk of a symmetrical family, their Stage 3 family. It is a small, nuclear family, home-centred, where the married couple both work, and share the central roles. They suggest that this Stage 3 family has been gradually developing since the early part of the century, starting with the middle classes and gradually spreading so as to become the dominant form of family structure. Goldthorpe and Lockwood (1969) in their study of the affluent worker assume the existence of a very similar structure, the 'privatized family'.

We need to ask how accurate a picture this is of family life in general. It is unlikely that there will ever be only one form of family structure. Young people may develop alternative styles of living arrangements, while the ethnic minorities in Britain already show us alternative models of family life. It is also important to remember that there is a more violent side to family life.

Violence in the family

The family can be a hostile environment, full of violent emotions. Vicious attacks on young children, the so-called 'battered baby syndrome', have led local authorities to maintain registers of children at risk. A high percentage of murders and violent assaults take place within the family. Marital violence remains an intractable problem.

Social scientists are still unclear as to the cause of violence within the family, although there does seem to be a pattern where some of those who are violent experienced violence as children. Marsden and Owens (1975) suggest that perhaps one in a hundred marriages have a violent side, giving a total of perhaps 140,000 violent marriages in the United Kingdom. Dobash and Dobash (1980) interviewed 109 battered wives in Scotland and estimated that these women had suffered 32,000 separate assaults.

Sociological concern with physical violence has been fairly limited. The pathological approach sees it as one of the potential dysfunctions of the family, and that it requires treatment or specialized help from social workers. Sociologists appear to show more interest in the analysis of psychological violence within the family. Those sociologists critical of the nuclear family have been able to make use of the insights provided by radical psychiatrists.

Cooper, in *The Death of the Family* (1971), and Laing, in *Sanity, Madness and the Family* (1964), explore the idea that love is used as a weapon to control and mould personality. The child is not allowed to develop freely, but is crushed into the roles required by the family. Laing's work on the 'causes' of schizophrenia suggests that the family, through the socialization process, forces the child to accept a particular view of the social world. In doing this, the family prevents its members from developing to the full the individuality of each human personality (for further discussion see Chapter 11, pages 330–1).

These critical approaches to the family are important to sociology. They act as a clear counter-weight to the functionalist view of the family as a source of stability. But perhaps the most powerful criticism of the nuclear family has come from the feminist perspective. Feminist sociologists have been concerned to show the way that the family has distorted the image that women have of themselves.

Women and the family

Most sociology has in the past been written by men, and therefore reflected the male domination of social life in general, and the academic world in particular. Sociology has tended to concentrate on the roles of men within the industrial, political and class systems. Women have been studied mainly in their supportive and expressive roles within the family. The growth of sociological work informed by a feminist perspective has helped redress the balance in the portrayal of the role of women within the family.

A complete sociology of the family must include an explanation of how women have become so closely identified with the domestic and maternal roles. Families socialize girls into a particular gender role which makes tenderness and passivity the perceived qualities of womanhood. The biological differences of sex have been translated into a social hierarchy of gender which anchors the 'normal' woman to the domestic hearth.

Sociological and anthropological research has seemed to suggest that the sexual division of labour, which allocated the woman a domestic role, was an inevitable and logical response to the biological differences between the sexes. In hunting societies it appeared unavoidable (with the exception of Mead's examples, quoted on page 218) that the physically stronger man would do the hunting, while the biological demands of motherhood would restrict the activities of the woman. Sociologists have suggested a near universal distribution of tasks according to sex, with women as food-gatherers, water-carriers, cooks and nursemaids. Oakley (1974) suggests that it is through this expressive function that sociologists have found an answer to the problem of order in society. The mother's role is to provide the child with the moral training and emotional security that would result in a stable adult personality.

The concern with the function of the family in maintaining stability is typical of the structural functionalist approach. But it can also be seen in the work of the psychologist John Bowlby. Bowlby (1953) in his book *Child Care and the Growth of Love* raised the key problem of the need for a strong mother–child relationship. Many public figures in the 1950s and 1960s used the mass media to express their concern about the 'danger' of maternal deprivation. Only recently has more emphasis been placed on the full participation of both adults in parenthood.

Sociology is now trying to develop a more realistic social history of women, which separates the biological from the social influences. The biological process for those women who opt for motherhood is bound to affect those women's opportunities in society, particularly if they are also expected to take the major share in child-rearing. Ortner (1974) argues that it is crucial to look at the way a society evaluates the biological role of women. The life of the woman has been linked to the natural world because it is so closely tied to the physical processes of menstruation, pregnancy and childbirth. Anthropological evidence shows that men have often seen these natural processes as polluting and potentially harmful. Ortner suggests that the male world has been seen as separated from nature. In both traditional and modern societies, men have predominated in politics, religion and the arts. The result has been to overvalue male-dominated cultural activities at the expense of the natural role of women in motherhood.

It is now becoming clear that women have always played a vital role in the family economy. In the pre-industrial family women were in charge of many of the essential agricultural tasks which sustained the family larder. At the same time, within cottage industry, they prepared the raw materials for the husband's work, for example, spinning wool. The growth of the factory system saw the wife as a wage-earner, and it was only towards the end of the nineteenth century that there was a drop in the proportion of married women working.

Social historians used to explain the drop in the proportion of working wives by reference to the work of Victorian philanthropists. The campaign to rescue women from dangerous work was paralleled by charitable work in the prisons, amongst abandoned children, and in the anti-slavery and temperance movements. Oakley (1974) puts forward an alternative explanation. She suggests that women were seen as rivals to male supremacy. A middle-class ideology grew up that stressed that the proper place for women was in the home, at the heart of a community sheltered from the corruption of the world.

The ordinary working man subscribed to the same ideology. Masculine pride was sustained by the knowledge that he could support his wife and children. Trade unions saw women as a rival source of labour, and even in war-time have been jealous of a man's right to the first choice of jobs. Even today, trade unions are weakest in those service industries where women are employed in great numbers, for example, amongst shop-workers and in the offices of small businesses. So both the middle- and working-class man saw the 'natural' role of the woman as that of housewife and mother.

The present century has seen a number of factors working to modify women's role in the family. Changes in the legal and social position of women accompanied their emancipation. There has been improvement in the educational opportunities for girls, although there is continuing evidence of female under-achievement in education (see Chapter 9, page 268). Legislation has removed some of the obstacles facing women, but has done relatively little to change social attitudes. Improvements in contraception and the greater availability of abortion have given women much greater control over their own fertility. The result of all these forces has been an increase in the number of women who go out to work, and women now make up nearly 40 per cent of the work-force.

Many studies have looked at the effect of mothers working while still having to care for young children. Such research reflects a traditional sociological concern with the ability of the modern family to carry out its basic functions. Myrdal and Klein (1956) suggest that mothers feel guilty about working, yet they know the value of their economic contribution to family finances. Indeed it may be that much of the working-class affluence of the 1960s may have resulted from the efforts of the affluent worker's wife. Myrdal and Klein felt that it was the educated middle-class mother who was most affected by the conflict between the roles of wife and worker.

Hannah Gavron's (1966) study of ninety-six North London mothers showed that many wives experienced a sense of freedom on marriage, but that this vanished with the arrival of children. The family then became a prison. Gavron suggested that the middle-class wives returned to work for social contact, while working-class wives returned with the motivation of extra money.

Rhona and Robert Rapoport (1977) suggest that the 'dual-career' family may offer a pointer to the future development of the family. Such a family is increasingly found amongst the middle classes, where both husband and wife try to combine professional or business careers with the demands of family life. However the Rapoports' work had its main focus on the emotional role conflict inherent in such a structure, rather than on the basic problems of time and money which confront ordinary families.

Gowler and Legge (in Rapoport *et al.* 1982) show that financial pressures have led to a growth in 'dual-worker' families in all social classes. Such families face three problems. Whose job or career is given the most importance? Must it always be the work of the husband that has priority? Secondly, what changes take place in the domestic division of labour? Thirdly, what arrangements are made for child-minding, particularly for working class families, few of whom will be able to afford residential help?

Ann Oakley's studies of the housewife (Oakley 1974) seem to suggest that it will be difficult to change the traditional domestic roles. Housework is seen as women's work, and many men are unwilling to concede that it is real work in the productive sense. The housewife is left economically dependent on her husband and has little chance to gain satisfaction from the repetitive monotony of the household tasks.

Oakley draws a distinction between housework and childcare. Middle-class husbands seemed to be more likely than working-class to help with the housework and childcare. It seems that our view of masculinity will continue to stress that small babies and the dirty tasks of childcare are still the responsibility of women. Oakley (1972) states that 'the presence of British husbands at the kitchen sink does not appear to mean that they are fast becoming househusbands'.

The domestic labour debate is crucial for a feminist sociology of the family. The family is servicing capitalism (and presumably other forms of society) by reproducing labour power. The wife keeps the husband in good working order for the factory or office by seeing to both his physical and his emotional needs. Women as mothers reproduce the future work force. The family, through the socialization process, then teaches the children to conform to the values and beliefs of society.

Feminists are now asking if it is possible for women to break out of these traditional domestic roles by themselves. Will the family, by its nature, always exploit women, or is this simply a feature of modern capitalist and state capitalist societies? The Marxist feminists seem to look for progress in the wake of revolutionary change, while the radical feminists prefer to look at the scientific advances in the regulation and modification of reproduction, and their potentially liberating consequences.

The state and the family

A commonsense view would seem to suggest that the family has remained free of state interference. But in reality the state has developed a very close relationship with the family. As mentioned, government has even gone as far as to consider the appointment of a Minister for the Family. The state can be seen to have developed its involvement with the family in three major areas; family law, formal schooling and welfare policy.

At the very simplest level, the state requires the family to register all births, marriages and deaths (see Chapter 12, pages 364–5). However, it goes further than this and actually creates the legal framework within which the family functions. The state decides on the laws that will regulate the forms and conditions under which people marry, and also the procedures that govern the official termination of a marriage contract. The factors that affect a particular state's attitude on legislation in such an area as marriage will obviously vary from society to society. England has seen a gradual easing of legislation on divorce, while Eire still prohibits it.

The state is also responsible for legislation on matters of sexual morality. Government, by setting a legal age of consent for sexual relationships, in fact helps to define what is acceptable behaviour. A good example of this can be found in the legislation passed by the

Labour government of 1964–70. Three major items of legislation in this field were: the Divorce Law Reform Act, the Sexual Offences Act, and the Abortion Law Reform Act. Such legislation was both a reflection of changes in public opinion, and an indication of the changing moral climate. Such legislation is likely to remain controversial. There has been constant debate over the working of the Abortion Law Reform Act, and politicians of all parties are subject to conflicting pressures from different interest groups. Similarly, the debate over homosexuality continues, particularly in the light of the failure of governments to extend the legislation across the border into Scotland. Governments in Europe still have similar legislative problems with abortion, divorce and family planning.

The range of legislation which affects the family is immense. The financial position of the family is invariably affected by the public expenditure policies adopted by government. The state determines the regulations which govern the sale of family property. When people marry, they automatically change the basis of taxation and welfare benefits.

Most of this legislation is open to public debate, and changes are made in public view. What is of greater interest to the sociologist is the indirect pressure that is placed on the family system. Althusser (1971) includes the family in his analysis of the Ideological State Apparatus. He argues that social behaviour can be controlled without the state resorting to physical force. The family, along with schools, the mass media and other public institutions, control our behaviour by making us believe in a particular ideological framework (see Chapter 4, page 102). The state can easily dominate the population because the family has trained the next generation of citizens in the habits of obedience. This process of ideological hegemony can easily be seen in the involvement of the state with the education and social welfare systems.

The state has a fundamental interest in population trends. It may show concern at a falling birth rate by offering financial allowances to parents, or by giving medals for motherhood. More commonly, governments have shown concern at rising population trends. This may lead a government to offer rewards to those not having children. The current policy in China exhorts parents to have only one child and offers special privileges to such parents. The privileges are withdrawn where a couple has two children, while parents who have three or more children pay a penalty. The state shows its concern for the quality of the future population by the provision of public authority health care.

The structure of the family is closely influenced by state action in the education system. The introduction of compulsory attendance at elementary schools in the nineteenth century had the effect of prolonging childhood. Any extension of the school-leaving age also delays the point at which children can be accepted into the adult world. This inevitably raises the age of marriage, and will have demographic significance by altering the average age of motherhood. Prolonged education also extends the period that the young are economically and psychologically dependent on their parents.

State policy on the structure of the education system will clearly affect roles within the family. A good example of this can be seen in government policy on pre-school education. If the family contains several young children under school age, it is obviously going to mean that the mother or some other responsible person must remain at home to look after them. Compulsory schooling prevented the family from using older children as baby-sitters while the mothers were out at work. However, the problems were partially solved after the Education Act of 1870 (the Forster Act), by the attendance of very young children in elementary schools. The proportion of the age group under 5 years of age in elementary schools rose from 24 per cent in 1870 to 43 per cent in 1900, a much higher proportion than today.

There is another significant example of state involvement in pre-school provision. During the Second World War, there was an urgent need to free as many women as possible to work in industry, and to provide a framework of services to cope with the mass evacuation of children from urban areas. Co-operation between the Health, Education and Labour ministries quickly produced 1450 full-time nurseries, opening for between twelve and fifteen hours a day. This system of childcare was rapidly run down once the war was over.

Clearly it is possible for the state to provide a high level of childcare support, which would allow for significant changes in the role of women as mothers. But in practice this has not happened. The number of children under the age of 5 in primary schools is much lower than at the start of the century. Governments have given their support to an expansion of nursery education, but have always been unwilling to devote adequate finance to it. The patchy provision of pre-school education has reinforced the domestic role of women. This is yet another factor which inhibits the development of more balanced role relationships in the early years between husband and wife.

The workings of the welfare state also affect the family. The state has used health and welfare measures to protect the national interest, and as a way of preventing the growth of internal discontent. The early welfare provisions of children, for example, school meals, the provision of milk, and of regular health inspections, all directly followed complaints about the inadequate health of army recruits for the Anglo–Boer War. Today, medical opinion suggests that many long-term mental patients should be cared for in the community, that is, at home. Such a medical ideology is seen by some critics as a means of saving money for the state at the expense of extra labour within the family.

The welfare system also continues the exploitation of women within the family. Land (1975) has forcefully argued that the Welfare State is based on the premise that a woman is dependent on a man, and so reflects society's patriarchal attitudes towards women and marriage. The Beveridge Report, on which much of the post-war welfare system was based, assumed that a woman would be supported by a husband. It was also assumed that women would have their working lives interrupted by childbirth. Beveridge further assumed that the rise in the number of working women was an exceptional situation brought about by the war. All benefits for a woman were determined by her marital status: a married woman received a lower level of sickness and unemployment benefit than a single man or woman. Land concludes that the state, through the social security system, is 'actively supporting not only the exploitation of women and unskilled men, but also patriarchy'.

The changing divorce rate

The annual publication of the divorce statistics usually produces a moral panic over the 'health' of the modern family. The rising divorce rate is seen as a major threat to the stability of the family. Goode (1971) explains that in western society our religious heritage has led us to view divorce as a tragedy. Functionalist sociology also reflects this concern with the stability of the nuclear family.

A divorce is the legal termination of a marriage relationship, a device acting as a safety-valve in this potentially explosive area of human relationships. Marriages can of course be terminated in other ways, for example, through separation or annulment. It should also be remembered that many unhappy marriages in fact continue and do not end in divorce.

The divorce rate varies from society to society. All western societies are showing an increase in their divorce rate. Britain has a lower divorce rate than the United States, Sweden and Denmark, but a higher rate than European neighbours such as France, Belgium and West Germany. But there are countries where the divorce rate has fallen as traditional family patterns have become modified, for example, Japan, Algeria and Egypt. (When you are considering these rates, remember the discussion on the use of official statistics in Chapter 3, pages 75-7.)

Sociologists agree on some of the factors contributing to marital breakdown. Marriages that cross boundaries of religion, class or ethnicity may experience extra pressures from friends and relatives. The divorce rate is higher in urban areas than in rural communities. The age of the couple at marriage is another crucial factor. This century has seen a trend to earlier marriage and the figures show that where the couple are both under the age of twenty, they are three times as likely to divorce. Young brides are also more often pregnant, a fact which must add stress to the relationship, and create housing problems for the young couple with their child. However, more efficient contraception and the availability of abortion has reduced the number of brides under twenty who were pregnant from 37 per cent in 1964 to 23 per cent in 1976. The improvement in life expectancy means that marriages can last longer, and increases the likelihood that a marriage will end in divorce rather than bereavement. Children can act as a bond in marriage, therefore childlessness is statistically associated with marital breakdown.

Another major factor in the increase in divorce is changing legislation. In the eighteenth century divorce was obtainable only by the rich via a Private Act of Parliament. Legal changes eased the situation, but at the end of the nineteenth century there were still only 500 to 600 divorces a year. This century has seen the gradual liberalization of the law on divorce. The introduction of the Legal Aid Scheme has meant that more people can afford the legal costs involved in a divorce.

The most important of these legal changes came with the passage of the Divorce Law Reform Act of 1970. Divorce was to be granted on the single ground of the irretrievable breakdown of marriage. This could be proved by evidence of separation, desertion, adultery or unreasonable behaviour. The Act allowed divorce by agreement following two years' separation, and for the first time, a divorce could be obtained against the wishes of one of the partners. The liberalization of British divorce laws reflects both the growing secularization of society (see Chapter 5, pages 139–40) and the belief that an unhappy marriage is a greater evil than a divorce.

In 1982 there were 147,000 divorces in England and Wales. Close to one in three marriages will now be ended by divorce. A significant number of divorces take place in marriages where there are no children. In 1982, 42,000 of the couples divorcing had no children. However, the other families involved in divorce contained over 158,000 children under the age of sixteen years.

Sociologists have attempted to explain why people have come to accept divorce more readily. It is clear that there has been a change in the British attitude to marriage. Secularization has weakened the religious attachment to marriage as a state to be accepted 'for better or worse'. The changing moral climate has weakened the stigma of divorce. But the most important factor is probably people's changing expectations of marriage. People see marriage without love and affection as stultifying, and therefore prefer to end the relationship and look elsewhere for personal fulfilment. The changes in legislation, the improved economic position of women, and the decline in the stigma of divorce, all encourage the partners in an unsuccessful marriage to try again, rather than continue an unhappy relationship.

The increase in the divorce rate clearly does not mean that marriage and the family have no future. As a society, we still believe in marriage. Over one-third of divorcees remarry within a year, showing that they still have faith in the institution of marriage. Perhaps sociologists have been asking the wrong questions about marriage. We need to know why people still want to marry and what they expect to gain from the relationship. Sociologists should also examine why some people choose not to marry. The answers to these questions might show us how successful marriage has been in terms of the participants' expectations.

Illegitimacy

The unmarried parent, with an illegitimate child, has been seen as a special social and legal case of an incomplete family. This form of one-parent family is often viewed as a social problem. Firstly, some see it as a moral threat to the nuclear family. Secondly, some see it as an unstable unit which is likely to collapse under economic and psychological pressures. The financial situation of many unmarried mothers also reflects the inferior economic position of women in society.

Social historians have taken a great interest in the history of illegitimacy, and have attempted to explain the great variation in illegitimacy rates. Peter Laslett's (1977) work from a sample of ninety-eight parish registers in England suggests a rough demography of illegitimacy. His figures show a rise in the proportion of illegitimate births in the second half of the sixteenth century, followed by a trough during the more 'puritanical' Parliamentary era. The trend was upwards during the eighteenth century and then took a sharp rise at the start of the nineteenth. The Victorian period shows an apparent decline in illegitimacy, only to see the rate rise again in the twentieth century to reach an all-time high in the post-war period.

The illegitimacy rate is a dubious statistic, because it is another good example of the socially constructed nature of statistics. How accurate were the early parish records? To what extent did moral disapproval affect the public acknowledgement of pregnancy outside marriage? How may extra-marital conceptions were hidden by a speedy marriage? How widespread was abortion? Without answers to these questions it is difficult to assess the accuracy of the official statistics on illegitimate births (see pages 75–7).

Shorter (1976) argues that there has been a sexual revolution in the twentieth century, and he suggests that pre-marital intercourse is now more common than at any time since the Middle Ages. He maintains that the illegitimacy rate fell precipitously everywhere in the period 1900–40, not because of a drop in intercourse, but because of the more widespread use of contraception. But then this sexual revolution led to a post-war boom in illegitimacy, despite the widespread availability of contraception and abortion in countries like England, which mostly reduced illegitimacy amongst older unmarried women. It has been teenagers who have represented the biggest rise in illegitimate births. The revolution in sexual activity has been such that it leads Shorter to contend that 'sexual activity has changed from a dangerous and marginal aspect of relationships between the unmarried, to a central part of dating and mating'.

By the end of the 1960s, one in twelve of all maternities was illegitimate, and for births to young mothers under twenty years of age the figure was nearer to one in four. Attempts to explain this rise in illegitimacy have frequently adopted a pathological approach. Eekelaar (1971) argues that the increase was the result of personality factors, and in particular the social environment that the young parents had experienced as children. He points out that the young people of the 1960s had been born into the unsettled conditions of war-time, and had then experienced the austerity of the post-war period. He saw illegitimacy as part of a cycle of deprivation that might repeat itself over the generations.

The picture changed in the 1970s. It seems that widespread sex education in schools and the availability of contraception may have reduced the number of births to girls under 16. Since 1972 there has been a fall in the number of births to this group, and since 1976 a drop in the number of abortions. However, the drop in the legitimate birth rate means that the national figures appear to show a rising illegitimacy percentage. In 1982, slightly more than 14 per cent of all births in England and Wales were to single, widowed, separated or divorced women.

Illegitimacy is easier to define than to explain: it is the result of sexual activity outside marriage, without using contraception, followed by the decision not to marry or terminate the pregnancy. But it is still difficult to explain the patterns of illegitimacy. The researcher is intruding into within the commune. Emotional clashes, together with financial condemns illegitimacy as a social problem. But there is concern over the financial plight of the unmarried mother, and concern over the relatively high infant mortality rate for illegitimate births. Sociology should perhaps pay more attention to the reasons why a birth outside conventional marriage cannot be tolerated alongside the traditional concept of the family.

Alternatives to the family

There have been many attempts to develop alternatives to the nuclear family. The 'counter-culture' of the 1960s reawakened interest in communal living as an alternative life-style. Kanter (1972) suggests that communes have been part of three broad critiques of the social order: the religious, the politico-economic, and the psychosocial. Rigby (1974) puts even greater emphasis on the variety of commune living. He suggests that there are six types of commune: self-actualizing, mutual support, activist, practical, therapeutic, and religious.

Communes are seen as a means of providing economic and emotional support for a group of adults and children, while still allowing the individual the personal freedom to develop their own unique identity. But communes face specific problems: the recruitment of new members, economic survival, the tension of collective decision-making, personal relationships, and the socialization of young children.

Abrams and McCulloch (1975) suggest that it has been easier to change the personal relationships between adults, than between parents and children. Women in communes may be freed from some of the household tasks, but often remain tied by their responsibilities to their own children. The unattached mother and child form one of the potentially most disruptive forces in the delicate balance of relationships within the commune. Emotional clashes, together and financial insecurity, are major obstacles to the long-term survival of any commune.

The commune movement is too small to undermine the domination of the nuclear family, but it does provide an interesting alternative model. Sociologists have perhaps been too quick to concentrate on the more exotic groups, rather than to look at communes based on political or religious beliefs, which may provide a viable new form of the extended family.

The Israeli kibbutz tries to create a communal environment which is held together by the voluntary identification of the individual with a socialist, Zionist philosophy. Kibbutzim vary in size, organization and ideological outlook, but a central feature of most is collective production, collective decision-making and collective consumption. Members may share administrative responsibilities and rotate work tasks over a period of time. The provision of clothing and housing may be a group decision.

The kibbutz has tried to weaken the parent–child relationship, while strengthening the bond between the individual and the community. From when they are six weeks old, children are increasingly cared for by a children's nurse. The nurse, rather than the parents, copes with the emotional and educational problems of childhood. Schooling is designed to develop the personality while building loyalty to the community. Parents do see their children, but the system is geared to avoiding some of the emotional conflicts found in the nuclear family.

It was hoped that kibbutz life would allow women to break away from traditional occupational roles. However, it seems that women in the kibbutz are still concentrated in the traditional female service occupations of teaching, childcare and catering. There is also a move in some kibbutzim back to stronger ties between parents and children. But the kibbutz can still show us ways of taking some of the burden of responsibility out of the nuclear family, and is still an alternative form of family structure.

Governments sometimes try to alter the structure and role of the family. One example can be seen in the Soviet Union following the 1917 revolution. Measures were introduced to release women from their largely domestic status so that they could play a fuller part in the political and economic life of a socialist society. Divorce was simplified. Birth control and abortion were made easily available. Communal facilities for childcare and for communal dining were developed. The law gave women equal rights.

But by the early 1930s, the USSR had a high divorce rate, a high abortion rate, and juvenile delinquency was causing concern. However, the disruption of the Soviet family probably owed more to the forces of social change than to any clear government attack on the family as an institution. Civil war, famine, the collectivization of agriculture and the reorganization of industry all took their toll on family life.

The Soviet government, alarmed by the falling birth rate, changed the direction of its family policies. The state took a stricter attitude towards lax morality and instead glorified parenthood. Abortion was made illegal in 1936, and stricter regulations were brought in on marriage and divorce. The Second World War saw a catastrophic loss of population, so further measures were taken to encourage large families. Family allowances were increased in 1944, starting with the third child, and decorations were given to those having five or more children.

Bronfenbrenner (1968) suggests that it would be wrong to assume that Soviet policy has swung back to support a 'western style' family. He suggests that there are two main features of post-war family policy in the USSR. East–West conflict requires that the population be maintained at a high level, therefore reproduction is encouraged. But the state expects to play a major role in child-rearing, and has tried to increase the amount of boarding education and day-care facilities for children. The Soviet government takes the view that the early experience of communal living will allow the state to supervise the physical, mental and ideological development of its future citizens.

Conclusion

It should be clear from this chapter that the sociology of the family is a large and important area for study. The development of a more historically informed sociology, together with a more realistic appreciation of the broader role of women in society, is likely significantly to raise the level of sociological debate in this field.

The family survives as one of the crucial institutions of society. It will continue to evolve, and the next few decades may see radical changes in its structure and roles. Scientific developments have given us the capacity to control reproduction. Already we have seen doctors playing a major role in 'test-tube conception'. Social engineering on a large scale may be possible in the twenty-first century. It is therefore likely that the role of the family will become even more of a major social and ideological issue. The sociological analysis of the family should offer the necessary framework for that debate.

Guide to further reading

There is a vast range of literature on the sociology of the family. A student should start with one of the books which attempt to give a general view of the subject. Wilson (1985), *Family*, is a comprehensive survey of the field, written for the student new to the subject. Probably the two best theoretical overviews are found in Morgan (1975), *Social Theory and the Family*, and in Harris (1983), *The Family and Industrial Society*. These studies look at both the traditional structural approach to the family, and at some of the more critical approaches.

Bell and Newby (1971), *Community Studies: an Introduction to the Sociology of the Local Community*, gives a good introduction to the field, particularly if placed alongside the companion volume (1974), *The Sociology of the Community: A Selection of Readings*.

An excellent overview of research can be found in Rapoport, Fogarty and Rapoport (1982), *Families in Britain*. A good little reader on alternatives to the family is Gordon (1972), *The Nuclear Family in Crisis: The Search for an Alternative*. Oakley (1974) in *Housewife* gives a readable introduction to the rapidly expanding literature of women in the family. Kitzinger (1978) shows how motherhood varies from society to society in *Women as Mothers*. Students should also sample the contents of the two readers edited by Barker and Allen (1976a), *Dependence and Exploitation in Work and Marriage* and (1976b), *Sexual Divisions and Society: Process and Change*.

9 Education

Patrick McNeill

In a pre-literate society, the younger members learn what they need to know in order to become fully-fledged members of the society without ever attending any institution which we would recognize as a school. They learn language, norms, skills, values and beliefs from parents and other relatives, and perhaps from the tribal elders. The culture and the structure of the pre-literate society is reproduced and kept in being by the activities of its members. There is no important difference between 'socialization' and 'education'.

In a complex society such as ours, the different elements of the socialization process are more separated from each other. Formal education is carried out in specialist institutions, called schools or colleges, by specialist people, called teachers and lecturers. It is formally organized in terms of what is taught, where it is taught, to whom, and for how long. The child's learning of approved knowledge is tested in public examinations, which are organized bureaucratically and impersonally.

Children and young adults in Britain learn the culture (see Chapter 5, page 123) of their society just as they do in simple societies. But the complexity and variety of the culture, and the amount of subcultural variation, is much greater. The content of any one person's or group's education is inevitably only a selection from the whole. It is important to consider what is selected, who makes the selection and why.

The most obvious characteristic of education in complex industrial societies is its size. Size can be measured in terms of how much money is spent on it: some £14.8 million in 1982–3; or by how many people are employed in it: over 500,000 teachers, plus administrators, secretaries, officials, cleaners, cooks, technicians, groundstaff, caretakers. Or you can note the fact that nearly everybody in our society attends school between the ages of 5 and 16, and many stay longer; one in five of the population is in full-time education. However it is measured, education is massive.

In addition, education has long been regarded as a most important cause of the successes and failures of our society, particularly in economic terms. It is argued that, if only we could get our education system right (whatever 'right' means) then we would have a less divided, more just, more economically productive society. Politicians, employers, trade unionists, the police, magistrates, journalists and clergy all, from time to time, blame schools for the shortcomings of our society and especially of its younger members. Everyone has something to say about education, because everyone has some first-hand experience of it.

Education and politics in society

We must be very clear, right from the start, about one very important aspect of education. It is, in the broadest sense of this expression, a political activity. This does not mean that it is a party-political activity, though the major parties do disagree about various aspects of it. It means that education is seen as, and used as, an important means of influencing, and perhaps changing, the kind of society in which we live and the kind of people who live in it. What kind of society we want is, clearly, a matter of disagreement, and what kind of society we get is a result of decisions made by those in power. Many of the decisions they make are concerned with education: how much education there is to be; how it is to be provided; for whom it is to be provided; what it is to include; how 'success' in education is to be measured; and so on. All these are aspects of 'social engineering', and are guided by overall views of what kind of a society and what kind of people are wanted. Those who argue that we should keep politics out of education are either naive or deliberately misleading. The two cannot be separated, in theory or in practice. It makes as much sense to say 'keep politics out of education' as it does to say 'keep the liquid out of water'.

A history of mass education in England and Wales

Education for all is a recent arrival in Britain, compared with other European countries. We have a long history of monastic education for clerics, many ancient schools (both public and grammar) established for the education of the elite, and the two ancient universities of Oxford and Cambridge, but education for the mass of the population is a relative newcomer.

The early nineteenth century

It was the social and economic changes of the early stages of the Industrial Revolution that resulted, in the early nineteenth century, in discussions of whether the children of the poor and labouring classes should be educated. On the one hand, it was argued, in parliament and elsewhere, that basic standards of numeracy and literacy were essential if workers were to do their work properly, and, most importantly, to be brought to understand the essential justice of the social and economic order. On the other hand, it was argued that it was positively dangerous to teach the poor to read, since they would then be able to read 'seditious literature' and acquire all kinds of dangerous ideas. They would begin to question their station in life, and this would cause social unrest. It was also unfair to the poor, who would develop hopes of self-improvement that must, inevitably, be doomed to disappointment. Only the early socialists, Chartists, and others argued for mass education as a means of social justice. The authorities regarded the question as one of economic efficiency, the question being whether the risks of political dissent were outweighed by the possibility of the curriculum (what is taught in schools) being sufficiently under the control of the dominant groups in society that the 'gentling of the masses' might proceed. The Victorian authorities appeared absolutely certain of the rightness of the social order of the time, and of their own right to be at the head of it. Typically, they did not regard education as a means of providing equal opportunity, or of enabling the poor to climb the social scale.

The mid nineteenth century

The immediate outcome of these debates was the establishment of an Education Committee of the Privy Council in 1839 to keep an eye on the provision of elementary education by voluntary agencies such as the churches. Then, in 1858, the Newcastle Commission's report appeared. It was highly critical of contemporary standards of elementary education as provided by voluntary agencies, but concluded that a compulsory system was 'neither attainable nor desirable'. Elementary education for the poor and the working class was distinctly different from that available to the middle class and the rich. There were separate educational systems in nineteenth-century Britain, consciously shaped to reflect the facts of class inequality. Elementary schools were for the poor, secondary schools for the better-off. There was no route from elementary to secondary education.

The late nineteenth century

The first great Education Act, the Forster Act of 1870, did not change this. Rather, it ensured universal elementary education by giving power to the local School Boards to provide elementary schools in areas where they were not provided by voluntary agencies (though attendance was not compulsory until 1880). The 1870 Act helps to explain why there are so many primary schools today still in buildings dating from a hundred years ago. Huge numbers of schools were built at this time, and many have still not yet been replaced.

The next major Education Act was passed in 1902. This Act empowered, but did not require, the newly created Local Education Authorities (LEAs) to establish schools 'other than elementary'. These were to be firmly modelled on the pattern of the existing grammar schools. This ensured that all forms of post-elementary education stayed in the traditional pattern of an academic, literary, non-technical education. The fact that LEAs could choose whether to establish such schools is one of the root causes of the differences and inequalities in secondary education from area to area that continue to the present day.

The twentieth century

In 1907 a further Act was passed which made it possible for selected 11-year-old children to transfer to a grammar school. Others stayed in elementary school until the end of their school career. Thus was the basis for selection at 11-plus established.

In 1918 another major Education Act raised the school-leaving age to 14, and abolished all fees for elementary education. The Act also made provision for health care, physical education, and some social facilities.

In the period between the two world wars, a series of official inquiries, notably Hadow (1926) and Spens (1938), published their findings. These were heavily influenced by the view of the psychologists, especially Sir Cyril Burt, that intelligence was mainly inborn and that an individual's success or failure in school could be predicted by the scientific measuring of IQ (intelligence quotient). They recommended that children should be tested when they were eleven, and allocated to secondary schools which suited their type and level of intelligence. The Norwood Report of 1943 recommended that free secondary education, for all children from 11 to 15, should be provided in three types of school – Grammar schools for the academic child, Secondary Technical for the 'higher grade' of child with a more practical intelligence, and Secondary Modern for the 'lower grade' practical children.

'In 1944 there were three types of school: elementary for the working-class, secondary for the middle class (to join which schools, one working class child in seven might aspire), "public" or independent for the upper class' (Pedley 1963). The educational system still mirrored the class system.

The Education Act of 1944

The Butler Education Act of 1944 created the 'tripartite' (three parts) system of secondary education recommended by Norwood. It also created 'primary' education from 5 to 11, and the stages of 'further' and 'higher' education to follow the secondary stage. The Act aimed to provide 'free secondary education for all' according to their 'age, aptitude and ability' in schools which would enjoy 'parity of esteem', that is, they would have equal status. It is this Act which remains the basis for our present system of education. The many changes that have occurred in education since 1944 have all been carried out within the framework of the 1944 Act.

The private sector

It should be noted that the independent public schools came through all these inquiries and legislation virtually unscathed. They were required to meet certain minimum standards of health, hygiene and educational provision, but fundamentally they continued to perform their task of educating the elite 5 per cent of children for the elite positions that they would occupy as adults in society. Many new schools, both public and grammar, were opened in the nineteenth and twentieth centuries, most of them in the same mould as the older institutions, though some experimental schools were established, in an attempt to reform education from within.

Since 1944, there has been a whole series of Acts modifying aspects of the Butler Act of 1944. Many of these changes, at least until the late 1970s, were much influenced by the findings of educational sociologists, as we shall see in the next section. The most recent initiatives, those connected with 'vocational education', have been less influenced and welcomed by sociologists, and we will consider them on page 272.

Sociology and sociology of education

As you will have understood from earlier chapters in this book, sociology underwent important developments in the late 1960s and early 1970s. If you are still unsure about these, you should reread Chapter 2.

The sociology of education has both suffered and gained from these developments. Interpretive sociology (interactionism and phenomenology) made its major impact on British sociology mainly in the areas of deviance and of education. The revival of Marxist sociology has been particularly influential in those areas of sociology that deal with culture, knowledge and ideas, and therefore in education.

So great have these changes been that it has become customary to talk of 'old' or 'traditional' sociology of education and 'new' sociology of education, the changeover being dated at around 1970, though in the 1980s a merging or blending of the two has become apparent.

Structural-functionalism in the sociology of education

Until the 1950s, there was no formal sociology of education, largely because mass education in itself was a comparative newcomer. Of the classical sociologists, Emile Durkheim paid most attention to it. Durkheim (1922) argued that 'Education is only the image of and reflection of society. It imitates and reproduces the latter in abbreviated form, it does not create it'. He argued that the task of education was to prepare the child (usually male) for life in the wider society, and particularly for the social level in which he would find himself through his occupation. Education is 'a social means to a social end – the means by which a society guarantees its own survival'. The origins of the functionalist view of education are clear (see Chapter 2, page 29).

As we have seen, sociology in the 1950s was dominated by the structural-functionalist tradition, inherited from Durkheim and carried on through the work of Talcott Parsons in America. In considering education, this approach asks, 'What is the function of education? What part does it play in the social system? How does it meet the needs of society as a whole? What is the need of society that education particularly responds to?'

Relying mainly on the work of Talcott Parsons, we can answer these questions thus:

(a) Education performs a socializing function, transmitting the culture of the society to the new generation. It ensures continuity of norms and values, and thus the continued equilibrium of the society and the handing-on of skills. In the Parsonian system, education plays a vital part in the integration of a society, thus helping to satisfy one of the four 'functional imperatives' that all societies face (see Chapter 2, page 26). Parsons (1959) argues that the classroom is a kind of miniature society, 'an agency through which individual personalities are trained to be motivationally and technically adequate to the performance of adult roles'.

(b) Education also performs an important selection and allocation function, placing people in the appropriate place in the stratification system. This argument ties in with the functionalist theory of stratification (see Chapter 6), and with a belief in the importance of social mobility.

The educational system is the mechanism within which competition and selection take place. Society sorts its members into the more and less able, teaches them the skills and attitudes that they will require to play their part in society, and ensures that they are appropriately rewarded. (It is important to see how this same basic insight has been repeated by Marxists. The crucial distinction is that the normative functionalist stresses the needs of society, where the Marxist stresses the interests of the ruling-class.)

Structural-functionalism is thus concerned with society's need to ensure that its members' talents are used in the most efficient way. Any wastage of talent would be regarded as dysfunctional.

Efficiency and social justice

This theme of efficiency, using the 'pool of talent' to full effect, has been important in educational policy since the beginning of this century. Another major theme has been the injustice of any educational system that provided widely differing educational opportunity for its members, depending on their social class. 'The hereditary curse upon

English education is its organisation upon lines of social class' (Tawney 1931).

In England in the 1950s these twin themes, efficiency and social justice, came together particularly in the work of Floud and Halsey. These two attacked the post-1944 system of secondary education on both grounds. They were by no means purely structural-functionalist sociologists themselves, being quite aware of the shortcomings of that theory, and wholly committed to reforms of what they saw as social injustice in England. Their work is, nevertheless, firmly within the functionalist framework. It concentrates on the interrelations between education and the other major institutions of society, particularly the economic institutions (Halsey, Floud, Anderson 1961).

As we have seen, the 1944 Act, and the tripartite system it created, were based on the belief that intelligence was inborn, independent of socio-economic status, and that it could be reliably measured at the age of 11-plus by IQ tests, the results of which determined which type of school a child would attend. The declared intention was that these schools would be separate, different, but equal in importance and esteem. In practice, the 11-plus examination quickly became regarded as a pass/fail test, with the failures (some 80 per cent) going to the secondary modern schools. (Only a small number of secondary technical schools were ever established.)

Social class and educational achievement

Sociologists of the 1950s took on the task of demonstrating that the 11-plus, and thus grammar school selection, was loaded in favour of children from middle-class backgrounds. 'Class' was, fairly crudely, defined in terms of father's occupation, and research was usually based on either the Registrar-General's scale, or the Hall–Jones scale (see Chapter 6, page 158).

There is a wealth of research from both sociologists and official government reports, demonstrating the pro-middle-class bias of our educational system in the 1950s, particularly in relation to the vital stage of secondary selection. For instance, Floud, Halsey and Martin (1956) compared 11-plus selection in Middlesbrough and in south-west Hertfordshire. They found that in 1953, in Middlesbrough, about 12 per cent of working-class boys were admitted to grammar school, but about 30 per cent of the sons of clerks. The figures for south-west Hertfordshire were about 14 per cent of working-class boys and nearly half of the sons of clerks.

The *Early Leaving Report* (1954) particularly stressed the fact that children from R-G Classes IV and V entered grammar schools less than half as often as they might have been expected to. Once there, they were much less academically successful, and tended to leave school earlier.

In 1959 the Crowther Report claimed to show a large scale wastage of ability especially among those just below the 'very intelligent' level. While 71 per cent of the male children of professional workers (R-GI) went to selective or independent schools, only 18 per cent of semi-skilled and 12 per cent of unskilled workers attended selective and none attended independent schools.

In 1963 the Newsom Report stressed that 'the essential point is that all children should have an equal opportunity of acquiring intelligence, and developing their talents and abilities to the full'. It reported that the educational system fell far short of achieving that target.

In 1963, also, the Robbins Report compared the higher education achievements of those with IQs of over 130 (the top group), in terms of their social class. Of the sons of non-manual workers with high IQs, 37 per cent went on to degree courses, compared with only 18 per cent of the sons of manual workers. Robbins referred to an 'untapped pool of ability' among working-class children.

There is so much data like this that Ivan Reid has referred to its collection as becoming 'a veritable industry'. By 1965, D.F. Swift could write:

The basic facts of social class performance in school are so well known as hardly to need repeating. As all teachers know, the children who do the best work, are easiest to control and stimulate, make the best prefects, stay at school longest, take part in extra-curricular activities, finish school with the best qualifications and references and get into the best jobs, tend to come from the middle class. [Swift 1965]

It is a very short step from demonstrating that such inequalities exist to theorizing about the causes of them.

In all these studies, the causes were identified as being to do with the child's life outside the school, whether it be the neighbourhood in which he or she lived, the attitudes of the parents to education, the actual physical surroundings of the home, the size of the family or even the diet and physical condition of the child. At this stage, no significant voice was raised to question what was happening in the schools themselves.

The most common conclusion drawn was in terms of a theory of 'cultural discontinuity'. Put simply, this meant that the subculture of the working class, into which the child was socialized in the family home, was so different from that of the school that the working-class child found that school was unfamiliar and alien.

Thus, in an important study published in 1962, Jackson and Marsden reported that 'grammar school culture is an extension of the middle-class child's home life'. They also found that those working-class children who did succeed tended to come from smaller families and to have been 'pushed' by their parents. In addition, one-third of their successful working-class children had parents with middle-class con-nections. In order to succeed, the working-class children had to learn consciously to reject their class's way of life, and they became alienated from it.

J. W. B. Douglas, in *The Home and the School* (1964), found that children from the upper middle class were four times more likely to go to grammar school than those from the lower working class. Half the high ability children from lower-manual working-class homes left school by 16; only one-tenth of upper-middle-class children of high ability did so. This study pinpoints the attitudes of parents as being crucial, and related to class, as well as family stability, family size and the child's position in the family (older children did better). Support and encouragement from parents could, however, override other disadvantages, but was found more often in the upper middle and middle classes, in any case.

The *Early Leaving Report*, as early as 1954, had specified the importance of 'the outlook and assumptions of parents and children in various walks of life'. It also referred to income differences (which were relatively unimportant), bad living conditions (which were important, affecting sleep, study facilities, homework, etc.), and the influence of the neighbourhood in which a child lived.

This last item brings us back to class subcultures. Jackson and Marsden (1962) have vivid accounts of the experience of being the only grammar school child in the street. Conversely, better educated parents will know more about schools, examinations, careers and so on. They can help with homework, have more books in the house, are able to afford more extras: the list goes on and on.

Geographical variations are also important. LEAs varied in how many grammar school places they provided. Douglas (1964) found that the proportion of children at grammar schools varied from 18.9 per cent in central southern England to 35 per cent in south-west England. In the London Borough of Barnet 35 per cent of children went to grammar school and 16 per cent to university. In Barking, the figures were 9 per cent and 3 per cent. Substantial inequalities existed, and still exist, between LEAs in terms of how much they spend per child per year on education, how many nursery places they provide, and in average class sizes. In 1968, 33 per cent of 17-year-olds in Cardiganshire were still in school, compared with 8 per cent in Middlesbrough.

On a smaller scale, the neighbourhood is important. An important aspect of class inequality in Britain is that people of similar class and status tend to live in similar areas. Since schools, especially primary schools, draw most of their pupils from the neighbourhood around them, 'middle-class' schools and 'working-class' schools emerge. The former may expect to receive more support from parents and more pupils who are committed to academic work. Teachers may prefer to work there. The school's sixth form will be large, so more money will be available. The school's academic record will improve, and more parents will try to send their children there, so the school can select its pupils. Standards will rise. Exactly the opposite tendencies may tend to operate against a school in a working-class area and, at worst, a 'sink' school may develop, unless local decision-makers take positive steps to prevent this.

All this research can be summarized in terms of a theory of cultural difference between working-class children and the predominantly middle-class value-oriented school. As we have seen (in Chapter 5, page 126), sociologists regard language as the crucial factor in culture, and Basil Bernstein has spent twenty years developing and refining a theory of the relationship between language and educational success. He also shows how these are related to the wider context of changes in social organization and patterns of power and authority.

Bernstein distinguishes between 'elaborated' and 'restricted' language codes. The difference is not primarily one of vocabulary, but rather of how language is used to communicate. The *restricted* code is used to convey meaning to the members of a group who already share the basic assumptions and knowledge of the speaker. To the outsider, it is vague and imprecise, even impossible to understand. Thus, for example within a family, members can talk to each other using a minimum of words, partial sentences, and various grunts, gestures and slang expressions. The *elaborated* code is used when the speaker wishes to give full details of what he has to say, including explanation and details in such a way that others who share the code can also share the experience he is trying to convey. This is particularly important when a speaker is talking about something abstract rather than just describing an object or telling a factual story to a group of friends.

The link with education is that, in Bernstein's view, formal education is based on the use of the elaborated code. Teachers use it themselves, and reward pupils who make use of it in answering questions, discussing etc. Therefore children who are accustomed to using elaborated code as well as restricted code, and to the patterns of thought and the cultural assumptions that go with it, will find school a familiar experience. Those whose language is usually limited to a restricted code will find school life more difficult to latch on to.

The final link is that, in Bernstein's view, the restricted code predominates in working-class speech and the elaborated code in middle-class speech. Middle-class homes also, of course, have their restricted code, but children from such homes are not limited to such a code.

Bernstein's point is then that children from working-class homes are judged to be educationally inadequate because they are judged in terms of a language code and a culture which is not theirs. Bernstein has been repeatedly criticized for implying that working-class children are actually deficient in language. He insists that he is only pointing to a difference (Bernstein 1971, 1975).

The question of intelligence

It will be obvious, by now, that sociologists attach little importance to intelligence as the major factor influencing educational achievement, or to IQ tests as useful measures of intelligence.

As we have seen, Cyril Burt's view that intelligence was inborn and fixed had a powerful influence on the 1944 Education Act. Burt's own work has been largely discredited in recent years, but his approach has been carried on by Eysenck in Britain and by the American psychologist Jensen. These two have emphasized the importance of heredity in intelligence, and Eysenck argues that it is highly probable that children will be of similar intelligence to their parents. Jensen claims that heredity largely explains the poor educational achievement of American blacks compared with whites.

Sociologists' arguments against IQ testing and the related idea of inherited intelligence are various. Even if IQ scores are accepted as measuring something, it is still the case that people with similar IQs but from different social class backgrounds have differing educational success. It is also argued that IQ tests are biased in favour of middle-class and white children since they ask questions which children from those cultural backgrounds are more likely to be able to answer, because of the cultural assumptions which they share with the testers.

The basic argument against intelligence testing is that it mistakes cultural variety for differences in intelligence. What IQ tests do is to identify those children whose cultural norms are those of the educational system, give them high scores, and then claim that their success in education shows how reliable a predictor the IQ test is.

Sociology of education and social policy

The research findings outlined in the previous section exercised a strong influence on educational policy-makers, whether for reasons of 'efficiency' or of 'social justice'.

Human capital theory

Those who favoured efficiency arguments developed what has been called 'human capital theory'. They argued that one of the assets a society has is the potential skills and work-power of its members. This asset, like any other, should be developed to the full. Thus 'investment' in education, that is, spending money on it, would produce a 'return' (a skilled and educated labour-force) on the original 'capital' (the children and young people). This argument was at the root of the huge increase in educational spending in Britain in the 1960s, the growth of higher education after the Robbins Report, and the raising of the school-leaving age in 1973. It also encouraged the countries of the Third World to invest in education. The cuts of the 1970s and 1980s show how this view has fallen from favour.

Comprehensive schools

The first focus of attention was on the move towards comprehensive secondary schools, and the abolition of the 11-plus examination. This story reveals, above all others, how decisions about educational matters are thoroughly political in origin.

Some areas, notably London, had had some comprehensive secondary schools since 1945, that is, schools which took all the children from a particular area into a school large enough to provide the full range of school subjects at all levels of ability.

However, the evidence produced against selection prompted the newly elected Labour government to issue in 1965 a circular to LEAs (Circular 10/65) asking them to submit their plans for reorganizing their secondary schools on comprehensive lines. The major arguments put in favour of this move were that such schools were more economical to run, that they encouraged social mixing of children from different classes, that they provided greater freedom of subject choice for pupils, and that there was less risk of the 'late developing' child being held back as he or she might have been in a secondary modern school.

Some LEAs were firmly opposed to the scheme in any form. Others felt there were grave financial and organizational obstacles. In addition, a spirited defence of the grammar school was conducted, largely through the 'Black Papers' by writers such as Bantock, Cox, Boyson and others (Cox 1969). Their basic argument is that there is an elite of the most able children who must be identified early on by means of testing. They must be educated separately in schools geared to serious academic study in which 'high culture' could be preserved and developed. Such children could be found at all social levels, and they must be given the superior education of which they are capable.

However, by 1970 31 per cent of state secondary school children were in 'comprehensive' schools, and by 1973 the figure was 48 per cent. Such figures must be treated with caution, however, since many schools were in areas where a proportion of pupils had been 'creamed off' into grammar schools – to say nothing of those whose parents could afford to have them educated in the independent sector.

The Conservative government of 1970 withdrew Circular 10/65. Comprehensive reorganization was not forbidden, simply less encouraged, and it continued its slow progress. In 1972 the National Foundation for Educational Research reported fifty LEAs with no 11-plus selection, fifty-six with selection in part of their area, and fifty-five still selecting.

The Labour government elected in 1974 passed the 1976 Act which, among other measures, required LEAs to reorganize on comprehensive lines. The direct-grant grammar schools, which offered both fee-paying and free places, were required to choose whether to merge with the state system or to become fully independent. Some LEAs resisted these instructions, and took cases to the High Court. However, the 1979 Conservative victory at the general election took the pressure off these LEAs.

By 1978, 80 per cent of all state secondary pupils were attending schools that were comprehensive, at least in name. In the second half of the 1980s the issue of how to organize secondary education has been superseded by the question of what should be taught in schools and how it should be assessed.

Educational Priority Areas

The other major policy outcome of social research findings in education was the Educational Priority Area, or EPA.

The Plowden Report of 1967, which studied primary education in England and Wales, had found huge variation in the standard of primary schools, with the lowest standards in deprived, inner-city, working-class areas. In line with 'human capital' and 'social engineering' thinking, it recommended a policy of 'positive discrimination' in these areas. This meant that extra money could be spent to provide better buildings, more equipment, and more teachers even than in the well-off areas. In this way, standards would be levelled up, and disadvantage counterbalanced. In addition, a collective effort should be made by all the agencies involved to attack all forms of deprivation. Perhaps the most famous example of the EPA in action was in Liverpool, where Eric Midwinter generated great enthusiasm for the 'community school'.

The EPA echoed similar thinking and policies in the USA where the Higher Horizons programme (1956), the Great Cities School Improvement Programme (1960) and Project Headstart (1966) were all aimed at creating greater equality of educational opportunity by diverting extra money and resources into deprived areas, especially the black ghettos of the big cities (see also Chapter 3, page 80).

Sociologically, the key idea on which all these programmes rested was that of 'cultural deprivation', for which 'compensatory education' would be provided. It was argued that children from 'disadvantaged' backgrounds were deprived in terms of language, culture and experience. They were therefore unable to take proper advantage of the educational opportunities offered them in primary schools. There was a 'cultural discontinuity' between home and school, as a result of the poor standard of the home.

The solution to this problem is to take steps to ensure that all children start their school life with a more equal chance of making the most of what is on offer. Hence 'positive discrimination', 'EPAs' and the expansion of nursery education in the early 1970s.

Changes in the sociology of education

Until the end of the 1960s, most sociology of education had been in the structural-functionalist tradition, and had concentrated on the question of equality of opportunity. Most research had been positivistic in method. The findings were used to guide policy-makers in their attempts to increase the efficiency and the fairness of British education.

The end of the 1960s and the early 1970s saw an important change in these traditions. The 'new sociology of education' emerged and became quickly established, especially in colleges and universities where teachers were being trained.

There are three main reasons for this change:

1   The changes in sociological theory generally which occurred with the appearance in England of micro and interpretive sociologies, whose main research method was participant observation (see pages 43–4; 70–1).

2   The revival of Marxism in England and western Europe (pages 31–6).

3   The unavoidable fact that the education policies of the 1960s, prompted by sociological theories, had not produced the effects expected of them. Middle-class children were still doing better at all levels of education than their working-class counterparts. Thus Jencks (1972) showed how, in the USA, despite all governmental efforts, there had been little change in inequality of educational opportunity. The influence of home and class on educational achievement remained paramount. He concluded that attempts to reduce social inequality through education are doomed to failure. Halsey wrote in 1972 that 'the essential fact of twentieth-century educational history is that egalitarian policies have failed'. In 1978 he wrote 'the conventional picture of a steady trend towards equality (of educational chances) has been an optimistic myth'. In 1969, Ford had shown that comprehensive schools could reproduce all the inequalities of grammar and secondary modern schooling, by dividing their pupils into 'streams' by ability, and treating them differently.

When considering these more recent studies, however, we must remember that the differences between the *-isms* and the *-ologies* of sociology are matters of emphasis rather than complete differences. They are aids to understanding rather than hard statements about what sociology is 'really' like (see page 44).

Recent researches in the sociology of education are the result of a variety of influences coming together in one piece of work. Very little research can be said to be wholly or only within this or that sociological perspective. None can be said to be entirely the result of the influence of one single school of thought. A preferred theoretical slant results in certain kinds of questions being asked and others not; a preferred model of the individual and society results in particular research methods being employed. But these matters are never clear-cut.

Marxism

Marx himself wrote very little about education. But there are two themes, related to each other, in Marx's writings, from which the Marxist influence on the sociology of education has grown. These themes can each be illustrated with a quotation from Marx:

1 'The sum total of the relations of production constitutes the economic structure of society – the real foundation, on which legal and political superstructures arise and to which definite forms of social consciousness correspond. The mode of production of material life conditions the general character of the social, political and spiritual processes of life' (Marx 1859). This is the clearest statement in Marx of his theory that the economic structure of society has a profound, even determining, influence on the way in which the other institutions of society are organized. Those who have economic power in captialist society, the owners of the means of production, the ruling class, also dominate all other institutions – including education.

2 'The ideas of the ruling class are, in every age, the ruling ideas: i.e. the class which is the dominant material force in society is at the same time its dominant intellectual force. The class which has the means of material production at its disposal, has control at the same time over the means of mental production. . . . The dominant ideas are nothing more than the ideal expression of the dominant material relationship' (Marx 1845). Here, Marx is arguing that the ruling class also controls the ideas and the knowledge that are available in a society. Ultimately, the most effective method of dominating others is not by force, but by controlling their thinking to such an extent that your power is entirely accepted, and nobody even thinks of challenging it. Yours is the dominant ideology.

Reproduction

For Marxists, then, education reproduces the existing class structure, with all its oppression and exploitation. It is reproduced both materially (that is, in inequalities of wealth and income) and culturally (that is, the attitudes and values of the members of the different classes).

For the Marxists, the fact that working-class children do not do as well in education as middle-class children is no mystery, but rather an integral part of the reproductive mechanism of capitalist society. It is a serious error to see education as a sorting system to sift out the talent in a society. Rather, it should be seen as the arrangement whereby inherited economic privilege and power is converted into a more socially acceptable form. The continued existence of the public schools, and the continued domination of the elite positons in our society by ex-public school products is further evidence of this process.

It follows from this analysis that no amount of tinkering with selection methods, comprehensive schools or EPAs will make any real difference. Only revolutionary changes in the ownership of the means of production, and hence in the whole society, will produce the desired changes.

Cultural reproduction is the vital element. For ruling-class domination to continue, it is essential that suitable ways of thinking, feeling and expressing oneself should be regarded as natural and inevitable. Assumptions that there are 'natural' leaders and 'natural followers', or that people can be shown to be more 'intelligent' than others, are ideology disguised as science. 'Intelligence' itself is not a scientific absolute. 'Operational definitions of intelligence are, in short, never value free; they always have social, cultural, ideological and political assumptions behind them' (Squibb 1973). Many sociologists would accept this statement; what the Marxist sociologist emphasizes is that the use of the concept of intelligence in education has served the political and economic interests of some groups to the detriment of others. Testing disguises privilege behind a scientific mask, and reproduces it.

Varieties of Marxism
Within Marxism, two major variations on this central theme can be identified. One follows in the more materialist and determinist tradition of Marxism, which argues that history progresses according to its own laws, and that there is nothing people can do to influence this. The other is in the more humanistic or voluntarist tradition of Marxism, which accepts the basic Marxist view but argues that, given the necessary insights, class-consciousness and organization, people can affect their own destiny by hastening the progress of history.

Louis Althusser, a French Marxist, belongs in the more determinist tradition. He argues that the state, the main instrument through which the ruling class dominates, is made up of two elements – the Repressive State Apparatuses (RSAs) and the Ideological State Apparatuses (ISAs).

The RSAs employ force and coercion, usually in ways that are regarded as necessary and legitimate. They include the police, the courts, the prisons and the armed forces. Their task is to repress dissent, with the use of legitimate force.

The ISAs' task is to develop and reproduce the values, attitudes and culture which will ensure the continued stability of the state. They include the family, religion and education.

Clearly, and vitally, the more successful the ISAs are in their task, the less work there is for the RSAs, and the more stable is the domination of the ruling class.

In our society, education has replaced the church as the most important ISA. It takes all children into compulsory schooling and teaches them skills and the dominant ideology. It ejects most of them into low-status occupations or unemployment at the age of 16; some are retained until 17 or 18 and are placed in middle-range and white-collar jobs; a selected few (mostly the children of the dominant class) are raised to the educational peaks, where they are trained in their future tasks as members of the ruling class, or their agents. Education is not free, but a servant of the state machine (Althusser 1971).

Antonio Gramsci, an Italian communist who did most of his important writing while being held in jail by the fascists in the 1930s, is in the more humanistic Marxist tradition. He places less emphasis on the structural aspects of education and class society, and more on the cultural aspects.

He argues that the most important weapon in the armoury of the ruling class is their 'cultural hegemony', that is, their ability to dominate culture, knowledge, etc., mainly via the educational system. But he believed that the superstructure of society, including ideology, is not an inevitable and fixed consequence of the economic base. He believes that it is possible for men working together in society to subvert, challenge and undermine the dominant ideology. In this way they can take the first steps towards changing the underlying economic relationships that are, in the end, crucial. It follows that the task of the revolutionary is to challenge 'cultural hegemony' and to develop the class-consciousness of the masses through, above all, the educational system.

A very influential book written from a Marxist stand-point has been *Schooling in Captialist America* by Bowles and Gintis (1976). They maintain that schools in America (and in all capitalist societies) reproduce skills, ideology and class-consciousness, and hence the social relations of the class structure. 'The social relations of schooling are best seen as reproducing the social relations of capitalist production, and thus the sort of personality attuned to working contentedly under that mode of production.' They make specific recommendations about the action that a revolutionary teacher, educationist or student might take.

Summary and criticism

Functionalists and Marxists thus ask the same macro-sociological questions about education, but come up with very different answers. Where the functionalist talks of the transmission of culture and the continued stability of the society, the Marxist talks of the reproduction of cultural hegemony and continued domination by the ruling class. Where the functionalist talks of the sifting of talent and the selection of the most able for the most important positions, the Marxist talks of the reproduction of privilege and the legitimation of class domination. Where the functionalist talks of order, the Marxist talks of domination.

As always with Marxist analysis, the whole argument rests on certain basic assumptions about the nature of capitalist society. Thus a criticism of Marxist theory of education cannot be separated from a general criticism of Marxist theory. Among Marxists themselves, the major debate concerns the 'structure/consciousness dialectic', that is, the argument about how far the processes they identify are inevitable and how far they can be changed by deliberate, conscious, collective action.

A more empirically-based criticism comes from those with an interest in social mobility. Halsey *et al.* (1980) specifically reject the thesis of the reproduction of the class system. They show that 'the educational system has undoubtedly offered chances of securing cultural capital to large numbers of boys to whom the ethos of the grammar and technical schools was new'. (See also pages 179 and 270-1.)

The enormous contribution of Marxist theory has been to remind us that education is inescapably bound up with the rest of the social structure. It successfully challenges the now rather naive-looking belief of the 1960s that education is in some way an independent element in society, capable of being manipulated so as to change the rest of the society. The other major contribution of Marxism has been to remind us that wherever disputes occur, they are resolved in a way that is more to the advantage of some people than of others. As far as that insight goes, it is not a monopoly of Marxism. But Marxism challenges us to reflect more deeply into the origins of the power that enables certain groups in society to ensure, over and over again, that the disputes and conflicts are resolved in their favour.

Symbolic interactionism

Functionalism and Marxism tend to ask the same kinds of questions about education, though answering them in very different ways. The novelty of the new interpretive sociology of education is that it asks completely different questions.

The interpretive perspective starts from the assumption that people (actors) make sense of the social world through their interaction with others. For example, pupils behave as they do in the classroom because they perceive it as a classroom, and they perceive it as a classroom because they interpret the behaviour of the other people there (teacher and pupils) in accordance with their previous experience of how people behave in classrooms. But they *could* choose to behave differently, they are not *forced* to behave as they do. The interactionist must consider the actor's definition of the situation. Behaviour is explicable when it is understood from the point of view of the actor.

When studying education, therefore, interactionists start in the classroom, which is where they claim the action is. The classroom relationship of pupils and teacher is the crucial relationship, for it is here that 'reality' is negotiated. It is here that pupils acquire the identity of being 'clever' or 'stupid', 'idle' or 'hard-working'. It is in terms of these labels that pupils and teachers interact with each other, and thus ultimately produce educational 'success' and 'failure'.

The criticism that symbolic interactionists level at both functionalists and Marxists is that they treat the school as a 'black box', into which children of varying classes and types are fed, and out of which they emerge, duly processed. The interactionist insists that it is essential to get into the school and into the classroom and to study how this process actually operates.

Early researches in the school

The application of symbolic interactionist research methods to schools is relatively recent in Britain, but there were signs of such work at the end of the 1960s. Earlier studies of schools as organizations had been made, but Hargreaves (1967), Ford (1969) and Lacey (1970) opened up new ideas by showing how subcultures emerged in schools as a result of the way in which they were organized. Hargreaves, by participant observation, showed that by the fourth year in a secondary modern school, two main subcultures had emerged, the 'academic' and the 'delinquescent', and he described them in detail. These subcultures reinforced the values of the homes from which the pupils came. Lacey found a similar situation in a grammar school, where he showed that, when the differences between the children were confirmed by 'streaming' (that is, grouping children into teaching groups according to their measured ability), an 'anti-group' was produced, which was opposed to the dominant culture of the school. Ford (1969) showed how, in a comprehensive school, the practice of streaming children by 'ability' tended to reproduce the social class difference previously found between grammar and secondary modern schools.

Though emphasizing the way in which the organization of schools created subcultures, these studies all included the idea that membership of these subcultures resulted in behaviour which 'fitted' with how the pupils saw themselves and their place in school. The most important organizational factor was streaming, but the particular theoretical point developed by symbolic interactionists is that streaming encourages in children an 'ability identity', that is, a view of themselves as clever, average or stupid. This identity results in the very kind of performance which it is supposed to reflect. Streaming thus becomes a 'self-fulfilling prophecy'. That is, children are placed in high or low streams according to their supposed ability; teachers and pupils interact in accordance with the label which has been assigned to the pupil; children labelled 'stupid' are treated by teachers as stupid children; their actions are interpreted in terms of the known fact of their stupidity; as a result, children come to accept the label, internalize the identity, behave accordingly, and thus fulfil the prophecy. In the same way, when a teacher interacts with a child to whom the label 'clever' has been attached the child reacts accordingly.

The question then arises: 'How do teachers decide that a child is clever or stupid?' Is it, as no doubt we would like to believe, a result of their unbiased assessment of the child's ability, based on evidence? Or is it the result of stereotypes (often learned in sociology courses) about 'poor homes', 'good homes', 'black children', 'culturally deprived', etc? Evidence from many sources supports the view that teachers, like all other social actors, respond to other people (in this case pupils) in terms of cues and clues given in their immediate appearance and behaviour, and interpreted in terms of class stereotypes carried in teachers' heads. Alan Little (1978) suggested, for example, that the relatively poor school performance of children of West Indian origin can partly be explained in terms of what teachers expect of them (although subsequent local surveys have produced contradictory evidence of performance) (see also pages 269–70)

Research in the classroom

Recently, symbolic interactionist studies have been firmly located in the classroom itself, and often overlap very much with more phenomenological questions. Researchers observe interaction between pupils and teacher and attempt faithfully to record what is going on, from the participants' point of view.

It is in the nature of this kind of research that it is impossible to sum it up briefly. It does not reach 'conclusions' about 'causes' of this or that event. It is descriptive, and descriptions cannot easily be summarized. Also, though many such studies have been made in the USA, they are fairly new in Britain. Nash (1973) tried to show the relationship between pupils' self-images, pupils' perceptions of each other, teachers' conceptions of pupils, and the result in terms of pupils' classroom behaviour and attainment. Hammersley (1974) tries to identify exactly what a teacher means by 'order' in class, how it is negotiated between teacher and pupils, and how a teacher recognizes whether or not it has been achieved. Hargreaves (1975) uses a version of labelling theory to study deviance in classrooms.

This kind of work, done in British classrooms, is well summarized in Delamont (1976). Some have studied how the physical layout of a classroom both reflects and influences the interaction that takes place within it. Others have shown how pupils and teachers build up their own 'meaning systems', that is, their own special way of understanding each other. Researchers have studied the role of teachers, and how individual teachers bring their own unique interpretation to the expectations of that role, within the limits set by the wider setting. Similarly, the role of pupil is described, and the processes whereby pupils and teachers 'size each other up' in the classroom. (See also Woods 1980a, 1980b.)

Teachers typically try to impose their definition of the situation ('I'm in charge here') by doing most of the talking and by trying to catch and keep pupils' attention, mostly by asking questions and insisting on answers. While talking, teachers define, directly or indirectly, what counts as good work, an intelligent answer, silliness and so on. Pupils are controlled largely through reward and punishment, especially the threat of public shame. Pupils' strategies are, mainly, to find out what the teacher wants and to deliver it. But if no gain is apparent, disruption is likely. Pupils seek approval from their friends and equals as much as from teachers. If what friends approve of is very different from what the teacher wants, there is likely to be a good deal of classroom conflict and of what the teacher would regard as deviance.

Summary and criticism

The most important criticism levelled at symbolic interactionism as it first developed in the USA, especially in connection with deviancy and labelling theory, is that it failed to take into account the fact that social interaction takes place in a wider context. In other words, that micro face-to-face relationships occur within a wider structural framework. This wider framework means that some people have more power than others to define situations, and to attach and to resist labels.

This criticism has been accepted by some interactionists studying education. Interactionist studies of schools and classrooms have often recognized that teachers have more power than pupils, and that this power is a result of wider authority relations in society, but also that teachers are themselves by no means free to choose how their classrooms will be run.

When reading and considering these detailed 'ethnographic' studies, the student must always be aware of the social structure within which the interaction described has taken place.

Phenomenology

Phenomenological sociology asks the basic question, 'How is it that social beings come to interpret the world around them in ways so similar to each other that social life is made possible?' The answer to the question is that actors are in fact creating or constructing social reality at the same time as they interpret it. Social reality is what people make it. People construct social reality by giving meaning to events. The process is all one.

This means that for the phenomenologist there is no fixed, final, absolute social reality. What counts as 'real' is that which is defined as real by the members of the social group in question. All facts are not absolute but *relative* to time, place and social context. Though most people, most of the time, take most of their experience for granted, this is only possible because we are equipped with a whole set of theories, categories and explanations which make it possible for us instantly to identify any situation. We do this so automatically that the world appears natural to us, and we take it for granted.

Phenomenological sociologists go about their business by suspending (or 'bracketing') all their taken-for-granted knowledge about society. They ask exactly the question that normally we do not ask: What kind of a situation is this? How do people know that it is that kind of a situation? How do they make it that kind of situation? What are the rules they are following that confirm to them and to others what kind of a situation it is? Why is it that and not some other way? Imagine, if you can, the proverbial visitor from another planet seeing your sociology classroom for the first time. They could have no idea what was going on and, if you asked them, they could only explain it in terms of some experience of their own. They would produce what you would regard as a hopelessly 'wrong' account of what was happening. Now think about how it is that you can recognize your classroom as such, and how your recognizing it makes you behave in a way that makes it a classroom. All these rules, rituals and routines are what the phenomenologist wants to identify.

M. F. D. Young's *Knowledge and Control* (1971) is a collection of essays, much influenced by phenomenology and by Marxism, which shows how very attractive the idea of 'relativism' is to those who wish to change the kind of society we live in. If it can be shown that what we take to be natural or inevitable ways of life are in fact relative, then it is at the same time proved that they could be different. Instead of merely analysing society, we can discuss the possibility of changing it.

Young argues that the weakness of the traditional sociology of education was that it took as its problems for study the same problems as educators identified, and it took for granted the same things as they did, for example, the problem of working-class failure in education. Since it failed to question the assumptions underlying these problems, it could not get any further than commonsense did, although in a more scientific-looking form. Young insisted that sociologists should 'make' rather than 'take' their problems, and should examine the taken-for-granted ideas underlying education and schooling.

The major objects of inquiry thus become:

1 The categories which educationists use, for example, 'clever', 'under-achievement', 'failure', 'intelligence', 'learning', 'deprivation', 'schooling'. What do these words actually refer to, and how are these social categories constructed by pupils and teachers on a face-to-face basis?

2 What counts as school knowledge and why? Why is some knowledge regarded as important and other as less so? Why are 'subjects' divided up from each other as they are?

The first question is of specialist interest, particularly for student teachers. The second question raises much more general points, and it is this one that we will pursue here.

The sociology of school knowledge

Of the vast mass of human knowledge, what is defined as suitable for teaching in schools? Even more importantly, why is it so defined, and by whom? Why do we learn algebra but not bricklaying? Why does an A-level in sociology count for more when going for a job than a knowledge of the income tax system? Why do human biology syllabuses include so much on reproduction and so little on contraception?

Answers to these questions are provided in terms of a more or less Marxist phenomenology, which says that the way knowledge is regarded in society is a result of who has power to define it, a view developed in feminist terms by Spender (1982) (see pages 128–30).

Young (1971) discusses the stratification of knowledge, and the way that some 'subjects' are given more prestige than others. (Max Weber had tackled this same question in an essay published in 1920 called 'The Chinese Literati'.) Young argues that the powerful in society define what is to be taken as school knowledge, and control the distribution and the 'ownership' of this knowledge. High-status knowledge tends to be abstract, literary and unrelated to practical everyday things. Young shows how schools distribute high-status knowledge to high-status pupils, and low-status knowledge to low-status pupils.

In the same book, Bernstein states: 'How a society selects, classifies, distributes, transmits and evaluates the educational knowledge it considers to be public reflects both the distribution of power and the principles of social control.' This is a most important statement of this approach, and the quotation is well worth considering carefully and at length.

In another essay Keddie combines symbolic interactionism and phenomenology in a study of what counts as knowledge in the classroom. She shows that, though teachers claim that they recognize ability in children regardless of their manner or class background, when they get into the classroom their judgement is related to their perception of a child's social class. She reaches the conclusion that 'it would seem to be the failure of high ability pupils to question what they are taught in schools that contributes in large measure to their educational achievement' (Keddie 1971).

Criticism

The major criticism made of this approach to knowledge is that it is endlessly relativistic. The problem is that, if all your knowledge is relative to social context then even the fact that you know that it is, is itself relative to social context, and even the fact that you know that ... and so on for ever. Thus there is no longer any way of distinguishing 'right' from 'wrong', 'good' from 'bad', or 'sense' from 'nonsense'.

The other major criticism is from those who argue that the stratification of knowledge, and its division into subjects, are not social constructs at all. Some types of knowledge *are* more important than, and superior to, others. It is not just a matter of social convention, and certainly not of the influence of powerful people. They may try to keep certain knowledge to themselves, but that is quite another matter (Pring 1972).

The hidden curriculum

The official curriculum is the subjects that are taught in school. The term 'hidden curriculum', coined by Jackson (1968), refers to the fact that pupils learn many things in school that are not actually taught, for example, how to respond to and cope with authority, how to get on with others, how to pass the time, how to deal with boredom, how to establish priorities, how to conform as one of a crowd, and so on. Studies of it have been especially popular with researchers who wish to show that, whatever the official goals of education may be, what actually happens is more to do with control, domination, and the consequent reproduction of social inequality.

The hidden curriculum can be traced in both the formal organization of schools, and in interaction in classrooms. Bernstein, Elvin and Peters (1966) showed how school organization emphasizes hierarchy, authority and power, and encourages these by way of competition, rewards and grading. 'The school itself symbolizes and celebrates the social order to come.' The basic value that is rewarded is conformity and obedience to authority.

The hidden curriculum of the classroom is set in the wider formal structure of the school, but can vary from teacher to teacher. Pupils have to learn the unspecified and taken-for-granted rules of the classroom, and of particular classrooms. Behaviour that is acceptable in the art room is not acceptable in a maths class. Pupils and teachers must size each other up and devise strategies for success and survival. Pupils must learn how to lie and to evade. There is an 'unwritten body of shared understandings which determines the behaviour of the classroom' (Gleeson 1977).

The more Marxist-influenced of these writers (for example, Dale 1977) would argue that the hidden curriculum is much more important than the official curriculum for the basic function of schooling, that is, the production of a labour-force with the 'right' attitudes to work and authority. The hidden curriculum was not hidden at all in the Victorian elementary school, but was open and applauded. It only became hidden when the rulers were satisfied that it was working.

Deschooling

The deschooling movement of the late 1960s and early 1970s was based on the same assessment of the hidden curriculum. Illich, Holt, Goodman and others argued that 'education', which they regarded as a liberating, creative process, was actually suppressed by schooling. True education can only be achieved in a free atmosphere, and schools actively repress that. 'The hidden curriculum of schooling initiates the citizen to the myth that bureaucracy guided by scientific knowledge is efficient and benevolent . . . and everywhere it develops the habit of self-defeating consumption of services and alienating production, the tolerance for institutional dependence, and the recognition of institutional rankings' (Illich 1971). The only way to create a truly open society with a truly free and educative culture is to abolish schools.

The deschoolers enjoyed a considerable vogue for several years, but are not so seriously regarded today. Hargreaves (1974) calls them the 'new romantics': they have romantic ideas but very little to offer in the way of practical policy.

Cultural deprivation reassessed

Keddie (1973) argued that 'cultural deprivation' is a contradiction. By definition, every social being has a culture of some kind. Everyone has a way of looking at the world and of interpreting what is going on. This is meaningful to them in their social context, and is adequate to their needs. So, what is the 'culturally deprived' child actually deprived of? Keddie's answer is that what is 'lacking' is 'mainstream' culture, and that this is white middle-class minority culture, which dominates school. The child is not so much deprived, or deviant, as different. But this difference is rejected by the educational system, and the child is 'failed' for it. Keddie suggests that, rather than expecting most school-children to adapt to the alien culture of school, and calling them 'failures' because they do not, schools should move closer to the culture and experience of the children.

Labov (1969) has criticized Bernstein's work on language codes. He maintains that the restricted code of working-class and black children recorded by Bernstein and others is to a great extent the result of the situation in which the research was done. Research interviews would be perceived as threatening by such children, and their defence is to become silent and inarticulate. When they talk among themselves such people are capable of expressing ideas just as abstract, subtle and universal as any white middle-class speaker. The greater command of syntax and vocabulary of the 'elaborated code' often conceals some very shallow thinking.

Bernstein (1970) attacks the associated concept of 'compensatory education' on similar lines. The phrase concentrates the attention on the supposed shortcomings of the individual and the family. It assumes that what schools are offering is unquestionably right and that the 'fault' for working-class failure lies in the children and their homes. But, says Bernstein, if education means anything, it means providing whatever will enable children to develop their potential. It must start where they are, even if this means challenging the schools' accepted culture and concepts of valid knowledge.

The public schools

To a visitor to Britain, the public schools, the elite of the private, fee-paying sector of secondary education, are perhaps the most remarkable aspect of the educational system, but little sociological investigation of them has been done.

In broad terms, the public schools continue to do what they have done for centuries, namely educate and train the children (mostly sons) of the social, economic and political elites for the elite positions in society. It would be wrong to under-estimate the changes in these schools in recent years as far as curriculum, teaching methods, community links, going co-educational and so on are concerned. But it would be even more mistaken to over-estimate these changes or the extent to which the schools have become open to the children of any social stratum other than the top.

Such research as has been done has mostly been of the 'black box' variety, that is, studies of the pupils entering the school and their social class position (the input), and of their careers afterwards (the output). Statistical details can be found in Reid (1977), Boyd (1973) and elsewhere, but the general picture is that two-thirds or more of the elite positions in the civil service, the courts, the church, industry and commerce, and Conservative governments are held by ex-public school pupils. Of the twenty-two senior members of the 1979 Tory government, twenty had attended public schools, six of them being Old Etonians.

There is very little research material on life inside public schools. There are some very personal accounts, either vigorously for or vigorously against the schools. Royston Lambert has, however, collected some accounts by pupils of boarding school life in *The Hothouse Society* (1968), and *The Cloistered Elite* by Wakeford (1969) is another important source. The concept of the 'total institution' developed in Goffman's *Asylums* (1961) also throws a great deal of light on these schools.

This lack of material reflects an important fact about sociological research: it is relatively easy to gain access to data about those lower down the social scale, but very difficult to collect data about the wealthy and powerful, who are in a position to keep the details of their lives to themselves.

Recent developments in the sociology of education

By the end of the 1970s, the main perspectives in the sociology of education were established. Work since then has largely been a matter of developing these approaches, and applying them to aspects of education that had hitherto received little attention.

For example, interest has continued to focus on inequalities of opportunity and of achievement in education. However, where social class was the key variable in the work of the 1960s and 1970s, gender and race have received much more attention recently.

Women and education

Chapter 12 includes a section on this topic, so only a few observations will be made here.

In the primary stage of education, girls' level of achievement in literacy and numeracy is at or above that of boys. After the primary stage, the position changes. In the 1950s and 1960s, the data showed consistent under-achievement by girls in secondary examinations, but the picture is now more complex. Girls now pass slightly more GCE O-levels and there is little difference at A-level as far as overall passes are concerned. Within this general picture, however, there are substantial differences in subject choice, where, despite the Sex Discrimination Act, various pressures still encourage girls towards the arts and domestic subjects and away from the physical sciences, mathematics and technological subjects. Beyond school, admissions to higher education are still predominantly male, and traditional subject choice is still apparant, with many girls in, for example, English degrees, and many boys in engineering. Though this picture is changing, the changes are gradual rather than overnight. In addition, cuts in higher education spending have tended to hit those areas which have attracted a relatively high proportion of women.

Explanations for female under-achievement have been similar to those for class under-achievement. Parental attitudes and support are often greater for boys than for girls, especially in working-class homes. Girls' expectations of their own future roles are formed in the home, in the peer group, and via the mass media. They may be reinforced in school, through classroom interaction (Stanworth 1983) and through the curriculum, both official and hidden (Spender 1982). Just as schools reproduce class privilege and inequality, so they reproduce male privilege and patriarchy, the associated exploitation of women, and the cultural values to legitimate such a system. Nevertheless, schools, as a part of the wider society, cannot be held entirely responsible, nor can they be expected to change things on their own.

Race and education

The educational achievement of children from ethnic minorities has attracted both official and sociological interest. However, there was little systematic research during the 1960s and 1970s, other than the ILEA Literacy Survey (Little 1978). The issue was not officially highlighted until the Rampton Committee was set up in 1979. The committee made its interim report in 1981 (Rampton 1981). Its final report, under the chairmanship of Lord Swann, included the statistics reproduced in Table 14.

Although these show a less uneven picture than did those of the Rampton report, the overall position is clear. In addition, ethnic minority children are under-represented in selective schools, over-represented in the lower streams of state schools, and over-represented in special schools (Coard 1971). Boys of West Indian origin under-achieve the most, followed by West Indian girls. Children of Asian origin have roughly similar levels of achievement to those of British-born whites. What explanations have been offered?

In such a sensitive area of debate, any explanation tends to be vilified by someone. It is clear, for example, that West Indian children's under-achievement is associated with poor housing, overcrowding, working mothers with poor child-care facilities and related problems. Further-more, it is argued, West Indian parents, while very keen to see their children do well in school, may be less able to provide the necessary support at home. This, combined with the view that there may also be language problems associated with the use of the Creole dialect, all sounds very much like the theories of cultural deprivation we have met before (page 250) and are therefore open to the same criticisms (page 266). Therefore, those who have suggested that the causes of under-achievement lie in the home background may be accused of racism. It may in fact be the case that what we are looking at here is best seen as

Table 14 *Educational achievement and ethnic origin in six LEAs (1981–2)*

	West Indian (%)	Asian (%)	All others (%)
CSE 1 or GCE O-level grades A–C			
(a) English Language	15	21	29
(b) mathematics	8	21	21
(c) in 5 subjects	6	17	19
GCE A-level pass in at least one subject	5	13	13
University degree	1	4	4
Other degree	1	5	5

SOURCE: Swann (1985)

working-class disadvantage aggravated by racial disadvantage.

To explain the difference between the achievements of those of West Indian and those of Asian origin it has been suggested that, whereas the cultural identity of Asians is relatively well-founded and supportive, West Indians' history of slavery and cultural devastation has left them without such an identity, and with a poor self-image. This is further compounded by their experience of racism in British society. Those who do accept British culture (whatever that is) will also learn to denigrate blackness, and will thus acquire a negative self-image.

Those who favour this culturally-based explanation of under-achievement advocate multi-cultural education, and perhaps the introduction of 'Black Studies', as a means of raising the status of ethnic minority cultures in schools. Such a solution is rejected by those who see the problem as essentially one of class and of social structure, which will not be changed by any amount of cultural activity.

Others (including the Rampton report) have looked to the educational system for their explanation. They argue that schools incorporate a white middle-class culture, which is apparent in teaching and assessment methods, and in an ethnocentric curriculum (i.e. centring on a white British way of looking at the world, as in history, geography, literature and so on), which devalues the black and West Indian experience and culture. The values of the school may lead teachers to interpret the differences of West Indian children as being deficiencies. In addition, pupil–teacher interaction may involve racist stereotyping by teachers, as well as genuine misunderstandings originating in culture clashes which operate to the disadvantage of the pupil. Teachers' attitudes have, according to Rampton, a 'direct and important bearing' on the performance of black pupils.

This analysis is confirmed by a sociologically far superior study (MSHE 1985). Both the survey and two detailed case studies carried out by Wright found strong evidence of discrimination against black pupils. Afro-Caribbean pupils met, or felt they met, racial prejudice from teachers and, in about the third year of secondary schooling, started to react with difficult behaviour and loss of interest in their work. As a result, they tend to be allocated to lower sets than their ability suggested they should be in. Though they started secondary school with an average reading age similar to that of other children, they left with fewer qualifications and much less chance of a job. Wright records many conversations with teachers which show that the pupils were justified in accusing their teachers of racism.

Social class and education

The work of the Oxford Social Mobility Group has produced a mass of data about the 10,000 men it surveyed in 1972, much of which is relevant to our concerns here. Halsey *et al.* (1980) used data collected by the main survey to look again at the link between education and class origins. They divided the population into a service class of managers and professionals (about 13 per cent), an intermediate class of clerical and service workers, people running small businesses, foremen, etc. (about one-third), and a working class of manual employees (just over half). They found that, while a higher proportion of working-class boys stayed on at school until they were 16 in the 1960s than had done so in the 1930s, this was largely accounted for by the raising of the school leaving age. Once school leaving age is past, the increase in numbers staying on, and of those entering higher education, is proportionately the same for service class as for working class. In other words, the relative advantages the service class enjoyed in the 1930s were still present in the 1960s. If anything, the service class has taken greater advantage of educational reforms than has the working class at whom they were supposedly aimed. Class differentials increased at each rung of the educational ladder.

What happens in schools?

There is a growing body of work which records, ethnographically, what actually happens in schools and in classrooms. As has been suggested before (page 261) it is impossible to summarize this kind of work. Woods (1980, 1983) has produced a huge number of descriptive accounts of how pupils and teachers negotiate their experience in school, describing their interactions and strategies for survival. Burgess (1983) is an ethnographic study of life in a comprehensive school.

One particular study, however – Rutter *et al.*'s *Fifteen Thousand Hours* (1979) – has attracted public and media attention as a result of its unorthodox findings. Though Rutter and his colleagues were trained mainly in psychology, they set out to investigate the sociological question of whether schools themselves influenced pupils' achievements. They collected evidence about 2000 pupils in twelve London comprehensive schools, and compared the schools in respect of the pupils' behaviour, delinquency outside school, attendance rates, and academic achievement. They found substantial differences between schools, which they said were due not to the home background of pupils or other external factors, but to what they called 'school ethos', the keystone of which is sound teaching by professional teachers who involve themselves in extra-curricular activities and inspire by their example. The term 'ethos' illustrates what sociologists most criticised about the book: its inadequate definitions and vague concepts, many of which seem to be based on the researchers' prior assumptions, rather than on the evidence. Their rejection of the importance of factors external to the school is based on unclear definitions. Gender and ethnic origin receive little attention. Their notion of a 'good' school is highly subjective.

The best of this work in schools does, however, try to show how the micro-processes of classroom interaction, and the freedom of pupils and teachers to negotiate social order, is limited by wider structural factors. In this, it follows the example of Paul Willis (1977) who claimed to show how, on a day-to-day basis, school ensures that 'working-class kids get working-class jobs'. He showed, from the standpoint of a group of lads who rejected their schooling, how the 'pro' and 'anti' school subcultures (the ear-'oles and the boys) emerge and are sustained. Just as the critics of small-scale interactionist studies deplore their failure to take account of social structure, so Willis maintains that abstract Marxist analysis is inadequate if there is no evidence to show how these historical processes actually operate on a day-to-day basis.

Education in the 1980s

The overriding reality of education in Britain since the late 1970s has been of cuts in real expenditure in all sectors and declining morale among teachers at all levels. This has been aggravated by the relative decline in their salaries, and by the closure or contraction of schools, colleges and universities. Huge sums are still spent on education, as we have seen, but the thinking behind the expansion of the 1960s (see page 252) is now deeply unfashionable among ruling politicians.

The only area where substantial new funding is available is in vocational and pre-vocational education in its various forms. The Great Debate, launched by James Callaghan in 1976, concerning the relationship between schooling and work has led to a bewildering number of initiatives in this field. TVEI (the Technical, Vocational and Educational Initiative) is creating courses in schools, distinct from GCE and CSE courses, to prepare 'non-academic' pupils for the world of work. The Certificate of Pre-Vocational Education, launched in 1985 in schemes involving cooperation between schools, colleges and employers, is the latest of such qualifications. In the colleges of further education, money previously channelled through the education authority is being withdrawn and replaced, sometimes on a larger scale, by money paid by the Department of Employment, via the Manpower Services Commission. The MSC, unlike the LEAs, is not an elected body but a 'quango' staffed by government appointees who are not accountable to the electorate. The MSC's Youth Training Schemes are, in some parts of the country, now the equivalent of a compulsory one or two extra years in education for up to half of young school-leavers.

What is the sociologist to make of these developments? From a liberal and functionalist stance, such changes are the result of society responding to needs created by social and economic development, and adapting to new circumstances and requirements. Those who see things from a more Marxist standpoint, and who relate these developments to a theory of political economy, see things more in terms of the state responding to a crisis of capitalism. It attempts to strengthen its ideological hold on the young, instilling in them the necessary disciplines and attitudes to prevent social unrest in the face of high unemployment, and to encourage good work habits in the interests of capital (CCCS 1981). Evidence of both racial and gender-based discrimination on MSC schemes strengthens such an analysis.

Guide to further reading

Every general sociological textbook (Haralambos 1980, O'Donnell 1981, 1983) includes a chapter on education. The publications of the Open University are always worth a look, especially the course readers, such as Dale *et al.* (1976), *Schooling and Capitalism*, Hammersley and Woods (1976), *The Process of Schooling*, and Cosin *et al.* (1971), *School and Society*.

Silver (1973), *Equal Opportunity in Education*, and Reid (1977), *Social Class Differences in Britain*, cover the traditional social class and education debate thoroughly. On the history of education, Ryder and Silver (1977), *Modern English Society*, covers the ground briefly but well, and Lawson and Silver (1973), *A Social History of Education in England*, is much more comprehensive.

In the last few years, most studies have focused on particular aspects of sociology of education, such as race and gender. Several have been mentioned in the text and will not be repeated here. Chapman (1986), *Sociology of Schools*, is the latest specialist text for the A-level student.

10 Work and industry

Jennifer Somerville

Work is regarded by sociologists as having a central importance in all societies because it provides the basic conditions of existence for their members. There is, however, no such thing as work in general. It is always organized in specific ways and by specific means. For example, the work force is differentiated according to certain criteria: the resulting division of labour is usually ordered in a hierarchy in terms of authority, status and remuneration; work practices have different rhythms and patterns; a variety of techniques are employed; a wide range of skills and knowledge are involved. The forms of organization different kinds of work take on depend to a large extent on other social institutions and social practices. The forms of political power, the forms of law, of family, of ownership, of knowledge are intricately related to the forms of work. The particular nature of the relationship between the organization of work and that of other social structures is a matter of major dispute among sociologists. It is these disputes which form the context of this chapter.

Sociologists tend to consider work to be the major factor determining a person's social class and social status. Indeed, those groups not directly engaged in paid employment may not even be considered. These social categories are discussed in other areas of sociological study. For example, the unemployed, the sick and the old feature predominantly in the sociology of the welfare state (Wedderburn 1974). Housewives have received recent attention in the area of women's studies (Oakley 1974a, 1974b) where the question of housework as domestic and productive labour has been raised. Students receive rather cursory treatment in the sociology of education (see Chapter 9), while those who live on unearned private income rarely get a mention since, as has already been pointed out in Chapter 3, page 77, the wealthy are well able to protect their privacy from the curiosity of social scientists!

Another social phenomenon closely related to work is that of leisure. A whole new specialization is growing up around the differential use of leisure time by different sections of the population (Parker 1971, 1976; Smith, Parker and Smith 1973). Some sociologists study the relation of these leisure activities to the new leisure industries, such as those which depend on, and indeed, generate, youth culture (see pages 145–8).

It is because of this fragmentation of sociology and the restrictions of space in a book of this kind that these aspects cannot all be considered in this chapter. Should you wish to pursue them in depth, you can try the various references given here.

Two further omissions from the sociology of work have been women and racial/ethnic groups. Recently, however, increasing attention has been paid to the location, distribution and status of these two social groups in the labour market for sociologists have become aware that they raise fundamental questions about traditional analyses of work. These will be touched on only briefly in this chapter for you will find fuller discussion in Chapter 12.

Work in non-industrial societies

Work in most non-industrial societies, for instance some Third World countries, tends to be centred on the household and organized towards providing for its maintenance alone. There is often little surplus over and above this level of provision, first because there is no call, given the limited nature of the market, and second, because the methods and instruments of production are relatively simple and labour-intensive. Generally speaking, then, the household is the main 'unit of production'. The labour-force consists of the working members of the family, the variety of operations or jobs necessary for production being allocated to the family members on the basis of a variety of criteria. Overall there is no need directly to involve people outside the household in the production process.

This is not to say that such societies are self-sufficient, although this idealized version of a traditional community based on a 'natural economy' has been popular with many sociologists. Contemporary studies of non-industrial societies have challenged this view and suggested that the exchange of products, that is, the market, has always existed. However, in non-industrial or non-capitalist societies, this exchange plays a minor role in deciding what and how much should be produced.

The point to be made here is that this non-industrial form of production has two important effects on the nature and organization of work. First, since the tasks of production do not require labour other than that provided by the household, specialization and the division of labour is limited. Second, as an effect of this, wages as such do not exist. Household labour has no price.

It is with the expansion of the market that production becomes more geared up to producing a surplus beyond that necessary for the household. This involves changes in the organization of production to increase productivity. One important change is the involvement of workers outside the household whose labour has to be paid, that is, the development of wage-labour. Another is the increasing differentiation of tasks and specialization of products which leads to a more complex division of labour. These two changes make it possible to produce goods entirely for sale in the market.

When the development of production geared towards sale in the market is the dominant form of production (what is called 'generalized commodity production'), work becomes differentiated and separated from other aspects of social life. In other words, it is when production becomes separated in time and place from consumption, from sale and from distribution, and when it becomes characterized by a complex division of labour in which wage-labour is the major form, that work becomes a separate activity, separated from that of leisure, of family, of political and cultural life. There is a general consensus among social scientists that this separation was a major factor in the decreasing participation of women in social production and the restriction of their activities to housework and childcare. Since the sociology of work developed in the context of this segregation of gender roles, it has been characterized from the start by a preoccupation with male, full-time employment.

It should be borne in mind, however, that to distinguish between non-industrial and industrial forms of production is not to say that there is an automatic historical development from one to the other. In the present day many of the countries which are classified as Third World nations have sectors of their economies which are highly industrialized and technologically advanced and other sectors which are not. Their development demonstrates the fact that the model of socio-historical development in Western Europe cannot be taken to be universal. Each society has its own specific form. There is no universal model of social evolution from 'simple' to 'modern' society. The whole question of development and the debates which that involves are well presented in the Open University course, D.302 'Patterns of inequality' (1976a).

Traditional approaches to the sociology of work

How, then, does work feature in sociology? Traditionally, it has not appeared as a single, general category around which research developed. Rather it has appeared only as a subdivision of the various subdisciplines of sociology, such as industrial sociology, the sociology of organizations or the sociology of professions.

Industrial sociology
Industrial sociology has concentrated on work in industry, particularly in the factory. One approach has been to examine the *formal* structures

of management and trade unions, the organization of the various tasks of production, and the effects of these on the formal differentiation of the labour-force. This then involves study of the organization of the labour-force, of the different forms of remuneration and of conditions of work.

It has often been approached through one of two perspectives summed up by Fox (1966) as the 'unitary' and the 'pluralist' frames of reference. The unitary perspective is associated with the notion of 'the harmony of interests', in which it is assumed that there is no fundamental conflict of interests between employer and employee, since the success of the business enterprise benefits both in higher profits and higher wages. The mutual interest concerned, however, is defined by management goals and policies, and any employee behaviour that does not correspond with these is seen as irrational.

The pluralist perspective recognizes that different interests do exist within the enterprise, as the consequence of a highly complex division of labour required by modern production techniques, and the hierarchical structure of administration that goes with it. However, this plurality of interests always exists within a framework of normative agreement between management and workers, settled by bargaining. It is this collaboration of divergent interest-groups which provides the basis for the system of industrial relations. The fact that employers and trade unions recognize the legitimacy of each other's interests and establish procedures through which agreements can be negotiated is understood in this way, as are the conciliation and arbitration procedures with which we are familiar in Western industrial societies.

This institutionalization of industrial conflict is taken here as proof of the decline of the significance of class and class conflict. It is regarded as the means by which the efforts of all those in industry are co-ordinated towards the common goal – the economic success of the enterprise. Communication is seen to be the most crucial factor here; lack of it or its temporary breakdown is the main cause of industrial strife.

Another approach has focused on the *informal* organization of industry, based on the occupational subcultures of workers. Industrial sociologists have been extremely interested in the way these informal structures affect productivity, the work practices of the shop floor, worker expectations, solidarity and militancy (see also Chapter 4, pages 104–6).

There is some measure of disagreement here. Some writers have emphasized the 'alienation' of workers from the work process (Mills 1956; Berger 1964). By this they mean the feelings of aimlessness, boredom and frustration generated by the monotony of assembly line production. From this point of view strikes and other forms of industrial unrest tend to be interpreted as 'expressive' rather than 'instrumental' behaviour. They express the workers' discontent, lack of commitment to the company and lack of job-satisfaction. As Knowles (1952) has put it, they are symptoms of 'industrial neurosis' derived from the difficulty workers have in adapting to changes in production necessitated by 'rational management' in pursuit of maximum economic growth.

In contrast, other sociologists have documented relatively high levels of satisfaction among workers under the same working conditions. Indeed Goldthorpe and Lockwood concluded from their now classic study of Luton car workers 'that these workers are disposed to define their relationship with their firm more as one of reciprocity and mutual accommodation rather than one of coercion and exploitation. And, in this sense at least, they are far from ' "alienated" ' (Goldthorpe and Lockwood 1968). This is explained in terms of the predominance of an 'instrumental' orientation to employment: workers expect work to provide them with an income, not intrinsic satisfaction. For interest, stimulation and self-expression workers look to their family life, their hobbies, their sporting enthusiasms, their various leisure activities. For the 'privatized' worker, work is important only in that it provides the conditions for the enjoyment of non-work. Nevertheless, it would appear that this very instrumentalism is in effect a matter of workers coming to terms with the fact that factory work cannot be self-realizing. Goldthorpe *et al.* do admit that this in itself may be an expression of alienation.

Some of this disagreement stems from the 'subjectivism' that characterizes much of the research. 'Subjectivism' refers to the theoretical approach that regards the consciousness of individual human beings as the determining factor of social structures and social relationships. In this view, to understand industrial relations, the sociologist should start with the opinions of those involved, for it is the shared meanings the workers attach to work situations which determine social action (see pages 43–5).

Gouldner's early book, *Wildcat Strike* (1954), is of interest here. He assumes that a certain 'harmony' or 'balance of tensions' is the normal state of industrial relations. His explanation of the strike at the gypsum plant, therefore, rests on the notion of workers' hostility to changes in management personnel and accompanying changes in the customary work patterns of the plant. These changes brought to an end the informal system of give-and-take, the 'leniency pattern', that the workers had come to expect from the management. This undermined the normative agreement between workers and management on which peaceful relations were based (see also page 108).

The point is that there is no account in the book of the course of the strike in terms of the actual negotiations between union and management or between the unions at the two plants involved. Nor is there any analysis of the economic and organizational interests which may have been at stake. Instead we are given a rather psychological account of the strike, seen through the eyes of the two leaders of the union cliques involved.

Similarly, although Goldthorpe and Lockwood's study tries to go beyond the narrow focus on the work place and takes account of the influence of external factors such as family, and social orientations, class attitudes, culture and political affiliations, its main slant is towards the personal significance which workers attach to work organization and work practice. 'The effects of technologically determined conditions of work are always mediated through the meanings that men give to their work' (Goldthorpe *et al.* 1969).

This orientation leads to a tendency to treat the organization of work as simply a series of external constraints on workers' attitudes, instead of considering that these objective factors may initiate, sustain and sometimes change those attitudes. As a result, sociologists who operate with a subjectivist methodology have difficulty in explaining the rapid shifts in workers' consciousness that are typical of strike situations.

The sociology of organizations

As far as the sociology of organizations is concerned, one might expect that it would cover a much wider range of enterprises than industrial sociology. It should include non-industrial work, such as that of commercial concerns, educational institutions, hospitals and other health-care facilities as well as the vast number of government departments, both national and local.

Its main orientation has been to analyse work in such organizations in terms of the formal chain of authority and responsibility, and the procedural rules and the organizational roles specified by them, particularly in relation to the established goals of the organization. In this respect it is influenced by Weber's ideal type of bureaucracy. Weber, however, was concerned to develop an ideal-type of a form of political organization of society as a whole. This he designated 'legal–rational', and characterized modern society as such. Much of the sociology of organizations, in contrast, has become synonymous with 'organizational theory'. This tends to look at the structure of any organization from the point of view of the practical problems associated with its efficient running, in pursuit of its stated goals. It tends to take as its starting-point the problems and interests of managers and bureaucrats in motivating, integrating and controlling members of the organization. It is within these terms of reference that the behaviour of the members, their 'role-play', their work-cliques and work-cults are analysed and explained. Work, in the sociology of organizations, tends to be managerial, concerned primarily with the problem of compliance and control of workers. Further discussion of this field of sociology may be found in Chapter 4, pages 104–11.

The sociology of professions

The sociology of professions, obviously, deals with that heterogeneous group of professional and semi-professional workers. It tries to explain what role, economic, political or cultural, they play in modern society that sets them apart from workers, managers and many other occupational groups.

Much of the conventional literature is characterized by what has been called a 'trait approach' (Millerson 1964). This begins by defining the characteristics of an ideal-typical profession. This then becomes the measure by which other occupational groups aspiring to professional status are assessed. The main features of this model include the possession of systematic intellectual knowledge, which necessitates extended education and specialized training and is tested by formal examination procedures. Such certification provides the basis for another ideal-type characteristic – the organization of qualified individuals into associations. It is claimed that these can be distinguished from trade unions and other occupational bodies on two related grounds. First is that a major concern of these professional associations is the regulation of the conduct of their members by ethical codes of practice, and, second, that they are more orientated to providing a public service than they are to enhancing their own self-interests. Indeed, Wilensky (1964) has suggested five necessary stages of this movement from occupation to profession: (1) the emergence of a full-time occupation; (2) the institutionalization of specialist training; (3) the establishment of a professional association; (4) the recourse to legislation to secure the recognition and protection of the association; (5) the formulation of a code of professional conduct.

The main problem with this model of professions and professionalization is that it consists of a list of elements abstracted from certain old established professions, mainly law and medicine. No other occupational group, developing under different circumstances, is ever likely to duplicate these characteristics and, therefore, will always fail the test. Further, a simple listing of features, often viewed though the rosy-coloured spectacles of the professionals themselves, cannot explain why those particular characteristics came to define what we refer to as 'professions'. Nor can it explain the relationship between these characteristics and the privileged and prestigious position of professions in modern industrial societies.

Much of the remaining literature concerns the socialization of professionals. It examines the rituals and processes by which new members are initiated into correct modes of conduct, how appropriate norms and values become integrated into the structure of the self during this process and how, in this way, the body of expertise that defines the profession is transmitted and maintained. Becker and Geer's study (1961) of the initiation of young medical students exemplifies this type of approach. It describes how the occupational role set by the professional association becomes part of the initiate's identity. This is seen to be the main factor in providing that level of commitment to and satisfaction from work which marks off the professional orientation to work from the instrumental, 'dissociated' attitude of other occupational groups.

It should be clear from this brief review of some of the areas of sociological study in which aspects of work form a part, that they tend to be largely descriptive. As might be expected, they are dominated by research either of the traditional positivistic variety or of the inter-actionist sort.

Overall, these areas concentrate on the normative structuring of social action, both arising from the work situation and the reaction to it. Studies are often organized round the 'formal–informal' couple, whether in relation to institutions, processes, work-groups' attitudes or motivations. They tend to be a-historical and a-theoretical. This partly accounts for the absence, in most of these studies, of any attempt to relate, in a systematic way, industrial relations, organizations, professions and the like to each other or to the economic, political and cultural context in which they are located, and which make up what we refer to as 'society'.

Industrialization and social change

'The imperatives of technology'

Work also features in a much more general way in sociology for it lies behind the concept of 'industrialization' and thus acts as the organizing principle for the work of another group of sociologists. From it they derive the claim that Western Europe and the United States can no longer be considered as capitalist countries. Rather, their development has led to a stage of highly advanced industrialism which has superseded capitalism. They are sometimes called, collectively, 'supersession theorists'.

Crucial to this claim is what Galbraith (1967) calls 'the imperatives of technology'. It is argued that the very pursuit of rational means to maximize profitability and efficiency, which was the driving force of nineteenth-century capitalism, led to the development of new types of technology which radically altered the organization of work processes, the form of financial investment and ownership and the class structure of those societies.

Technology breaks down the process of production into component parts, each of which relates to an area of specialized knowledge. The division of labour becomes more elaborate and encourages a high degree of specialization, not only in terms of technologists, technicians and manual skills, but also in terms of co-ordinators and planners of the production process.

This search for increased efficiency and economy leads to two main developments. One is the rise of large scale production and distribution, combined with complex organizational bureaucracies. The other is the increasing involvement of the state, since only the state can take the risks attached to certain spheres of modern industry. For example, the state can underwrite the costs of development; it can provide a reliable market for the product; it can finance, through the education system, the necessary knowledge and skills in the work-force. In other words, in advanced Western societies planning comes to replace the market forces, so avoiding the worst effects of competition. In this way capitalism, entirely identified here with its so-called *'laissez-faire'* phase, is transformed into a new type of society with a corresponding form of state. This is variously called 'post-capitalist society', 'the new corporatism' or 'the new industrial state'.

These so-called imperatives of technology are said to have far-reaching effects on the social structures of such countries. Indeed, in some variants of the supersession theory it is claimed that all societies 'converge' as they reach an advanced stage of industrialism.

This 'convergence thesis' emerged in the late 1950s and early 1960s, mainly in the United States. It is particularly associated with the Inter-University Study of Labour Problems, the conclusions of which were published as *Industrialism and Industrial Man*, by Clark Kerr *et al.* (1962). This thesis held that industrialism in itself generates the same problems for all societies in which it occurs and that the solutions to them are necessarily similar. These solutions impose certain changes on major social institutions and processes, such as the education and occupation systems, the class and status systems, industrial relations and the family, so that they become of a uniform type. These changes produce a socially, geographically and occupationally mobile and flexible society characterized by the values of individualism and achievement. Any remaining political or cultural differences between such countries tend to be regarded as residues and peripheral to the general long-term pattern of convergence. For Raymond Aron (1967), another famous advocate of the convergence thesis, the differences between capitalism and socialism, based on their respective forms of ownership of economic resources, are outweighed by the problems which are common to both – the rational planning of economic growth.

However, the theory that capitalism in Western countries is being superseded does not depend on the proposition of convergence. What differences exist between these writers on the question of convergence are overridden by their agreement that changes in the social structures of Western Europe and America have made redundant the application of Marx's analysis to them.

One major element of this argument, first put forward by Berle and Means (1968), as early as 1932, is the thesis of the separation of ownership and control. This thesis claims that the development of joint stock companies and their expansion beyond the control of their owners have led to a division between nominal owners – the shareholders who are increasingly widely dispersed throughout society – and the managers who control the day-to-day running of the organization. This is said to lead to a conflict of interests between these two groups, with the shareholders' interest in profits increasingly clashing with that of the managers in the growth, efficiency and productivity of the company as a whole – 'the soulful corporation' as Professor Carl Kaysen (1957) put it. Although the most obvious and extreme version of this thesis is to be found in James Burnham's *The Managerial Revolution* (1945), in which he envisaged the emergence of a new ruling class of managers and bureaucrats by the 1970s, it is still present in a more limited version in Dahrendorf's concept of the 'decomposition of capital' (Dahrendorf 1959).

However, this debate has been dealt with in Chapter 6 (page 172). What is more relevant to the present chapter are the arguments that relate to Dahrendorf's twin category of 'the decomposition of labour'. This relates to post-war changes in the occupational structure of Western societies, in particular the decline of manual jobs and the increase and expansion of non-manual ones. These shifts give rise to the claim that the working class which provides the social base for socialist parties is disintegrating, and with it the likelihood of a revolutionary transition to socialism. Central to this claim is the assertion that knowledge has replaced capital as the most important resource in post-capital society.

A major proponent of this thesis is Daniel Bell (1974). In an analysis of the changing patterns of employment in the United States, Bell points to the significance of the decline of manual occupations, the most important aspect of which is the continuing decline within the productive sector – what Bell calls the 'goods-producing sector'. This has resulted from the introduction of new technologies, such as numerical control machine tools, electronic computers, instrumentation and automatic controls. (Today, one might add the whole micro-chip technology.)

He shows that employment has shifted from production to the service sector. This has overtaken industrial employment in the share of total employment so that he estimated that by 1980 there would be a ratio of service to production workers of 68.4 per cent to 31.7 per cent. While a major factor here is the growth of government employment (national and local), even within manufacturing the proportion of white-collar workers continues to increase. From this evidence Bell concludes that advanced societies have become white-collar societies and that this increase is not just in female labour but also in male employment. The bulk of these male white-collar jobs, Bell identifies as 'management, professional or technical – the heart of the upper middle class in the United States'.

This gives us the clue as to what Bell wants to make of these shifts in the occupational structure. He wants to draw from them certain implications for changes in the class structure:

Instead of the industrial worker, we see the dominance of the professional and technical class in the labour force – so much so that by 1980 it will be the second largest occupational group in the society and by the end of the century the largest. This is the new dual revolution taking place in the structure of occupations and, to the extent that occupation determines other modes of behaviour . . . it is a revolution in the class structure of society as well. This change in the character of production and of occupations is one aspect of the emergence of the post-industrial society. [Bell 1974]

This so-called revolution is identified as the move from a capitalist society dominated by a concern for the *quantity* of goods produced to a post-industrial society characterized by 'the *quality of life* as measured by service and amenities'. Thus, the middle classes, whose work is concentrated in such areas as the finance, distribution and co-ordination of large-scale industry, in the organization of the infrastructure of society, and in educational, environmental, health, social community and cultural services, come to displace the working class.

In such a society, Bell goes on, information and knowledge become the most important resource and the most important source of power when it is located in organizations. This brings us to the crux of Bell's thesis. The most powerful groups of people in post-industrial society are not those with capital, but those with knowledge, particularly those who control information through education and training. They protect and transmit their knowledge and skills through their organization in professions, and these become the criteria for positions within society. Knowledge is said to replace capital and at the same time a plurality of expert elites replaces owner–managers of industry as the dominant group in society.

However, these very developments towards communal concerns within post-industrial society give rise to demands for participation and consultation by the general public, and this comes into conflict with the new professionalism. It is this conflict of interests between the experts and the laymen over communal and public interest issues like the environment, education, crime, municipal services and so on which, Bell predicts, will replace the conflict between management and labour. The problems of class become peripheral.

This view is not restricted to American liberal-pluralism. It is one which has been shared by a large section of the British intelligentsia and has had important effects in Labour party programmes and ideology. Wilson's 'great white heat of technology', coupled with Crosland's aim to equalize opportunity through educational reform, were the strategies of the 1960s which were geared to reshaping British society towards a new era of social justice and planned efficiency sustained by continued economic growth (see page 252).

What all these theories have in common is the attempt to show that Marx's theory of social class and social change has been falsified by empirical observation of major social changes in industrial societies over this century and that these changes are rooted in the work process. This attempt is dominated by what is called a 'technicist' conception of social development, that is, that technology *in itself* is the major determinant of social institutions and social change.

However, it is not too difficult to argue that Marx's theoretical enterprise is not demolished by these theories though they have brought attention to certain of its limitations.

The Marxist view

Although Marx is often criticized, if not written off, by sociologists for his economic determinism (that is, the view that economic structures provide the foundation for the forms of other political and cultural structures) he has a much more sophisticated view of the economy than do most of his critics. For Marx, the economy is not simply the technology employed to produce goods and services. Rather, the economy is conceived of as a combination of 'forces of production' and 'social relations of production' in which the latter are always dominant.

Marx had a great belief in the capacity of 'the productive forces' (that is, the harnessing of natural resources by human labour, enhanced by technology) to liberate humankind from the vagaries of nature. Thus, Marx regarded capitalism as progressive to the extent that, in the pursuit of profit, it encouraged technical innovation and so accelerated the development of productive forces. However, the productive forces are always situated in the context of certain sets of social relations. The organization of production, the distribution of the social product among members of society, and the type of technology employed depend on definite forms of social relations of production.

By the 'social relations of production' Marx meant the system of access to the ownership and control of the means of production. Groups of people are distinguished from each other on the basis of their relationship to the means of production, that is, whether or to what extent they own and control the various resources necessary for production to take place, and whether or to what extent they are separated from the ownership and control of those resources. Social groups are differentiated from each other in this way and identified as social classes by their position in relation to the means of production (see also Chapter 6, page 152).

A further qualification is necessary. The notion of the ownership of the means of production in Marx does not simply refer to juridical relations – to those who *legally* own them. Rather it refers to the capacity to control the functioning of the means of production and the labour process. Thus 'ownership' in this context indicates an economic power, the power to provide the unit of production with the means of production, and to withdraw those means. As such it becomes identical with the notion of 'possession' of the means of production. Thus, although it may be said that *legal* ownership of private industry has become diffused in modern society, with the spread of small shareholding and the investment of trade union pension funds and life assurance premiums in business for example, it in no way follows that the concentration of effective possession and control, that is, 'possession', has likewise become dispersed. The two are not at all incompatible.

Given this point, it is clear that for Marx social classes exist on the basis of economic relations and are differentiated with respect to the possession of and separation from the means of production. The possession of the means of production by one class always involves the separation of another class from those means. The separated class, in order to be able to live, must gain access to the means of production. This places the separated class under the economic control of the possessing class. Marx locates the origin of economic exploitation in the relationship between the possessing and non-possessing classes. The relationship is, therefore, characterized by the opposition of interests between the two classes.

In a society where commodity production has become generalized (see page 276), labour too becomes a commodity to be bought and sold on the market. This, however, is not possible unless workers have been radically separated from the means of production. So long as workers have the necessary resources to provide adequately for their own living, they will not be willing to sell their capacity to work on a continuous basis. This provides Marx with his two main criteria for defining capitalism: the existence of extensive commodity production geared to profit, and generalized wage-labour. Capitalist society is thus characterized by two main classes – a capitalist class which possesses the means of production and a proletarian class which sells its labour-power, mental or manual, to the former.

However, Marx (1867) makes it clear that the possession/separation of the means of production is not confined to those directly involved in the production of commodities. The capitalist class is not confined to the industrialists. Bankers and merchants are also capitalists. How is it that they are considered part of the capitalist class and may even outnumber the industrialists, when they are not directly involved in the production process?

Marx's answer lies once again in the possession of the means of production. The industrial capitalists may not be in possession of all the means necessary for production. Or they may not have all the money required to expand production.

Here the bankers enter the scene. They provide the industrialists with the required money and in return gain interest. The latter is a part of the profit that would have belonged to the industrialists had they not needed to borrow money. The credit system is central to developed capitalism and the creditors' (bankers) position as capitalists is a consequence of their possession of capital, money which is required by the industrialists to run and expand their business.

Further, since the industrialists cannot at once sell all the commodities they produce to the final consumers, they cannot immediately 'realize' the capital initially invested in production and its accrued profit. Commodities have to 'circulate' in the market. It is at this stage that the 'merchants' enter the scene. The merchants (wholesalers and retailers) buy the commodities from the industrialists and advance them the money necessary to renew the process of production. The merchants in turn sell the commodities to the final consumers and make a profit out of it. The profit that comes to the merchants is a result of their possession of money-capital which is necessary for the industrialists to continue production. Once again, this profit would initially have gone to the industrialists, had they possessed all the necessary capital for further production.

Thus, although the merchants are not directly involved in the production sphere, they can, because they have capital, exert a certain control over the process of production. It is precisely because they possess certain of the means of production that the merchants are considered to be a section of the capitalist class.

The point, however, is that the social relations of production are by no means confined to the sphere of production. They also include relations which affect how certain means of production (in my example, credit) are distributed to the unit of production. These relations also extend to the sphere of circulation of commodities (that is, trading and selling) which forms the link between production and consumption. They provide conditions for what Marx terms 'the circulation and realization of commodities'.

Given this analysis, production cannot be regarded as referring simply to sets of techniques combined with human agents, but also includes other conditions necessary for production which may well fall outside the immediate production process. If this is the case, the possession/separation of the means of production is not restricted to the sphere of production. Therefore, social classes are not simply those groups involved in the immediate production of commodities, that is, a homogeneous working class comprised of industrial workers and a homogeneous capitalist class comprised of industrialists. Rather, it is the relations of possession/separation in the process of production *as a whole*, that is, a process that includes production, distribution, circulation and realization, that differentiates classes in what is termed 'the social division of labour'.

It has been pointed out already (page 284) that the technicist sociologists identify social classes according to their position in the occupational structure, as determined by the technical functions that they perform. Marx, on the contrary, argues that the '*technical* division of labour', that is, the division of technical functions in the unit of production, is itself prestructured by a '*social* division of labour'. The latter, as we have seen, is the division of society into classes on the basis of the relations of possession/separation.

Technical functions, for Marx, do not order *themselves* into a hierarchy. The hierarchy is the effect of the social relations, the class relations which characterize that society. It is these which are most significant in defining the criteria of selection for occupations, access to them and remuneration for them.

This account of Marx's argument is, of course, qualified by the fact that, despite the impression given by sociologists, Marx nowhere in his work develops a rigorous theory of social class. The chapter entitled 'Social classes' in volume 3 of *Capital* amounts to no more than a few lines, his death having curtailed any further elaboration. It is, therefore, via his *general* analysis of the capitalist economic system in *Capital* and other works, that Marx provides us with elements to attempt a conceptualization of classes.

Nevertheless, we may deduce certain positions from his work which directly confront those of the supersession theorists:

1 Technological innovations are not autonomous forces determining the form of social structures, for there can be no technology outside social relations.
2 Knowledge, therefore, cannot replace capital. The application of knowledge to the production of commodities is not determined by the nature or direction of the applied sciences but by practical problems determined by social and economic factors. Thus, the particular class of occupations to which the applied sciences have given rise are also specified by those factors. Under capitalism, scientific and techno-logical knowledge has always been a necessary adjunct to capital.
3 It follows that there can be no simple identification of occupation with social class.
4 In addition, it follows that the identification of manual work with the working class and mental work with the middle class has little meaning for Marxists.

The new sociology of work

It is on the basis of the positions summarized in the last section that a new sociological approach to work and industry has arisen in recent years. It criticizes both the tendencies within the traditional sociology of work which have been considered in this chapter, viz. the tendency to fragment work into a number of discrete fields, and that which unifies them into a technological conception of social development. Instead the new sociology of work tries to show how the organization of work, in all its various forms, is an effect of wider economic, political and ideological structures. In particular, this new sociology of work concentrates on relating work organizations, work technologies and work practices to capitalist economic organization. It is heavily influenced by Marxism. The Open University course *People and Work* (1976b) and its course reader edited by Esland, Salaman and Speakman (1975), provide a good example of this new development and an excellent source of references.

The writers who are loosely associated with this approach see work as the most crucial sphere of activity in capitalist society, for it constitutes the fundamental factor in securing and reproducing capitalism. Though these writers willingly concede that political and ideological institutions and practices have important roles to play in providing certain conditions necessary for the functioning of capitalism, it is in the workplace that capitalism is crucially generated. They believe, following Marx, that the possession/separation of the means of production is what determines one's position in those economic structures which profoundly affect all the other spheres of social life. It is the capitalist class's possession of the means of production which enables it to continue to make profits and accumulate more capital which, of course, is then reinvested in a variety of profitable enterprises. Conversely, it is being separated from the means of production that maintains the workers as workers. This is not to say that individual workers may not become capitalists, nor that, occasionally, individual capitalists may not fall to the ranks of workers. It is simply to say that, regardless of individual class mobility, the class system remains (see Chapter 6, page 180).

Important here is the claim that profit is not simply made by selling products for more money than they cost, but that it also involves the exploitation of workers. Now this notion of 'exploitation' does not appear in *Capital* as simply a term of moral repugnance by which to denounce capitalists. It has a particular economic sense. By exploitation, Marx meant the way in which the capitalist class is able, by its possession of the means of production, to buy the workers' *capacity to labour* – their 'labour-power' – for a certain number of hours each day. During that time, the workers have to work under the discipline, surveillance, direction and to the specification of their employers. In return for this labour-power, the workers are paid wages – the price of their labour-power, that is what it costs to feed, clothe, house them and bring up their families according to the generally accepted standards of the time.

Marx argues, however, that the workers create through their labour-power more value in the form of commodities than that for which they are compensated in the form of wages. This extra value – 'surplus value' – goes to the employers. Out of it they pay certain costs of production, such as rents and taxes, and purchase raw materials, technology and other utilities for further production. What is left is profit. Thus, it is argued that all profit can be reduced ultimately to surplus value, that is, unpaid labour.

However, not all those writing within this recent approach to work are committed to this 'labour theory of value', although it is a theoretical assumption behind many of the texts. What does seem to unite all these writers is the recognition that possession/separation of the means of production is the dominant organizing principle of capitalist society. This means that its effects are not limited to private business but structure all the economic and occupational institutions in such societies, regardless of their *legal* ownership. Thus, the industrial, commercial and administrative enterprises of the state are equally subject to capitalist forms of work organization, of calculation and of work ideology.

There is, then, according to this view, a fundamental conflict of interest between those who possess the means of production and those who do not – employers and employees – between the needs of the former to make a profit (or in the case of government agencies, to keep labour costs down to the level determined by their budgets) and the needs of the latter to make a living. So long as the work processes of Western industrial nations are organized on the basis of such social relations, those societies remain capitalist, regardless of the technology introduced. There can be no 'decomposition of labour', as Dahrendorf suggests, so long as the majority of the population are excluded from responsibility for and control over the production and consumption units that dominate their lives.

The work of Braverman – 'proletarianization'

Indeed, one major writer, the influential American Marxist, Harry Braverman, claims that the opposite is the case. He claims that, rather than the working class withering away, it is actually growing in number and absorbing whole groups of workers previously regarded as middle class.

In *Labour and Monopoly Capital* (1974), Braverman argues, along classical Marxist lines, that there is a built-in tendency of capitalism to increase productivity so as to reduce the price of commodities on the competitive market. This has as its effect the continual revolutionizing of the means of production, above all by technological innovation. The resulting increase in costs is offset by the capacity of technology to decrease the size of the labour-force and, therefore, the proportion of labour costs.

This is part of the process of the development of capitalism in which smaller companies, less able to invest in new expensive technology, become swallowed up by those which can so invest, by means of take-overs, amalgamations and by bankruptcies. Production, distribution and circulation become dominated by a few large-scale, complex, capital-intensive enterprises, the investment programmes of which are diversified into a number of fields in which they control the most significant share of the output. Economic possession of the means of production becomes concentrated into fewer and fewer hands. This phase of capitalist development, characterized by the 'concentration and centralization of capital' has become known as 'monopoly capitalism'. This does not mean that competition between enterprises has been abolished but that, by means of cartels and trusts, these corporations attempt to control prices, the volume and type of production, and various other conditions of the market, in their own interests.

The ever-increasing scale and complexity of capitalist organization requires an increase in the number of workers employed in the supervision, regulation, co-ordination and control of the whole cycle of production, distribution and sale. In this way, Braverman explains the relative decline in the number of manual workers directly engaged in production and the corresponding expansion of white-collar jobs. However, unlike Galbraith, Bell and others, who interpret this shift as a decrease in the working class and an increase in the middle class, Braverman argues that the majority of white-collar workers are in a position in relation to the nature of their jobs and conditions of employment that is not dissimilar to that of manual workers.

Most of the accounting, record-keeping, planning, scheduling and supervisory functions in a previous stage of capitalist development were accomplished by a relatively small number of clerks. Their privileged position and status was a consequence of the then scarce possession of skills of literacy and numeracy. These functions have been increasingly divided up, segmented and diffused among a wide variety of departments in the modern enterprise. There, such functions have been further reduced to component operations which amount to no more than the repetitious performance of mechanical tasks. The result, says Braverman, is that in much mental labour, 'the brain is used as the equivalent of the detail worker in production, grasping and releasing a single piece of data over and over again'.

The same processes of 'rationalization' which have been applied to so-called blue-collar work are now overtaking white-collar occupations. The same investment in mechanization, automation and micro-electronics which has transformed the labour process in the sphere of production is now having similar effects on office work. Even the specialized knowledge skills, information and experience once necessary for semi-managerial work are now being undermined by this same development. This decreases the value of the office-workers while at the same time it makes them more easily subordinated and controlled, since key information is removed to higher levels of management. Ultimately, of course, this must lead to a reduction in the size of the mental labour-force as routine clerical tasks are taken over by machines and electronic calculation and communications systems.

Braverman concludes that there are no grounds for distingushing between manual labour and mental labour of this type. Whereas for Bell (and for many other sociologists) the white-collar workers are identified with mental labour, for Braverman they are largely the manual workers of the office. They constitute a mass of subdivided detail workers employed to perform routine, standardized tasks which involve no understanding of the total process in which each of their jobs is one small component.

Clearly this has important implications for the assessment of the class position of such workers. The view that they constitute a new middle class is unacceptable to Braverman. It is based on what he considers to be certain superficial and secondary characteristics, such as the fact that they are often paid salaries rather than wages, that they do not have to 'clock on and off', that they have more secure tenure of employment and that they work in quieter, cleaner and more comfortable surroundings. As far as their position in the labour process and their related class and social position are concerned, Braverman argues that these are not being improved but undermined by technology in what he refers to as 'the de-skilling process'. The rationalization, simplification and mechanization of office practices have led, he writes, to 'a polarization of office employment and the growth at one pole of an immense mass of wage-workers – the creation of a large proletariat in a new form'.

At the other end of this pole, Braverman distinguishes between two groups:

1 Senior executives, whom he regards as the functionaries of the capitalist class. They act professionally on behalf of capital and thus must be regarded as part of the capitalist class.
2 Middle levels of management and technical experts, whose specialist knowledge and delegated authority allow them 'a petty share in the prerogatives and privileges of capital'. In terms of function they collate and analyse information, organize and control the mass of labour in the interests of capital. They are also the source of recruits for higher management. Nonetheless, since their privileged position depends on the scarcity and functional indispensability of their particular kind of labour-power, Braverman suggests that they also share characteristics with the proletariat. If such labour-power became rationalized in the same way that industrial and clerical

occupations have been, this intermediate stratum could well become 'proletarianized'. For these reasons Braverman somewhat reluctantly designates them 'the new middle class'.

Braverman attempts to show that Marx's analysis of capitalism is as relevant as ever to contemporary societies in the West. He rejects the idea that the working class is disintegrating and proposes the opposite, i.e. that it has been expanded by the proletarianization of workers previously considered to be middle class. Furthermore, he rejects Bell's thesis that the end of class politics has been reached. Rather, he claims, the very conditions of alienation – the subjection of rationalization, routinization and deskilling – engender in workers a spontaneous and authentic opposition to capitalist work organization. This in turn produces revolutionary politics.

Braverman's analysis, however, is not without its problems:

1 By concentrating on immediate work processes, Braverman ignores the ways in which much of the framework in which work is located is determined outside it, in political, legislative, legal and cultural spheres.

2 Braverman assumes that once you have decided to which social class a social group belongs, you can fairly accurately predict its political behaviour. There are serious theoretical objections to this reduction of political affiliation to economic position, as well as the fact that empirical experience in the last decade has shown such predictions to be at least partial.

3 Braverman seems to measure work in advanced capitalist societies against a rather idealized conception of craft labour in the past. It is doubtful whether the artisans of the pre-industrial period got much job satisfaction given their generally cramped, badly lit, often dangerous work conditions and their vulnerability to the whims, defaulting and demands of their patrons. Braverman allows a nostalgia for small-scale commodity production to blind him to the fact that it is unlikely that any labour process under any form of production would be entirely without some division of labour, and certainly not one which takes the problem of scarcity and inequality seriously and contemporary standards of health and welfare for granted. It would appear that the worker has always been and always will be separated from some aspect of the total labour process.

The reserve army of labour

One aspect of the new sociology of work which has generated a veritable industry of research is its rediscovery of Marx's concept of the reserve army of labour.

Marx, in opposition to most political economists of his day, argued that unemployment is not an occasional and abnormal side-effect of capitalist production but a necessary condition for its continuation as a result of the following characteristics of capitalist economies:

1 As investment moves out of and into branches of industry chasing higher returns, employment levels fluctuate, so that there will always be some structural and regional unemployment.
2 In periods of economic recession, employers will shed labour until such time as wage levels are low enough to reduce production costs and so encourage re-investment.
3 The drive to increase the productivity of the labour force, and so reduce the cost of commodities and make them more attractive to customers, leads employers to introduce more efficient forms of work organization and increase mechanization. The long-term tendency as a result is a progressive decline in jobs.

The unemployed workers produced by these processes constitute a reserve army of labour. Marx argues that while individuals may move in and out of this labour reserve, *structurally* it exists as a permanent pool of unemployed or under-employed workers.

Sociologists in the 1970s finally began to realize that the preoccupation with full-time male employment in the sociology of work had become increasingly out of step with the facts of the occupational structure. While the shifts from manufacturing to service occupations in all Western economies were very well researched, their full implications were not recognized.

Most significant was a radical change in the relative proportion of men and women in the labour force. In Britain, for example, between 1966 and 1976, more than $1\frac{1}{2}$ million jobs in industry disappeared, most of them men's jobs. In the same period, the expansion of the public sector generated over a million jobs, mainly in the service sector and they were almost entirely taken up by women. Another significant change was that most of the jobs which vanished were full-time jobs; a large number of the new ones were part-time.

These changes have very important repercussions on wage levels and on trade union organization. Women's traditional domestic responsibilities leave them little time and energy for activities at work, and this socially induced lack of participation often results in a lack of commitment to work. This marginalization results in low wage scales, a lack of opportunities for responsibility and promotion, and a greater willingness to do temporary or part-time work.

Braverman argues that the characteristics of female labour – low wage rates, lack of organization and temporary/part-time status – qualify the mass of women workers for inclusion in the reserve army of labour in that they provide employers with a cheap, docile and disposable labour force. Feminists have been quick to develop this kind of analysis. Examples may be found in Amsden (1980), Coote and Campbell (1982), Crompton and Jones (1984) and West (1982).

The other aspect of Marx's notion of the reserve army of labour which has interested sociologists of work is its function as an effective weapon to divide and control employees. This has been developed by sociologists to account for the position of racial and ethnic groups in the occupational structure. Castles and Kosack (1973) argue that in the post-war boom it became increasingly difficult for European capitalism to maintain an indigenous industrial reserve army, partly because of the general shortage of labour and partly because of the vastly increased strength of the labour movement. The solution was to employ immigrant workers from poorer areas of Europe and the Third World either as migrant labour or as settlers. Immigrant workers took unskilled and semi-skilled jobs in those sectors of the economy which have the lowest pay and the worst conditions of work. This had important socio-political consequences: the line between consistently employed workers and the reserve army of labour became identified with race and colour. The relatively privileged indigenous workers try to maintain their position at the expense of the immigrant worker. This produces institutionalized discrimination which maintains the low socio-economic position of these racial and ethnic groups into the second and third generations. Thus, this reserve army based on race/ethnicity both serves to keep down the general level of wages and fragments the subordinate classes, obstructing any unified political organization and strategy.

The main problem with the use of the notion of the reserve army of labour in these contexts is that as an explanation it tends to be circular. For example, are women in the reserve army of labour because of their characteristics *as* women, or do these characteristics arise from the fact that they are in the reserve army of labour?

Competition and conflict at work

A central focus of the new sociology of work is the way in which the conflict between capital and labour takes place in the context of competition. Competition between enterprises seems to be endemic to capitalism despite the regulation of prices and wages, of working hours and conditions of work, of markets, and of industrial relations.

As well as direct competition between firms producing similar goods, there is also the indirect competition of companies producing dissimilar goods, for at the margins of consumer expenditure many people have to choose between a colour television and a freezer, a newer car and a holiday. It is worth noting here that this also applies to enterprises outside the private sector. For example, there is the rivalry, especially fierce in the 1960s, between the British state-owned industries of gas, electricity and coal to capture that 25 per cent of total national energy use represented by domestic consumption.

One could add to this the very obvious penetration of foreign companies into markets traditionally dominated by domestic capital, for example the import of Japanese cars, and the attempt by the British industry to involve the state in its defence via protectionist policies. There is also the threat to smaller, less developed companies presented by large enterprises, sometimes multi-national, with vast resources of capital available for technological innovation, diversification and expansion. These threaten to alter radically the market and the structure of production. This complex situation of multiple competition, then, is what provides the framework of employment for the vast majority of those who depend on selling their labour-power. The competition between employers generates and maintains competition between employees.

In this view, trade unions take on quite a different role. For writers like Hyman (1975), they are no longer regarded as one among many pressure or interest groups. Rather they are a fundamental economic institution of capitalism.

In the first place, any attempt by individual workers to improve or defend their pay or conditions of work is almost guaranteed to fail, given the ability of the employer to substitute another worker. It can succeed only by collective action. It is in this sense that the basis of trade unionism is said to lie in the common situation of all those who sell their labour-power. The trade unions provide a defence of the working classes against the competition between employers that drives them to hold down labour costs.

In the second place, since the work force is differentiated by technical function, by educational and social criteria, by various modes and levels of pay and by other conditions of employment, the general interest of employees as sellers of labour-power is fractured into a multiplicity of group interests. Since the first commitment of a trade union is to the immediate interests of its members, trade unions end up by protecting the sale and use of *particular* labour-powers rather than labour-power in general.

Instead of describing the institutional structures of trade unions, the sociologists' emphasis is now on the different forms of strategy which different unions can pursue. For example, craft unions use the specialized skills of their members to gain higher wages and better conditions. They maintain these by operating policies on apprenticeships, training, and job demarcation which restrict access to the work. These may well increase competition among employees in other sectors of the labour market, but they do lessen that among workers in the same sector who are constantly threatened with dilution and rationalization by employers. At the other end of the scale, general unions have developed strategies based precisely on the *lack* of skill of their members. Of course, all these strategies and policies depend also on particular circumstances brought about either by national economic policies or by local conditions.

Strikes are understood not as some irrational expression of worker 'anomie', but as the ultimate collective sanction available to employees in response to a common work situation. As sellers of labour-power, workers, in the last instance, can resort only to withdrawing that labour-power. In earlier stages of dispute there are other sanctions available to them, such as overtime bans, working-to-rule, demonstrations, sit-ins, blacking goods, appeals to the public and various forms of sabotage. Some of these may be regarded as variations of strike action in that they are either partial withdrawals of labour or threats to withdraw labour. Whatever is the case, such industrial action is understood as the result of a series of rational calculations by workers of what is to be lost or gained, and is based on an assessment of the interests of the various groups involved.

This is not to say that strikes are, therefore, always right. Labour leaders, official or unofficial, may make an incorrect evaluation of the situation, or they may have inadequate or false information. But these are not reasons for misinterpreting rational calculative behaviour as irrational and neurotic. Trade union activity, including strikes, is understood as a series of strategies concerned to defend the interests of its members against attempts to undermine wage levels or working conditions.

Looked at in this way, the traditional sociological separation of occupations, professions and industrial relations becomes nonsensical. Once sociologists stop focusing on the details of the type of work and its institutional form and concentrate instead on the strategies of particular workers in the context of the competition between employers, a rather different picture emerges. It is by shifting the emphasis in this way that Johnson (1972) can conclude that occupations can best be distinguished according to 'the institutional forms of *control* of occupational activities'.

This control may derive from particular specialized skills or from specialist knowledge. These qualifications enable the skilled practitioners to distance themselves from their clients, whose lack of knowledge makes them ill-equipped to judge the service or product for which they are paying. This very ignorance of the consumers enables the occupational group to mystify their expertise far in excess of the actual complexity of its content. As Johnson puts it, 'the greater the social distance, the greater the helplessness of the client, then the greater the exposure to possible exploitation and the need for social control'. It is clear from this that one definition of 'professions' is those occupations which have most developed this potential for social distance and autonomy from clients.

However, the extent to which this potential is realized depends on other linked factors. The social tension that is generated by these tendencies of specialist groups leads to the development of mechanisms to control them. Johnson identifies three major forms of institutional control:

1 'Collegiate control', where the relationship between practitioners and clients has been dominated by the former. They have set the standards of their service through various forms of colleague control and have determined who should receive their services. Examples of this would be the self-disciplining, professional bodies which developed in the nineteenth century, controlling the content of the service, the recruitment into and training for it. Obvious cases are law and medicine.

2 'Patronage control', where the clients have defined their own needs and the manner in which they were to be satisfied. Here the practitioners are attached to great aristocratic houses or, in more contemporary times, they are in the service of large business enterprises or government agencies, for example, engineers.

3 'Mediative control', where the relationship between consumers and practitioners is mediated by a third party which defines the needs of the former and the services which the latter are to provide. The clearest example here would be social work. The clients of social workers were created by the state on the basis of criteria like poverty, social need or criminality. Their needs were thus officially defined and the occupation of social worker created to provide for them.

Of course, Johnson admits that there is some overlap between these categories, and gives the example of the British National Health Service. Here the state, though it brought almost all GPs into a state medical scheme and determined that all British citizens should be entitled to free medical services, left the British Medical Association to control medical practice and the remuneration of its members. It therefore represents a combination of categories (1) and (3). Such overlaps are partly due to the particular historical circumstances in which an occupation emerged and the ways in which it adapted itself to subsequent changes in demand for and control of its services.

However, these forms of occupational control acquire *explanatory* power only when located in the context of the relationship between occupations and the economy as a whole. Johnson attempts to do just this in a much more abstract article, which places his analysis in a Marxist framework (Johnson, T. 1976). As we have seen, for Marx the economy involves both the production and the circulation of commodities under definite social relations. It also requires that labour-power is 'reproduced', that is, the employees at all levels acquire all that is necessary for them physically, socially and intellectually to perform their labour adequately.

Johnson argues that each of these areas of economic activity involves a different labour process: each generates a variety of occupations and has its own institutionalized forms of control. The aim of the production area for instance, is to increase the surplus value embodied in commodities. This process then requires bureaucratic systems of control and surveillance, involving a hierarchy from foremen to work-study engineers and managers.

Within the circulation area, where commodities are bought and sold, the main labour process is concerned with large-scale systems of calculation and control necessary for the 'realization' of profit. The foremost occupation here is modern accountancy. Within the area of reproduction, the labour process involves the institutionalization of certain health, educational, social and cultural standards. This clearly generates a number of new professions as well as adding to the importance of some existing ones. However, such centralization and formalization also involves the intervention of the state, through its agencies. On the one hand, state agencies authorize and legitimate the exercise of occupational skills by controlling the granting of certificates of qualification to practise. On the other hand, they try to usurp the authority of occupations and their clients to decide what professional services should be and how they should be carried out. Johnson calls this attempt 'state heteronomy'. The extent to which the state succeeds depends on a number of factors, as we saw in the case of social work and medicine.

Johnson concludes that the emergence, expansion or decline of occupations is related to the requirements of capital, but that this relationship is cut across by other factors. Not the least of these is the ideology of professionalism itself and the occupational control over forms of knowledge. Further, Johnson suggests that, where an occupational group or part of an occupational group is directly involved in defining the categories that go into the 'appropriation' and 'realization' of surplus value or the reproduction of labour-power, that group shares the functions of capital, as well as its power and privilege. (By 'categories' Johnson means categories like 'profitable' and 'non-profitable', 'productive' and 'non-productive', as well as 'educationally deprived', 'criminal', etc. All of these are part of the process of production and reproduction. Occupational groups which are in a position to define who, or what activity, belong in each category, are, of course, very powerful.) Such groups are the powerful, relatively independent professional associations which most closely approximate to his category of 'colleague control'. What maintains and protects their privileged position is their ability to control entry and training, to determine how different work activities are stratified in the occupational group, and to bind their members by ethical codes of conduct. This marks them off from those occupations or parts of occupations which merely apply these definitions as part of a routine labour process, as in the case of what are some-times called the semi-professions. These groups are much more vulnerable to the 'de-skilling process' and 'proletarianization' described by Braverman.

Summary

The main contribution of this recent sociology of work has been to insist that the organization of work and all that it involves is not simply the effect of administrative and technical demands but of the nature and type of society within which work occurs. In examining present-day societies, the sociologists concerned are convinced that the social and economic forms of what we call 'the West' must still be considered capitalist. That is, their economic, social and political institutions and policies are oriented towards the pursuit of profit above all else; their work-forces are increasingly separated from the control of the means by which they make a living; and their enterprises remain related to each other through competition in the market.

What interests these writers is the way in which the structure of power produced by a capitalist economy relates to the organization of work. What they have introduced into the sociology of work is 'the politics of work'.

Conclusion

It was stated at the beginning of this chapter that much of the literature in the sociology of work can be best understood as a debate about the relationship between the organization of work and other social, political and cultural institutions. That debate is most concerned with the role of technology.

Simplifying the positions somewhat, on the one hand there are those, loosely identified with liberal pluralism, who see technology as the determining factor of the social and technical organization of the work place and of society in general. Certain skills, knowledge and normative standards generated by the complexity of modern technology stratify the occupational system, the educational system, the class system and the political system. Society, consequently, becomes characterized by a multiplicity of interest groups, each with their own elites, each competing with the others for national resources and national honours. This very competition, it is said, guarantees democratic government, since each interest group has to rely on its respective public for support. A democratic system of checks and balances on institutional power is thus claimed to be one major attribute of 'the imperatives of technology' (see also Chapter 7, pages 208–12).

On the other hand there are those, loosely linked with Marxism, who argue that technology always takes place within definite sets of social relations. Specific aims and interests do not penetrate technology from the outside subsequent to its construction. Rather they actually constitute the fabric of the technical apparatus.

The importance of Western technology to Third World countries is often cited by Marxist economists as a classic example of how certain forms of technology, once installed, bring with them certain forms of social relations. They argue that the acquisition of technology by underdeveloped societies cannot be viewed simply as the importation of a set of techniques and sophisticated machinery. Once a certain form of technology is established a certain form of work organization, including a division of labour and a labour-force equipped with specific skills and knowledge, hierarchically evaluated, will be required. The maintenance and reproduction of these arrangements then require the form of social relations which initially accompanied the technology in the country of origin. It is clear that, in this example, the operation of technology has a double effect on the importing country. First, it introduces changes in the indigenous labour process, and second, it establishes certain political and economic links between the importing and the exporting country, which may not be to the former's advantage.

For Marxists, you will remember, social relations always involve the ownership and control of the means of production, so that it is not technology as a set of techniques and instruments which structures social and economic organization; it is the ownership and control of technology. This, they argue, is becoming increasingly concentrated in the hands of a few large-scale enterprises – the great corporations and the capitalist state. This concentration of the means by which the majority of the population earn their living results in the very opposite of democratic control. Rather, it leads to a diminishing of the control that people have as producers and as consumers. As workers, their jobs become increasingly tightly defined and narrowed by modern management techniques designed to secure the greater productivity, control and compliance of the work-force. As consumers, their choice becomes increasingly limited as the type, quality and price of commodities and services are standardized, despite the appearance of an ever-greater number of consumer goods on the market. As citizens, their impact on political and public affairs is diminished as more and more of the issues are seen to be 'too technical' for the ordinary person and are removed to closed committees of experts.

It should be noted that in the debate between these two positions there is little disagreement about what changes in social, economic, political and scientific institutions and policies have taken place in Western industrialized societies during this century. What is in dispute is how these changes are interpreted and explained.

Despite these differences, however, both positions in their respective ways retain the notion of technology as a neutral embodiment of rationality. Marxists, with some justification, attack the pluralists for assuming that the *existing* social relations of capitalist production are also the technically necessary, and, therefore, inevitable ones. For Galbraith and others, social divisions in modern society are determined by technical imperatives. Such social divisions therefore assume a certain political innocence.

This idealization of the neutrality of scientific–technical development leads writers like Marcuse (1964) and Habermas (1975) to argue that science and technology have taken on the functions of legitimating political power. Not only do science and technology structure, in the service of capital, the organization of work for the majority of the labour-force, but they also provide 'a background ideology that penetrates into the consciousness of the depoliticized mass of the population'. Once technology and science become fused with capitalist industry they become a major ideological force in society. The logic of scientific progress provides the justification for the specific forms of social organization, for the limitation of democratic decision-making to the choice between alternate sets of political and administrative experts, and for the spiral of consumerism which, by keeping people in increasing comfort, prevents them from recognizing the political domination that is part and parcel of 'technical reason' (see also pages 212–15).

Nevertheless, behind more orthodox Marxist writings lies the notion of a neutral technology – the slumbering potential of the forces of production which, once delivered from the restraints of capitalism, may be utilized in the establishment of socialism. In analysing the capitalist system, sociologists influenced by Marxism have most persuasively shown how technology cannot be considered without reference to certain sets of economic and political interests. Yet they continue to believe that it is possible to rescue that very technology unsullied from capitalist relations of production and to establish it within a socialist society.

This ambiguity is a result of the tendency to regard technology as all of one piece instead of a number of different technologies. By insisting on the primacy of the social relations of production these writers have certainly helped to demystify prevailing ideologies of technical rationality and political neutrality. But they have neglected to analyse the social implications of a variety of technologies in relation to each other.

In this respect, John Mathews's article 'Marxism, Energy and Technological Change' (1980) is extremely relevant. Using the example of energy policy, Mathews argues that, given the scale, penetration and destructive capacity of modern technologies, Marxists must turn their attention to the *intrinsic* characteristics of different forms of technology.

In comparing nuclear power to alternative energy sources, he argues that the logic of technology does have definite social and political effects. In the case of nuclear power he points out that:

1 the inseparable connection between nuclear reactors for the generation of electricity and the production of *material* for nuclear weapons amounts to an almost insurmountable obstacle to any political breakthrough on the question of disarmament;
2 the huge escalation of costs associated with safety measures means a drain on national resources which might otherwise be available for socially useful endeavours;
3 the advanced nature of the theoretical physics involved and the risks to public safety mean that the control of the means of energy, whoever owns/possesses them, must lie outside the work-force or the consumers and in the hands of an obsessively secretive technocracy;
4 the deadly nature of radioactive materials necessitates authoritarian structures of command and security both inside and outside the plant. This undermines the civil liberties and trade union freedoms which we currently possess.

Mathews claims that there is an intrinsic logic in nuclear power, and that it works in favour of a highly centralized, bureaucratic, authoritarian monopoly with virtually no public accountability. The social impact of nuclear technology, therefore, is the same whatever the social relations in which it is situated. 'Nuclear surveillance and nuclear disasters do not discriminate between socialist and capitalist enterprise.'

By contrast, Mathews points out the *potential* in the alternative energy technologies for decentralization, increased levels of employment, worker and consumer participation and a variety of social experiments in ownership and control.

His argument indeed extends beyond the case of nuclear power. Its lesson is not to underestimate the importance of the central power to control the production process; to determine the type, quantity, quality and price of what is to be produced; to hire and fire workers; to close down one production unit and open another at will. The conclusion is not to substitute one form of technological determinism for another. It is to argue that one of the tasks of the social scientists engaged in the study of work and industry is to analyse and identify the likely social, political and economic implications of different technologies and, thus, to provide a thorough basis for choosing between such technologies on *social* grounds.

Guide to further reading

As you will have noticed, several suggestions for further reading have been included at the appropriate points in this chapter. Many of the relevant texts are rather difficult and assume a familiarity with theories and concepts beyond the scope of the A-level syllabus. For this reason, the suggestions for further reading are rather limited.

Weir (1973), *Men and Work in Modern Britain*, provides a basic reader. For an account of the debate about industrialization and social change, try Turner (1975), *Industrialism*. Parker *et al.* (1977), *The Sociology of Industry*, represents traditional approaches to work, while Nichols (1980), *Capital and Labour*, is a useful Marxist primer.

See Blauner (1967), *Alienation and Freedom*, for an attempt to operationalize the concept of alienation in four different industries. Beynon (1973), *Working for Ford*, presents a vivid account of the experience of workers in large-scale process production, and the effects on worker organization, strategies and consciousness. The shortest and easiest exposition of Marx's theory of capitalist exploitation can be found in his two pamphlets, *Value, Price and Profit* and *Wage Labour and Capital*. A classic text on the growth of monopoly capitalism is Baran and Sweezy (1968), *Monopoly Capital*.

Many of the issues raised in this chapter are discussed in Abercrombie and Urry (1983), Giddens and MacKenzie (1982), and Stewart and Blackburn (1980).

11 Deviance and social problems

Roger Gomm

Words do not stand alone but take their meaning from whole patterns of ideas – usually called 'perspectives' in sociology. Thus the term 'deviance' changes its meaning as we move from perspective to perspective. I will, therefore, make it clear from the outset what I consider to be the most useful definition of deviance, and this will give you an idea of the position from which I am commenting on other uses of the term.

Deviance as a complaint

The term 'deviance' is not often used in sociology in the statistical sense, meaning 'unusual' or 'uncommon'. Being an Olympic medallist or a Nobel prize-winner is certainly more 'deviant' statistically than being a burglar or a suicide case, but only the latter would be regarded as examples of deviance in sociology. Let us say that we are dealing with deviance when we hear people say: 'it's wrong', 'something ought to be done about it'. That's deviance, and it may range from a complaint about mispronunciation to one about murder, and from breaking crockery to breaking and entering. It is very important not to restrict the term deviance only to its most dramatic examples such as murder, rape, drug addiction or treason. Deviance of a less dramatic kind is an ordinary feature of everyday life.

When people make such complaints they are pointing to some 'rule' to which they think other people should conform. Deviance and rule, then, are two sides of the same coin; if you make rules you set up conditions for deviance to occur. Since it is impossible to imagine social life without people judging matters as good or bad, or without making rules about how they and others should live their lives, deviance is an ordinary part of any ordinary society. There is nothing sociologically surprising about the existence of deviance in society. What is of interest are the different forms taken by deviance in different social settings.

Deviance as social reaction

I approach the study of deviance through what is sometimes called the 'social reaction approach', which derives from 'symbolic interactionism' (see Chapter 2, page 38). It is also consistent with Marxist and other 'conflict' approaches to deviance. It is not consistent with most psychological explanations of deviance nor with a functionalist approach (see below).

Next we need to examine the term 'social' as it occurs in 'social reaction'. Whatever the term 'society' means, it has something to do with people, and people do not necessarily agree with each other as to what is right or wrong. It is quite possible for something which is regarded as deviant by one group of people to be regarded as right and proper by another, and there is no activity which has always been regarded by all people everywhere as deviant. Deviance is 'relative' to whoever is making the judgement and where and when. Whose reaction, then, are we dealing with?

The topic of deviance thus links directly with the topic of inequality, through the question of who is able to make and enforce the rules and standards against which deviance is judged. Being able to make rules and enforce them successfully against others is a very important aspect of power and inequality, of the class structure, the age structure, of the relationships between ethnic groups and between sexes.

Social problems

'Social problem' is an awkward term. The most useful way of thinking about social problems is to see them as political phenomena: as the occasions when individuals or groups have been able to mobilize the support of others to translate their personal interests, concerns or objections into an issue for public debate and public action (Mills 1959). In the same way as with deviance, whether some matter is viewed as a 'social problem' or a matter for individual conscience, or (say) as an 'economic problem' or a 'social problem' depends upon who is successful in defining the problem in the political arena. There is no way in which the sociologist can decide that (say) abortion or homosexuality are social problems or problems on which individuals should consult their consciences. This is a matter which is decided in the real world of politics.

The study of social problems should really lie with the study of political campaigns in general. Though attempts by sociologists to outline the stages through which social problems develop is a step in this direction (Butterworth and Weir 1972), social problems have often been considered apart from politics. A major reason for this is the confusion within functionalist sociology between social problems and the problems of society (see below). A further confusion to avoid is that between 'social problems' and 'sociological problems'. The latter refers simply to those matters which interest sociologists and is dealt with in more detail in Chapter 3, page 79.

For the social reaction approach, which I favour, the key question with regard to both deviance and social problems is always, 'Says who?' Treating deviance as a social reaction is to focus on the questions, 'Why do people make a fuss about it?' and 'What sort of fuss do they make and why this sort?' or 'Why do they react as they do?'

Now this of course turns the usual commonsense approach to deviance on its head. When we are faced with someone's behaviour we find objectionable, we don't usually ask, 'Why is it that I find this objectionable?' What we usually ask is, 'Why should they do such an objectionable thing?' These are two distinct sorts of questions. Both are interesting sociologically and it is important to seek answers to both sorts. Usually, however, there is more sociological mileage in the question 'Why is it considered deviant?' than in the question 'Why did the deviant act occur?'

An example may make this clear. Down's syndrome – or 'mongolism', as it is popularly called – is a congenital defect which produces people with a low intelligence and a number of physical abnormalities. We know exactly how this condition is caused; by a mistake in transferring genetic information from parent to child. Some really interesting sociological questions would be, for instance, 'Why do we view Down's syndrome as a problem?' 'What sort of problem do we view it as, and why?' and 'How do people react to Down's children and their parents, and how in turn does this determine how they feel and behave?'

Over the last 100 years attitudes and beliefs about 'mongols' have continually changed: they have been viewed as 'evolutionary throw-backs', as punishments from God, as the result of dietary habits, as pathetic and harmless, as dangerous and frightening, as needing firm discipline and segregation from ordinary folk, or as needing love, affection and integration with 'normals'. In each case the causes of Down's syndrome have remained the same, but it has been a different sort of deviance, and the differences have been produced through different types of social reaction.

This introduction establishes my standpoint regarding the definition of deviance and social problems. Now we must catalogue the various different approaches to deviance to be found in the sociological literature. You will note that I include both psychological and sociological perspectives, because until recently many sociologists did employ psychological theories to explain deviance (some still do), and because all types of sociology make some assumptions about the human personality; that is to say, all sociologies imply a psychology of sorts.

Perspectives on deviance

In order to make a simple catalogue of theories of deviance, I will use a grid with two axes (Figure 6). The first axis divides psychological theories from sociological ones. Psychological theories locate the causes

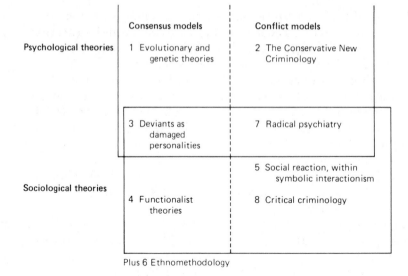

Plus 6 Ethnomethodology

Figure 6   *Catalogue of theories of deviance*

of deviance within the make-up of the deviant him/herself; deviance is thus due to there being 'odd people'. Sociological theories on the other hand see deviance as arising out of the 'way in which society works', or 'fails to work properly'. There is an important area of overlap where deviance is seen as resulting from the way in which societies work to produce people with odd personalities.

The second axis divides theories of society into those based on:

1 'Consensus models', which view society as either being based on a widespread agreement about what is right and wrong ('value consensus'), or as being in an imperfect state when such agreement is lacking. Given such a picture of society, deviance stands as evidence that some people are deficient or confused because they won't or can't share the values of others, or that 'society isn't working properly'. Such views of deviance are often called 'pathology models' because they entail the idea of deviance as an individual or social *sickness*.
2 'Conflict models', which view society as containing groups of people with different interests and values, and usually involve the idea that some groups are subjected to the interests of others. Looked at in this way deviance is unsurprising. It appears as part of an on-going struggle between people to get their own way.

I have located some theories of deviance on the grid and numbered them in the order in which they appear below. Remember though, that a grid like this is really too simple to capture the full complexity of different theories of deviance. It is a model, as explained in Chapter 3, page 62.

1 Born deviants: evolutionary and genetic theories of deviance

No treatment of the history of ideas on deviance is complete without a mention of Cesare Lombroso (1867, 1911), sometimes called 'the father of modern criminology'. Lombroso was an Italian doctor whose hobby was doing post-mortem examinations on the bodies of executed criminals. In splendid style he describes how the resolution of the puzzle of deviance dawned on him:

> This was not merely an idea, but a flash of inspiration. At the sight of that skull, I seemed to see all of a sudden, lighted up as a vast plain under a flaming sky, the problem of the nature of the criminal – an atavistic being who reproduces in his person the ferocious instincts of primitive humanity and the inferior animals. Thus were explained anatomically the enormous jaws, high cheek bones, prominent superciliary arches, solitary lines in the palms, extreme size of the orbits, handle shaped or sessile ears found in criminals, savages and apes, insensibility of pain, extremely acute sight, tattooing, excessive idleness, love of orgies, and the irresistible craving for evil for its own sake, the desire not only to extinguish life in the victim, but to mutilate the corpse, tear its flesh and drink its blood. [Lombroso 1911]

In his own times Lombroso's ideas seemed perfectly credible. He was writing at a time when the idea of 'evolution' was being applied to virtually every facet of intellectual life. People then did not merely think of the evolution of species as organisms, but of the *biological* evolution of habits (tattooing for instance), intelligence and moral sensibility, and many were quite convinced that European and American males of the intellectual classes stood at the pinnacle of the evolutionary tree. What more sensible then than to imagine that 'deviants' appearing among the 'advanced races' were evolutionary throw-backs to an earlier period of evolution? Lombroso's theory of 'atavism' explained crime, and especially political and violent crimes in this way, but was paralleled by similar theories for other kinds of deviance. Down's term 'mongol' is a contraction of 'Mongolian idiot': for Down's 'mongol' children represented throw-backs to a Mongolian stage of evolution through which the advanced Caucasoid races had passed. Mongolian peoples, such as the Chinese, were of course all seen as 'idiots' by comparison with white Europeans, only appearing as intelligent because they had copied European ways (Gould 1980).

Such grand evolutionary theories are no longer taken seriously, but similar ideas still appear today piecemeal. Thus among the extreme right wing in the West and in South Africa, black people are regarded as 'less evolved' and hence as more prone to crime, and there are elements of this sort of thinking in attempts to explain the educational failure of black pupils in the USA in terms of the idea of a lower level of *inherited* intelligence (see Chapter 9, page 252).

In the contemporary literature of deviance there are many attempts to find genetic causes for deviant states or behaviour. Down's syndrome – although it has nothing to do with atavism – is an uncontroversial example, so are some forms of blindness, deafness and muteness, and some physical disfigurements which impair people's lives. Beyond this, however, there have been many attempts to prove that behaviours such as crime, drug addiction, alcoholism, homosexuality and some forms of 'mental illness' are inherited defects. To say the least, these attempts must be regarded as unproven, and to some degree mistaken (see also Chapter 5, which considers biology as ideology on page 134).

The major shortcoming of this approach to deviance is that it assumes that deviance is caused by the existence of deviant people, and that it only asks how it is that such deviant people appear in the population. It leaves out all the interesting 'social reaction' questions about why some states of being or some behaviour is regarded as deviant and how other people deal with it. We may consider an example of these shortcomings in the work of the most sophisticated exponent of such biological theories: Hans Eysenck (1970). Eysenck's theories all have a similar structure, so our comments on his thinking on criminality apply also to his thinking on phobias, homosexuality, compulsive gambling, and various forms of 'mental illness'.

Eysenck believes that people can be placed along a continuum ranging from 'extraversion' to 'introversion', and that their position on this continuum is determined by their genetic make-up. The 'extravert' is not necessarily the outgoing, fun-loving type, nor is the 'introvert' quiet and contemplative. The terms refer instead to scores achieved on various extraversion and introversion tests; for instance, extraverts make more mistakes in completing a pencil-and-paper maze, and are less able to sustain a rhythm when tapping with a pencil. Eysenck regards these as indicators of extraversion/introversion. Eysenck claims that, when people in prison are tested for extraversion, more extraverts are found than in the general population. Since extraversion is claimed to be inherited, this must be the inherited basis of criminality. The mechanism which links extraversion with ciminal behaviour is that extraverts take longer to 'condition' than introverts. (The idea of conditioning is the behaviourist psychologist's picture of learning, in which people learn the behaviour for which they have been rewarded in the past, and fail to learn the behaviour for which they have been punished: the image is that of dog-training.) Thus the argument goes: because it takes extraverts longer to learn the rules, they are more likely to break them, and therefore more likely to end up in prison.

This is an extremely flimsy set of ideas. They are important, nevertheless, because they are widely believed by psychiatrists in mental hospitals, prisons and in the education service. We can use them to show the shortcomings of positivistic methodology (see also Chapter 3, pages 59-60).

First, by starting with the characteristics of imprisoned criminals, Eysenck assumes:

(a) that they are all guilty;
(b) that the tests he uses measure essential characteristics of criminal personality, and not the effects of being imprisoned;
(c) that the people who commit crimes and get caught are a representative sample of all those who commit crimes. At the most, Eysenck has a theory about convicted criminals, and not about people who commit crimes in general.

Second, Eysenck's view of the 'rules of society' is absurdly simplistic. He writes as if there were an unambiguous, fixed set of rules, known by and approved of by everyone. If, on the other hand, we imagine that some children at least will grow up in households where they are taught to break the law effectively, then criminality should sometimes correlate with 'introversion'. Indeed, by Eysenck's own theory, introverts should be 'naturally' better at the sort of crimes which involve elaborate organization and split-second timing. Without becoming too fanciful, however, we should note that the rules of social life are in fact ambiguous, shifting, and subscribed to in different degrees by different sorts of people. There is no way in which learning to be a competent member of society can be compared to learning to be an obedient puppy.

2 The war of good against evil: neo-classical theories of deviance or the Conservative New Criminology

There is a theory of deviance currently popular in the USA, with a few 'neo-classical' sociologists: the Conservative New Criminology (Wilson 1968, 1975; van den Haag, 1975). It treats human nature as essentially competitive and self-seeking, and, although a minority of people are seen as incorrigibly 'bad', no reason is given as to why this should be so. Deviant behaviour, particularly crime, is seen as a choice to do wrong, and although it is recognized that people may have different conceptions of right and wrong, those who think differently from the writers are viewed as being in error. Life seems to be seen as a war between good people and bad people; in the American context this comes very close to a view of social life as a war between whites and minority groups such as blacks, Puerto Ricans or Chicanos, and between the poor and the better-off.

Sociological and psychological theories purporting to explain deviance are regarded as unproven. Deviance is taken for granted as a fact of life, as are the laws which define what is criminal and the norms against which deviance is judged. The whole weight of this sort of theorizing is thrown into the discussion of how best to prevent crime through policies of deterrence, punishment, prison security and effective policing.

Despite the fact that this theory is proposed by sociologists, it is a thoroughly unsociological theory. It is important, however, because it accords so closely with the views of many judges, police chiefs, politicians and members of the public.

3 Socialization gone wrong: deviants as damaged personalities

An enormous amount of the literature on deviance has taken the view that deviance arises because the deviant person has been *improperly socialized*. In such theories there is usually the idea that 'human nature' requires certain conditions which must be satisfied if people are to develop 'normally': otherwise people will grow up bitter and twisted, disorganized, inhibited, violent, anxious, repressed and so on. With this view – which derives from the developmental psychology of Freud – the causes of deviance can be traced back to sets of factors which distort or damage the personality.

Two things need to be said about these ideas. Firstly, there are many contrasting notions about what constitutes a 'proper environment' for socialization. They range on the one hand from statements about the need for firm discipline, order and regularity in the child's life, to notions about the need for freedom, self-determination and non-judgemental love. So there is precious little agreement among psychologists about the 'proper' environment for socialization. Indeed, it can be shown that whatever is popularly thought among child psychologists to be necessary for healthy mental development bears a very close resemblance to the way in which the intellectual middle classes are bringing up their children at a particular point in time (Gomm 1976). More sophisticated exponents of this view recognize that the 'proper' environment in one society or cultural group may be different from that in another, and that the important thing is for people to be socialized in such a way that they 'fit in' (Mead 1970). Even so, the connections between the way in which people are brought up and the way in which they behave in later life is only tenuously understood – despite a century of research (Clarke and Clarke 1976). (The topic of socialization is dealt with in more detail in Chapter 4, pages 90–5.)

Secondly, theories of this sort also vary according to how much they focus on personality development, and how much on the social circumstances in which socialization occurs, that is, how psychological or how sociological they are. For brevity we will look at just one example of a body of research leaning towards sociology: the work of D. J. West and his colleagues at the Cambridge Institute of Criminology (West 1969).

One of West's largest research projects was a study of all the male children aged 8 years old in all the primary schools in an inner London Borough. West and his colleagues collected a great deal of information about these boys, at 8 and at later stages.

Their findings were unsurprising. The boys who were already official delinquents by the age of 14 were drawn mainly from the boys who at the age of 8 were living in the families with the lowest incomes, and with the lowest standards of housekeeping. They had the lowest standards of school work, and tended to be unpopular with their fellows and teachers. There was more likely to be marital discord in their homes and they were most likely to have parents who were unco-operative with regard to the survey.

Now West himself writes about having a 'multifactorial theory of delinquency', but it is quite evident that the many factors he correlates with delinquency are made to hang together with the simple notion that 'growing up in adverse circumstances creates delinquent tendencies'; that is, a damaged personality model.

Although West's research is very sound in many respects, it doesn't necessarily lead to his conclusions. Perhaps the key criticism is this: West assumes that all these factors correlated with delinquency have a *causative* influence, in the sense that they predispose a child towards law-breaking. From the evidence that West produces, however, there is an alternative explanation. It may be that such children do not commit any more delinquent acts than others, but that, being known to come from 'bad backgrounds', to have a 'poor record' of school work, etc., makes them more likely to be prosecuted than other children. (For West's own answer to this criticism see West 1973.)

This idea of the deviant as a damaged personality appears as an explanation for a wide range of deviant behaviour, from property crime, through homosexuality, rape and mental illness, wife- and baby-battering, alcoholism, drug addiction and suicide. This model of deviance has strong links with other topics in sociology. For instance, it is the key to understanding the idea of the 'cycle of deprivation' explanation for both poverty and educational failure; viz. parents with inadequate personalities inadequately socialize their children who in turn become inadequate parents.

As you can see, this way of thinking has the effect of focusing attention on the personality of the deviant and on the way in which the personality was formed in the past. In so doing, it makes 'society' appear as if 'it' were merely the result of personality types reproducing themselves. Such thinking makes a direct connection between the idea of a deficient child-hood and the commission of deviant acts. It ignores the very complex processes through which people come to be regarded as deviant by others, and sometimes by themselves. This is a theme we will return to later.

Summary: Psychological theories in the definition of social problems

The theories we have looked at so far are all essentially psychological. As with any other theories they would not be so important if it were not for the fact that they become active in the world; in this case, through the way in which deviant behaviour is made into a political issue. Whenever we are faced with what people call a 'social problem' we should look to see who it is who is most successful in convincing others that their definition of the problem is the right one, and that the solutions they propose will work. 'Experts' such as psychologists or sociologists are only one sort of contributor to the definition of social problems. This process also involves other occupational groups, political parties, pressure groups, the media, influential personalities, and from time to time even the general public. So far as our psychological theories are concerned, there is a fairly clear relationship between theories and their popularity with particular political views: genetic, biological and neo-classical theories are generally more popular with the political right, while damaged personality theories are more popular with the social democratic centre, with its interest in social reform.

For some groups, making sure that decision-makers accept a particular version of a social problem is a very important matter. Behaviourist psychologists, for instance (such as Eysenck), gain considerably from being able to convince politicians that deviance arises from faulty conditioning, because this leads to the establishment of facilities for re-conditioning and de-conditioning people and provides careers for psychologists. Again, the widespread acceptance since 1945 of the damaged personality model has been crucially important in the emergence of the occupations of psychotherapy and social work – both of which groups claim to have the skill to remedy 'personality disturbances'. A clear example of the way in which a theory comes to be translated into action is the Children and Young Persons' Act of 1969. This was based on the notion that young offenders are not so much 'bad' and in need of punishment, as 'deprived' and in need of social work. This Act (thoroughly unpopular with policemen and magistrates), enormously increased the role of local authority social workers and hence their career prospects. Changes in legislation since 1969 have generally been based on the notion that young offenders are morally bad and in need of discipline and punishment.

4   The system isn't working properly: functionalist theories of deviance

The term 'functionalism' covers a wide range of thinking about society and refers to a variety of theories of deviance. We can make some general remarks, however. All functionalists have some conception of society being a system made up of interlocking parts. Modern societies are not seen as static systems but as tending to evolve towards becoming more complex. This raises the possibility that, in the process of changing, social systems are always at risk of 'going wrong', at least temporarily.

Thus functionalists have usually (not always) associated deviance with social change.

To understand this more fully we must recall some other elements of functionalist theory. Firstly, there is an image of human nature as being highly motivated to achieve the good will, respect and esteem of others. This is the same as saying that people are highly motivated to conform to what others expect of them. Secondly, there is an assumption that social systems stay stable (despite change) by making sure that the members of society have the ideas which the system needs them to have. This is seen to be done mainly through the process of socialization, which is here seen as a process of learning to do the things which gain the individual the good will of others. For functionalists, socialization is learning to conform. The social system is seen to offer rewards to those who conform (wages, promotion, honours, respect, etc.) and punishments for those who do not (stigma, imprisonment, execution, etc.). All this is called 'social control'. The set of common beliefs and values which the social system needs people to subscribe to was called 'the collective conscience' by Durkheim, and the 'central value system' by later functionalists.

Thirdly, functionalists accept that people are different biologically, with different attributes and potentials, and, to different degrees, functionalists assume that problems will arise if 'the wrong people' get to occupy 'the wrong position' and if 'talented people' are not allowed to rise. Nearly all functionalist theories are 'meritocratic' when they deal with modern societies, i.e. they maintain that those in the top positions are there on merit. The classic statement of this position is that of Davis and Moore, called the 'functional theory of stratification', and is dealt with in Chapter 6, page 181.

Furthermore, functionalists have classified social phenomena into those which promote social stability, and those which threaten it. From the 1940s these were labelled 'functional' and 'dysfunctional' respectively. It is important to note that not all types of deviance are seen by functionalists as dysfunctional; some are seen as functional. For instance, Durkheim recognized that some forms of deviance gave people the opportunity to express their support for important social values. Accusing and trying a witch might promote both a feeling of unity among the social group and serve as a way of publicly demonstrating abhorrence at all the bad things represented by witchcraft. Many social anthropologists have argued that the stereotype of the witch in African societies, and the risk of being accused of being one, constitutes an important means of 'social control'. For instance if witches are known to be mean, greedy and bad-tempered, this is a very good reason to be generous and good-natured. In our own times, the ritual surrounding some forms of deviance, especially the criminal trial, and the extensive coverage of deviance in the mass media, might be said to perform the same function, with regard to some people at least. For instance the image of the 'social security scrounger', displayed forcefully about once every four months in the popular press, is a very important deterrent against claiming social security benefits (Golding and Middleton 1979).

Functionalists have also recognized that some forms of deviance, while they may be dysfunctional, have functional aspects. Crime, for instance, provides employment for policemen, prison warders, probation officers, locksmiths and security firms. The sudden disappearance of crime would have rather severe social consequences.

Deviance may also be seen as functional in the sense that today's deviance is the forerunner of tomorrow's conformity: that is to say, because the public attitudes which define some activity as deviance are 'lagging behind' what the system 'really' needs. As an example of this, functionalists might cite the case of birth control in the UK. With the falling death rate during the nineteenth century, combined with a high birth rate, the population of Britain was growing so rapidly that it threatened social stability. So the pressure groups which campaigned for artificial techniques of birth control in the last quarter of the nineteenth century were actually suggesting something which was functional for British society. However, public attitudes which had been appropriate for a society with a high infant mortality rate persisted and people regarded the advocation of artificial techniques of birth control as a form of deviance, and put birth controllers on trial for the crime of obscenity (Davis 1948).

It is true that what is regarded as deviance at one period of history may become normal, or even desirable, at another, but to accept this functionalist view in its entirety you have not only to agree that population growth in the nineteenth century did threaten social stability, but also that in some mysterious way the 'social system' produced the mechanism 'it' needed to deal with the problem, in the form of the birth control movement.

Finally, functionalists allow that some forms of deviance have biological origins. Durkheim, for instance, suggests a special category of deviance called 'biological deviance' (Durkheim 1893), while Talcott Parsons (1952) regarded illness as deviance. In these cases the origins of deviance are not what is sociologically interesting – for they are outside the social system. What are interesting are the mechanisms devised by the system to minimize the disruptive effects. Thus Parsons argues that illness prevents people from performing their normal roles adequately. To minimize the effects of illness on the smooth workings of the social system, societies have developed systems of health care. However, since illness may be used as an excuse to avoid performing social roles, there is always a risk that this 'loophole' might be abused. Hence societies have developed ways to limit access to the sick role to those who are 'genuinely ill'. The use of medical certificates is an obvious example.

Parsons also notes that sickness carries with it obligations which prevent it from being the 'easy way out', for example, the obligation to want to get better, the obligation to follow the treatment prescribed. Parsons does not recognize that the idea of being genuinely ill is problematic in itself.

Durkheim and anomie – the origins of a functionalist theory of deviance

Durkheim is probably best known for his concept of 'anomie'. Like all the founding fathers of sociology, Durkheim was particularly concerned to understand the transformation of small-scale rural societies into modern industrial ones (Durkheim 1895). His picture of small-scale traditional societies was of societies with very strong community sentiments and a strong moral consensus. Most people would agree on what was right and wrong, and the rules for living would be clear and unambiguous. As he saw it the transformation into modernity swept away moral consensus and community spirit and left people feeling isolated and unsure about morality – in a state of anomie. This is a very familiar theme in early sociology, and indeed in non-sociological thought about society. It has been called the 'loss of community' theme (see also page 112). It provides a ready-made theory of deviance, in so far as it can be argued that:

(a) when people are unsure about 'the rules' they are always at risk of breaking them;
(b) when people have to make their own way in the world without the support of others, they sometimes can't cope. Durkheim (1897) uses this idea in formulating the category of 'anomic suicide' (see Chapter 3, pages 67–8).
(c) when people are not involved in close social relationships with others they are less likely to seek approval of others for their own behaviour, or to censure the behaviour of other people of which they disapprove. 'Community' is equated with strong social control.

Durkheim had doubts about whether the moral life was in fact possible under modern industrial urban conditions. He gives a great deal of attention to the function of education in spreading a new appropriate morality throughout a modern society, and to 'the professions' as the moral conscience of modern societies (Durkheim, 1922). One thing he seemed to be sure of, however, was that social stability under modern conditions could not be achieved unless societies were so structured that people were able to achieve their biological potential; he focused on this point particularly in an attack on inherited wealth and position (Durkheim 1897).

In Durkheim's work, which was completed around the turn of the century we have all the themes to be found in later functionalist theories of deviance: the idea of lack of moral consensus and loss of community; the idea of deviance being generated by rapid social change (urbanization, industrialization and migration); the idea of thwarted potential and frustrated expectations.

The Chicago school of social ecology

Working from Chicago University between the two world wars, the 'old Chicagoans' (Park 1925, McKenzie 1933) produced a theory of deviance which is merely a refinement of Durkheim's, although this tends to be hidden away by their use of language drawn from biological ecology. They were particularly concerned with the mapping of deviance. The Chicagoans found that the city could be described in terms of zones, each of which differed according to types of building, types of activity and types of people. In the centre of the city is the 'central business district' of offices, shops, leisure facilities and hotels. The next zone out is where the oldest and most run-down residential property may be found. In English terms, it is property which is under 'planning blight', because the city centre is expanding and sooner or later decrepit houses can be sold at a large profit for redevelopment as offices. Thus this zone is called the 'zone of transition'. Because it contains the least desirable and the cheapest houses or rooms, it is here that the poorest people live. In the American context, this tends to mean whichever group of immigrants had most recently arrived in Chicago. Not surprisingly, the Chicagoans found that most crime was committed, most criminals lived in, most suicides occurred in and most admissions to mental hospitals were from, the zone of transition.

Their explanation for this rests heavily on the notion of community, and in two ways. Firstly, there is the idea that these areas were 'socially disorganized', and that the sort of social controls present in 'organized' areas were lacking. This is an argument which is both circular and doesn't really fit the facts. It is circular because of the problem of defining 'social organization/disorganization', namely: 'Why is there deviance?' 'Because the area is disorganized.' 'How do you know?' 'Because there is deviance.' It doesn't fit the facts, because Chicago in the inter-war years is the epitome of highly *organized* crime, with the Sicilian mafia on the one hand and the Irish political 'bosses' on the other.

If the first explanation rests on the idea of not enough community, the second rests on the idea of too much. The argument is that the zone of transition is populated with people of diverse origins who form tight groups, each with its own norms and values and way of life and with a loyalty to the group rather than to 'American society' as a whole. What may be quite legitimate behaviour within the group is deviant from the viewpoint of 'American society'. For instance, drinking alcohol was considered a perfectly legitimate activity among Italian and Irish Americans, but since this was the time of prohibition it was illegal.

The term used by the Chicagoans for these diverse groups was 'subculture'. It almost goes without saying that the Chicagoans confused the preferences of white Anglo-Saxon Protestant Americans with 'American culture', and it is from this viewpoint that subcultures are seen as deviant. In the American context the problem which is being identified, rather coyly, is ethnic diversity, and the Chicagoans are tacitly racist in their assumption that the ways of life of ethnic minority groups are inappropriate to modern America.

This is also a version of the idea that social change causes deviance. Here urbanization and immigration have brought together various groups, but in such a way that they are able to perpetuate ways of life which may have been functional once, but are now 'out of date'.

The prescription for reducing deviance is obvious: make sure that subcultures are broken down and cultural differences ironed out. The roles of mass education and the mass media are particularly obvious here, although the Chicagoans do give some attention to the importance of opening up avenues of opportunity for social mobility among the members of minority groups: the thwarted opportunity theme again.

Mertonian anomie and subculture (Merton 1938)
Robert K. Merton is probably the most sophisticated functionalist writer, and his work changed the meanings of both 'anomie' and of 'subculture'.

The most acute intellectual problem of functionalism is the problem of distinguishing between what promotes social stability (functional) and what tends towards social disintegration (dysfunctional). If you remember that social systems are seen to be in a state of change, you will see that some changes have to be labelled 'functional' and some 'dysfunctional'. To make matters worse, when things stay the same we are not allowed to assume that this means they are functional; it could be that failure to change threatens the survival of the system. With a little plausible reasoning it is quite possible to argue that any social phenomenon is functional or dysfunctional, as you choose.

Merton did not solve this problem, but he ducked it fairly successfully by assuming that some social phenomena could be functional at one level of society and dysfunctional at another. Merton's anomic theory of deviance is one possibility which arises from this assumption.

Merton assumes, with other functionalists, that social stability is based on a very strong consensus of values, which nearly everyone comes to share. He also assumes that modern societies need to make sure that the most suitable people come to occupy the most appropriate positions, and that everyone is highly motivated to want to do what the system requires of them – essentially the functional theory of stratification (see page 181). However, while society requires everybody to be highly motivated to achieve certain rewards, it is assumed that only a handful of people can actually be rewarded; we can't all be president, a millionaire, or a film star, but we will only get a good president, millionaire or film star if we ensure that everyone wants to be one and joins in the contest. Merton puts matters like this: he says that societies devote a great deal of propaganda to certain *cultural goals*, but that the access to the *legitimate means* of achieving these goals in limited. From this he generates what Laurie Taylor has called, rather rudely, 'the fruit machine theory of deviance' (Taylor 1971). More politely it is called Merton's 'anomic paradigm'.

For Durkheim, anomie was a state of normlessness; a combination of moral confusion and uncertainty. For Merton anomie refers to the mismatch between what people are encouraged to want to be/do, and their ability to do/be it, as decided by their access to legitimate means. This mismatch is experienced as a personal problem to which the individual adapts by adopting one of the strategies in Table 15.

We will now run down the list of 'modes of adaptation', starting with conformity, which refers simply to the acceptance of the legitimate means of achieving the accepted goals. Let us assume that the cultural goal in question is being wealthy: the 'innovator', then, is someone who accepts the desirability of being wealthy but doesn't limit his/her efforts to the legitimate channels: he cheats and robs banks, defrauds his employer, or finds an entirely new legal way of making money through some new type of enterprise. The 'ritualist' adapts to the problem of anomie by forgetting all about the goals his society wants him to achieve and putting all his interest and energy into working the legitimate means: Merton gives the example of the stereotypical bureau-crat who is more interested in seeing that the correct forms are followed than in wondering what the forms are for. The 'retreatist' and the 'rebel' reject both the cultural goals of their society and the legitimate means to achieve them; retreatists drop out and develop alternative life-styles; rebels prepare themselves for the overthrow of society and the institution of new, better, cultural goals. Merton lists drug addicts, bohemians (hippies), suicides, alcoholics and utopian religious sects among the former group, and political deviants among the latter.

While Merton accepted that anomic deviance was likely to be present in any society where competition was important, he believed that American society could be, and should be structured more efficiently to

Table 15   *Merton's anomic paradigm*

Modes of adaptation	Legitimate means	Accepted cultural goals
Conformity	+	+
Innovation	−	+
Ritualism	+	−
Retreatism	−	−
Rebellion	±	±

damp down its anomic problems. Merton's work is a mild critique of the 'American Dream', complaining particularly that while American culture stresses the value of egalitarianism, American society is structured in a grossly unequal way. This is seen to produce not only anomic deviance but also a situation where the social system does not benefit from all the available 'talent', since many people are blocked in their pursuit of cultural goals through lack of legitimate means. Merton's criticism of American society, then, is a complaint that capitalism isn't working as efficiently as it might, rather than a radical appraisal of capitalism itself.

The main intellectual problem with Mertonian anomie is that it asks us to believe that the central value system of America (in the 1930s) was very widely disseminated; that virtually everyone really wanted to live up to the American dream, including even those people who 'retreated' or 'rebelled'. The retreatist or the rebel is seen as someone who 'really' believes very strongly in the values of American society, and because he/she can't achieve them, freaks out. This assumption has the curious effect of deriving deviance from conformity. Deviance, in the form of anomic strategies, really arises because, deep down, people conform to American values!

Merton's anomic theory treats deviance as an individual reaction to a personal problem, though a problem created for the person by the social structure which limits his opportunities and by the culture which gives him unrealizable aims. The picture is given almost as if each individual deviant made up his deviant behaviour anew, without learning from others. However, Merton's paradigm was quickly united with the Chicagoan notion of subculture (see above), and with Edwin Sutherland's insistence that deviant behaviour was learned behaviour. This combination produced one of the most influential packages of ideas in deviancy theory (Sutherland 1955).

If we add Merton's paradigm to the notion of subculture, we get a picture of whole ways of life being developed by groups of people as a solution to anomic problems which they have in common. Note that this changes the Chicagoan notion of subculture. For them subcultures were basically anachronistic ways of life left behind by progress. In the new formulation, subcultures appear as ways of life which have developed as a response to the way such groups see themselves placed with regard to the legitimate means of self-improvement. Subcultural studies of this kind have been particularly common in the fields of juvenile delinquency and poverty.

So far as working-class juvenile delinquency is concerned, the usual analysis entails an assumption that working-class youths lack status and authority both as youths and as working class. At school and later at work they will be subjected to 'middle-class' authority. They perform badly at school and will go on to do jobs of low esteem with poor prospects. Like working-class males in general, they care little about activities where they are subjected to the authority of others and they seek their satisfaction in non-work, leisure activities. They structure these activities in such a way as to reject the society which denies them status, and this may take the form of adopting values which are the reverse of 'middle-class values'; for instance, groups of youths may place a high value on success in acts of physical violence, in property destruction, obscenity, or at school or work in thwarting the plans of teachers or management. These subcultural values enable members of the group to achieve status within the group, even though they are denied status outside it, and indeed even though 'wider society' may punish them for it. There is an 'alternative system of honor', as Goffman puts it (Goffman 1963). (For English studies on these lines see Downes 1966 and Willmott 1966.) The main theme is the idea of subcultural behaviour as an adaptation to an anomic position. A subsidiary theme is usually the idea of personal inadequacy in the form of a poor self-image, that is, a lack of faith in one's own abilities. Thus the idea of anomie is made to fit neatly with the idea of the deviant as a damaged personality.

The problem here is that, in order to accept these accounts, you have to accept that the behaviour of these groups of delinquent youths is caused by their rejection or exclusion from 'wider society'. This is to attribute to them a problem they may never know they had and to treat their behaviour as an adaptation to that problem. For instance, David Hargreaves's well-known study of a secondary modern school (1967) focuses on the differences in attitude and behaviour between A-stream and D-stream boys. The latter take great delight in everything that the teachers disapprove of, including delinquent behaviour. Hargreaves analyses this as if the boys' behaviour is evidence of their rejection of an educational system which has rejected them. It is equally plausible to argue that the education system rejected them because of their behaviour.

The use of the idea of subculture in the analysis of poverty, and of all the forms of deviance which tend to go with it, is closely associated with the anthropologist Oscar Lewis (Lewis 1961, 1966). His studies of slum life in Mexico and Puerto Rico proceed from the assumption that the pattern of life has evolved to protect slum-dwellers from personally damaging feelings of failure. The fact that slum-dwellers believe strongly in luck or God's will, disbelieve in the value of education, take little interest in life beyond the slum, go for easy-pickings, often in illegal activities, rather than taking honest jobs, and generally live for the immediate present rather than planning for the future, are all seen in this way. Lewis argues that although this 'culture of poverty' arises as a defence against feelings of failure, it becomes a self-fulfilling prophecy. Once adopted it prevents slum-dwellers and their children from climbing out of the slum. (For an English version, see Klein 1965.) This argument comes dangerously close to blaming the poor for their poverty by treating poverty as a state of mind rather than a state of being which is structurally determined. Lewis tends to write as if changes in attitude, and the dissolution of the subculture, would enable individuals to take advantage of the opportunities offered by wider society. This, of course, assumes that such opportunities are there. Other writers (Valentine 1968 and Ryan 1971) have pointed out that they are not, and that the slum-dweller's fatalism and his/her tendency to live in the immediate present without thought for the future may actually arise from a very realistic appraisal of a situation which offers little future (see also Chapter 3, pages 85–6).

Linked to the idea of 'the culture of poverty' is the idea that such a subculture produces inadequate personalities. The theme of anomic subcultures and the idea of inadequate personalities together suggest particular social policy programmes. Perhaps the best known in the sociological literature are the suggestions from Cloward and Ohlin (1960); they attribute much juvenile delinquency to 'blocked opportunities' for lower socio-economic groups and suggest programmes of special education to compensate them for their disadvantages, and to help them overcome their hostility to wider society. In the USA Lyndon Johnson's 'War on Poverty', which included the educational programme 'Headstart', was very much an institutionalization of these ideas, particularly in so far as 'cultural deprivation' was used as an explanation of educational failure, and educational failure as an explanation for delinquency and drug addiction. The idea of 'cultural deprivation' is simply subcultural theory's contribution to the sociological literature on education (see Chapter 9, page 254).

The functionalist approach to social problems: social problems as social sickness

Functionalists have tended to regard social problems as the same as 'the problems of society' and to see public debate about some problem as representing the social system itself signalling 'its' problem to people so that they might take appropriate action – rather as a body signals damage to itself through the nervous system, as pain. A little thought shows that this is an absurd way of thinking, for societies cannot have problems, only people can, and what one person regards as a problem may well arise from the advantages enjoyed by another. It is easy to see how functionalists fell into this trap. Because of their assumption that a society is a system which needs to maintain stability, and that in the long run social stability is to everyone's advantage, they make no distinction between 'the problems of society' (staying stable), 'social problems' (articulated by people) and 'everyone's problem'. The ideological result is an approach to 'social problems' which identifies the problems of dominant groups as 'the problems of society'. Referring back to Cloward and Ohlin's approach to juvenile crime, especially juvenile black crime, it can be argued that the problem was defined when it was, in the way it was, and acted upon in the way that it was in the 1960s, because of the growing political militancy, contempt for the law, and disenchantment with the 'American way of life' of young blacks and other minority groups. This was felt as a threat by better established groups. It was their problem which was being dealt with, not a problem of society (Sears and McConahey 1973).

5   Groups make rules: the social reaction approach to deviance

This is the perspective with which I introduced the chapter. It originated with a later group of sociologists at Chicago University, especially in the work of Howard Becker (1963, 1964) and was carried on in Britain by the National Deviancy Conference (Cohen 1971, Taylor and Taylor 1973). It is symbolic interactionism's contribution to deviancy theory and hence the crucial issue is always a question of 'meaning'. Deviance is not seen as an act or a state of being which exists independently of the sense people make of it, but as an interpretation. For instance, in the real world, types of deviance are often classified not by reference to some physical reality, but by reference to the intangible idea of 'intention'; the difference between murder and manslaughter is an intention to kill; between accidental death and suicide, an intention to kill oneself; between theft and forgetfulness, an intention to steal. Social reaction theorists stress alternative interpretations are always possible and usually present. Deviant acts are the acts people 'label' as deviant, but the effect of this depends on how successful someone is of convincing others of his/her point of view. In Becker's words: 'Social groups create deviance by making rules whose infraction constitutes deviance, and by applying these rules to particular people and labelling them as outsiders' (Becker 1963).

Much of this approach centres around the idea of 'labelling'. A particularly dramatic example is Rosenhan's pseudopatient experiment (1973). Rosenhan arranged for a group of people to have themselves admitted to a number of American mental hospitals by reporting to the admissions office claiming to be hearing voices. Apart from falsifying their names and symptoms on entry they otherwise behaved as 'normally' as possible and gave accurate information about their lives and previous experiences. They actually found it very difficult to behave 'normally', since the routines of a mental hospital are very different from those of everyday life outside. However, their nursing notes described them as co-operative patients. In the hospital they were diagnosed as 'schizophrenics' and the staff acted on the assumption that they were mentally ill. So, for instance, the pseudopatients kept notes of their experiences and this led to comments from staff such as 'There's no need to write it down; if you forget, just ask the nurse'. On one of the pseudopatient's nursing notes is written, day after day, 'Patient manifests writing behaviour'; writing is obviously being seen as a symptom of mental illness.

The label 'mental patient' evidently provided a set of meanings in terms of which the staff interpreted the pseudopatients' behaviour. It also determined the way in which staff and pseudopatients interacted. As part of the research project pseudopatients made requests of the staff, such as other patients might make. Now usually when someone speaks to another, they listen, make eye-contact and make some attempt at an answer. However, many of these interchanges took on 'insane' forms such as:

'Excuse me, Doctor. Can you tell me when my case will be discussed at case conference?'

'Ah, good morning, Mr X, and how are we today? Feeling a bit better, eh? Good, good. Carry on the good work.'

The point is that, rather than the patient's actions producing the label 'schizophrenia' – as commonsense would suggest – the label provided the framework in terms of which the staff interpreted the patient's behaviour. Routine interaction between staff and patients was organized around the label, and in such a way that staff were most unlikely to query it.

Mental illness labels are particularly 'sticky', for while patients with physical ailments are usually discharged 'cured', mental patients are discharged 'in remission' with the assumption that the problem might return. This is obviously important for the ex-mental patients' own conception of themselves and for the way they will interpret their own feelings and behaviour in the future. Furthermore, histories of mental illness follow people in the form of records stored by employers and health authorities and thus have important implications for a person's future prospects. You will see the obvious similarities with criminal records, school reports or word-of-mouth reputations.

The idea of labelling leads fairly easily to the idea of 'deviancy amplification': the harder they try to stamp out deviance, the worse it gets. Actually there are two sorts of deviancy amplification, which are not always distinguished. One I call 'the iceberg effect'. This is where someone or some agency determines to reduce some form of deviancy, and in investigating it finds a far higher incidence than was suspected. They then assume that the problem is on the increase. Jock Young (1971a) points out that the formation of Drugs Squads in the 1960s resulted in more and more cases of drug abuse being discovered, and in turn more and more pressure being placed on the police to eliminate it, and so on in a 'deviancy amplification spiral'. Again, the appearance of a new label may suddenly bring old forms of deviance into sharp focus in a new way. The effect of the British media's adoption of the American term 'mugging' to reclassify offences such as 'thefts in the open', 'snatching' and 'assault' gave the impression of the sudden appearance of a new type of crime (Hall *et al.* 1978). The role of the mass media in creating such spirals has attracted a great deal of sociological attention (Cohen and Young 1981).

The other type of deviancy amplification might be called a 'reaction effect'. This is where the labelled group reacts to attempts to control them by becoming even more deviant. Armstrong and Wilson in their study of Easterhouse 'gangs' describe Easterhouse youngsters who had been subjected to intensive policing as reacting by committing more serious offences (Armstrong and Wilson 1973). In a more elaborate argument Jock Young (1971b) proposes that the way in which the police attempted to *control* the 'drug problem' actually *created* a real drug problem out of what had previously only been a fantasy on the part of the police and the mass media.

Most of the work of symbolic interactionists in this field consists of detailed ethnographic studies of deviant groups, produced through participant observation (see Chapter 3, pages 70–1). The main effect is to show how rational and understandable are the views of groups labelled as deviant once matters are seen from their point of view. These are of course descriptions of 'subcultures'. However in this tradition subcultures are not seen as deviant variants on a mainstream culture. Everyone belongs to a subculture, and other symbolic interactionists have provided descriptions of the subcultures of medical men, nurses, factory managers and so on. One theme which such studies of deviance do share with functionalist subcultural studies is the notion that, in part, the behaviour of the deviant group can be seen as a reaction to rejection and labelling.

This genre has produced some of the most readable sociological literature, but its journalistic quality has attracted adverse criticism. Firstly, the tendency to choose as research topics, bizarre and exotic subcultures has led to the charges that these studies have been produced to satisfy the voyeuristic desires of 'straight' society and that they celebrate deviance rather than explain it (Gouldner 1973). Secondly, there is the problem associated with participant observation that researchers come to see things through the eyes of their subjects: 'going native' (see Chapter 3, page 71). For instance, Jock Young's study (1971a) of drug-takers is an account of how the mass media and police stereotype and label drug-takers. At the same time it stereotypes and labels police officers (Young 1971b).

Symbolic interactionists pay more attention to the results of social reaction than to the reason why people commit the initial acts which others label as deviant. Critics point out that in many studies it almost appears as if there were no reason for deviant behaviour except personal choice or bad luck. However, labelling theory does provide a partial answer to this criticism. David Matza (1964), for instance, uses the term 'drift' to suggest that people commit minor acts of deviance without much thought, but that labelling by others ensures that some are forced further and further down the deviant road and into the company of other labelled deviants. This allows for a considerable amount of luck in the process, and would go some way towards explaining why people in the same sorts of situation do not all end up being labelled 'deviant' (see also Lemert 1972).

Theories of deviance in the real world

By focusing on social reactions to alleged deviance, symbolic inter-actionists place themselves in a position to be able to study the way in which social problems are constructed through the actions of interested parties, who offer theories to explain and recipes to control what they define as a problem. (For instance, see Cohen's study of how the activities of youngsters at seaside resorts was built into the problems of Mods, Rockers and youth violence: Cohen, S. 1972).

It is important always to remember that theories purporting to explain deviance or social problems are not just ideas but are often ideas which are put into action as social policy (see Chapter 3, pages 79–81). Deviance is a decision-making process, and the theories of people such as legislators, magistrates, social workers, police, psychiatrists, coroners, and so on are important parts of the total process. This is shown in Figure 7. This is a more complex version of Figure 3 in Chapter 3 (page 73).

The diagram is drawn as a model to illustrate the process of deciding who gets officially labelled as a juvenile delinquent. It could be redrawn for virtually any other sort of deviance. You will see from the diagram that who gets the deviant label depends upon what ideas about deviance are held by the people who make the decisions. Imagine, for instance, that the members of the juvenile bench have read D. J. West (see page 312-13) and are convinced that the really serious cases of juvenile delinquency come from 'bad homes' and are likely to have 'poor school records'; and that the social work report on an offender shows that he has such a background. If this is so, it seems likely that they will deal with our juvenile delinquent as a 'serious case' warranting a custodial sentence, and not (say) as an 'unfortunate lapse', warranting a conditional discharge.

Now imagine that a sociologist analyses the output from this juvenile court and finds that a high percentage of the offenders who receive custodial sentences come from 'bad homes'. He might well claim that this proved that 'bad homes create delinquency', but all he could legitimately claim would be that the estimation of home circumstances as 'bad' is likely to lead magistrates to classify a case as one requiring

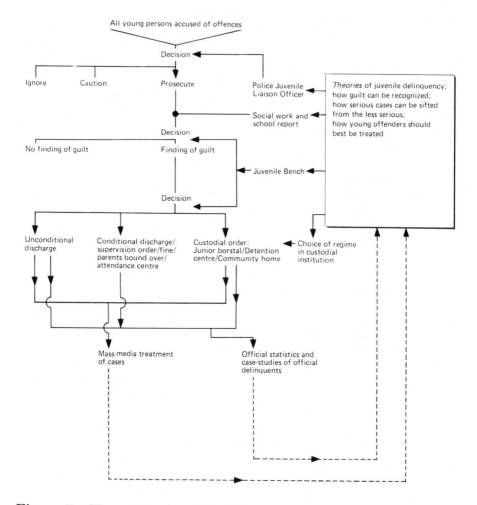

Figure 7   *The application of theories of juvenile delinquency*

custodial treatment. You might like to redraw the diagram, inserting other sorts of deviancy theory in the box on the right.

Many of the routine procedures for dealing with deviants tend to have the effect of confirming some prevailing theory of deviance. Young says that the prevailing picture of drug abuse in the courts in the 1960s was of rather foolish young persons being led astray by evil-minded, profit-motiviated drug-pushers. When in court, drug-users gained more lenient treatment by representing themselves as having been 'led astray'. In doing so, they hid the fact that marijuana was distributed not by the stereotype 'drug-pushers' but, in a small-scale amateur fashion, by the drug-users themselves (Young 1971a). Similarly, Braginski and Braginski (1969) show that one of the most important things which happen to a mental patient in a mental hospital is that they learn to be mentally ill 'properly', by learning the symptoms appropriate to their diagnosis. Using videotapes, they were able to show that patients were able to display symptoms of mental illness which were serious enough to avoid being discharged from the hospital, but not serious enough to prevent their being granted the run of the hospital and grounds. Patients were thus in a position where it paid to confirm the prevailing control theory of mental illness.

Having considered the symbolic interactionist approach to deviance there are three directions in which we can go:

One is to look in much more detail at the processes people use to make sense of some phenomenon and to find it deviant – ethnomethodology;

Another is to take the viewpoint of the labelled deviant more seriously than that of the labellers – radical psychiatry;

The third is to take seriously the question of 'who makes the rules?' – critical criminology.

6 Constituting deviance as an everyday activity: ethnomethodology

Ethnomethodology is about investigating the methods people use for making sense of social life. One of the most useful ethnomethodological studies in the field of deviance is Max Atkinson's study of how coroners *create* suicides by interpreting deaths and reaching verdicts; suicides are the result of the coroner's methods for reaching suicide verdicts. (This is dealt with in more detail in Chapter 3, page 72–3). A study linking the topics of deviance and education is Hargreaves *et al.*, *Deviance in Classrooms* (1975). This is a report of an investigation into the ways in which teachers make sense of pupil behaviour in order to 'find' that they are particular types of pupil, and how they make use of these concepts of pupil types to make sense of pupil behaviour: yes, the process is circular, but that *is* how people make sense of the world.

Ethnomethodological studies show that the 'rules' of social life are never clear. They are always shifting, and because deviance is defined in relation to rules this makes deviance problematic. For instance, in the Hargreaves study it is shown that the rules of the classroom imposed by teachers shift from minute to minute. It is never quite clear as to whether it is 'paying attention time', 'working at your books time', 'clearing-up time' or so on. Thus it is never quite clear what the rules are that have to be broken for deviance to occur. Pupils can always attempt to defeat a charge of deviance by the teacher by claiming that the rules under which they have been charged were not in play ('But sir, it's clearing-up time'), or that the rules were not clearly signalled ('But sir, you never said'). In so doing, of course, they may run the risk of being charged with other types of deviance – insolence, inattention, etc.

The same study also appears to show that labels – in this school at least – are tentative and provisional. Children do come to be regarded as of particular types, but people do change their minds about them. Further, when pupils are labelled there is no automatic consequence. They themselves may be unaware or mistaken about others' views; they may conform to a label of, say, being 'dim' by giving up, or it may act as a spur to work harder (see also pages 260–1).

What goes for deviance in classrooms may not apply to deviance in other settings. In settings such as mental hospitals (see Rosenhan, above), a label may determine the totality of a person's relationships with others. Some forms of labelling are surrounded by dramatic rituals which leave no doubt that the label is being applied and what it means to the labellers – so called 'degradation rituals' (Garfinkel 1956). Even so, it seems wise to assume that those who are labelled still have some room for manoeuvre in their own interpretations (Sykes and Matza 1957).

In commonsense thought we tend to view what we see as 'normal' behaviour as almost automatic, and deviant behaviour as something rather special. However, ethnomethodologists demonstrate that 'being normal' is something which people have to work at very hard. Garfinkel's study of the transvestite 'Agnes', by showing what he/she had to do to appear as a normal female, also shows what 'normal females' have to do in order to give a convincing performance of femininity (Garfinkel 1968). Moreover, not only do we work hard at giving an impression of ourselves as being normal, law-abiding etc., but we also engage in artful practices to make sure that people do not think otherwise. Next time you are in a help-yourself store, watch out for the people who are 'doing-not-shop-lifting'; walking about holding what they want to purchase at arm's length to make sure that no one could mistake them for a shoplifter. In ethnomethodological studies, then, deviance often appears as a charge made successfully against others because they are socially incompetent.

If ethnomethodology illuminates the details of the processes of making sense of the world and of giving competent social performances, it does very little else. It is very much about 'how' things happen, rarely about 'why'.

7   Only the mad are sane: radical psychiatry

This approach to deviance refers mainly to conditions labelled 'mental illness'. It rejects the idea that mental illnesses are 'illnesses' on the grounds that there are no norms of mental health, like the norms of physical health, against which behaviour can be designated as 'ill'. As Szasz says, treating objectionable behaviour as 'illness' is like calling the television repair man to complain about the content of TV programmes (Szasz 1972). Mental illness diagnoses are seen as labels which confuse rather than illuminate. For instance, 'clinical depression' may confuse the fact that someone is very miserable for good reasons. It just designates the person as 'work-for-the-doctor'.

These writers do present some fairly convincing case-studies of mental patients to show that their apparently insane view of the world is actually quite rational, given their circumstances and other people's reactions to them (Laing and Esterson 1970).

Many people would agree with the case-studies, but would say that, even while the views of such patients make sense, their insanity lies in the way in which they are out of touch with 'reality'. Laing (1970) and Cooper (1968), however, would argue that the 'mentally ill' are actually more in touch with reality than are the 'sane', and that is what their problem is. They lack the capacity for self-delusion, for playing along with the trivial rituals of life, and see right through to the awful truth about the human condition.

Radical psychiatry has much in common with the interpretive approach of symbolic interactionism, but it is usually underpinned by a Marxist critique of capitalist society. This is used to explain why it is that most people exist in a state of 'false consciousness' (see Chapter 6, page 183) and live out of touch with their real selves (alienation), and thus why it is that seeing reality is regarded by others as mental illness. Many people who would accept this view if it were applied to the case of the dissenters in the Soviet Union who are diagnosed as mentally ill (Medvedev 1969) are loath to accept it as a critique of Western psychiatry.

The Marxist critique links radical psychiatry with critical criminology, with which I deal below. However, it must be said that accepting the idea of radical psychiatry – that the route to the truth about the human condition lies through madness – requires a great deal of faith in the reader.

8 Deviance and the power structure – critical criminology

Critical criminology is a reaction against orthodox criminology, and thus the latter must be understood first. The employment of psychiatrists, psychologists, medical doctors and sociologists as 'criminologists' is the result of the state and voluntary agencies putting up the money for the study of why people commit crimes and the discovery of how they can be stopped. In this sense, orthodox criminology has been 'correctionist', and the same might be said about orthodox psychiatry, research into troublesome pupils, or suicidology. Looking back over the theories of deviance reviewed so far, it is fairly easy to see that only some can be accommodated within orthodox criminology. Theories of deviance which locate the causes of deviance in the deviant's biological make-up, or his early childhood experience, or in the odd ways of a local subculture, all suggest remedies which do not involve changing much, except the deviant or his immediate surroundings. Theories of deviance which refer to 'blocked opportunities' are likewise acceptable, at least to social democratic politicians.

However, from an orthodox criminology point of view, a theory which says 'the cause of crime is the law' is a non-starter, because criminologists are paid to uphold the law and not to question it – although some of course do, to a limited extent. Theories of deviance which say that the causes of deviance lie deep in the structure of capitalist society – as in critical criminology or in radical psychiatry – are definitely out of court for the orthodox criminologist. Symbolic interactionists, radical psychiatrists and critical criminologists would all say that orthodox criminology is neutered because employment as a criminologist prevents the right questions being asked. Furthermore, orthodox criminology actually helps to perpetuate the deviancy it purports to study, through processes such as deviancy amplification, and through helping to uphold the power structure which is the root cause of deviance.

Critical criminology starts with a critique of this orthodox criminology and then builds on symbolic interactionism to follow up the question of how deviance is related to the power structure of society. This is an obvious path to take, once you have accepted that deviance follows from the successful making and enforcement of rules.

Critical criminology is an explicitly socialist theory. Exponents see themselves as contributing towards the transformation of capitalist societies into socialist ones (Taylor *et al.* 1973, 1975). Like most Marxist theory, it has to be read in part as an attempt to answer the question of what prevents capitalism collapsing, and hence of what delays the establishment of socialism. It is interesting at this point to compare critical criminology with an important theme in functionalist deviancy theory. The latter assumes that modern industrial societies, if they are to be stable and efficient, need to be meritocratic, and thus that departures from 'equality of opportunity' lead to deviance and other problems. Equality of opportunity, however, is only an equal opportunity to compete for positions in an unequal society. For critical criminologists on the other hand it is inequality itself which lies at the heart of deviance.

Critical criminology, then, treats many forms of crime and deviance as thoroughly unsurprising. They result on the one hand from the ability of the powerful to 'criminalize' and stigmatize what threatens their interests, and on the other from motivations – such as self-enrichment – which are the same whether pursued through legal or illegal means. In this regard, much property crime, and offences committed in the course of industrial disputes or at political meetings, can be viewed as aspects of the 'class struggle', even though the 'criminal' may not be conscious of this. Critical criminologists view crime as a political act. Other forms of deviance, criminalized or otherwise, may be viewed as arising out of the unpleasant living and working conditions and distorted human relationships which characterize the lives of the majority under capitalism. Examples of the latter might be wife- or baby-battering, suicide, alcoholism or 'mental illness'.

The notion of alienation in two of its many forms is thus important in critical criminology. In the first sense the working class are seen to be alienated from the product of their labour, and hence of the power to determine their own lives. Reactions against this are criminalized by those who benefit from exploitation. In the second sense capitalism is seen to alienate people from each other, preventing them from making meaningful relationships, and from their own selves, which results in bizarre, sometimes self-destructive behaviour (see 'radical psychiatry' above). In addition we can include, as part of critical criminology, all the notions of labelling and deviancy amplification produced by symbolic interactionism.

With regard to crime then, the question is not 'Why does crime occur?' but 'Why doesn't it occur more often?' For instance, why is there not more property crime in a society like Britain, where 7 per cent of the population own 84 per cent of the privately owned wealth? Or, if the Marxist account of exploitation is correct, why is there not more industrial militancy to be criminalized, and why not more militant left-wing action to be made illegal?

These considerations set critical criminology on the road to tracing the links between crime and power, through investigating the way in which the dominant class controls the under-classes. The Marxist account of this has already been dealt with at various points in this book, but we will have to pick up a few points here in order to explain critical criminology (see Chapter 5, page 130; Chapter 7, page 191).

First, there is the assumption that the state under capitalism, with its various social control agencies – the law, the police, the courts, social work, etc. – functions in a way that is broadly consistent with the interests of capital and against the long-term interests of other groups, particularly against the working class (see pages 212–13).

The criminal law is assumed to encode the interests of the ruling class. Evidence for this might be: the fact that most of the criminal law is about the protection of property; the fact that the courts deal relatively leniently with, say, property developers who destroy listed buildings and relatively harshly with youthful vandals who spray the walls with aerosols; and the fact that some areas of activity which concern profitability are only weakly sanctioned by the law, for example, industrial safety legislation, environmental pollution or the regulation of the stock exchange. However, power in modern capitalist societies is not simply the ability to influence the way the law is made, or the ability to call on police forces to protect your interests. It is also the power to influence the way in which people think. Here the key idea is 'ideological hegemony', which in Marxist thought occupies the same position as does the idea of a central value system in functionalist thinking. Ideological hegemony, however, refers to a dominant set of beliefs and values, widely held, but which actually only serve the interests of the ruling class. These ideas are disseminated through schools, the mass media, the courts and even through the way in which ordinary people bring up their children. It is from this dominant ideology that standards of normal or good behaviour come, against which deviance is defined, and in terms of which social problems come to be defined and acted upon (Hall *et al.* 1968). Perhaps the two clearest examples of this are the way in which the law, the mass media, and, according to public opinion polls, most people, view supplementary benefit fraud as a much more serious offence than tax evasion, in spite of the fact that, in terms of cost to the Exchequer, the latter is enormously more expensive (Golding and Middleton 1979).

The second example is the way in which 'the crime problem' tends to be equated with working-class crime – much of which is relatively trivial – and not with the arguably much more important category of 'white-collar crime', including systematic fraud by white-collar employees (Sutherland 1961) and the evasion of the law by corporations. In the words of an attorney-general of the USA (scarcely a critical criminologist):

Illicit gains from white collar crime far exceed those from other crimes combined. . . . One corporate price-fixing conspiracy criminally converted more money each year it continued than all the hundreds of burglaries., larcenies, or thefts in the entire nation during those same years. Reported bank embezzlements cost the nation ten times more than bank robberies each year. [Ramsay Clark 1970, quoted in Taylor, Walton and Young 1975]

And note that these comments are about 'illegal' activities in the white-collar field. It can be argued further that the way in which the law is structured enables the powerful to inflict considerable damage on other people without breaking the law at all. In Al Capone's words, 'Business, dat's jest der legitimate rackets' (Pearce 1973).

Within a Marxist framework of ideas the term 'subculture' changes its meaning yet again, so that working-class youth cultures especially, come to be seen in one way or another as ways of life which are developed as reactions to the alienation and oppression experienced under capitalism (see also Chapter 5, pages 147–8).

The attempt to trace the links between the power structure and deviance is obviously a fruitful exercise. Criticism of critical criminology really requires a critique of Marxist theory as a whole, which space forbids here. However, the following points should be borne in mind.

Firstly it is by no means clear that all criminalization relates to upholding the interests of the ruling class. It requires some convoluted reasoning to argue that a husband assaulting his wife, a suicide, or a homosexual offence actually threatens the international capitalist class. Let us take one detailed example to illustrate this point: illegal immigration. It can be plausibly argued that the employing classes benefit from a free flow of labour (an absence of immigration legislation) because, under such conditions, immigrant labour can be used to keep the price of wages down; and because racialism among the work-force prevents the development of a united class-consciousness among the working class; and because the problems of areas with immigrants can be blamed on immigrants rather than on the workings of capitalism. Yet immigration legislation in the UK has become more and more restrictive since the war (see Chapter 12) and many types of immigration have become criminalized. How can this be explained? A critical criminological view says that we should explain criminalization by reference to ruling-class interest. Yet in this instance, changes in the law appear to have gone against ruling-class interest.

It is possible to use the Marxist notion of 'contradiction' to solve the puzzle, thus: the racism of British culture is functional for capital in so far as it divides black workers from white workers, but (and here is the contradiction), the same racism has generated a strong demand among the electorate for restrictive immigration laws which has been picked up and passed into law by the politicians. So, while capital gains from racism in one way, it loses in another. (Note the similarity here between the Marxist idea of 'contradiction' and the Mertonian notion of 'functional' at one level, 'dysfunctional' at another (see page 28).)

Does this explanation suffice? It does seem reasonable to ask whose interest is served by the criminalization of an activity. However, it is quite another thing to say that an activity was criminalized because it served some ruling-class interest. The idea of a contradiction of capitalism really does not get the argument off the hook.

As a second general objection to critical criminology, we might say that there are power centres in modern societies other than property ownership and control; there are politicians, organized labour, professional bodies, pressure groups, people in the mass media and, at a local level, community groups, all of whom have their own interests and are able to influence the definition of social problems and of what is deemed criminal and deviant. This may be done in ways that do not necessarily correspond either with the interests of capital or of the working class.

This is not to deny the great importance which must be attached to power in the analysis of deviance, but to remind the reader that there are models of the power structure other than the Marxist one, particularly those which derive ultimately from Max Weber. While there is at present no neo-Weberian deviancy theory, it is fairly easy to imagine what it would be like. As with critical criminology, it would emphasize the relation between power, deviance and conflict. But it would allow for a more wide dispersal of power, and for conflicts other than class conflicts.

It would have an emphasis similar to that in symbolic interactionism, on the importance of understanding the meaning of deviance, both to deviants and to accusers.

Guide to further reading

Carson and Wiles (1971), *Crime and Delinquency in Britain,* is a book of useful short readings on crime and delinquency, covering most perspectives, except for ethnomethodology and critical criminology. Becker (1964), *The Other Side: Perspectives on Deviance*, Rubington and Weinberg (1968), *Deviance: the Interactionist Perspective,* Cohen (1971), *Images of Deviance*, and Taylor and Taylor (1973), *Politics and Deviance* all cover symbolic interactionism very well, with a large number of readings. Cohen includes a paper by Maxwell Atkinson which is probably the best example of ethnomethodological method for A-level. Boyers and Orrill, *Laing and Anti-Psychiatry*, is the standard reader on radical psychiatry. On critical criminology, read Taylor, Walton and Young (1973), *The New Criminology* and (1975), *Critical Criminology*. In the latter volume, Jock Young's paper 'Working class criminology' is probably the best introduction for the A-level reader. The 'new subcultural theory' arising from critical criminology is well represented by Hall and Jefferson, *Resistance through Rituals*.

On social problems, Weinberg and Rubington (1973), *The Solution of Social Problems*, provides a reader organized into perspectives, and Butterworth and Weir (1972), *The Social Problems of Modern Britain*, provides a large number of readings, rather less well organized or edited, but better representing the British situation. Note, however, that the literature on 'social problems' repeats much of what is dealt with under the headings of 'deviance' or 'crime and delinquency'.

12 Gender

Carol Gray

When considering 'inequality' it is not unusual to think first of social classes; and yet, along with race, gender comprises one of the most fundamental bases of inequality in our society today. Half the population is placed at an immediate disadvantage from the moment of birth. Although a number of factors may have sharpened our awareness of this, it is of course not something new, nor something confined to Britain.

Accusations of 'chauvinist' and 'sexist' are regularly heard in conversation and such references are not uncommon in the media. The wide usage of these labels, however, does not necessarily indicate that everyone understands them to mean the same thing. Try constructing your own stereotype chauvinist - how does it compare with the description drawn up by the person next to you? *Chambers' Dictionary* (1975) defines chauvinism as: 'An absurdly extravagant pride in one's country, with a corresponding contempt for foreign nations: extravagant attachment to any group, place, cause, etc.' How often is this what is meant today?

Biology and culture

Two terms which are easily distinguished and understood are sex and gender. The first refers to the physical difference between males and females. It is *biologically* determined – an ascribed status. The second is concerned with the difference between masculinity and femininity and is *culturally* determined.

In trying to assess whether a biological or a cultural argument is most valid in explaining sexual divisions, emphasis must be on both male and female roles. They operate as a system and one cannot be understood without the other. This now seems to be acknowledged by the publication of several books on masculinity, and by the growth of men's groups. Also many women now realize that a change in their own position can only come about when men move away from their traditional roles.

Table 16   *Some stereotypes*

Women	Men
Passive	Active
Unaggressive	Aggressive
Irrational	Rational
Weak	Strong
Easily distracted, scatter-brained	Persistent, dogged
Small	Large
Timid	Brave
Submissive	Dominant
More emotional	Less emotional
More nurturant or caring	Less nurturant or caring

'Natural' explanations

The continuity of gender roles throughout time, as well as cross-culturally, has been used as the major argument supporting a biological basis for gender differences. Supporters of this claim maintain that all societies could not have independently arrived at the same arrangements unless there was a strong biological foundation. And yet, if there are biological differences, should they affect the way in which society is organized? Use of the term 'natural' can be very misleading when trying to discover whether or not innate biological and temperamental characteristics do exist to separate the sexes. Indeed 'natural' is sometimes used to describe actions simply because there is no readily available alternative explanation. Similarly people may refer to 'natural' in an effort to support how they think things should be; e.g. 'It's natural for women to want children.' (See page 132–3.)

Although none of the evidence is conclusive concerning the relative importance of biological and cultural factors in producing gender identities, many people do believe that differences between the sexes can be explained biologically – giving rise to *naturalistic* explanations. They think women and men possess different inherent capabilities. It is on the basis of such beliefs that sexual stereotypes like those shown in Table 16 are established (although few people exactly fit the images).

Such stereotypes can be damaging if they are used either to exclude one sex from certain activities or to suggest their unique suitability for others. (This occurs even when the images are inconsistent.)

Throughout the nineteenth century in countries such as Britain and the USA, warnings were given against women entering further education or involving themselves in voting. Some writers claimed that mental work was likely to damage women's 'maternal organs', and fears grew about their reproductive potential. Although we would no longer contribute to such arguments, other authors have more recently maintained that fundamental biological differences do influence our social roles. Talcott Parsons, for instance, turns to biology to support the following statement:

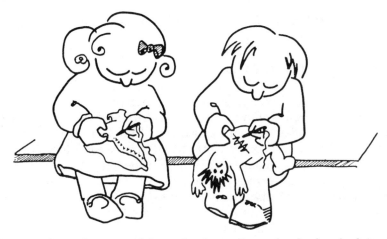

'If women have the manual dexterity for sewing, why do they lack it when it comes to . . . surgery?'

In our opinion the fundamental explanation of the allocation of roles between the biological sexes lies in the fact that the bearing and early nursing of children establish a strong presumptive primacy of the relation of mother to the small child. [Parsons 1956]

Therefore, since women are biologically the only ones able to bear children, they are seen as better suited to rearing them and establishing a strongly emotional bond. (Parsons's argument should be set within a strictly functionalist framework considered later in the chapter.)

It is from a similar standpoint that George Peter Murdock (1949) sees biological differences as the basis for the sexual division of labour in society. He simply suggests that biological differences – such as the greater physical strength of men, and the fact that women bear children – leads to clearly defined gender roles out of sheer practicality: 'The advantages inherent in a division of labour by sex presumably account for its universality.' It is worth remembering that survival today in the West, as well as in many Eastern countries, is no longer dependent on physical strength.

At the beginning of the current Women's Liberation Movement there was some rebellion against biologically determinist ideas, since such arguments had been used in a variety of ways to justify and maintain the *status quo*. Although biological arguments allow some flexibility in the way gender roles are played, they suggest little chance of actually abolishing them, whereas most feminists believe social change in this respect is possible. During the 1970s women increasingly concerned themselves with issues surrounding women's health and were anxious to understand the functioning of their bodies. Such a concern was seen as a means to an end in establishing safe means of contraception as well as abortion. Thus, although biologically determinist arguments were rejected, an interest in health care resulted in a better understanding of biology.

Biology – a cultural evaluation

Another belief which dominated Western thought for centuries was the 'Great Chain of Being' which perceived a hierarchy headed by God, followed by man, then woman, animals, plants and finally minerals. (The 'chain' was racist as well as sexist in that European man was ranked highest, with other races being fitted in between European man and animals.) The consequence was that black people, like women, were portrayed in much eighteenth- and nineteenth-century writing as less intelligent, more animal-like and more liable to be dominated by instinct and passion than by logic and reason. The man=culture and woman= nature equations were established.

Historically, Western society has shown more respect for culture than nature, since the former is seen to control and regulate the latter. For example, through the invention of hunting weapons and techniques, man was able to capture and kill animals. Brown and Jordanova (1981) claim it was during the nineteenth century that the 'nature–culture distinction' was predominantly applied to sexual divisions. The result was more rigid stereotypes and the growth of two separate spheres of power, each with their own positive and negative features. Women were thus seen as the principal characters in the private familial domain, while men dominated the areas of politics, warfare and work comprising the public domain. From this point of view the subordination of women is not explained biologically, but through the cultural evaluation of biological make-up.

The gender socialization of young children

Whether or not one contributes to the above explanations, the process of socialization cannot be ignored. From birth one is socialized into a gender role according to the norms of one's culture. Although, theoretically speaking, what is 'masculine' in one society could be considered 'feminine' in another (e.g. wearing make-up and jewellery or adopting a child-rearing role), we know there is a high degree of consistency cross-culturally.

All of us can probably recall childhood experiences which introduced and then reinforced gender differences. And yet such sex-role stereotyping begins well before the age to which our memories can stretch. For instance, the choice of a name (there are relatively few unisex forenames) and the colour and style of clothing (maternity units show no signs of dispensing with the tradition of wrapping boy babies in blue blankets and girl babies in pink ones).

Research carried out at the University of Sussex has revealed interesting differences in the attitudes of adults towards boy and girl babies of just a few months. Psychologists were keen to find out just how early sexual stereotyping begins. They chose two boys and two girls to be amused for ten minutes by eight mothers of newborn babies. The children spent half the time in frilly pink dresses and were called Jane, and the other half in blue stretch suits and were called John. Dr Barbara Lloyd, a social psychologist at Sussex University, noticed that the first toy offered when the baby appeared as a boy was usually a hammer-shaped rattle. For a girl it was a soft pink doll. When the baby was assumed to be male, then, it was encouraged to be active, to play with moving toys, and to explore and discover; in contrast, when it was thought to be female its limb movements were restricted while it was cuddled and caressed. Other studies of mother–infant interaction with children up to six months old have seemed to show that girls are also fed more quickly, left to cry more often and for longer, are played with less frequently and discouraged from exploring.

Parents, relatives, siblings and peers continue to anticipate different behaviour patterns in boys and girls. How often are small boys told not to cry but to be brave when they are hurt, and little girls chastised for getting their clothes dirty? Approval is crucially important for young children – as we saw in Chapter 4, early socialization consists of the child being encouraged to imitate certain patterns of behaviour and discouraged from others. Faced with the continuity of these expectations from so many other areas of society, the child is unlikely to question their validity.

One important and interesting aspect of early gender socialization is seen in children's books and toys. Many young children's books and comics are still flagrantly stereotypical in their protrayal of girls' and boys' activities, although some publishers now recognize the influential effects of such literature and have started to publish 'non-sexist booklists'. (Of course this may have something to do with the growing number of parents demanding non-sexist books.) Toy shops, too, continue to display toys and games for children of all ages under the separate signs of Boys' Toys and Girls' Toys. Typical are tool kits, toy cars and trains, an assortment of weapons, Meccano and Lego sets for boys; and dolls' houses, baby dolls, make-up, vacuum cleaners and kitchen gadgets for girls. Similarly, birthday cards differ considerably in what is illustrated according to the sex of the recipient. Television advertisements also continue to show boys in the more active and exciting leadership roles.

These few examples illustrate how society has different expectations of pre-school-age boys and girls. Young children are supremely conscious of adult reactions, particularly parental ones. Clearly, in any society children are being prepared, both conspicuously and subtly, for their future adult roles, and play is a very important part of this learning process.

Gender differences in education

Social role conditioning, then, is firmly established at home in the pre-school years, and this is reinforced as children enter the education system.

The primary school

Just as play is of great importance for the under-fives, so later on learning to read is vital in developing independent access to information. At this influential stage children are presented with a reading scheme which all too often shows boys exclusively involved in active leadership positions and girls in passive domestic roles. Glenys Lobban (1976) found, in her analysis of six reading schemes, that of 225 stories only two showed women who were not engaged in domestic tasks. Of the two exceptions one was a shop assistant and the other a school teacher! Males, however, were portrayed in a wide range of roles. As Lobban (1977) concludes, British curricular materials portray 'males as superior in everything except the ability to cook, dust, clean and smell flowers'. Clearly, then, reading schemes, while teaching children to read, also have the effect (intentional or not) of presenting to them images of the way society is organized.

Children quickly discover that the structure of the school bears some resemblance to that of the home. To help children feel secure in their new environment some features of the home such as curtains and carpets are, where possible, reproduced in the classroom – and of course primary school pupils are cared for mainly by women. The men who are involved in their early school experiences are either in positions of power or those such as caretaker (controlling a predominantly female workforce) whose jobs keep them outside the immediate 'domestic environment'. 'In all co-educational schools almost without exception, girls will see a community where responsibilities are held by men.' (Wood 1973)

Teachers have different expectations of boys and girls in their classroom activities. Research clearly shows that labelling and a self-fulfilling prophecy occur on the grounds of gender as well as class and race. (See Chapter 9, page 260.) Almost unconsciously teachers reinforce established patterns through their requests of young children. Tasks of a physical nature demanding a degree of strength are assigned to boys, while the more domestic cleaning and tidying roles go to girls – who indeed come to school with notions that part of their lifestyle includes performing tasks for others in the domestic arena. Similarly girls learn early on to be dutiful and attentive listeners. Despite the stereotype image of chattering little girls (developing into gossiping women), research shows that girls talk far less than boys in the classroom (Spender 1978). Many teachers see girls as passive, compliant, polite and non-aggressive and thus frequently easier to teach *because* of their docility and diligence. Boys on the other hand ask questions, challenge teachers, protest and demand explanations and therefore receive a greater amount of attention and probably a better understanding of information. Criticism levelled at the work of boys and girls is interestingly patterned and hinges upon teachers finding fault with the presentation of boys' work, and the content of girls' work. It can be seen that the former is the easier to rectify, and the latter could undermine confidence in the future.

Secondary education

Sex discrimination in education is unlawful and most schools abide by the letter of the law (even if there is little enthusiasm for its spirit). However, a number of factors contribute to traditional subject choices being made in the secondary school.

The impact of sexist textbooks should not be under-estimated for, even though many individual examples may be trivial, the influence of daily contact over a school career is undoubtedly powerful. Illustrated physics books for instance rarely show experiments carried out by girls, just as cookery textbooks seldom show boys. Pupils will also be affected by the 'masculine' or 'feminine' presentation of certain subjects and reach the conclusion that these are either male or female preserves. Another institutional influence may be the advice and counselling offered to pupils, since boys and girls are frequently encouraged to opt for 'suitable' courses. Finally, peer group and parental influence are important. For instance, once it becomes the done thing for girls not to like science, or to find mathematics difficult, the pressure is put on other girls to conform to the norm. As Brewster (1980) argues, 'It is often far more threatening to be unfeminine than to be an under-achiever.'

Thus, by the stage at which subject choices have to be made, prejudices are firmly held and traditional options taken. Not surprisingly, alternative conceptions are also held of 'the future'. 'Work' and 'career' feature more prominantly in the plans of adolescent boys, whereas girls stress marriage and families. This helps explain why a similar number of boys and girls are entered for CSE and O-level examinations but a greater proportion of boys stay at school to take A-level courses.

Single-sex education

It could be claimed that girls would benefit from being taught separately. Numerous studies have shown that boys demand more of teachers' time in the classroom, and Sheila Wood (1973) has even claimed that '... too many schools are boys' schools with girls in them'.

Spender suggests that boys and girls are familiar with their classroom roles even before entering school, i.e. males should have the floor while females should listen attentively. Whilst teaching the topic of 'war',

Table 17 *Stamford School experiment*

| | Test marks % | | |
	Oct. 78 init.	Nov. 79	Feb. 80
All-girls set	59	55	55
Girls in equivalent mixed set	58	50	44
Boys in equivalent mixed set	59	59	56

SOURCE: Schools Council

John Elliot (1974) was disturbed by the lack of female participation in discussion; but when he encouraged any girl to comment she was ridiculed by the boys who considered it to be 'their' topic. Elliot came to the conclusion that he was forcing girls to be 'unfeminine' by asking for their comments.

More commonly, however, girls who do take verbal initiative can be reprimanded for being 'loud', 'aggressive' or 'bossy'. In the single-sex classroom, however, girls do not experience the same constraints, since a range of verbal roles is available to them instead of purely subordinate ones.

Attempts to improve girls' performance in mathematics have been made by some schools which have experimented with teaching single-sex groups within a mixed school. Their long-term results are interesting. Table 17 shows the second-year mathematics results for girls at Stamford High School in Tameside. Those taught in single-sex sets did consistently better than those being taught in mixed sets.

Girls educated in single-sex schools frequently experience a broader range of opportunities as well as a better chance of examination success. However, such an arrangement could be seen as avoiding the issues rather than providing an answer. Later on, interaction with the opposite sex, both in competitive and non-competitive situations, can be difficult.

Higher education and beyond

Beyond the secondary school age, more girls than boys enter some form of further education, but boys generally go on to the more prestigious courses. Thus, more girls enter colleges of education or nursing, secretarial and catering courses, whereas more boys study for degrees. In addition, approximately four times as many boys as girls are given block or day release by their employers (DES 1978). The UCCA statistics for 1984 show that 28,000 more men than women applied to universities. Although a higher proportion of successful applicants were female, there were still 40 per cent more male entrants (UCCA 1985).

The subjects studied in both higher education and further education almost completely replicate the pattern in schools, although males and females have equal likelihood of success. Despite this there is an over-

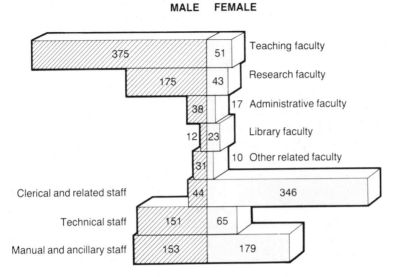

MALE FEMALE

375	51	Teaching faculty
175	43	Research faculty
38	17	Administrative faculty
12	23	Library faculty
31	10	Other related faculty
44	346	Clerical and related staff
151	65	Technical staff
153	179	Manual and ancillary staff

Figure 8 *Sussex University: total number of staff by categories, 31 Dec. 1983*

representation of males at postgraduate level, and financial cutbacks in the 1980s have fallen primarily on those areas (arts, social sciences and education) where women have been most successful.

A similar pattern is reflected in the staffing of universities. Figure 8 demonstrates the situation in the University of Sussex, and clearly shows the concentration of men in faculty positions and women in subordinate clerical work.

Class v. gender divisions in education

A problem with studies of gender differences in the hidden curriculum of education is that no explanation is given of the conflict between the definition of 'masculine' as aggressive, independent, competitive and 'superior', and the expectation that working-class children are thought to learn passivity and subordination in schools along with resignation to failure, and inferiority. Conflict may similarly arise for girls, particularly those from middle-class backgrounds, in trying to equate a training of 'femininity' which avoids competitiveness and self-assertion with a school system that encourages 'achievement motivation'.

The employment of men and women

Historical changes

There are some occupations in which women are concentrated and others in which men are concentrated. The term *occupational segregation* is used to refer to the division of the labour market into predominantly female or male occupations. These have been subject to historical change. For instance in 1851 clerks were, without exception, men, whereas clerical work is now a thoroughly female domain. In the pre-industrial economy, the household was a collective working group with all family members involved in production. Although the man was the head, the survival of the family was dependent on the efforts of his wife and children, so the notion that women entered the workforce for the first time in the twentieth century is mythical.

The decline of cottage industries with the building of factories, added to the loss of land due to enclosure, forced women (like men) to leave their homes and sell their labour for a wage. In many parts of the country women were a permanent feature of the agricultural labour force, while they also worked in factories, mills, workshops, and even in mines. However, the Victorian ideology that a woman's place was in the home coincided with the exclusion of women from certain trades and the growth of new areas of industrial work (railways, steel) which came to be defined as 'men's work'.

Historically, women have been excluded from particular occupations. They were not allowed to enter the professions, medicine or law until feminist agitation opened them up to women during the nineteenth century. Many were excluded from craft occupations since the rules of guilds would not permit women members, and to gain entry to an apprenticeship one had to be a guild member. By the turn of the century the number of married women with 'extraneous occupations' had fallen to 10 per cent from its 25 per cent fifty years before.

New forms of paid employment became available for women when conscription of men for the Second World War brought a severe labour shortage. But it is also a myth that the war introduced thousands of new workers to the labour market since most women who entered at this stage had been employed previously. It was assumed that at the end of the war women would leave their work in industry, transport and offices and disappear back into domestic service and 'women's trades'; and although many were reluctant to leave, the government, employers, unions and men forced them to make way for men.

The Second World War and after

Despite 10 per cent unemployment at the start of the war, mass mobilization quickly absorbed this and by 1940 it was clear that women were needed again to provide extra workers. As in the previous war, women entered many male-defined jobs, quickly learning the skills and performing them efficiently. Although excluded from fighting, many women worked at very dangerous and physically demanding jobs, such as in the munitions industry. But the decade following the war again saw a general reaction against women staying in their jobs and they were urged to return to the home. However, the relative independence experienced by many women meant they were not prepared to work solely at home, isolated from other people, and the post-war decades saw an increasing number of married women in the workforce.

Apart from a major labour shortage produced by the early post-war boom in economic growth, several other factors contributed to this including earlier marriage, smaller families, reduced housework (owing to household gadgets and convenience foods) and an increase in the tertiary sector of work. Because of the labour shortage employers were forced to revise their attitudes and looked on women as a reserve source of labour. A great army of women workers were 'freed' from the home, some would say for exploitation. Indeed, it is important to recognize that employers often see the employment of women as advantageous in many sectors of work. For example, women may be seen to have greater 'dexterity' than men for light manufacturing industry, or be viewed as a more flexible and more docile source of labour. But as Massey argues:

It is not the fact that these people are biologically female which explains their characteristics and their new availability for the wage work force ... but the fact that certain kinds of (patriarchal) social relations construct them as having these characteristics. [Massey 1983]

Status and promotion

In 1981 about 50 per cent of *all* women were in the labour force, although, of course, the proportion of women of *working age* (16–59 years) is much higher. However, women are not employed evenly throughout the occupational structure: they are concentrated in low-paid low-status jobs with fewer opportunities for promotion and more likelihood of redundancy. (We should not, however, assume that all men in contrast have secure, highly paid, good-status jobs with promotion possibilities.)

Many women's jobs can be seen as extensions of their domestic roles within the family, such as nursing, teaching, social work, catering and cleaning. Mary Benet (1972) even maintains that some office work is the business equivalent of housework since it is concerned with tidying and restoring order rather than actually producing anything.

Almost all women interrupt their working years to have children. If they return to paid employment it is often on a part-time basis to fit in with the family responsibilities. In 1979, 69 per cent of women without dependent children were working compared with 52 per cent of those with dependent children. Seventy per cent of working mothers worked part-time – 26 per cent working without dependent children. Just over 40 per cent of working women have part-time jobs compared with just over 5 per cent of men. Society continues to define dependent children as the responsibility of women. This results in working mothers *either* finding jobs which enable them to collect children from school, stay at home during the school holidays and take time off in case of illness, *or* entering into complex arrangements (usually with other women) to cater for these eventualities. Many women in poorly paid jobs have been in flourishing careers. However, only a few years out of the labour market puts them irrevocably behind in the promotion race. During their years at home, their colleagues will have climbed the career ladder, leaving them at an older age, a few rungs below, with little or no hope of catching up.

Thus, despite the increased participation of women in a wider range of jobs, they are still not proportionately represented in high-status, decision-making positions. In Britain in 1976 only 5 per cent of the female labour force, compared with 20 per cent of the male labour force, was classified as 'professional employers or managers'. Furthermore, the fact that so many women are concentrated in 'women's jobs' makes legislative measures such as the Equal Pay Act (1975) partly ineffectual. For example, in 1981, occupations in which women comprised over 70 per cent of the labour force were clerical and related, catering, cleaning, hairdressing and other personal services.

Perhaps not surprisingly, men tend to earn much more than women. For example, in April 1984 full-time women workers earned an average of £117 per week, compared with £179 for full-time male workers.

Many women see their major role as that of housewife and mother, and the importance given to work is secondary to family considerations. Furthermore, women usually see themselves as secondary breadwinners compared with the male head of household. A whole family is far more likely to move house or area to further a husband's career than it is for a wife, and promotion of course is frequently dependent on residential mobility.

The fact that women have increasingly participated in the labour market and yet failed to end the sexual division of labour has led some writers to suggest that women as a group must gain control over part of the forces of production.

Work in the home

We usually think of the workplace as separate from the home and the 'worker' as someone who travels to and from work and stays there for a certain number of hours. This is true of people in paid employment (apart from those who work from home). But if not as 'work' how else can we define the activities of the housewife at home?

Apart from the obvious difference in financial reward there are four major distinctions to be made between housework and paid work. Firstly, housework is done for oneself and family rather than for an employer. Secondly, it is done in isolation rather than with the cooperation of others. Thirdly, it is difficult for the houseworker to distinguish between work and non-work. Are mothers, for instance, ever 'off-duty', whether it be day or night? Finally, the houseworker retains control over day-to-day activities (within certain confines) whereas paid employees are subject to employers' control. Houseworkers are accorded very little prestige and do not have the chance to join a union to represent their interests, and yet they make a substantial contribution to the economy by acting as unpaid nurses, cooks, teachers, cleaners, laundresses, and so on.

Despite the common assumption that conjugal roles are becoming increasingly joint, housework is still seen as predominantly women's work. Although some husbands are willing to help with the 'chores' in the home, the emphasis is still very much on helping rather than sharing, even when both partners work full-time.

Men in the home

On the whole, men do play a very limited role in the home. Just as we saw earlier how women's upbringing prepares them for a subservient role, so men are socialized to believe that they should be the providers.

We should be aware of how this works to men's advantage and disadvantage. The married man, for instance, benefits from living in a family. Compared with a single man (as well as a married woman) he is more likely to have a successful career, a higher occupational status and better mental and physical health. The evidence suggests that marriage actually brings out these effects. In contrast there is plenty of evidence to show that wives (unlike unmarried women) suffer considerably more stress, anxiety and depression and are less physically healthy. Wives are supposed to soothe away the stress and tension encountered by men at work, to act as emotional sponges mopping up male anxieties.

But why is it that men have to rely on their wives to perform this role? Being a man in our society carries the expectation of emotional strength. Thus, men are not supposed to cry, nor to discuss their hopes and fears with other men. Many men find it difficult to express emotion even within the close perimeters of the family. For instance, fathers frequently interact physically with their children only through playing mock rough games rather than kissing and cuddling them. This especially applies to sons for whom kissing usually stops at an early age. Many fathers also see very little of their children during the week, leaving for work early and arriving home just in time for their bedtime. (One of the few beneficial effects of increased male unemployment has been that some fathers have got to know their offspring better and have realized what a lot they have missed before.) We only have to look at the way courts deal with custody cases to see who society considers a 'better' parent – it is still rare in contested cases for men to be granted care and control of their own children.

Gender roles in other societies

Primitive societies

In the 1930s Margaret Mead studied three cultures in New Guinea in which she claimed sex roles were acted out very differently from those in Western culture. She refuted the existence of any universal 'masculine' or 'feminine' personality, claiming that characteristics were either undifferentiated by sex or they were the reverse of the stereotypes found in modern industrial society. The Tchambuli, for instance, reversed many of our accepted differences by producing strong, dominant women and nurturing, emotional men. Both sexes of the Munduqumor were said to favour an aggressive 'masculine' character, while the Arapesh were a passive, gentle and non-hostile people, all of whom took responsibility for looking after children (Mead 1950).

Mead's study has been cited frequently to demonstrate the malleability of human nature. However, when Fortune revisited these societies his findings contradicted those of Mead. He concluded that even in the Arapesh society, males retained ultimate power and were solely responsible for waging war and other organized aggression. Could a similar criticism, however, be made of Fortune to that made of Murdock (i.e. that the data were interpreted through male Western eyes and therefore an objective assessment of gender roles was not made)?

Some of the assumptions held in Western society about role association lose their universal credibility when anthropological evidence is considered. Varying types of masculinity and femininity further undermine the system of sexual stereotyping. It is useful here to examine some of these assumptions surrounding sex and gender differentiation.

A deeply-held belief is that the responsibilities of motherhood (pregnancy, breastfeeding, daily attention to the child's needs) necessarily mean she must give up work. However, most small-scale societies do not ban physical exertion during pregnancy, lactation or the early child-rearing years. In many of these societies women continue with their usual agricultural and domestic work until the baby is delivered. They then return to normal work after a rest period of about three weeks (or sometimes, even, just a few hours). The idea that lactation restricts the mother's movements is not a problem in many small-scale social groups since they have institutionalized the practice of communal breastfeeding, whereby each child is regularly fed by several women.

Modern society also continues to emphasize (although to a gradually lesser extent) the importance of the mother–child bond. Continuous contact with its mother is thought to result in a child's greater security. However, this emphasis is again not found in all societies. Since parenthood involves both mothers and fathers, men and women tend to share the task of child-rearing. The Trobriand Islanders, for example, have been renowned for their ignorance of the father's biological role in reproduction and yet they have stressed the importance of the father's role in raising offspring.

A second common assumption is that both maternity and domestic work demand fairly low levels of energy and strength. Traditionally, however, domestic work has required enormous physical stamina: for instance carrying water for long distances, and pounding grain. In addition, of course, many aspects of child-care are both mentally and physically tiring. For these and other reasons some societies do put child-care among the occupations carrying high, rather than low, status.

A third assumption is that women have, throughout history and cross-culturally, confined themselves to a domestic role, contributing little to the economic welfare of their society. The employment of women outside the home is certainly not a Western twentieth-century phenomenon. In many parts of Africa women have been the main cultivators of the land for centuries while the male role was to fell trees, hunt and fight. Men thus became under-employed as the last two roles became redundant. Detailed studies of the role of women in agriculture among African peoples, conducted between 1940 and 1962, showed that even at this late date women did between 60 and 80 per cent of the total agricultural work.

The fourth, and last, assumption is that women lack the physical strength and size of men and this excludes them from certain activities. Actually, of course, there is no overall distinction between female and male size, and in any case strength is not always dependent on size. Certainly if one sex is more involved than the other in tasks demanding strength, they will develop a superior capacity for those tasks. Thus where males customarily fell trees and hunt large animals they become well-suited to doing these things, just as where women carry water and pound grain they necessarily display both energy and strength. Undoubtedly, individuals of one sex can adopt themselves to activities of the other sex. This was demonstrated in Western societies during the First and Second World Wars, when women entered many men's jobs which involved heavy work and mechanical skills. This instance combined with several others of women hunting and fighting show how flexible gender roles are.

Returning, then, to the assumptions of Western society, the only universal male–female contrast is the reproductive distinction, and different societies interpret this and related activities in different ways.

USSR and Eastern Europe

Although Russia has the highest percentage of working women (85 per cent) in the industrialized world, they are concentrated in the lowest paid and lowest status sectors of society. Despite familiar Western images of the female construction worker, heavy manual labour is on the lowest rung of both status and income in fact. Therefore, far from women being sufficiently liberated to enter these jobs, they are more often than not limited to them.

Three-quarters of Russia's doctors are women, but there again medicine is a poorly-paid occupation with little prestige. Women predominate at the lower end of the hierarchy while men occupy surgical and higher administrative posts. Similarly, in industry and on collective farms, women are rarely found at management levels. This pattern is repeated throughout government departments.

Women have therefore adopted a vital role in the workplace while retaining exclusive responsibility for housework and child-care. (Although day-care facilities do exist they are inadequate, and institutional supports such as paternity leave have not been introduced.) The situation, then, in the Soviet Union, as well as in other communist countries of Eastern Europe, is one of modified role change with women performing two roles (only one of which is paid) and men maintaining power.

China

In pre-revolutionary China women were confined to their homes and families and excluded from public life. Since that time the position of women has been reformed but not revolutionized. For instance, women are now educated, but very few progress to the higher levels attained by men. Communal nurseries have been established but, like elementary schools, these are entirely staffed by women. Young children attend a crèche at the mother's, rather than father's, place of work. Although many women are involved in politics at the local level, very few occupy positions at regional or national level.

In the mid-1980s the government of China began to introduce 'free market' principles to many aspects of the Chinese economy. It remains to be seen what impact, if any, this development will have on the relations and positions of men and women in China.

Israel

One of the major institutional modifications of Israeli society is communal living (although this is far from universal). The pioneers of Kibbutzim aimed to bring about a revolution in gender roles whereby the conventional roles of each sex would become common responsibilities. However, evidence has shown that most men on the Kibbutzim occupy traditionally masculine occupations while most women are engaged in 'feminine' tasks. Furthermore, an interesting 'masculinization' seems to have occurred, in that physical strength and aggressive leadership have come to be valued highly while work which lacks economic reward has been devalued. The most obvious example of the latter, of course, is domestic work and child-care. As in the USSR and China, men predominate in decision-making and positions of power.

Sweden

The early 1960s saw Swedish society revising its attitudes towards the entire gender role system. Legislation was introduced whereby either parent could claim an income for six months after the birth of their child, and sick pay allowance was available to either parent. Extensive child-care facilities were also established to allow both partners more occupational choice. Thus young people in Sweden have grown up in an environment favourable to shared roles in which practical measures like child-care centres and parental allowances exist to make this a realistic option. There have also been government attempts to abandon sex-stereotyping in education and to emphasize to men and women the openness of all careers.

And yet, despite all these measures, traditional attitudes predominate. There is no noticeable difference between the career biographies of this generation and those of their parents. The country's power structure is mostly male-dominated and role models in families and local communities remain conventionally sex-based. There seems, then, to have been a mismatch between official policy and traditional ways of thinking, the latter enjoying both psychological and social support.

Some cross-cultural comments

A common feature throughout this discussion has been the Western world's predisposition to allocate a powerful public role to men, and a subservient domestic role to women.

The examples show that male domination can exist in very different types of society and cannot be attached to any one kind of socio-economic structure. However, although a pattern has emerged in the developed world which even government legislation in some cases has failed to dislodge, we should not forget the arrangements common in primitive societies. Perhaps the situation in Alor described by Cora du Bois (1944) could be adapted to a wide range of circumstances: '. . . although there are distinctions between the (economic) roles of the sexes, it is not thought unhealthy for anyone to take on the other sex's work – rather they are admired for possessing a supplementary skill'.

The women's movement

It is difficult for most women in developing countries to fight for their own liberation when they struggle against other forms of exploitation alongside their menfolk.

Although, in recent years, some women in Third World countries have been documenting their experiences (which more often than not add up to multi-faceted exploitation), there is still an obvious lack of information about women who live beyond the industrialized West. Because of the danger of presenting a vague, while at the same time specialized, picture in this field, emphasis will centre on what the women's movement means to people living in Europe and America. Just as women in developing countries have to devote their thoughts and energies to practical problems, so, activists in modern industrial societies are disproportionately women from middle-class, well-educated backgrounds who have both knowledge and time to invest.

Origins of the movement

Newcomers to feminism in the 1960s wanted to learn about the activities of earlier 'rebellious' women. Many were surprised that the suffragettes at the beginning of the century had been fighting for more than the vote. Like many of us today they had a stereotyped image of suffragettes chaining themselves to railings, throwing themselves under horses, and waging hunger strikes in prison. Despite the failure of the suffragette movement to publicize their aims and achievements, we know that winning the vote was viewed by them originally as a means to an end, the 'end' being social reform. However, for some, the vote was seen as an end in itself and this gain alone became quite obsessional.

In the period following the granting of the vote (in 1918, and 1928), society underwent a massive economic decline. This made it difficult for women to pour their energies into the political arena, as they fought to survive the depression.

The new wave of feminism

Just as new feminists in the 1960s were surprised to find women almost a century ago had been campaigning for 'liberation', so older women in the 1960s could not understand why so much publicity was suddenly given to a movement which had existed for generations. There was, however, one particular event which sparked off the interest of the media. In 1968 a group of women in Atlantic City staged a protest against the Miss America Pageant, arguing that it degraded *all* women. Beauty contests, they said, called on certain values to define 'beauty' (more often than not 'white' standards) and claimed such artificial forms of assessment were an insult to both the contestants and the viewers. Unaware of the way their actions would be manipulated by the media, they threw their underwear in a 'freedom trash bucket'. One particular news agency added imaginary flames which resulted in the phrase 'bra burning'. Just as the suffragettes were the victims of selective reporting, so these women had their protest presented in such a way that it looked ridiculous, and the serious issues were ignored.

Nevertheless, a new wave of feminism was established as women began to organize themselves, discussing their daily lives. 'Consciousness raising' resulted as they drew political conclusions from their private oppression. They began to question the assumptions made about their responsibilities for child rearing and housework, realizing these were not simply private arrangements but part of a sexist ideology on which society relied. Female solidarity was seen as an essential pre-condition for women's liberation. By 1969 a few women's groups had independently emerged in Britain, although the US experience no doubt served as inspiration.

They focused their attention on gaining equal education and job opportunities along with equal pay. They also saw a need for free contraception and abortion on demand and extensive nursery provision. Later on, women campaigned against the discrimination shown towards lesbians and demanded the right to define their own sexuality. Finally in 1978 a declared aim was:

Freedom from intimidation by threat or use of violence or sexual coercion, regardless of marital status, and an end to all laws, assumptions and institutions which perpetuate male dominance and men's aggression towards women.

Although the earlier demands were of course important in drawing attention to particular issues, the final bid goes further in recognizing that sexism penetrates every area of society and changes in legislation have to be accompanied by attitudinal changes. Since the inception of the women's movement campaigns have been organized about issues such as male violence, abortion, educational opportunity and child-care. Women have also become more recognized in, for example, publishing, film-making and the 'peace movement', and degree courses are now available in Women's Studies. Above all, the movement has given a great many women the confidence to question their position and make informed choices.

Radical feminism and socialist feminism

Since the early 1970s some women in the movement have defined themselves as either 'radical feminists' or 'socialist feminists' (while many more feel reluctant to label themselves at all). The crucial difference between these groups is where they lay the blame for their own oppression. The argument of radical feminists is taken from *biological determinism*, claiming that pregnancy and the rearing of young children have channelled women into a domestic role – enabling men to seize power over women unhindered by these responsibilities.

In modern society, of course, women devote a relatively short time to these functions since pregnancies are regulated. And yet as we have seen, society continues to emphasize the mother–child bond as well as the dependence of women upon men. This leads some radical feminists to recommend a separate identity from men, living apart and accomplishing 'not just the elimination of male privilege, but [of] the sex distinction itself' (Firestone 1972).

To achieve this would involve artificial means of reproduction. Other radical feminists maintain that a period of separatism is necessary for women to free themselves from their social and economic dependence on men. Since patriarchy would then hold no meaning, men and women could come together in new, equal, relationships.

Clearly, then, radical feminists see men as the enemy to be fought in the battle for liberation. Socialist feminists adopt a rather different view. Stemming from a commitment to left-wing politics, they argue female subordination should not be separated from class oppression. Men oppress women not because of their biological maleness but because capitalism is rooted in exploitation and men are channelled into patriarchal roles. Thus, men are not rejected, but are seen as both the oppressors and the oppressed. The question is – would a truly socialist society be non-sexist (as well as non-racist)?

The legal status of men and women

Considerable changes have taken place since the mid nineteenth century in the legal status and position of men and women in Britain. This is seen in areas such as voting rights, employment legislation and in the legal rights and responsibilities of parents. To take the latter instance, under the 1832 First Reform Act a married woman's children legally belonged to her husband. In 1839 the Custody of Infants Act gave women limited access to their children if separated from their husband under particular circumstances. Improved access came gradually, but not until 1925 did the Guardianship of Infants Act give mothers equal rights with fathers to *apply* to courts for custody of their children. Finally, as recently as 1971 the Guardianship of Minors Act gave women equal rights with men on matters of custody, access, etc. As mentioned earlier, it is unusual today for fathers to win contested custody cases, and so 150 years has seen society reverse its thinking on the rights of parents: a change perhaps from the sublime to the ridiculous? (See Table 18.)

A selected sample of legislative moves cannot tell the whole story, and indeed a true picture is impossible since no reference is made to the campaigns and Bills which were hard-fought but failed to become law. Indeed, rather than simply being seen as episodes which in themselves restructured gender relations in society, legislation is better viewed as reflecting and mirroring already existing social, economic and political pressures for change. Here it is interesting to note that some commentators argue that the economic and social restructuring which has taken place in Britain during the 1980s, much of it based on government legislation and related activity – for example, in changing the welfare

Table 18 *The changing legal status of women in Britain, 1792–1980*

1792	Mary Wollstonecraft's *Vindication of the Rights of Women* presented the first clear statement of the need for political and civil equality for women.
1842	Mines Regulation Act – women and children prohibited from underground work in coal mines. The first example of discriminatory protective labour legislation.
1857	Matrimonial Causes Act – allowed a man to divorce his wife on the grounds of adultery but a wife had to prove an additional grievance. A wife was allowed separate use of any property acquired during a legal separation, but she still had no rights over property/possessions owned on marriage. Possibilities of access to children increased.
1870	Married Women's Property Act – allowed married women to retain £200 of their own earnings. Education Act provided elementary education for girls as well as boys.
1882	Married Women's Property Act – removed husband's automatic rights to his wife's property on marriage.
1884	Matrimonial Causes Act – made a women no longer a 'chattel' but an independent and separate person.
1894	Local Government Act – parish, rural and district councils created for which women could vote (and if propertied could sit).
1903	Women's Social and Political Union formed by Emmeline Pankhurst and her daughters Christabel and Sylvia, to campaign more militantly for female suffrage.
1918	Representation of the People Act – gave the vote to women over 30. Women entitled to become MPs.
1923	Matrimonial Causes Act – gave wives equal rights with their husbands to petition for divorce on the grounds of adultery alone.
1928	Representation of the People Act – gave women over 21 the vote in parliamentary and local elections.
1969	Divorce Reform Act – liberalized divorce laws by granting divorce on any grounds showing an 'irretrievable breakdown' in a marriage.
1970	Equal Pay Act – employers given five years to implement equal pay for equal work.
1975	Sex Discrimination Act – made discrimination between men and women unlawful in employment, education, housing, advertising and other services. Sex discrimination defined as treating a person less favourably than another on the grounds of his or her sex. Left untouched the area of social security, other fiscal policy and protective legislation.
1980	Social Security Act – equalized social security system. From 1984 women eligible for supplementary, unemployment and sickness benefits on same terms as men.

state and education system – has significantly harmed the position of women and the opportunities available to them.

Theoretical approaches to the sociology of gender

In addition to the feminist thoughts already considered, it is important to look at two alternative approaches to the roles of men and women. These are Marxism and functionalism.

Marxist perspectives

Although there are many varieties of Marxism, a quote from Lenin which would be accepted by many Marxists is:

Woman continues to be a domestic slave, because petty housework crushes, strangles, stultifies and degrades her, chains her to the kitchen and to the nursery, and wastes her labour on barbarously unproductive, petty, nerve-racking, stultifying and crushing drudgery.

For Marxists, the nuclear family is one of the main units through which the class system is reproduced. It is here that children are socialized into accepting the values of hierarchy, deference and obedience, all essentials for the maintenance of capitalism. Gender roles are learnt in the family, resulting in clearly distinguishable adult roles. Capitalism allocates women the responsibility of housework and the home where she is seen as the central character in maintaining a loving and supportive environment. Because she can provide her partner with physical, emotional and sexual needs he is able to operate as a stable and efficient worker. Similarly the man is given the responsibility for financially providing for his family. He is encouraged to work hard to keep a regular job so that he can pay the bills. His bargaining power is weakened as withdrawal of labour brings hardship not only to him, but to his wife and children too.

At the same time the capitalist-controlled media raise people's material aspirations. The major unit of consumption, the family, is encouraged to purchase more and more goods and see these as worth while in themselves.

We have seen that socialist feminists view women's oppression as part of the class struggle, and yet some Marxists say feminism is harmful in its rejection of the class struggle. Concern over sexist ideology is thought to divert people's interests and energies away from the only significant struggle – the class struggle.

The campaigning activities of miners' wives in the 1984–5 miners' strike provide an example of working-class women involving themselves in a class struggle and drawing feminist conclusions from their experiences. An understanding of their public oppression led many women to identify their private subordination in the home.

Functionalist perspectives

As we saw in Chapter 8, the sociology of the family was for many years dominated by the functionalist approach. But, as variations occurred in family processes, functionalists found it more and more difficult to explain them and for some time maintained that nothing very important was happening.

Nevertheless an important change which could not be overlooked was the greatly increased divorce rate, and it was on this that Parsons commented. He argued that it was because spouses were straying away from their distinct gender roles that tension was occurring in their relationships, leading to separation and divorce. He advocated one partner being responsible for the home and the rearing of children, while the other concentrated on the breadwinner role. Although he referred to these roles as the 'mother role' and the 'father role', he maintained that either sex could occupy either position. Strain would occur, however, if both parents attempted to pursue two roles – such a situation would be dysfunctional for individual family members and society at large.

We can clearly see, then, that functionalists believe harmony can best be preserved if men and women adopt responsibility in separate and distinct spheres.

Man-made language

Just as the activities of many women have been excluded from historical documents (his story?), so a lot of what is written has a male bias. Many people claim that words such as 'chairman' do not qualify as sexist, and yet it becomes difficult to accept this when faced with a long list of similar vocabulary. Here are a few examples to which you can undoubtedly add: manager; man-made; manufacture; statesman; craftsman; man-in-the-street. Do these terms reflect our thoughts on whom we expect to occupy certain positions? Would we be surprised to find the manager of the local bank is a woman? Even words like actor and author are still not 'unisex', since modifications are sometimes used for women in these professions.

The subject of titles preceding people's names has caused some controversy too. A campaign to introduce the title of Ms for women has been only partially successful. One of the problems with this term is its ambiguous pronunciation; more importantly though, the ideology behind its creation has been misinterpreted so that it is sometimes assumed that only feminists and those ashamed of their single or married status want to make use of it.

If we wish to continue to use titles then it would seem sensible to have one word referring to males and another to females, rather than subdividing women into married and unmarried (which incidentally can affect whether women are permitted to enter into credit agreements).

However, when filling in forms, women are now in the strange position of being either Miss, Mrs or Ms – instead of the categories being narrowed, and therefore equalling Mr, the gap has in fact widened.

Nevertheless, the fact that Ms is now an offically recognized title signals a small victory for the women's movement. The incorporation of feminist ideas into our language may in time influence public opinion.

Concluding comments

If we return to what is meant by 'sexism', it is useful to consider how Raymond Williams (1983) interprets the term: '. . . critical descriptions of attitudes and practices discriminatory against women.' Again we can draw a parallel here between sexism and racism since in both cases notions of superiority and inferiority have been superimposed upon what are simply distinguishing features. Biological differences between blacks and whites and males and females have been repeatedly misunderstood, or twisted into something they are not, and then incorporated into elaborate theories which define the exploited group as inferior. For example, in the days of slavery, white Westerners came into contact with people whose cultural organization was different from their own. They conveniently interpreted such a culture as barbaric and its people as savages. Given the context in which the two groups came into contact, whites were able to confine black people to an inferior and dependent role.

While retaining the definition offered by Williams we can now consider the inferior and dependent role occupied by women through classifying them as a minority group. This is the approach adopted by Helen Mayer Hacker, who uses Louis Wirth's definition of a minority group:

. . . any group of people who because of their physical or cultural characteristics, are singled out from others in the society in which they live for differential and unequal treatment, and who therefore regard themselves as objects of collective discrimination. [Hacker 1972]

Hacker refers initially to women's 'high social visibility' and then to the attributes ascribed to them by the majority group. Women have been regarded by men as inconsistent, emotionally unstable, irresponsible and lacking in both logic and intelligence. Prestigious qualities like reason, objectivity, independence, authority and leadership are seen as male-based – and it is not uncommon for women who are successful in business careers to be labelled as 'thinking like a man'! The power of the dominant group (men or whites) is then strengthened as a substantial number of the minority group (women or blacks) accepts the position and confines they have been allocated – filling low-pay low-skill low-status jobs.

Finally, it is important to recognize that some readers may judge this chapter to be sexist, in that it gives far more attention to women than men. (Although ask yourself, too, why this textbook has only two female contributors.) The bias in this chapter certainly breaks with tradition, for conventional sociology has been accused of making women 'invisible'. For example, although women may have been given attention in family studies as housewives and mothers, there has been little consideration of them as workers.

Ann Oakley (1974) maintains that stratification theory, one of the major areas of sociological study, makes certain basic assumptions about class membership which guarantee women's invisibility. Three of these assumptions are:

1 The family is the main unit of stratification.
2 The family's social position is determined by the man's status.
3 The social position of women is almost always determined by the status of the men, fathers or husbands.

In reality, of course, 58 per cent of households are not nuclear families and the majority of single-parent families are headed by women. Also, if assessed separately on occupational criteria, many wives would be in a different class from their husbands. Finally, in terms of social status, women often do not share their husbands' status but are accorded a lower ranking as 'housewives'.

Oakley's ideas on women's invisibility gain support when we consider the Oxford mobility studies. This, the most thorough examination of social mobility made in this country for over 30 years, omitted all women and focused entirely on the male working population. One of the consequences of this is that any *comparative* comments about men and women in the stratification system cannot be made until well into the twenty-first century.

Guide to further reading

For students who are interested in some general reading on gender socialization, an easy starting point is Elena Gianini Belotti's *Little Girls* (1975), or Joyce Nicholson's *What Society Does To Girls* (1977). Dale Spender has written at length on women in education, and *Invisible Women* (1982) dispels the myth of equal opportunity in schools. Eileen Byrne also uncovers the 'hidden curriculum' of sex-typed educational practices in *Women and Education* (1978). Deem (1978) provides a full account. A comprehensive guide to the women's liberation movement can be found in *Sweet Freedom* (1982) by Anna Coote and Beatrix Campbell. One of the most radical demands for alternative arrangements in the future comes from Ann Oakley who recommends abolishing the family and thus breaking the pattern of gender socialization: *The Sociology of Housework* (1974).

Finally, a consideration of men's personal and domestic roles, particularly as fathers, can be found in *The Father Figure*, edited by Lorna McKee and Margaret O'Brien (1982).

13 Population & health

Roger Gomm

Introduction: vital statistics as social products in two senses

Statistics of births, marriages, deaths, population movements and other measures of population must be regarded as social products in two senses.

Firstly, such statistics reflect social processes at work which determine the frequency of births, deaths and so on. Thus we may read such statistical material as evidence about the way in which societies 'work'. In Table 19, for instance, you will see that the death rates take on a pattern which is very much like that of social class. We would not get very far in explaining these figures by investigating each death in turn – although some case-studies would be interesting. Instead, the obvious patterns in the statistics suggest that we should seek an explanation in terms of the 'structure of society' and the social processes which

Table 19 *Mortality of men (usually aged 15–64) by social class: standardized mortality ratios*

| | Registrar-General's social classes | | | | |
	I	II	III	IV	V
1910–12*	88	94	96	93	142
1921–23*	82	94	95	101	125
1930–32	90	94	97	102	111
1949–53	98	86	101	94	118
1959–63	76	81	100	103	143
1970–72	77	81	104	114	137

(OPCS Series DS no.1, Occupational Mortality. Decennial Supplement, 1970–72. HMSO) 1976

*The figures prior to 1923 are calculated in a slightly different way from the later figures.

How to read this table: in the top line under Class I you will see the figure 88, and under Class V, 142. The average for all men in this age group, and for the line is 100. Thus the death rate for Class I was 12 per cent below average, and that for Class V was 42 per cent above average.

distribute incomes, job opportunities, wealth, health *and* premature death. Data like these, which can be taken as indicators of an underlying social structure, are often called 'social facts', following Durkheim (1895, 1897).

Secondly, such statistics are a record of the processes used to define, count and classify population data. For instance in Table 19, while the classification of deaths by age presents few problems, the classification of men by 'social class' relies on the use of a scheme of classification based on a rather hazy idea of 'occupational prestige'. The table only tells us obliquely about the relationship between premature death and income, or occupational hazards. The allocation of particular occupations to 'social classes' is an extremely arbitrary procedure. To make matters worse the definition of social classes by the Registrar-General is not the same for different years, and thus the horizontal lines in the table are not directly comparable (see page 158–60).

In handling vital statistics, then, we should always be aware that we are dealing with the results of two sorts of social process: the social processes which determine the frequency and extent of what it is that the statistics measure, *and* the social processes of defining, counting, classifying and analysing the statistics. The problem is to disentangle one from the other. (For further discussion of this matter, see Atkinson 1978; see also pages 75–7.)

The social context of measuring populations

The collection and manipulation of population statistics is an arm of government. These are the most important implications of this:

1 Official statistics provide information for state activities. Governments could not make any coherent policy decisions without some statistical picture of 'the state of the nation', now and in the future.

2 The statistical categories into which individuals are mapped represent aspects of their relationship to the state. Date of birth, place of birth, marital status, numbers and birth dates of children, place of residence and so on, are what we might call 'official status-markers' which determine important obligations. Just consider the importance of 'age' in establishing legal rights and obligations. Note also how such information has to be 'official' to count. Writing of an American social welfare agency, Zimmerman (1974) says:

An applicant had told [the social worker] that she could not find her citizenship papers that were to be used to verify her age – a critical issue in determining her eligibility for a certain category of assistance. The applicant went on to say that at one time she had copied her birth date on a piece of paper, which she then handed to the worker. The case workers greeted the story with laughter.

Growing concern has been expressed recently over the process by which individuals are mapped into official categories. With modern systems of electronic data storage and retrieval, the collection of information about individuals, and the possibilities of collating data collected for one purpose with data collected for another, gives rise to acute problems of confidentiality, and to threats to the individual's civil rights.

3 Statistical data add a dimension to the political process so that statistics become important resources to quote in justifying or criticizing policies. In Britain, what passed for sociology in the nineteenth and early twentieth century – the so-called 'British Empirical Tradition' was to a large extent a process of analysing official statistics and collecting additional ones to influence public policy.

From this it follows that we cannot see official statistics as a kind of neutral objective portrait of the nation. Instead, we should expect them to be a reflection of current political debates, and of the interests and policy commitments of those involved. The same is true, of course, of the statistics collected by pressure groups attempting to influence government policy (Irvine *et al.* 1979).

4 Statistical material helps to transform what it purports to describe. For example, it was intended that a question on ethnicity should be included in the 1981 census. The idea of counting numbers of black people very obviously arises from the political arena. This question was dropped from the census after a pilot census in Haringey showed how much hostility it aroused among blacks. In the USA groups representing blacks are very favourably disposed towards ethnic questions in the US census, because such questions help to define certain areas with large black populations as deprived areas for special government assistance. By contrast, in the UK opposition to the ethnic question on the census is based on the fear that some future government might use the census returns as a basis for a policy of repatriation (BSSRS 1979). Place of birth, place of residence and ethnic affiliation are transformed in significance when they are recorded. An area with large numbers of black people is not quite the same thing as the same area covered by detailed statistical information.

Populations: how they change

The expression of births or 'fertility'
There are various ways in which births can be expressed, for instance the number of babies born in a given time period in a given territory: in Britain in 1983 the number of live births was 694,000. This is obviously an important figure, especially for those who have to plan facilities for babies and children. Sociologists however are usually more interested in *rates*. The 'crude birth rate' is the number of births in a given time period

per 1000 of the population. For Britain in 1983 this was 12.7 per 1000. Rates are useful because they allow us to standardize the size of population, to make comparisons between two populations, or between two points in time. Crude birth rates are useful for rather crude comparisons. More refined rates can be used for more precise analyses. The 'fertility rate' is the number of births per year per 1000 women aged 15–44: for Britain in 1983 it was 60 per 1000. We could also use the 'married women's fertility rate', the 'teenage fertility rate', the 'West Indian fertility rate' or others, depending upon which groups were of interest, always expressing the number of births to the chosen group of women per 1000 of the 'population at risk' (that is, married women, teenage girls, West Indian women within their child-bearing years).

Since it is only women between certain ages who can give birth, fertility rates usually give a better indication of reproduction in a society than do birth rates, and a special fertility rate expressing the number of births per woman over a number of years and called a 'period fertility rate' may be calculated. In the past the same sort of measure was provided by the notion of 'average completed family size' which is the number of births per woman (or per married woman) when she has reached the end of her child-bearing years. The problem with this measure is that it cannot be computed with accuracy until women have indeed reached their middle forties, although some good estimates can be made for women aged thirty plus or even younger, especially when backed up with surveys of family intentions (Dunnel 1979).

The expression of deaths or 'mortality'

As with births we can simply count deaths and classify them by sex, age-group, region, cause and so on. We can compute a 'crude death rate' – the numbers who die in a given time period in a given territory per 1000 of the population: United Kingdom, 1982: 11.8 per 1000. 'Age specific' mortality rates may be used: numbers of an age group dying per 1000 of that age group. Among age-specific rates are various measurements of infant deaths defined in Table 20. These death rates are widely used for international comparisons, because they are taken to be sensitive indicators of standards of living (see Table 21).

As a variant on ordinary rates, standardized mortality ratios may be used, allowing comparisons between age, sex, class or regional groups in terms of their deviation from an average figure set at 100 (see Table 19).

Lastly, deaths may be expressed in terms of life expectancy. This is an estimate of the length of life of an 'average person' of a given age. Life expectancy for boys born in 1981 is 69.8 years, for girls 76.2 years in the United Kingdom (see also Figure 14).

Table 20 *Still births and infant deaths by social class of the mother, England and Wales 1980; and illegitimate births*

	I	II	III_n	III_m	IV	V	All classes	Illegit. births
	Registrar-General's social classes							
Still birth rate: (deaths before birth or at birth of foetuses over 28 weeks gestation per 1000 total births)	5.0	6.0	6.2	7.9	8.0	9.5	7.2	8.9
Perinatal death rate: (still births plus deaths during the first week of life per 1000 total births)	9.7	11.1	11.8	13.0	15.0	17.0	13.3	16.9
Neonatal mortality rate: (deaths during first 28 days of life per 1000 live births)	5.7	6.4	6.7	7.1	8.7	9.8	7.6	9.7
Infant mortality rate: (deaths of infants 0–1 year per 1000 live births)	8.9	9.5	10.2	10.7	13.5	16.0	11.2	16.7

SOURCE: Macfarlane and Mugford (1984). See also Figures 14 and 15.

Table 21 *Early childhood mortality*

	Death rates	
Region	*0–1 year (per 1000 live births)*	*1–4 years (per 1000)*
West Africa	161	30
Middle Africa	173	30
East Africa	145	35
Mid-South Asia	136	14
Southern Africa	118	30
South-East Asia	116	8
Northern Africa	131	28
South-West Asia	115	10
Tropical South America	99	7
Middle America	70	6
Caribbean	65	3
East Asia	58	2
Temperate South America	72	3
Oceania	28	1
USSR	28	1
Eastern Europe	25	1
Southern Europe	24	1
Western Europe	15	1
Northern Europe	13	1
North America	15	1
World	83	8

SOURCE: WHO/FHE Estimates based on a variety of sources.

Population growth

The rate at which a population grows or declines is determined by the relationship between births and deaths ('natural' increase) and between immigration and emigration ('migration balance'). Beyond this simple statement things become more complicated, firstly because of the large number of factors involved which influence natural increase and migration balance, secondly because births, deaths, immigration and emigration are not independent of each other but interact in complex ways. Figure 9 gives some indication of the interplay of factors determining fertility, and we will see how other factors play a part in the historical survey which follows.

The history of population in England and Wales

Figure 10 shows the birth and death rates for England and Wales between 1750 and 1980, during which time the population grew from about 4 million to about 49 million.

Fertility

Figure 10 shows that the birth rate fell from a high level to a low one between the eighteenth and the twentieth century. In the period before the industrial revolution the birth rate was high by modern standards, but still fell far short of the maximum possible birth rate for a human population.

The major reason for this appears to be associated with the fact that a very high percentage of people spent the period between 8 and 25 years old as living-in servants in other people's households, or more rarely as apprentices (Macfarlane 1978). Although their parents must have benefited to some degree from the earnings of their children in service, the economic advantages of having children would have been quite different from those in a peasant society, where each extra child would have been an extra pair of hands to work on the family enterprise. England was not a peasant society like this. Thus the lower-than-possible birth rate in pre-industrial England must be attributed to both the lack of economic incentive for child-birth and late age of marriage, rising sometimes to 29 years, associated with single, living-in servants.

Although the data are problematic it is usually reckoned that the development of factory industry raised the birth rate by lowering the average age of marriage, and by increasing the illegitimacy rate. Opportunities for wage-work which did not involve staying single, lowered the age at which young people would become economically self-sufficient. Exactly why the illegitimacy rate rose is difficult to establish, although it is often assumed that urban industrial life offered more opportunities for pre-marital sexuality. (For further details on illegitimacy see Chapter 8, pages 237–8) For some women, at least, high factory earnings gave an opportunity to do without husbands at all, and

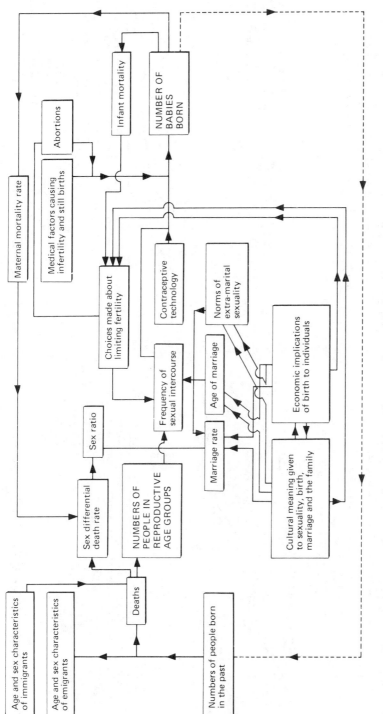

Figure 9 *Some important factors determining the number of babies born in a society*

Note: Regard each box as a range of variables, e.g. read the diagram as if immigrants were mainly young, with a balanced sex ratio; emigrants mainly elderly and male; the sex ratio in the reproductive age groups 50:50, and so on. Then read it again making different assumptions. Note that to determine the *birth rate* you have to make assumptions about the age structure of the population as a whole and not just for the reproductive age groups.

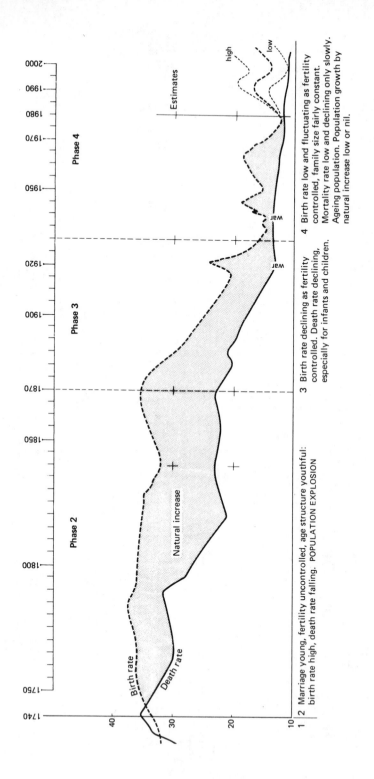

Figure 10 *Crude birth and death rates, England and Wales 1740–2000 (per 1000)*

1

2 Marriage young, fertility uncontrolled, age structure youthful: birth rate high, death rate falling. POPULATION EXPLOSION

3 Birth rate declining as fertility controlled. Death rate declining, especially for infants and children.

4 Birth rate low and fluctuating as fertility controlled, family size fairly constant. Mortality rate low and declining only slowly. Ageing population. Population growth by natural increase low or nil.

in the textile towns of the 1850s a whole generation of children were born to unmarried mill-girls.

Factory work and other industrial employment, and wage-work by labourers on the land, at first gave abundant opportunities for the employment of children, and although childbirth reduced a woman's earning capacity there must have been a great advantage in having a large family of earners to spread the risks of unemployment and sickness. Given this, it is not surprising that the birth rate remains high throughout the first three-quarters of the nineteenth century. Remember also that because this is a rapidly growing population it is also a young population with a high potential fertility. However, we can tell that children were not always wanted by the high rates of infanticide, child abandonment, and death of infants by wilful neglect.

Because of the falling rate of child and infant mortality, family size increased to reach its maximum of an average of six for women married in the 1860s. From then onwards, however, the birth rate begins to fall.

The fall in the birth rate from the 1870s
The birth rate does not fall equally for all sections of the population. It begins to turn down for the middle class in the mid 1870s and by 1911 this tendency has spread to all sections of the population.

The period 1870–90 is often called the 'Great Depression', a period of declining rents and profits. There is some considerable doubt about the severity of this depression, but it coincides with major increases in necessary expenditure for the middle and upper classes if they were to maintain the life-style to which they had become accustomed. Servants' wages were rising in competition with a growing choice of alternative jobs, and children were becoming much more expensive to support for the middle class. From 1850 onwards it became important to have academic qualifications if children were to occupy the same middle-class status as their parents. The most obvious result of this was the development of highly exclusive and expensive public schools for the rich and 'private schools' for the not-so-rich.

With nursery maids and nannies, governesses and tutors, school fees, expensive toys and fashion clothing and the necessary social round of balls and receptions, children were becoming very expensive for the middle class at the same time as more and more survived after birth. One result of this seems to have been the purposeful limitation of family size by middle-class couples so that they might concentrate all their resources on fewer children; another result was a rise in the average age of marriage for the middle class, and another, a rise in the number of life-time spinsters and bachelors. The trend towards smaller families was certainly consolidated by the dramatic fall in the infant mortality rate after the 1890s, and smaller families probably contributed to the fall in the infant mortality rate (Banks 1954).

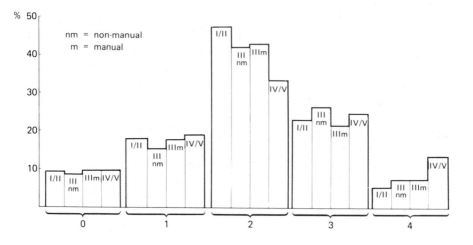

Figure 11 *Social class and family size: number of children born to women in Classes I–V (Registrar-General's scale), who were married 1956–65, after ten years of marriage. See also Table 22.*

It is probable also that the growing influence of feminism among middle-class women persuaded them of their right to dispose of their own sexuality:

During the last few years, and since the rights of women have been so much insisted upon and practically carried out by the 'strongest minded of the sex', numerous husbands have complained to me of the hardships under which they suffer by being married to women who regard themselves as martyrs when called upon to fulfil the duties of wives. [Acton 1857, 'Functions and disorders of the reproductive organs . . .', quoted in Comfort 1968]

For the working classes children became an economic burden rather later in the century. Throughout the nineteenth century, legislation made it more and more difficult for children to work and earn a wage, and in 1880 universal elementary education was made compulsory. Despite very high truancy rates up to 1914, the employment prospects of children were greatly limited. Attempts by the working class to limit families are probably best understood against this background, although women frequently faced great opposition from their husbands when attempting to limit their families (Davis 1978). In many working-class families the burden of bringing up children fell entirely on the wife, who had to budget out of whatever percentage of her husband's wage he chose to give her, or from her own earnings. Working-class families remain significantly larger than middle-class families until the late 1960s when class differences in family size become less significant (see Figure 11).

The means by which people limited their families in the nineteenth and early twentieth centuries are somewhat mysterious. Infanticide and abortions were common, particularly among the very poor, and so were illegitimacies. It is probable that most people knew the technique of *coitus interruptus* (withdrawal), and condoms, vaginal sponges and douches have a long history in Britain, although usually associated with extra-marital sex before the 1880s. By the 1880s it is certain that people were using a variety of contraceptive techniques and devices, either prescribed by doctors for their fee-paying patients, or purchased over the counter. The development of rubber technology in the early twentieth century provided the basis for the manufacture of cheap and effective contraceptives, and from then onwards contraceptives became more widely available, later to include the birth pill and the coil (McLaren 1978).

Fertility declines almost continuously from the 1880s onwards, although with occasional upswings. In the period following each world war, fertility rises. However, this is mainly a phenomenon of postponed births. Births which would have happened during the war, but didn't, are added to those which would have normally occurred after the war: remember, however, that there are also a number of 'lost' births, that is, those where the prospective parents were killed in the war. This has been estimated at about 600,000 for the First World War, and far fewer for the Second World War.

Since the Second World War there have been fluctuations in the birth rate, but average family size has remained fairly constant, at between two and three children. Thus fluctuations in the birth rate are mainly due to two factors:

1 The number of women in the child-bearing age groups, itself a result of earlier birth rates, plus the pattern of immigration and emigration.
2 The choices people make about *when* to have their children.

The upswing in births between 1954 and 1964 seems to have been due mainly to a change in timing. Whereas previously many women had married and had continued to work after marriage for a number of years before having children, between 1954 and 1964 a large number of women chose to have their babies immediately after marriage. The result was as if twelve years' births had been crammed into ten years. During the 1970s, when the birth rate actually fell below the death rate in 1976, timing habits changed again with many women postponing births for several years after marriage. Some of the upswing in the birth rate in the period after 1978 is due to these same women having their babies in their late twenties and thirties, and some is due to the fact that women born between 1954 and 1964 are themselves reaching their child-bearing years. For this reason it is expected that the birth rate will continue to rise until the 1990s (Dunnell 1979).

In the post-war period, then, we see a population which is exerting a considerable amount of control over births through using contraceptive techniques, but with a very strong preference for a family size between two and three children. We would expect, therefore, that birth rates in any particular year would be a sensitive reflection of people's thinking about the family, marriage, standards of living, the economic future and so on. One factor which stands out clearly in the pattern these days is the economic activity of women, so that families are now often planned with the wife's employment in mind. This in itself is an indication of the considerable improvement of the wife's status *vis-à-vis* her husband, and the reader will be able to relate this to the changing pattern of family life as described in Chapter 8, pages 222–38.

There are other less obvious factors, however. Firstly, the decline in the birth rate has meant an enormous improvement in female health and life expectancy, since childbirth under nineteenth-century conditions was one of the most dangerous 'occupations'. Secondly, although the birth rate has dropped dramatically since 1880, far more women have babies today. In the 1880s only a small percentage of women accounted for the average family size of six, because so many remained unmarried. In 1871 60 per cent of women over 15 were unmarried, but by 1975 the percentage was only 16 per cent. About 65 per cent of women are married at any time. Most marriages give rise to children, and there is even a small-scale tendency for women to choose to give birth while remaining unmarried. Parenthood has become a more common attribute of the fully adult person. People who are not parents are even misguidedly looked upon with pity or suspicion by some people, but clearly there is a proportion of unmarried and married couples who freely choose not to have children.

Age structure

The age structure of a population refers to the numbers and percentages of people in different age groups. It is a reflection of the effects of birth rates, death rates and migration.

Figure 12 shows the age structure of England and Wales in 1891 and 1971 – these should be compared with Figure 10. Note that the pyramid for 1891 has a broad base which reflects a high birth rate. The pyramid for 1971 by contrast 'bells' towards the middle age groups, reflecting the fall in the birth rate from the 1920s onwards, and in its finer detail reflects the ups and downs of the birth rate since then. In addition the 1971 age structure shows a greater percentage of the population in the older age groups. This is a result of increasing life expectancy and, more importantly, of the fact that the people who were elderly in 1971 were born at a time of higher birth rates. This phenomenon is called the 'ageing' of a population and is characteristic of the populations of all the

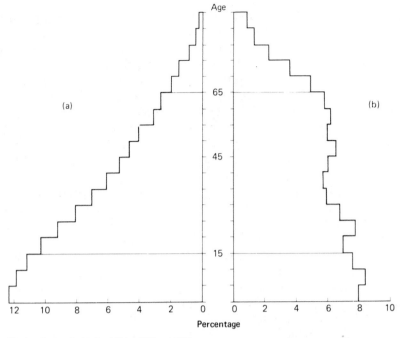

Age

65

45

15

(a)

(b)

12 10 8 6 4 2 0 0 2 4 6 8 10

Percentage

Source: *Census, England and Wales, 1891 and 1971*

Figure 12 *Population pyramid for England and Wales, 1891 and 1971: (a) 1891 (both sexes): (b) 1971 (both sexes)*

advanced industrial nations. For Britain the percentage of elderly in the population will continue to increase into the 1990s and then decline, for by then those who are elderly will have been born at times of lower birth rates.

The ageing of the population is sometimes described in terms of the 'dependency ratio': that is the ratio between those in the economically active age groups on the one hand, and children, the elderly, the chronically sick and the handicapped on the other. While it is true that providing health and welfare services for the very old is extremely expensive, a picture is sometimes given of a declining middle-aged population having to work harder and harder to maintain an ever increasing number of dependents. This is misleading for three reasons. First, large numbers of elderly people do not of themselves lead to high levels of expenditure on services. The expense is the result of a moral decision that the elderly deserve services. Secondly, dependency is not a fact of nature; it is a social arrangement. If we were short of productive workers we could raise the retirement age, lower the school leaving age or import workers from overseas. Thirdly, modern technology is increasingly reducing the amount of labour required.

Really, the problems presented by an ageing population are of two sorts. First there is the political problem of charging earners high taxes to pay for the pensions and other benefits consumed by the elderly. Secondly, there is the problem which arises for three- (and even four-) generation families, which were not particularly common in the nineteenth century. A combination of large numbers of elderly people, fewer young relatives to care for them and greater geographical mobility makes the family care of the elderly more difficult than in the past. However, remember that in the nineteenth century the mass of the population was too poor to prevent their elderly relatives ending their days in the workhouse, and for richer people the care of the elderly was performed by servants and paid companions.

In itself the age structure of a population is relatively unimportant. What makes it important is the way in which age is used as a principle of social organization. For example, a population with a large percentage in the child-bearing age groups may have a high birth rate, but only if social attitudes favour reproduction rather than celibacy. In a society such as ours, chronological age is used to batch people into groups with particular rights, obligations and expected patterns of behaviour. Batching by age is especially important with regard to the relationship between the individual and the state. Thus certain welfare services and benefits are granted only to persons of a certain age, and certain kinds of behaviour is required only of certain age groups; compulsory attendance at school for example. Changes in the birth rate, which feed through to cause fluctuations in the numbers of people in particular age groups, then have considerable implications for state services which have been designed to cater for more or fewer in that category.

For example, both the post-war baby boom and the rise in the birth rate from 1956 to 1964 led to a shortage of primary school places and primary school teachers and crash programmes of building and training. Note, however, that 'shortage' here refers to political decisions about the need for children to go to school, the amount of space each requires and an acceptable pupil–teacher ratio.

Similarly in the mid 1980s the number of 18-year-olds in the population reached a peak and began to decline. The government of the day used this as an argument to reduce the number of places in higher education (universities, polytechnics and colleges of higher education). Close inspection of the evidence shows, however, that most of the fall in the birth rate which caused a decline in the number of 18-year-olds had occurred in working-class families. As Table 22 shows, the birth rates of the university-going classes had remained buoyant. In addition, by the 1980s a growing percentage of working-class pupils was seeking entry to higher education, more and more girls were applying for higher education, more and more people were obtaining the entry qualifications, and more people in their twenties and thirties (especially married women) were making applications. While the number of 18-year-olds

Table 22 *Legitimate live births by social class, for selected years, England and Wales*

| | Classes | | | |
	I/II	III	IV/V	Total number
1950	15.6	53.3	25.5	697,097
1964	15.3	47.1	27.1	875,972
1970	18.9	48.1	21.4	784,486
1980	25.1	41.8	18.3	656,234

SOURCE: MacFarlane and Mugford (1984)

was falling, the demand for higher education places was rising. The important point is that sheer numbers of people in a particular age group is of itself unimportant. What makes such a factor important are the political decisions about who deserves what kinds of services, at what level of provision, and the social expectations and patterns of behaviour of the people in an age group.

Mortality, 1750-1980

Over the whole period we can say that the main causes of death have changed from the infectious epidemic diseases in the earlier period to the so-called 'degenerative' or 'chronic' diseases today. In the eighteenth century the following diseases, plus accidents, were among the major killers: smallpox, typhus, enteric fever (typhoid and paratyphoid), diphtheria, rheumatic fever, whooping cough, measles, scarlet fever, tuberculosis, influenza and pneumonia (Howe 1976). Only the last two are major killers today, and in the 1970s over 80 per cent of all deaths were accounted for by heart and circulatory diseases, cancers and diseases of the respiratory system (bronchitis, pneumonia, etc.).

Thus the fall in mortality over the historical period is due largely to a decline in fatalities from epidemic diseases. Two sets of factors are of overwhelming importance:

1 Changes in the environment which make the transmission of epidemic diseases less likely; this is mainly a question of environmental engineering in sewage control and water supply, and later in housing and town planning.

2 Changes in food production, distribution and consumption. Diet is extremely important because in general epidemic diseases produce far higher levels of fatality among badly nourished people. While we regard measles or whooping cough as 'childhood ailments', though with damaging side effects for a minority, the same diseases are killers when nutritional status is low, as in many Third World countries (McKeowen 1976; Howe 1976).

The reasons for these changes can be conveniently summarized in Figure 13. The least important factor in the mortality picture is curative

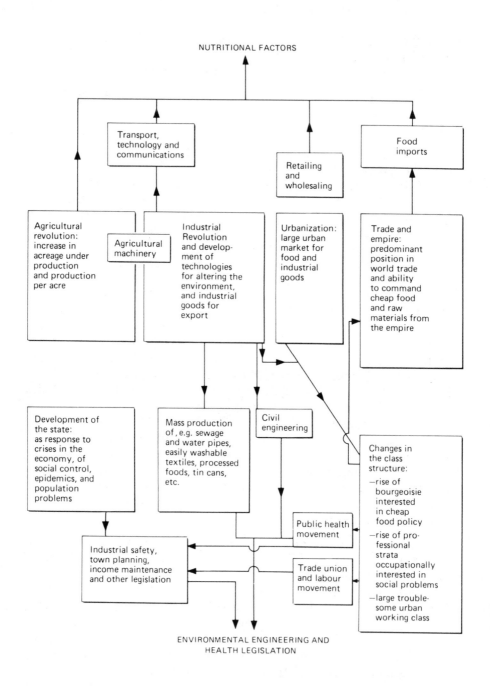

Figure 13 *Major factors in the decline in the mortality rate in England and Wales in the nineteenth century*

medicine (McKeowen 1976; Powles 1973). With the exception of smallpox vaccination from 1863, virtually no improvements in mortality can be attributed to curative medicine before the 1930s, by which time mortality rates are down to a 'modern' level. From the 1930s curative techniques of various sorts and immunizations do become important, but their effects on the death rate are very small compared with nutritional and environmental factors coming into play in the preceding century.

Figure 13 indicates that changes in the mortality rate are not due to any simple set of factors, but are the accompaniment of the transformation of a whole society. For instance, technological changes within agriculture were important in increasing the home-produced food supply, but they were only able to have an effect on the death rate because of the industrial developments which led to changes in transport technology, and because of the emergence of wholesaling and retailing agencies which accompanied the development of large urban populations. Again the importation of food from abroad depended on the production of industrial goods against which food imports were traded. However, for this to happen on a large scale required a change in the power structure within Britain, which shifted national economic policy away from one which limited imports, which favoured the land-owning aristocracy, and towards 'free trade' favoured by the rising bourgeoisie of industrial employers. Thus this component of the fall in mortality follows from radical changes in the class structure. Moreover, the environmental improvements which were put into operation during the nineteenth century through voluntary effort and state intervention were themselves only one aspect of attempts to solve the political problem of dealing with a large and unruly – as well as unhealthy – urban working class. In many ways the growth of the state (which was the basis of much environmental engineering and of legislation about safety at work, food hygiene or town planning), must be seen as a response to the internal political problem of preventing revolutionary activity by the working class, and the external problem of finding and protecting markets in which to sell British products through the development of empire (see Figure 13).

Changes in child and infant mortality

During the first ninety years of the nineteenth century, the main downward movement in mortality was for adults and older children. Indeed, during the second half of the century the infant mortality rate rose from 148 per 1000 in 1851 to 153 per 1000 in 1901. From the 1890s a new pattern begins to show itself: a fall in the infant mortality rate and greater survival chances for young children. Figure 14 expresses this in terms of life expectancy at birth.

The increase in life expectancy *at birth* has improved considerably since 1900, because infant and child mortality rates have fallen.

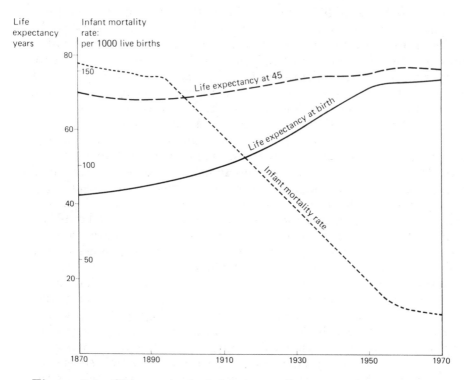

Figure 14 *Changes in the infant mortality rate and in life expectancy,*
England and Wales, 1870–1970
SOURCE: Powles (1973).

Improvements in life expectancy for older age groups have declined less
dramatically, and those who are 75 in 1980 have a life expectancy which
is only marginally greater than those who reached 75 in 1880.

The fall in infant mortality must owe a great deal to all the factors
already mentioned, but there are some additional ones.

1 The fall in infant mortality coincides with a fall in the birth rate. In
   smaller families more care and resources can be lavished on each
   child. The fall also coincides with a decline in the number of married
   women workers. In addition it can be suggested that both the fall in
   the birth rate and the fall in the infant mortality rate are associated
   with changing attitudes to children (Newson and Newson, 1974).
   They coincide with the beginning of there being a distinct period of
   'childhood' for working-class children, as they are increasingly
   excluded from the work-place and placed in schools. Additionally,
   there is the development of a literature about child health and welfare,
   much of it in mass circulation magazines aimed at women (Newson
   1974).

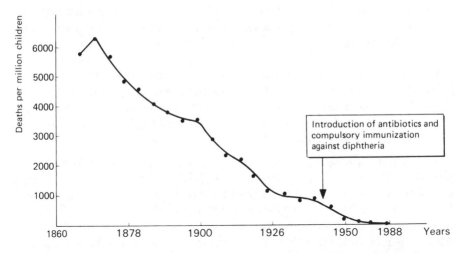

Figure 15 *Deaths of children under 15 years attributed to scarlet fever, diphtheria, whooping cough and measles, England and Wales*
SOURCE: Porter (1971).

2 The fall in the birth rate was accompanied by acute concern about the 'decline' of the British population, which brought into being a quite impressive array of government and voluntary services for mothers and children, ranging from antenatal clinics to the school medical service, between the beginning of the century and the 1930s.

Again, modern medicine does not begin to play a part until the advent of the 'wonder drugs', such as sulphonamides and antibiotics, and of routine immunizations from the 1940s and 1950s: see Figure 15. From then onwards, modern midwifery and obstetric techniques probably do play a significant role in reducing the infant mortality rate.

The modern way of death
Heart disease, circulatory diseases and cancers are sometimes called 'diseases of affluence'. This is very misleading since they are most likely to lead to the early death of the *poor* in affluent societies. However, these diseases can be linked to the way of life in a modern industrialized society.

1 Increases in life-expectancy themselves are likely to increase the incidence of some diseases; we might say that we have saved people from death by smallpox at an early age, to die of heart disease at a later one. Everybody, after all, has to die sometime.
2 The deaths of people who are born with congenital defects are now an important component in the adult and adolescent death rates. Previously such people would have figured in the infant and child mortality statistics.

3 There is a considerable body of evidence linking modern diseases with
   a modern way of life. The suggested link between smoking, cancer and
   heart disease is well known. There is abundant evidence linking some
   forms of cancer with modern industrial processes involving oils,
   plastics and substances such as asbestos and perhaps glass fibre
   (Cole 1972). And there are strong suspicions that other fatal diseases
   are linked to modern dietary patterns: bowel cancer and lack of
   roughage in modern diets, heart disease and high intakes of refined
   sugar or of animal fats (Powles 1973).

The same high technology which brings us modern medicine also
places us at risk of dying from the effects of modern chemicals, highly
processed foods emerging from the food processing industry (Politics of
Health Group 1980), or motor-car accidents. Perhaps the most frightening consideration concerns the extent to which medicine itself has
become a risk to health. Each year there are large numbers of deaths
from drugs prescribed by doctors, and the widespread use of antibiotics
in medicine and farming has enabled disease organisms to develop
immunity against them.

Health and class inequality

As in the nineteenth century, so today, the distribution of illness is closely
associated with social class as is shown in Tables 19, 20 and 21. The
Black report of 1979 (Townsend and Davidson 1982) shows that manual
workers and their families suffer more from virtually every serious
illness and are more likely to die at an earlier age. The Black report
suggests four main kinds of reason for these class gradients in illness.

1   Health as an influence on class
The first is the idea that it is ill health that assigns a person's class
position, so that the less healthy sink to the bottom of the class structure
and the most healthy and vigorous rise. It is of course true that children
who are in poor health may do less well at school and that adults who are
unhealthy may experience downward social mobility towards less well-
paying jobs or a life as welfare claimants. However, research into social
mobility as a whole (see page 178) suggests that health is only a small
factor in determining social mobility. Moreover the suggestion that
health causes class position fails adequately to explain why it is that
people become unhealthy in the first place.

2   Quality and quantity of services
A second explanation for class differences in health suggests that
working-class people are less well served by the health services than are
the middle and upper classes. There is considerable evidence that this is

so and two factors are cited especially. One is the availability of services to different classes, and the other is the greater difficulty working class people have in using health services effectively.

It is generally true that the poorer an area the less well-served it is with doctors, clinics and hospital beds and the lower is the quality of these. The contrast between the quality of health services in the affluent south-east and the poorer regions such as the north-east of England is especially marked. This effect is extended by the existence of the private health care sector. However, private health care is on a very small scale in the UK, covering only 6 per cent of the population and tending to specialize in routine treatments of non-life-threatening conditions. It is most unlikely that private health care influences the class pattern of illness greatly.

In much the same way as the schools place working-class pupils at a disadvantage (see Chapter 9, page 248), many working-class patients find it difficult to communicate with doctors (Cartwright 1967). It seems that more effective communication between middle-class patients and their doctors leads to earlier and more expensive regimes of treatment. Working-class people can also find it more difficult to get to surgeries, clinics and hospitals if they are not close at hand, and if private transport is not available. This is the case especially for many poor people living in rural areas.

However, there are difficulties in arguing that class differences in the care obtained from the health services are an important factor in explaining class differences in illness or early death. There is no good evidence on which to decide whether receiving medical treatment actually improves health. In affluent nations there is a strong *positive* correlation between the numbers of doctors per head of the population and the death rate (Cochrane *et al.* 1978). The evidence from strikes by doctors seems to suggest that death rates fall when doctors go on strike and rise when they return to work. The main reason for this seems to lie with the risks of death accompanying treatment, especially surgical treatment of non-life-threatening conditions (Roemer and Schwarz 1979). Some writers such as Illich (1976) go as far as to say that modern medicine has become a major threat to health. Illich presents a great deal of convincing evidence that many routine medical treatments are themselves dangerous or ineffective. However, Illich overstates his case, for the truth of the matter is that evidence about the effectiveness of medical treatments is piecemeal. We do know that some widely used treatments are ineffective (intensive care units for coronary patients, for example), some are more dangerous than the condition they are designed to cure (many drug treatments), and that some are definitely life-saving or life-enhancing (accident services or hip-joint replacement). However, about the vast majority of treatments there is very little evidence at all, and most medical interventions are for conditions which would probably improve whether they were treated or not. In the light of this it is difficult to pursue the argument that class differences in medical treatment are important in the picture of class differences in illness or early death.

The other two explanations in the Black report focus on class differences in *vulnerability* to illness.

3 *Vulnerability*

It can be suggested that the greater vulnerability of the working class to illness is due to material inequalities, such as low incomes, dangerous working conditions, poor housing and diet and unhealthy local environments. The facts that the prevalence of illness is greater among poorer people in countries poorer than Britain, and that the health of the British population has risen historically as the standard of living has risen, lend credibility to this argument. So does recent work which correlates illness, early death and unemployment, for manual workers are much more vulnerable to unemployment than are other employees (College 1981, Gomm 1982).

Diet is regarded as an extremely important factor in health, and the National Food Survey shows each year that there are marked class differences in diet (Table 23). To a great extent these differences can be attributed to differences in income: indeed there is evidence that middle-class families with good knowledge about healthy diets trade down to a poorer diet when they fall on hard times.

A direct link between illness and class inequality of a material kind would suggest that equalizing health chances requires a radical redistribution of income and wealth. This view is similar to the structural view of poverty discussed in Chapter 3.

4 *Knowledge about health*

Cigarette smoking, which is probably the most dangerous hazard which people choose, is more prevalent among manual workers (Townsend 1979), whereas the market for health foods, health magazines and health sports is decidedly middle class. It can be suggested that equalizing health chances can be accomplished by educating people out of their unhealthy habits rather than changing the material circumstances of their lives.

Table 23 *Income and nutrition: ounces of particular foods consumed each week*

	White bread	Sugar	Potatoes	Fruit
High-income group	18	9.3	29	33
Low-income group	31	15	52	17

SOURCE: National Food Survey (1980)

Such an argument tends to shift the blame for illness away from the structural features of society and on to those who fall sick (or their parents), as with subcultural theories of poverty (see Chapter 3). Health education programmes of various kinds are undoubtedly worth while, but very often the propaganda of the health educator confronts more powerful campaigns by commercial interests encouraging people to maintain an unhealthy life-style. For example, in Britain the national budget for all health education in 1982 was some £8 million, while the tobacco companies alone spent £80 million encouraging people to smoke.

The phenomenology of illness

So far we have been discussing illness as if it were a simple fact of nature. However, illness is a social construct and has to be understood as an idea which people use to organize their experience and to cope with situations. Labelling deviance was discussed in Chapter 11, and in much the same way illness has to be regarded as that which is labelled as such.

Sociologists sometimes make a distinction between 'illness' and 'illness behaviour'. The former term they apply to the biological effects of the virus or the bacteria or the broken leg, and the latter to the social behaviour which accompanies it. Whether one screams with pain, or keeps a stiff upper lip, takes to one's bed or struggles on, is not a matter which is determined solely biologically; there are also social conventions. Something that every child learns is how to be ill properly.

What is 'illness'?

One way of looking at illness is to see that defining someone as ill is defining them as work-for-the-doctor. What are 'illnesses', and what are not, is a matter of how an occupational group defines the boundaries of its work. An important feature of the twentieth century has been the extent to which more and more conditions have been defined as medical work.

Some conditions have indeed *ceased* to be medical work. Homosexuality ceased to be an illness in the USA after a vote of the American Psychiatric Association, and there are many diseases from which people died in the nineteenth century such as 'fatty heart', from which it is impossible to die today because they are no longer recognized by doctors. However, on the whole the number of areas of life into which doctors claim the competence to intrude has grown larger. Some sociologists even write of the 'medicalization' of life (Zola 1975). Thus it is only recently that being fat has been redefined as 'obesity'; drinking heavily as 'alcoholism'; disliking school as 'school phobia'; and being unable to read as 'dyslexia'.

Surveys which screen large numbers of people for all kinds of medical conditions have found that up to 90 per cent of the population is suffering from some condition which, if presented to a doctor, might be regarded as a disease or disability (Last 1963). In this sense illness is the statistical norm. Yet at any one time only a minority of people think of themselves as ill and seek treatment. Given that most people could be regarded as ill, why is the illness label applied to only a few? The question is rarely whether someone is ill or not, but whether they are ill enough to deserve to have the benefits or disadvantages of being treated as ill.

The process of self-diagnosis which precedes a person's appearance in a surgery is very important. We might divide the factors involved in self-diagnosis into two kinds. First there is the knowledge that lay people have about illness which helps them decide whether this unpleasant sensation is in fact a 'symptom'. Secondly there is the question of what people gain or lose by being defined as sick.

We actually know relatively little about lay medical knowledge. In the UK what ordinary people believe seems to bear a close relationship to the way doctors thought thirty or more years ago, mixed with rather haphazard and often muddled additions gained from school learning, from personal encounters with the medical world and from the mass media. If anyone had to rely on the latter as their major source of information about illness, their ideas would be dominated by dramatic epidemics, medical disasters (such as have been associated with the side effects from some drugs), and medical 'breakthroughs'. The fact that ordinary people do not share the same ideas as doctors is a good example of the social distribution of knowledge mentioned in Chapter 5, and relates to the way in which medicine is a closed world where an occupational group monopolizes a body of knowledge and practice. Nonetheless, somehow or other people have to use what knowledge of illness they have in order to decide whether to seek medical treatment.

For some people the problem is more acute. Most non-Euro-American cultures have a traditional body of knowledge about illness, but Western medical ideas have now spread throughout the world. Thus many people in the world have a choice between defining themselves as ill in terms of Western medical ideas and seeking treatment from doctors or hospitals, or defining themselves as ill (or otherwise) in traditional terms and seeking help from traditional healers, religious functionaries or counter-witchcraft specialists. Even in Europe and America there are flourishing 'alternative therapy' movements, which not only offer different treatments for illness, but also allow people to define themselves as ill in ways not recognized by orthodox medicine.

Social advantages and disadvantages of illness

Being ill offers certain benefits and disadvantages which will influence whether or not someone seeks to enter the 'sick role'.

One of the benefits of being defined as ill is of course that it gives one a right to treatment. In addition, in our culture, to claim to be ill is to claim the right to be treated with special care and consideration and to be remitted from normal social obligations. If I claim to be ill I may be claiming the right not to go to work, but to receive sickness benefit and to oblige someone else to put themselves out to look after me. Illness also provides a legitimate reason to evade unpleasant situations. It is probably significant that people who report low levels of work satisfaction also take more time 'off sick'.

Because of the opportunities illness gives for evading social obligations it is frequently associated with suspicions of 'malingering'. This suspicion is itself a deterrent to using illness as an excuse for evasion of work or other obligations, but in addition illness is 'policed'. Doctors not only offer treatments, but authoritatively decide who have the benefits of being defined as ill.

One of the advantages of being defined as ill is that of not being defined as deviant in some other way. 'Feeling under the weather' is usually a good excuse for having been bad tempered or slothful; and the difference between a 'truant' and a 'school phobic' is that one is bad and needs punishing, while the other is sick and demands our sympathy. The effect of defining some problematic behaviour as an illness is to shift the blame for the deviant behaviour away from the person to the condition. This is especially the case with so-called 'mental illness' (see Chapter 11).

While some people may seek the sick role, others have it thrust upon them. If I claim that *you* are 'ill' I may well be claiming that you should not be allowed to go to the disco, or that you should resign your job, or that what you are saying should not be taken seriously. Thus while the sick role may offer advantages it may also be a way of denying people rights that they would otherwise have.

Claiming and attributing illness, then, may be caught up in the politics of families and organizations: a family member may put pressure on the others by claiming that their behaviour makes him ill; children may be controlled by the claim that they are 'not well enough' to do something, or that doing something will make them sick; managing directors of companies who have lost the confidence of the board resign 'for health reasons'; incompetent teachers are rarely dismissed, they are more usually 'invalided out'.

Health statistics

The decision on whether to consult a doctor is thus a crucial element in the official statistics of illness. The discussion above of the complicated processes involved in making that decision should alert you to the fact that official statistics on illness show the same kinds of deficiencies shown by other official statistics. That is to say, they reflect the *way* in which cases become officially recorded as well as the *incidence* of particular conditions and behaviours.

This is why most discussions about the social distribution of ill health use statistics of premature mortality rather than of illness, for the statistics of death do not present quite so many difficulties as the statistics of illness.

Taking the diagram in Figure 7 in Chapter 11, which refers to juvenile delinquency, you might like to draw a similar one for illness. The second half of the diagram would refer to the way in which doctors reach diagnoses. This is discussed below.

Social effects of the practice of medicine

Sociological and other studies of how doctors reach diagnoses show how idiosyncratic individual doctors are and how haphazard the process is. In a recent study, for example, ENT (ear, nose and throat) specialists and paediatricians shown slides of tonsils rarely agreed on the preferred treatment. What is more, unbeknown to them they were shown the same slide twice, and only in 50 per cent of cases did the same doctor make the same decision twice (Bloor 1976). Similarly a recent Scottish study checked the causes given for death on death certificates by carrying out autopsies. In about 30 per cent of cases the doctors doing the autopsies diagnosed causes different from those on the certificate.

One of the reasons for the apparently haphazard nature of diagnosis lies in the way in which medical practice is organized. For example, the average GP consultation lasts for approximately five minutes, and in this time the doctor has to make a quick decision about what are often ill-defined symptoms incoherently described by the patient. Under-standably doctors often seem to draw on social stereotypes to assist them in coming to a conclusion. Some doctors seem to have quite entrenched ideas about women who come to the doctor simply to 'seek attention', working-class men who are 'malingerers' consulting only for the sake of a day off work, and black patients who 'make more fuss' than white ones.

David Sudnow's study of admissions procedures in American hospitals shows clearly how the way the staff perceived the social status of a patient determined what diagnosis was given. He focused on accident admissions where it was unclear as to whether patients were dead or not. Sudnow found that the decision was always made to attempt to resuscitate children; but among adults, the older they were, the poorer they appeared to be, and the more evidence there was of drinking, the more likely it was that they would be diagnosed as 'dead on arrival', and despatched to the mortuary (Sudnow 1967).

Other features of the organization of consultation also seem to be important. In fee-for-service medicine, where doctors are paid according to the number of operations they perform, more people are diagnosed as in need of surgical operations. Roth (1963) studied tuberculosis treatment in a sanitorium and showed that patients negotiated with their doctors as to the speed at which they moved through the various stages of treatment. Those patients who were anxious to be discharged persuaded their doctors to define them as fit quicker than others who were content to stay in the sanitorium.

Sometimes doctors choose a diagnosis to write on a medical or a death certificate so that it does not upset or disadvantage the patient. For example, doctors often choose not to use the diagnosis 'infant cot death syndrome' on a death certificate, but write in another such as 'upper respiratory tract infection', because they feel that parents may blame themselves for a 'cot death'. Less justifiably, doctors with consultancies with industrial concerns have been known to avoid diagnoses which make the company liable for compensation payments, and deaths and disabilities caused by medical incompetence are sometimes disguised with an alternative diagnosis.

Health, medicine and the social structure

Functionalist writers tended to see medicine as a social response to society's problem of having the efficiency of its members impaired by biologically caused illnesses. Similarly early Marxist writers often saw the development of health care systems as a necessary price that had to be paid by the ruling class for a healthy and efficient workforce. However, as more and more doubt has been thrown on the effectiveness of medicine in delivering health, writers have looked around for other functions which medicine might perform. Most recent sociological writing on medicine and health does not view health care systems as being simple social responses to a problem of illness. Instead they see organized medicine as part and parcel of a kind of society helping to reproduce its most important features. A question which crystallizes the issues involved is: Why is it that modern health care systems have developed to produce high-technology cures, rather than towards preventing people becoming ill in the first place?

Ivan Illich is well known as a critic of modern medicine. His view of industrial society is as a pathological form of life on its way to destruction. Illich's writing on professionalism (1979) argues that professional groups capture and monopolize certain areas of knowledge, and practice and develop them to the advantage of the members of the profession and to the disadvantage of everyone else. For Illich medicine has been developed in a high-technology curative form delivered by complex organizations to maximize the earnings and status of doctors in a way that keeps everyone else in ignorance of how to be healthy. To this extent doctors have a vested interest in people becoming ill.

Illich's view is rightly criticized by Marxist writers for treating professional occupations as more powerful then they really are. By contrast Marxist writers argue that if professional groups such as doctors have high earnings and high status, this is because of the way their activities promote the interests of ruling-class groups. Such writers claim that the way organized medicine has developed has to be understood in terms of its role in the development and reproduction of capitalism. Two notions are especially important here.

First, health care is an important market for the products of capitalist enterprises. The pharmaceutical industry, for example, is one of the world's largest and most profitable industries. Its main objective is profit and it has an interest in maximizing the consumption of drugs. In countries where there are few controls over the labelling of drugs, they are marketed as cure-alls, and larger doses are recommended than in those countries where there is stricter government supervision. Where doctors do not have a monopoly of prescribing drugs, companies use all the techniques of modern advertising and retailing to sell direct to the public. Where doctors monopolize prescribing they act as 'retail-outlets' for the pharmaceutical multinationals, who invest large sums of money in persuading doctors to prescribe their wares. It has been shown that drug companies make it extraordinarily difficult for doctors to judge the truth of their advertising claims. Marxist writers argue that in capitalist economies it is unsurprising that the form of medicine that will develop is one which makes the greatest profit for shareholders, and that this is likely to be so even where health care is nationalized, as in the UK.

Secondly, it is argued that medicine constitutes a mystifying ideology. In this view one person's good health, power and high standard of living is another person's sickness, powerlessness and stigmatization. An economically 'healthy' industry yielding high profits for its owners may do so only by offering dangerous working conditions and low wages to its workers. Better working conditions, more controls over environ-mental pollution, higher wages or higher taxes to provide health for the masses may mean lower profits for the owners of industry.

The kind of information contained in the Black report (discussed above) does suggest that if we wish to improve people's health, then this can only be done by radically restructuring society. Marxists argue that by focusing on the cure of sick individuals and the biological causes of illness, modern medicine distracts attention away from the social, economic and political conditions which makes people vulnerable to illness. To coin a phrase, people are encouraged to believe that they are sick and in need of a doctor, rather than sick of capitalism and in need of a revolution.

Women, medicine and health

In this section I want to review some of the themes which appear earlier
in the chapter in the different context of gender relations.

Women have a longer life expectancy than men. This seems to be
partly genetic since it is true of most human populations, but these
biological differences are probably increased by the fact that women are
less likely to engage in dangerous work or leisure pursuits. In the UK
until the turn of the century childbirth was a major cause of female
mortality; but with a fall in the birth rate and better obstetric techniques
the gap between male and female life expectancy widened. Indeed, in
talking of the ageing of the population we are talking mainly of an
increase in the female elderly. One of the effects of this increased life
expectancy has been to increase the number of lonely and elderly
widows.

On the other hand, steps towards sex equality since the war are
associated with rising rates of female mortality from the conditions
which had previously mainly killed males. For example, while smoking
among men has levelled off, smoking among women goes on increasing,
as do female deaths from lung cancer and coronary heart disease, both
smoking-related diseases (Jacobson 1982).

Paradoxically, while the death rates suggest that women are on the
whole more healthy than men, women are in fact more frequently
diagnosed as ill. One reason is that women more frequently consult their
doctors. This may be due to the fact that it is easier for the housewife or
part-time female wage worker to get to the surgery than it is for a man
working full-time; but it has also been suggested that the process of
being socialized as a female encourages help-seeking, while being
socialized as a male encourages self-sufficiency.

Gender and the division of labour in health care

In looking at health and gender relations it is important to note that the
majority of doctors in the UK are male. This is itself part of the sexual
division of labour in which women are denied access to the more elite
occupations (see page 344). It is still the case that female applicants for
many medical schools need higher A-level grades than do males, while
in the long medical training childbirth and child rearing often severely
disrupt a woman's medical career. Most nurses and almost all midwives
are female. In the medical workplace, as in many others, males
dominate females.

Within medicine the sexual division of labour has developed over the
last 150 years. Prior to the professionalization of medicine there was a
wide variety of healers, many of them female. The organization of
medicine in the name of higher standards of care was at the same time a
process of excluding women from healing. There were in fact more

women doctors in the 1830s than there were in the 1900s. The professionalization of nursing by Florence Nightingale was an attempt to develop a profession parallel to and equal in status to that of doctors – hence Nightingale's recruitment of upper-class women to nursing. However, almost inevitably nurses (as women) came to be subservient in the workplace to doctors (as men). Indeed, the female nurse and the male doctor have come to be one of the most powerful images of masculinity and femininity in contemporary popular culture.

More contested was the way in which the midwives were brought under doctor control. There was much in the claim made by doctors in the nineteenth century that midwives were inept and unreliable and contributed to high rates of maternal and infant mortality, but much the same could be said about male doctors. What was also at issue was that midwives competed with doctors for the fees paid by women in childbirth at a time when there were more doctors than the market could provide with an adequate income. Over a period of fifty years the male medical establishment used the male domination of parliament to have legislation passed which by the 1930s meant that midwives could practise only in cases surpervised by doctors.

It is also worth noting that the vast majority of unpaid 'nursing care' is performed by women as members of families: another aspect of the way in which women's unpaid labour plays a vital role in the political economy (see page 268).

For feminists the domination of female health workers by male health workers is only one aspect of a patriarchal system which subjects women to male control. In medicine this included the control by men (as doctors) over the bodies of their female patients.

Gender definitions of 'illness'

Nineteenth- and early twentieth-century medical thinking was full of ideas about how women differed essentially from men (Ehrenreich and English 1976). It would not be too far off the mark to say that medicine treated women as defective men, and found all that was peculiar to the female anatomy a source of illness. Thus while for men the cause of tuberculosis was seen to be exposure to germs, for women it was a dysfunction of the ovaries. Upper-class women, who could pay doctors' fees, were cultivated as a market for medical attention, with childbirth, menstruation and menopause defined as serious illnesses.

At the same time medicine found 'scientific' reasons why women should not compete with men. Women were seen as 'naturally' wives and mothers, their whole biological lives revolving around the womb. Thus it was argued that if women studied (like men) they would overtax their female brains and divert energy away from their reproductive organs, causing them to wither and making it impossible for them to give birth. The image persists in the cartoon tradition of dumb, busty women, and scraggy intellectual ones. Similarly women were ascribed with a 'delicate' nervous constitution which would make it dangerous for them to enter politics, business, the law or medicine. Equally, female desires to compete with men might also be taken as symptomatic of illness. It is the definition of what is 'natural' that lies at the basis of the definition of a disease.

As Ehrenreich and English (1976) say, medical ideas depicted upper-class women as ineligible to compete with men, but highly eligible to be the fee-paying patients of male doctors. Working-class women, however, were depicted differently in medical thought. They were largely neglected as patients by orthodox medicine, except as the subjects of medical experiments, and instead seen as the source of infections which might spread to the more respectable classes. Working-class women were, after all, the servants, the shop girls, the factory hands and the prostitutes whose work brought them into contact with the better off. That nine-teenth- and early twentieth-century male-dominated medicine should provide two distinct images of women – one for each class – is a good example of the way in which the ideologies of class and patriarchy interact.

Modern feminists claim that medicine still provides an ideology which assists men to dominate women. For example, most tranquillizer prescriptions are for female patients and a majority of those who are diagnosed as suffering from 'clinical depression' are housebound working-class housewives (Brown 1978). From a feminist viewpoint it can be argued that the dissatisfaction that women feel from serving men as housewives and child rearers is medically transformed into an illness, and that the real conflicts of interest between men and women in marriage are thereby banished from view.

Childbirth control

An issue which has particularly interested feminist writers is the male control of childbirth. Childbirth is one of those aspects of life which has been 'medicalized' in the sense of being defined as work-for-the-doctor, and for feminists this also means male control over a female function. Feminists (and others) object that giving birth to children is a perfectly healthy and normal activity which does not require the kind of high-technology medical intervention to which it is now subject. In Britain 95 per cent of births now occur in hospitals. Prior to the fall in the birth rate in the 1970s there were far more home deliveries by midwives and GPs; but thereafter hospital obstetricians were able to demand that an increasing share of the dwindling supply of babies should be born on the hospitals wards they controlled.

Most obstetricians claim that hospitalization makes the process of childbirth safer, because the hospital has all the high-technology equipment necessary to deal with emergencies. Critics claim that deliveries in hospital are actually more dangerous because the presence of high-technology equipment encourages unnecessary medical interventions such as inductions, forceps deliveries and the use of anaesthetics, each of which carries its own dangers. They also point out that when a woman is wired up to a fetal monitoring machine, this means she has restricted movement, and thus feels pain more severely. This in turn encourages the use of anaesthetics which in turn limits her ability to participate actively in the birth, and in turn calls for the injection of drugs to contract the uterus, the use of forceps or caesarian deliveries. Similarly it can be argued that the use of incubators for newborn babies prevents the development of a good relationship between mother and child immediately after birth (Rakusen and Davidson 1982).

In fact there is no good evidence that hospitalizing childbirth makes childbirth more or less hazardous, though it certainly makes it much more expensive, and for many women makes it a highly alienating experience. The same example also illustrates an argument about the development of technology, to the effect that those technologies which are developed are those which serve the interests of groups who are already in control. Marxists would argue that the new technologies of childbirth are primarily in the interests of the companies which produce them. Feminists would point out that such technological arrangements place the (usually male) obstetrician firmly in charge of childbirth, and de-skill the female midwives to the level of machine minders. Both would point out that the hazards of childbirth have less to do with the immediate dangers of giving birth, and much more to do with the standard of living of the mother before and during pregnancy. It is empirically true that most still births and most handicapped babies are born of low birthweight, and that low birthweight is associated with maternal poverty (Macfarlane and Mugford 1984) (Figure 16).

Guide to further reading

On the dynamics and measurement of population, try Kelsall (1979), *Social Structure of Britain: Population*; and on the social and political context of population statistics, Irvine *et al.* (1979), *Demystifying Social Statistics*. On fertility, *Birth Counts* by Macfarlane and Mugford (1984) is an impressively thorough treatment of the statistics of pregnancy and childbirth in Britain over the last 100 years. Fertility and childbirth as feminist issues are dealt with in the essays in Roberts (1981), *Women, Health and Reproduction*.

On mortality, Howe (1976), *Man, Environment & Disease in Britain*, is a readable historical survey. From a Marxist viewpoint historical and contemporary mortality is well-covered by Doyal (1979), *The Political Economy of Health*. Tuckett (1977), *An Introduction to Medical Sociology*, provides perspectives on health other than Marxist ones, and

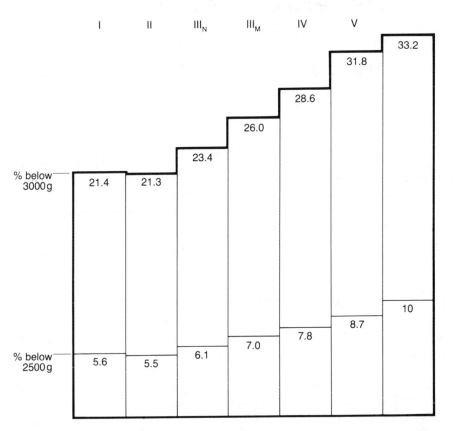

LEGITIMATE BIRTHS   **ILLEGITIMATE**

Figure 16 *Babies born at different birthweights by social class and legitimacy, England and Wales*

together the two books will provide the beginning reader with a comprehensive coverage of the sociology of health. Empirical material on class inequalities in illness and death are found in Townsend and Davidson's (1982) edition of the Black report, *Inequalities in Health*. Specifically on gender and health, Leeson and Gray (1978), *Women and Medicine*, provides an overview.

14 Development, under-development and migration

Roger Gomm

Chapter 13 covered births and deaths. Later in this chapter we shall look at migration which is the third major aspect of population. It is necessary first to consider the topics of 'development' and 'under-development' because the key to understanding the movements of people lies in understanding the political and economic fortunes of the areas people move to and from.

Global and regional inequality

In an advanced industrial nation such as Britain there are marked regional and local inequalities. As one moves north from the south-east of England, so the percentage of employed people who are manual workers rises, average wages fall, fewer people own cars or houses, unemployment rises, and average life expectancy is shorter. In the industrial lowlands of Scotland, for example, men are 25 per cent more likely to die before they reach 65 than in the south-east. In the most deprived area of Britain, which is Northern Ireland, unemployment reaches its highest level, average wages are lowest, the cost of living highest and the standard of housing lower than elsewhere in Britain. On a smaller scale the same kinds of contrasts may be drawn between the British inner cities and the more affluent suburbs.

The global pattern of inequality is even more stark. Seventy per cent of the world's population lives in the poorer countries, but these countries have only 17 per cent of the world's income. Fifty per cent of the world's population has no clean water supply and 60 per cent have no organized health care. In the Third World, (outside of Africa and the socialist countries), 75–90 per cent of people are landless labourers – 800 million people live on the very edge of survival.

In the twentieth century the large-scale movements of people from country to country and area to area have been from the poorer areas where opportunities for a secure livelihood have been limited, to areas where opportunities are better. This is hardly surprising, but what is a more complex issue is the question of why it is that some areas are economically buoyant and politically stable, and others are economically 'under-developed', riven with strife, and vulnerable to disaster. This question is the central topic of the 'sociology of development'. The first part of this chapter reviews the various theories of development and under-development to be found in sociology.

Modernization theory

Modernization theory is an amalgam of functionalist sociology and orthodox economic thought. For some modernization theorists the 'good society' looks remarkably like the capitalist society of the USA, and for others it looks more like Sweden with its mix of private and public ownership and high welfare expenditure. These are 'developed' societies. In terms of these theories 'development' refers to steps on the way to (or beyond) such a situation, while an 'under-developed' society is one that has not got there yet.

'Under-development' then, is a kind of social and economic immaturity, and modernization theorists look to the history of the now affluent nations for clues as to how development might be fostered in the Third World.

The economist Walter Rostow (1960) has been particularly influential in explaining the social changes which amount to modernization. He places the emphasis on capital investment. He argues that once investment in machinery, roads, and so on, reaches a certain point, industrial development will 'take off' and be self-sustaining, as happened in nineteenth-century Britain, or early twentieth-century America. However, for this to occur it is necessary that all or most of the institutions of a society are receptive to modernization. For the sociologists who belong to the modernization tradition the important issue is what it is about a society that makes it amenable to change along the capitalist road.

Weber's classic *The Protestant Ethic and the Spirit of Capitalism* is an early example of this kind of approach (see page 452). Weber argues that capitalism arose in Western Europe and New England, and not in the Islamic world, India or China, because the culture of Western Europe already contained features conducive to capitalist development. Specifically Weber argues that Protestantism was a religion which stressed personal responsibility and individual initiative and allowed individuals to serve God in their everyday activities rather than through joining religious orders. Thus the otherwise mundane activity of making money could be glorified as serving God and a religious motivation was put behind economic enterprise.

Modernization theory maintains that those societies which have 'developed' have been those which already had characteristics which made capitalist development easy, while those societies which remain under-developed have characteristics which make it difficult for them to change. Thus the social organization of under-developed societies tends to be seen in terms of what was once appropriate and functional for a pre-industrial society, but which now stands in the way of development towards a modern capitalist type. A great deal has been made of the 'conservatism' of Third World peoples, their 'resistance' to new ways of doing things and the way in which they continue to believe in and value activities which are out of date 'in the modern world'. Closer inspection has often shown that Third World peoples have very rational reasons for rejecting change.

Meritocracy and achievement

For functionalist sociologists one of the most important features of 'modern' societies is that they are meritocratic. That is to say they are thought to have a pattern of inequality where those who occupy the most important and powerful positions are those who have 'ability'. This is expressed in the 'functional theory of stratification' (see pages 181–6), which argues that in a modern society meritocratic stratification ensures that those with talent are placed where they can best use their ability to serve 'society' as effective leaders, skilful investors, producers of knowledge and so on. The same theory argues that inequality is a necessary feature of modern societies because it stimulates everyone to want to achieve, so that people are motivated to work hard, compete seriously, and find more efficient ways of doing things. The image of a modern society is one in which competitiveness is a necessary psychological state.

Explanations for why capitalism developed earliest in Northern Europe, and why some societies are still under-developed, rest heavily on the ideas of meritocracy and achievement motivation. This is well seen in functionalist thinking about the family and industrialization (see also pages 219–20). In many traditional societies kinship forms the backbone of social organization. Who you are, what roles you play, who you may marry, what land you may farm, who you may support politically, who you worship with, may all be determined by birth. Functionalists have argued that this kind of social organization works against modernization for various reasons:

1 It does not stimulate achievement motivation, because there is nothing to achieve and because the individual's welfare is not dependent on his own efforts.
2 If the individual were to achieve anything by his own efforts, obligations to kin would mean that he would have to share the results with them.
3 If social position is determined by birth rather than by achievement, then there would be no relationship between an individual's social

role and his ability to perform it: the best people would not be placed in the most important positions.

4 It is argued that strong kinship organization inhibits people from moving in response to the needs of the economy. Functionalists have argued that as societies have industrialized, so kinship organization has withered away, leaving the isolated nuclear family as the family type 'best adapted' to a modern society. It is seen as 'best adapted' because it can move in response to the labour needs of the economy, because it fosters achievement motivation in so far as its members do not have to share the results of their own efforts and have to rely on their own efforts rather than upon kin for their welfare. Functionalists imagined that in the absence of kinship obligations people are promoted to positions in society which match their ability rather than according to the accident of birth.

In empirical terms there is a great deal wrong with this argument. I shall not dwell on this here, but point simply to the fact that a heavy emphasis is being placed on the importance of *attitudes*: it being necessary for a 'modern' society that people are motivated to want to work hard, and consume greatly, and to show the qualities of economic entrepreneurship.

If we put the economic and the sociological thinking of modernization theory together, we get a package which includes the idea that capital investment is the essential ingredient for economic growth, that economic growth is a good thing in itself, and that capital investment will occur and have successful results where people have the 'right' attitudes for industrial development.

Education

Within modernization theory sociologists have placed great emphasis on the importance of education in fostering development. This includes not only the more obvious matter of teaching literacy and numeracy, work skills or modern agricultural knowledge, but also using education as an agency of cultural change to instil work discipline into a population or to encourage people to want to consume more manufactured goods. Functionalists have always argued that in modern societies families cannot be left with the sole responsibility for socializing children, since this would result in children growing up with widely different sorts of knowledge, attitudes and beliefs, and loyalties to their kin, neighbourhood and ethnic group rather than to the wider society. Often in newly independent countries, as in the USA or Australia, the education system is explicitly used to foster a sense of national identity among a population of heterogeneous ethnic groups, and the mass media may be used in a similar way.

We can see the parallels here between modernization theory and other areas of sociology. Functionalist sociologists have often attributed social problems such as crime or poverty within industrial societies to the subcultural attitudes passed on from parent to child, and have sought a remedy in education. Educational failure itself is attributed to the inability of working-class or ethnic-minority parents to prepare their children adequately for schooling, and the usual remedy has been earlier and more intensive government intervention into the socialization process. Working-class subcultures have been seen as reservoirs of 'outdated' attitudes which stress loyalty to relatives, neighbourhood, fellow workers and class rather than the individualism which an efficient modern society is said to require. It is a common explanation for the economic decline of regions in Europe and the USA that workers there are unwilling to adapt to modern technologies and misunderstand the modern requirement to trim labour forces and moderate wage claims. Ethnic minority subcultures have been viewed as especially problematic because they keep alive ways of life which diverge from the dominant culture of a society. In modernization theory functionalists have viewed whole countries in much the same way, so that whatever is distinctively non-EuroAmerican is seen as 'unmodern' and in need of change. This is hardly surprising when the model of a 'developed' society is America or Northern Europe and the most 'progressive' elements of such developed societies are seen to be the white middle classes.

Economic policy - free-market or Keynesian?

Within modernization theory there are two distinct wings of economic thought. Rostow, mentioned above, believed that 'the free market', unhindered by government intervention, was the most effective means of generating economic growth. Historically the industrialization of Britain and the USA was carried out largely through 'free enterprise'. However, not all modernization theorists subscribe to this kind of economic thinking. In the early stages the industrialization of countries such as France, Germany and Japan was planned and orchestrated by governments, and many modernization theorists subscribe to Keynesian economics which see governments and international agencies as having an important role to play in fostering development.

The two wings of modernization theory offer somewhat different prescriptions for the economic policies which poor countries ought to pursue in order to develop economically, and the policies which the now industrialized countries should pursue in order to sustain their economic growth. 'Liberal' economists - like Rostow - believe that left alone 'market forces' will generate economic growth and that economic growth will produce high standards of living and a better quality of life for everyone - though not everyone equally. Renamed 'monetarism', this essentially nineteenth-century brand of economics has become central to the policies of the Reagan administration in the USA and the Conservative government in the UK in the first half of the 1980s. It prescribes that governments and international agencies should interfere with the economy as little as possible. 'Social expenditure' by governments which raises the standard of living of the poor is seen as a drag on economic growth because it requires high taxation which destroys the incentive to work and invest and diverts capital away from areas of profitable investment. The best hope for the economic development of poor countries, or the economic regeneration of depressed areas within the industrialized world, is to establish a climate in which small businesses can be profitable and to make the areas attractive to investment by multi-national corporations. This, it is said, will generate local employment and more local purchasing power, which will in turn stimulate the growth of more industry, while the incoming investment by multi-nationals will 'transfer' new technologies and new work skills from richer areas to poorer ones. The appropriate policy to effect this is one of low taxes, low levels of welfare expenditure, weak anti-pollution and safety legislation and government activity to restrict the activities of trades unions. Rostow's book *The Stages of Economic Growth* is sub-titled 'a non-communist manifesto'. Like Davis and Moore's 'functionalist theory of stratification' (see page 30) it was written when there was a moral panic in America about the subversion of the American way of life by communists. Both works issue a warning that nothing but harm will come from government attempts to make people more equal.

Free-market economists can of course point to a number of development success stories in countries which have followed these policies to some degree. Japan, Taiwan, Singapore, Hong Kong and South Korea have made dramatic economic progress since the war with policies along these lines; and in the USA industry has moved away from the high-tax, well-unionized north-east, into the 'sun-belt' states of the south and to the West Coast.

Modernization theorists who belong to the Keynesian wing are still committed to an image of the good society which is basically a capitalist society, but believe that the state has an important role to play in orchestrating the economy and alleviating hardship. The economics of John Maynard Keynes developed in response to the great recession of the 1930s when millions of people throughout the world were thrown out of work and into poverty by the near collapse of the American economy. To Keynes and others of like mind it appeared that free-market economics had failed, because while this was an efficient policy for producing goods, it was a very ineffective means for producing the purchasing power to buy them. Capitalist economies had developed a huge productive capacity without providing people with sufficient income to purchase what was produced. The Keynesian solution is for governments to act in the economy to keep supply and demand in balance. Thus when the demand for goods falls and industrialists begin to cut back production and lay off workers, governments should use tax-payers' money to purchase goods, increase welfare benefits to increase the purchasing power of the poor, and expand government employment so that more people are paid a wage they can spend.

Keynesian economics became economic orthodoxy in most non-socialist countries from the end of the war into the 1970s. It was the policy which lay behind the huge economic reconstruction programme funded by American loans that allowed for the rapid redevelopment of the war-shattered Japanese and European economies. From the war until the 1970s these policies did appear to have the effect of sustaining economic growth and high living standards and of keeping unemployment at a low level in the industrialized world. In this context 'welfare state' expenditure is not just a device to improve living standards but a way of managing the economy to avoid violent booms and slumps.

Transposed on to the world stage Keynesian economics gives a role to the government of Third World countries in stimulating economic development by spending on infrastructure or even establishing state-owned industries. International agencies such as the International Monetary Fund and the World Bank, originally established for the post-war reconstruction of Europe and Japan, widened their brief to loan money to governments all over the world to fund economic development projects, while individual countries, United Nations Agencies and the EEC have been active in giving aid to poorer countries for economic and social development.

Keynesian economics lost its glamour with the world recession of the 1980s, when global economic growth fell, and unemployment rose all over the world and no economic policy seemed effective for dealing with the problem. Liberal economists are inclined to blame 'excessive' government interference – particularly 'excessive' expenditure on welfare – while Keynesians put the problem down to insufficient or ineffective economic management. The Brandt report (1980), for example, was commissioned by leading statesmen of a Keynesian persuasion such as Herr Willie Brandt of West Germany and ex-premier Edward Heath of Britain. It diagnosed the cause of world recession in the lack of economic growth in Third World countries, and argued that the best response would be to increase aid to poor countries, allowing them to purchase more goods from the industrialized world, and to industrialize more rapidly themselves.

Modernization theory does not see the process of development as complete. As a branch of functionalist thought it is an evolutionary theory which sees the world moving towards ever more efficient ways of producing goods and organizing societies. Trends detected in contemporary industrialized societies are extrapolated forwards to predict a 'post-industrial' society. This is a society in which modern technology takes the effort out of work, and produces a large amount of leisure time for everyone. Cheap consumer goods will be available to all and living standards will be levelled up (the embourgeoisement thesis – see page 173). Class differences will be eliminated because social position will depend on merit and parents will be unable to pass privilege on to their children. Managers and bureaucrats will constitute the new ruling elite, and they will obtain their positions by ability and not according to family background. In private enterprise the power will shift from owners to managers and companies will tend to be run more for the public interest than for the interests of their owners. Education, a free mass media and democratic systems of government will mean that politicians are more accountable to the public. One thread of this argument predicts that the capitalist systems of the West will become more socialist, and the communist societies of the East will develop a more free-enterprise economy, because the industrialization process produces a similar kind of society irrespective of political ideologies (Kerr *et al.* 1973).

In this scenario the now industrialized societies will move into their post-industrial phase and slough off their more traditional heavy and assembly-line industries, which will be adopted by industrializing countries. The post-industrial societies of the world will specialize in the high-technology industries and in providing services such as international banking and insurance. The decline of heavy industry in Europe and America, and the way in which the Japanese have abandoned such activities as textiles, is taken as evidence that this is indeed occurring. The unemployment and regional decline associated with the run-down of traditional 'smoke-stack' industries is seen as a transitional problem in the necessary evolution of industrialized societies into post-industrial ones.

Marxist theories of under-development

Marxists present a very different picture of the way the world is going. Marx's own theory of development (Marx 1867) has all societies developing through a series of stages of which capitalism is the penultimate and communism the last. Each stage, except communism, has the seeds of its own destruction built into it. For Marx one of the self-destructive features of capitalism is its tendency towards overproduction or under-consumption. For capitalists to make a profit and re-invest it, they must pay their workers less than the market value of the goods they produce. Purchasing power must always fall short of the value of what is available for purchase, and Marx predicted a falling rate of profit which would undermine the capitalist system. The prediction is that employers will react to a falling rate of profit by cutting wages, or replacing workers with machines, and that this will provoke the working class into revolutionary action – which will lead to the establishment of a communist system.

Marx was writing during the nineteenth century and expected capitalism to be overthrown during his lifetime. He expected this to occur first in the most developed societies of the time such as Britain where the self-destructive logic of capitalism would work itself out soonest. What actually happened was that those proletarian revolutions which have occurred have happened in societies where capitalism was less well developed – such as Russia in 1917 – or scarcely developed at all, such as China in 1939, or Cuba in 1959.

Lenin, in his work *Imperialism: the Highest Stage of Capitalism* (1915), argued that although the collapse of capitalism was inevitable in the long run, capitalists can stay one jump ahead of the crisis by constantly expanding the capitalist economy into less developed areas of the world. On this view the development of empires by the European powers extended the life of capitalism in the West. It provided capitalists with new markets, cheap sources of raw materials, and cheap labour, lowering their production costs. Where, as in many Third World countries, wage work is combined with subsistence farming, capitalists do not even have to pay wages sufficient to feed and clothe their workers and their workers' children. Because producers in the less developed world could be paid very low wages, the working class in the developed countries were able to enjoy increasing living standards and their revolutionary potential was sapped. The Western working class has been allowed to share the benefits of capital's exploitation of workers in poor countries, and the harsh effects of capitalist exploitation have shifted out of the richer countries into the poorer ones. In Eric Hobsbawm's phrase, exploitation was exported (1969). This is why socialist revolutions tend to occur in under-developed rather than developed societies.

Capitalism and colonial exploitation

Unlike modernization theorists who view under-development as a stage prior to development, Marxist writers use the term to refer to the dislocations caused by the expansion of capitalism from Europe, America and now Japan, into other parts of the world. 'Under-development' refers to the results of capitalist exploitation in one place, which provides the means for 'development' to occur in another. For Marxist writers the poverty and strife to be found in Third World countries today is to be explained in terms of the continuing history of relationships between rich and poor countries, during which the latter have been systematically under-developed to the advantage of the former.

From the sixteenth century onwards the societies and economies of the Third World have been moulded as economic satellites to supply the needs of the richer societies in Europe and North America. The West Indies, for example, were developed – or under-developed – to provide sugar and other agricultural products for Europe. West Africa was under-developed to provide the slaves to work the West Indian and American plantations. In West Africa itself powerful kingdoms such as Asante or Benin grew up to supply European slave traders with captives from the surrounding tribes they conquered with the guns made in the factories of Europe and New England, laying to waste whole societies around them. In India the traditional metal and textile industries were actively destroyed by the British in favour of British manufactured goods, and the sub-continent was milked for taxes for the British exchequer. In other areas of the world such as Australia, South Africa, North and South America, native peoples were dispossessed of their lands, and sometimes actively hunted down and killed to make way for 'white' settlers, or plantation companies. It was not necessary for an area of the world to be formally colonized for it to be incorporated into the system of colonial exploitation. Argentina, for example, while never a British colony, was nonetheless developed to supply cheap grain and meat for Britain, and as a market for British manufactured goods.

In each case, under-development took the form of fostering the production of cheap agricultural goods or mineral raw materials, and discouraging the development of any industries which might compete with the industries of the colonial power. Some writers argue that without the profits made from its colonies, capital investment in Europe would never have reached Rostow's 'take-off' point.

Neo-colonialism

Since the Second World War, most colonies have obtained their political independence, but their economies continue to be distorted towards serving the needs of the developed countries for minerals and agricultural products – so-called 'neo-colonialism'. This leaves their economies heavily dependent on the export of a few commodities. The world market for tropical agricultural goods is especially unreliable, with prices fluctuating wildly from year to year. Moreover, since 1972 most commodities have fallen in value: to buy the same tractor a Third World farmer has to produce three or four times as much today as in 1972. While a tonne of sugar in 1975 would buy 42 barrels of oil, in 1985 it would buy only three.

Whether in copper or tea, vegetable oils or uranium, world trade in most of the commodities poor nations depend on is controlled by a handful of giant multi-national corporations who are able to set poor nations in competition with each other and secure low prices. Against the falling prices of commodities, and in need of export earnings to buy industrial goods, the governments of Third World countries have tried to produce more and more of their staple commodities. Dependent on the export earnings of a few unreliable basic commodities the poorer countries of the world find it difficult to diversify their economies.

Marxist writers see the poorer countries of the world as playing the following roles in the capitalist world economy. First, they supply cheap raw materials and industrial goods for the more developed countries. It is worth pointing out that in the world as a whole, poor countries with malnourished populations send more food to the richer countries with well-nourished populations, than vice versa.

Secondly, they provide cheap labour, whether locally or in the form of immigrant workers. Thirdly, they provide locations for production processes which have been banned in more developed countries or which are made expensive by anti-pollution or safety legislation. For example, the dangerous processes associated with the manufacture of asbestos goods are now largely carried out in Third World countries, while the more polluting activities of the petrochemical and agrichemical industries are being relocated in countries with little anti-pollution legislation.

Fourthly, Third World countries have been, and continue to be, developed as markets for the products of the developed world. Marxist and other commentators have pointed out that the development of Third World markets is often detrimental to the interests of local people. For example, with the decline in the birth rate in the Western nations the baby-milk companies turned their attention to the high-birth-rate countries of the under-developed world. Not only is infant formula a more expensive way of feeding babies than breast milk, but baby milks mixed with polluted water are lethal. Similarly, with the levelling out of smoking in the West, tobacco companies are engaged in the hard sell of cigarettes in the Third World. Again, many of the herbicides, pesticides and pharmaceuticals which enter the Third World market are banned as unsafe in their country of origin.

Ruling elites in the Third World

In contrast to modernization theorists, Marxist writers view developing nations as containing different social groups with opposed interests. The development of a country to serve the interests of its ruling elite is not necessarily in the interests of the majority of the people. Indeed, World Bank evidence shows that since the war 75 per cent of the additional income generated by development in the Third World has gone to the most prosperous 40 per cent of the population. Third World elites are seen as sharing many of the interests of capitalists from the developed world. Thus, when multi-national corporations establish subsidiaries in poorer countries, it is common for them to offer director-ships to memebers of the host government. Much of the export earnings of Third World countries are spent on military technology which is used to keep the ruling group in power, and the children of Third World elites are often educated with the children of the upper classes of Europe or America.

Investment or exploitation?

Modernization theorists have laid great store by the development role of capital investment and technological transfer from multi-national corporations. However, as Marxist writers point out, the jobs provided by multi-nationals in the Third World are usually for unskilled or semi-skilled workers, who learn little of value on the job. Expatriates are brought in to perform the more highly skilled tasks. Multi-national corporations do not bring much capital into countries but raise it in the countries where they establish subsidiaries, and their high-technology production techniques may require the importation of expensive raw materials.

For example, throughout the Third World small soap making industries using cheap locally available raw materials have been replaced by the subsidiaries of the world detergent giants which use expensive imported oil as raw material, employ far fewer people and make more expensive products. The profits of multi-national corporations are remitted 'home' to their shareholders in Europe, America or Japan, so that the poorer countries of the world are net exporters of capital.

Attempts by Third World countries to derive more benefit from the activities of multi-nationals have often been thwarted by alliances between multi-national corporations, local right-wing opposition parties or the military, and the governments of richer countries. In Chile, where the socialist Allende regime nationalized the American-owned copper mines, the Western banks cancelled their loans, the American government reduced its aid to almost nothing, and the CIA and a group of multi-national corporations engaged in a destabilization campaign which brought a right-wing government to power. In Jamaica, where the prime minister, Michael Manley, increased taxation on the aluminium ore exported by Western multi-nationals, these companies helped to finance the election campaign of his right-wing opposition opponent, Edward Seaga. In Nicaragua, the left-wing Sandinista government overthrew the dictator Samosa, seized the lands of USA fruit corporations and distributed it to the peasants. American businessmen are financing the 'Contra' guerrilla movement which aims to reinstate the Samosa regime; the American government is aiding the guerillas, and blocking loans to Nicaragua from the World Bank.

OPEC

The one apparently successful attempt by poorer countries to derive more benefit from their own resources illustraties the way the world economy works to the disadvantage of the poorest nations and the poorest people within them. In the 1970s many of the oil-producing nations of the world banded together into the Organisation of Petroleum Exporting Countries. They believed that the American and European oil companies were paying too little for extracting oil, and that when the oil was exhausted they would have derived little benefit from it. OPEC raised the price of world oil. The increase in the price of oil raised the price of industrially produced goods. However, industrialized countries were able to pass price increases on to Third World countries, so that they had to produce more cotton, or tea, or sugar to purchase the same quantity of industrial goods.

Large sums of money began to flow into the OPEC countries. As they were unindustrialized most of this money found its way quickly back to the developed countries. It was spent on industrially produced goods, on contracts with multi-national builders for roads, hospitals, hotels and offices, and much was simply invested in Western companies and Western banks. The banks found themselves with a 'cash mountain' of OPEC money, which they lent to poorer countries.

The world inflation which was caused by the increase in the price of oil meant that at first non-oil-producing Third World countries were able to pay the interest on their loans; such loans are cheap when inflation is high. Brazil in particular experienced an 'economic miracle', with economic growth rates as high as six or seven per cent a year in the 1970s. However, with the onset of world recession in the 1980s and a fall in demand for all goods, more and more Third World countries have been unable to service their debts. This constitutes a serious problem for the Western banks. A refusal to repay by a country such as Brazil could lead to the collapse of the world banking system. Loans have been 'rescheduled': that is to say, debtor countries are lent more money to help them pay the interest on their existing debts. However, the rescheduling has strings attached: usually conditions that force the debtor country to give priority to producing goods for export which will earn the money to pay interest. Many debtor nations now use as much as 25 per cent of their export earnings to pay loan interest. This entails cutbacks in health, education, housing and welfare expenditure, wage freezes and wage cuts, and often repressive policing to deal with opposition. One does not have to be a Marxist to see that the very poor in debtor countries are being squeezed to make sure that the interests of the shareholders of the Western banks are upheld.

International aid

Marxist sociologists see aid as a further device serving the interests of powerful groups in both the rich north and the poor south. A lot of aid, for instance, is given by governments only on condition that it is spent on the products of companies in the donor nations. Such tied aid represents a transfer from the taxpayers of a rich country to the shareholders of companies in the same donor countries. Often the projects built with such aid have been irrevelant to the needs of the majority of people: prestige airports in countries where most people do not fly, or military equipment to keep an unpopular government in power. The major source of aid has been in the form of loans from the World Bank and the IMF. Marxists point out that these organizations are dominated by their biggest donors, America and her allies, and by the private bankers from these countries.

Multi-national corporations

By contrast with the 'post-industrial society' view of functionalist sociologists, Marxists view the world moving into a stage of 'monopoly capitalism'. The most important feature of this is the emergence of huge multi-national manufacturing and finance corporations more powerful than national governments. Indeed, the hundred biggest multi-national companies do have incomes bigger than the hundred poorest nation states. These companies are seen to be run in the interests of the tiny group of people who own most of the shares and are powerful enough to influence the policies of governments to their advantage.

Marxists point to the importance of the corporate financing of political parties and the control over ideas they exert through their ownership of the 'free-world' mass media, and the way in which politicians, top civil servants, military leaders and capitalists tend to be drawn from the same social background. However, their main source of power is seen to be their ability to affect the economic fortunes of a country. Investment decisions by multi-national companies raise and lower the economic indicators by which the success of governments is judged: unemployment levels, balances of payments and the value of a country's currency. Governments thus have to adjust their policies so as not to upset multi-national companies. This limits a government's capacity to tax capital to provide health and welfare, or to impose stringent anti-pollution or safety regulations on corporate activities.

With regard to the under-developed world there are two main variants within the Marxist view. Some Marxist writers such as Frank, who are often called 'dependency theorists', see Third World countries as being in a state of permanently arrested development – always being sucked dry by the capitalists based in the rich north and their allies among Third World elites. The more orthodox Marxist position is to say that, although the poor countries of the world are grievously exploited by international capital, this is a 'progressive tendency' because it will lead eventually to the emergence of a world working-class revolution: just as capital has become 'internationalized', so eventually will labour solidarity.

Social stratification on a world scale

Elsewhere in this book you will have learned about Marxist notions of social class, but mainly as they apply *within* industrialized countries. The topic of development forces us to look at social stratification on a world scale.

As noted above, modernization theorists have argued that the end product of capitalist development is a 'post-industrial society' in which the distinctions between social classes become less marked. The embourgeoisement thesis is one element of this. Such theories look credible when viewed solely in terms of a single industrialized society. However, viewed on the world scale, from a Marxist perspective, it appears that what gains the Western working class made towards a middle-class lifestyle were supported by exploitation of low-paid workers in the poorer countries of the world. More recently multi-national corporations have begun to relocate their production capacity in the low wage areas of the world, and this is beginning to have a fundamental effect on the global class structure with a loss of employment prospects and bargaining power for workers in the West.

The embourgeoisement thesis is closely associated with the 'affluent' car workers of Britain in the 1960s. British car assembly line workers are no longer affluent, even among British manual workers. In the 1980s the car industry has become organized so that the production of components and the assembly of cars is spread throughout the world. Workers in a particular factory in one country no longer have the bargaining power they used to have, since a company faced with an industrial dispute in (say) Britain can simply increase production in Spain, or Brazil, South Africa or elsewhere. In the last resort attempts by workers to raise their wages can be met by the closure of a factory and its relocation elsewhere in the world. From a Marxist point of view, rather than the industrialized countries of the world moving towards a better post-industrial future, it seems likely that they in their turn will be 'under-developed' as jobs are relocated and the living standards of the Western working class are forced down in competition with workers in the low wage areas of the world.

Under-development and the critique of industrialism

Marxists and modernization theorists are agreed that industrial development is a progressive movement. Other writers, such as Ivan Illich, see the industrial urban society as a wrong turning for humanity. In direct contrast to modernization theorists who see economic development since the war in terms of an increasingly efficient and rational use of the world's resources, these writers view modern technology as increasingly inefficient. 'What', they ask, 'is efficient about Western agricultural systems that use 100 calories from oil to produce ten calories worth of food?' Such writers make many of the same points as do Marxists about the adverse effects of imperialism on the Third World, and stress especially the environmental destruction which has occurred in pursuit of rising living standards and profitability. They see little 'progress' in the permanent destruction of South American rain forests for the temporary production of meat for North American beefburgers.

The main thrust of this position is that the earth's resources are finite and unable to support a population of 5000 million two-car families in semi-detached houses with freezers and televisions. True development is not the pursuit of American standards and styles of living but the cultivation of locally self-sufficient ways of life which do not destroy the earth's resources: stability, self-sufficiency and local control over local resources are the goals rather than economic growth. The development 'problem' does not lie with poor countries but with the rich ones who squander the earth's resources and provide a misleading image of progress to poorer societies.

Most of the remedies lie in persuading the rich to give up their wasteful lifestyles, and the poor to limit their birth rates (see below).

Women and development

Recently feminist writers have begun to turn their attention to the topic of development. Most adopt a basically socialist position and their writing may be seen as a feminist elaboration of certain elements of Marxist thinking. They argue that in the Third World the processes of development – or rather, under-development – far from liberating most women, have either subjected them further to male domination, or have left them unsupported and impoverished. This is a re-run of the Marxist-feminist reading of the history of industrialization in Europe and America.

They point out, correctly, that most development programmes in the Third World have been directed by and at men. Thus the huge post-war drive to increase the production of cash crops for sale and export in Third World countries has often meant that the best land has been taken for cash-crop farming by men who use their wives' unpaid labour, while women have been left with the worst land and most of the burden of producing food crops to feed themselves and their children. Where peasants produce Third World commodities these can be sold at very low prices because women and children are supported mainly through the unpaid labour of women. Similarly where male migrant labour is common, as in South Africa, low wages can be paid, because female subsistence farming feeds the children and reproduces a new generation of labourers at no cost to the companies employing their husbands. It has always been a tenet of Marxism that if men had to eat in cafes, take their sex in the brothel, and purchase on the open market all that their wives do free, then they would demand such wages as would make capitalist production unprofitable. Similarly parallels have been drawn between the way the 'housewife–mother' provides a subsidy to capital in the north, and the way the subsistence farming sector gives a subsidy to capital in the south. Marxist–feminists claim that in the south it is again generally women whose unpaid work allows for capitalist profitability.

Feminist writers have also noted that, just as the textile mill owners in nineteenth-century Britain preferred to employ women and children, because they were a more docile labour force, so in the newer garment and electronics assembly-line industries in the Third World, young women and children form the majority of the workforce.

Under-development theories and the world 'population problem'

Malthusianism and neo-Malthusianism

World population is currently about four and a half billion and increasing by 200,000 per day. Birth rates are indeed falling in most areas of the world, but in most areas life expectancy is increasing. Even if world population reaches a state where it is merely replacing itself, we can expect a world population of some six billion by year 2050, five billion of whom will live in Third World countries.

The birth rates of the poor have often been seen as problematic by the better off. In the late eighteenth and early nineteenth century, Reverend Thomas Malthus attributed poverty, lawlessness and a great many other ills to the high birth rates of the poor. Malthus was living at a time of rising population, though as we now know this was caused more by a fall in the death rate than by the much smaller rise in the birth rate. What was dramatically obvious to Malthus was the growth in the numbers of the rural poor caused by the agricultural revolution, and the growth in large lawless urban populations in the new industrial towns. It might be said that when Malthus and his peers wrote of 'over-population' they were using this idea as a metaphor for social disorder. What is more, the growth in the number of poor people was also a growth in expenditure on poor relief, meaning higher taxation for the better off.

Malthus propounded a principle which has never since been far away from debates about population. He argued that population had the capacity to grow faster than the development of the means to support it, and that therefore famine, war and pestilence would always be part of the human condition, unless people exercised 'moral restraint' and limited their reproduction. More important than Malthus's principle is its policy implications. It implies that relieving poverty is counter-productive, because supporting the poor simply encourages them to have more children and to create more poverty. Equally it implies that redistributing wealth from rich to poor will lead to the birth of more poor people rather than the elimination of poverty. Understandably Malthus's thinking was very popular with the better off of his time. Variants on this theme have remained popular ever since, although these days they are more often applied to the relations between the poor of the under-developed world and the better off in the rich north.

Malthusian thinking has been criticized in three main ways. First it is said that Malthus failed to realize how dramatically technological innovations would increase the production of food and other necessary goods. The history of Britain seems to bear this out, but it is worth remembering how rising living standards were based on the importation of food from poorer areas of the world; by 1907, 70 per cent of Britain's cereal requirements were imported. Since the Second World War writers have begun to point to the finite capacity of world resources and ecosystems, and to claim the ultimate truth of Malthus's principle when the earth's population reaches this or that number of billion people. This view is closely associated with the critique of industrialism and with much of the 'ecology movement'. It is interesting to note that just as Malthus articulated his principle of population when the traditional pattern of social control in Britain was breaking down, and the poor were demanding more assistance, so the neo-Malthusian theme begins to be articulated in the 1960s as the colonial regimes of the European powers begin to collapse in the face of nationalist movements, and as aid begins to be disbursed to the Third World.

Secondly it has been claimed that Malthusian thought fails to understand how birth rates are associated with economies and societies. Population is an issue which divides modernization theorists here. Those of a liberal economic persuasion are also likely to be technological optimists, who believe that growing population means growing productivity and consumption and that technological breakthroughs will always occur to support the world's population increase. Population growth is indeed often seen as the challenge which brings technological innovation and makes it worth while. This, however, will only happen if it is the free market which is left to cope with the situation. This position rejects Malthus's gloom about the future of mankind, but accepts his view that aid for the poor is counter-productive. This was the position adopted by the Reagan administration in the USA in the first half of the 1980s.

Other modernization theorists adopt a position which illustrates the functionalist nature of their thinking nicely. As functionalists they believe that the 'stable' society is one in which all the institutions and the culture subscribed to by everyone are in phase. The history of population in the now industrialized societies shows a very characteristic pattern which is usually called the 'demographic transition'. (Figure 17). The population histories of the now industrialized countries have shown much the same pattern (A), which is drawn schematically in B. Stage 2 is a phase of population explosion of high birth rates and falling death rates, while stage 4 is the modern pattern. In most industrialized countries now birth rates and death rates are very similar. Most Third World countries today are in stage 3, but since their

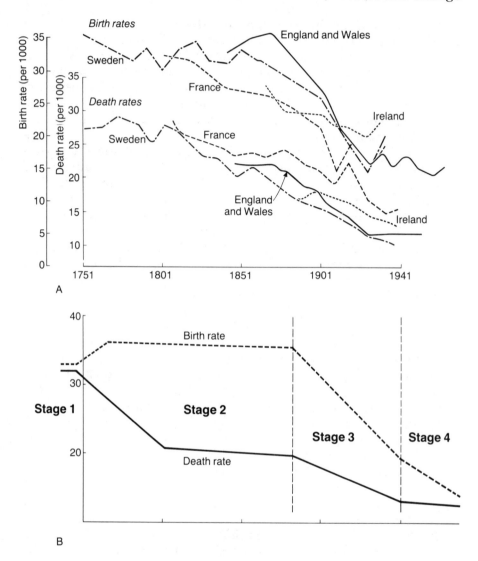

Figure 17   *The demographic transition*

death rates are falling faster than their birth rates their populations are still growing.

It seems that there is something about the process of industrialization which leads inevitably to falling birth rates. Among other things the demographic transition involves a cultural change away from attitudes and values favouring high birth rates, towards a cultural disposition for lower ones. In functionalist thinking it is as if the society's 'need' for a lower birth rate is somehow signalled through the system to result in a cultural change which makes this possible.

In relation to less developed societies, the key question has been that of when the demographic transition will occur: when will birth rates begin to turn down? Functionalist writers vary in their emphasis here. Some have argued that the demographic transition will only occur when the industrialization process is well under way. Others have argued that by providing contraceptive technology and birth control education a reduction in the birth rate can be accomplished sooner. This approach places a great deal of emphasis on culture as the key factor in determining birth rates.

The argument goes that while it may be 'functional' for people in a society with high rates of infant mortality to value high rates of reproduction, it ceases to be so when rates of infant survival increase. Their cultural knowledge (about family limitation) and their cultural attitudes (favouring many pregnancies) have become out-dated and need to be changed.

Three main findings have emerged from the last 20 years of intensive birth control campaigning in the Third World. First there is a very characteristic pattern of take-up of family limitation. The better off are much more responsive to birth control programmes than are the very poor. This parallels the way in which family limitation in England started first among the middle classes (see page 371). Some writers have simply attributed this to the more 'intelligent', more 'modernized' attitudes of the better-off, seeing the attitudes of the poor as 'lagging' behind.

However, the second major finding is that the key factor is economic security. In societies with little or no social welfare system, large families are an insurance against illness, unemployment and old age. This is especially so when there is a market for child labour. Note again the parallel with the nineteenth-century working class in Britain (see page 223). Far from it being an irrational clinging to out-of-date attitudes, or a kind of fecklessness, having large families is a rational response to the realities of life in the lower strata of a poor society. An implication of this is that it is not the degree of industrialization of a society, nor its gross national product, which is important in reducing the attractiveness of large families, but the way in which its wealth is used to provide economic security for its people. Even among catholics and members of other religions which proscribe birth control, otherwise devout believers tend to limit their families when they have achieved economic security. This adds credence to the notion that it is economic rationality rather than cultural belief which determines family size.

Lastly it is apparent that birth control programmes are more successful where development raises the status of women and gives them more power over their own bodies.

The third major criticism of the Malthusian view points out that it is not the numerousness of people which causes world poverty, but the way in which power and resources are distributed between them. Marxists take this line as do a large number of other writers. Thus they point out that since the Second World War, world food production has more than kept pace with the growth in world population, at roughly 110 per cent of what would be required to give everyone a reasonable diet. Much of the increased production has actually been in countries where there are hungry people. In addition there have been large increases in the production of non-food crops, and an increasing percentage of cereal and pulse production all over the world is being used as animal food to increase the proportion of meat in the diets of rich 'northerners'. The root of the problem of world hunger does not lie in numbers of people, but in the fact that there is no profit to be made in producing food for poor people, and that in a capitalist world it is profitability which determines what gets produced, and purchasing power which determines who consumes it. The 'food mountains' of the EEC and the payments made to American farmers not to grow crops appear as another example of the kind of over-production and under-consumption which Marxists see as inevitable under capitalism.

Development, under-development and migration

Everybody knows that most people on the move are looking to improve their living standards or their safety. What is more sociologically interesting is how it comes to be that some areas are safer to live in than others, and why some offer better economic prospects. This of course is what sociologists try to explain in the sociology of development and we will use the previous discussion as a background for understanding migration.

Migration within Britain

The general picture of migration within Britain over the historical period is one of a movement from the countryside to the towns, and from the fringes of the British Isles to the industrial centres. In the twentieth century the flow begins to be diverted towards the south-east and the west midlands as the traditional industrial centres of the north and South Wales decline. From the inter-war period onwards we see the movement of people out of the city centres and into the suburbs, commuter villages and new towns.

The capital investment in agriculture which constituted the agricultural revolution sent hundreds of thousands of people from rural areas into towns (Levine 1977), where at the beginning of our period profits from agriculture were invested in factories and housing. Much of this migration was short-range, and the various areas of large cities seem mainly to have been populated by people from the immediately adjoining countryside (Levine 1977, Anderson 1971). This is the pattern with regard to Third World towns today. It is probably wrong to think of the movement to the towns as being an unorganized rush. The pre-industrial population was anyway quite mobile, some villages changing their population by 60 per cent by migration in a generation, with young people often travelling far from home as servants or labourers (Macfarlane 1978). A significant minority of the population – such as craftsmen, drovers, pedlars, seamen, soldiers and seasonal agricultural workers – travelled widely and sometimes never returned to their place of birth.

People probably went from rural areas to nearby towns which they already knew, to stay initially with or near friends, ex-neighbours or relatives. The historical evidence suggests that kinship took on a new meaning with urbanization, and that kinship links were used as a device to cope with the industrial environment; kin assisted with housing, finding work, and offered aid in times of sickness and unemployment, in much the same way that Jewish and Asian immigrants to the UK have used their kinship networks to cope with a new environment. It is not until the development of urban-industrial working-class areas that we begin to find groups of married brothers or three-generation households living under the same roof in any great numbers. Far from destroying the extended family, urbanization seems to have created it, if by 'extended family' we mean a group living under one roof (Anderson 1971).

Nineteenth-century towns were not static. They grew rapidly in size not just because of migration, but also through births, because most of the people who migrated to the towns were young and therefore had a high birth rate. People not only moved to towns but within towns. Economic success would take a migrant from a poorer area to a more desirable one. In addition towns were constantly being redeveloped as housing was pulled down for new roads, canals, factories or railways, and working-class communities were continually being destroyed and reformed. Once established, however, local people attempted to exert a control over the housing stock and the labour market, and attempted to exclude outsiders. In the nineteenth-century there was considerable hostility between townsfolk and rural migrants, and employers exploited this by recruiting gangs of countrymen as strike breakers.

The period between the two world wars saw an agricultural recession which pre-dated the depression of the 1930s and made agricultural land available for building at cheap prices. The middle class who had occupied larger 'family houses' built for households with servants in the inner suburbs, began to move out to detached and semi-detached houses in the outer suburbs, built for families without servants. This move thus coincides with a change in life style for the middle classes. Partly it was a response to rising servants' wages, partly to falling birth rates among the middle class, and partly to the development of suburban transport networks and private car ownership which allowed the better off to live at a distance from their work in the city centres. The large Victorian family houses in the inner suburbs were converted into bedsitters and flats to house working-class people and young, single, white-collar workers.

Already by the First World War British industry was becoming uncompetitive by comparison with German and American industry. The war, however, created a boom situation in industries such as metals, shipbuilding, armaments and textiles and temporarily staved off industrial decline. The 'affluent workers' of the period were those in the armaments and shipbuilding areas such as Tyneside, but by the 1930s Tyneside had become the epitome of the poverty associated with the great recession. The most famous of the hunger marches of the period started from Jarrow, on the Tyne. The global recession of the 1930s began with the American stock market crash of 1929, but behind it lay the fact that world industrial capacity had expanded much more rapidly than world purchasing power and all over the world factories and mines closed or laid off workers. In the industrialized world unemployed workers and their families moved to those areas which continued to offer employment in the newer industries such as motor vehicles, chemicals, aerospace or electrical goods. In America the recession accelerated the movement westwards to the Pacific coast states and was swelled by the widespread bankruptcy of farmers in the middle-west and by the soil erosion in states such as Oklahoma. In Britain, with a third of the workforce unemployed, there was a general drift out of the older industrial towns of the north and South Wales to the west midlands and the south-east. Areas such as Luton and Dagenham with their car assembly lines constituted bright spots of opportunity in an otherwise tight labour market. An 'industrial transference scheme' organized the migration of young persons from the declining areas to areas where there were better opportunities. This was widely criticized by the labour movement as a means of undercutting wage rates in areas which remained relatively prosperous.

During the inter-war period cities had grown enormously in extent, though not in population, and governments had become increasingly worried about urban sprawl. The result was a number of restrictions on urban growth which became the post-war 'green belt' policy. However, since the war residential development has simply leap-frogged the green belts and so large areas of the countryside within commuting range of city centres became dormitories for commuters (Pahl 1975).

While the countryside near towns has been suburbanized, more isolated areas have experienced a different kind of population change. Young people have tended to move away because of a lack of jobs, and people from the higher income areas have purchased rural housing as second or retirement homes. The influx of middle-class newcomers has pushed up house prices beyond the means of local people, causing considerable local resentment: in Wales, for example, there are sporadic arson attacks on holiday cottages. More recently the sale of rural council houses to their tenants has meant that housing which used to be ear-marked for local people is beginning to pass into the hands of incomers. The second-home phenomenon has been made possible by the widespread ownership of motor-cars. This has a second effect in rural areas of undermining public transport services, so that the rural poor without cars are greatly disadvantaged. Closely associated has been the closure of village shops, unable to compete with the supermarkets in the towns which car-owning villagers can reach and non-car owners cannot. Since most incomers are middle-aged to elderly, and those forced out of the villages are young, many rural areas are becoming very elderly in their population, stretching local medical and welfare services.

After the Second World War, the outer suburbs and the metropolitanized countryside began to be settled by working-class people, in part as owner occupiers, but mainly through council re-housing schemes developed to clear the slums and the war-damaged areas of the inner cities. While most such schemes were housing estates with minimal amenities, the most distinctive were the new towns which were designed to be complete communities providing housing, employment and all other necessary services. In fact the new towns were not as successful as they might have been in rehousing inner urban slum populations. This was because the kind of industry which was willing to move to a new town tended to require high levels of skill. New towns like Stevenage with its aerospace industry recruited not so much from the slums of inner London, but from among skilled workers all over the country.

The inner city has been transformed in two ways. Near business and commercial areas the growing demand for office space from government and big business produced a situation where it was highly profitable to invest in inner urban sites for office building. Especially during the period 1964 to 1974, speculation in property by banks, insurance companies and pension funds forced up the price of inner urban sites. Factories with sites in the inner city sold up, realized a profit on the deal and opened new factories elsewhere, causing a collapse in the inner urban market for manual work. Local authorities found it very difficult to afford to buy inner urban land for residential council development, so they built their council estates in the outer suburbs, in market towns, or in the countryside. Another kind of urban transformation occurred in areas of the city less favourably sited for office development. In the north and in South Wales this has affected whole towns. Here declining industries simply closed down, or profitable industries re-located their factories elsewhere in Britain or overseas.

Since the war the inner cities have lost population at a considerable rate. Most of the out-migration has been of working-class people, though because job losses have been more pronounced than population movement the inner cities have high rates of unemployment. However, there has also been a re-colonization of the inner city by the middle class. The more soundly built working-mens' cottages, many of the Victorian family houses which had been sub-divided, and abandoned factories or warehouses have been converted and have passed into owner-occupation so that once working-class areas have been 'gentrified'.

The areas of Britain which have experienced economic growth in the 1970s and 1980s have been outside the big cities. The string of towns along the M4 motorway, between London and Bristol, for example, has seen a rapid growth in high-technology industries, earning it the nick-name Silicon Corridor, while many small market towns have benefited from the re-location of insurance and other commercial enterprises. There are many factors at play in this development. High-technology industries and financial concerns are not tied to any particular place and can be located with an eye to providing pleasant environments for their employees. Some – more in America than in the UK – are clustered around universities so that there is an easy interchange of ideas between academics and industrialists. In other cases, such as in printing, new investment has been outside the areas in which strongly unionized workers can resist the introduction of new technologies. It is often claimed that the high rates levied in inner urban areas to pay for the welfare services of depressed populations force companies to move elsewhere. Since rates rarely account for more than 4 per cent of a company's turnover this seems unlikely.

Since the war there have been many programmes by governments to stem the loss of jobs from the inner urban areas or from the declining regions. Most offer companies incentives to locate their operations in a declining area rather than elsewhere. Incentives include tax reductions, and the building with public money of factories to rent cheaply, or direct investment by government in the enterprise. Governments throughout the world now compete with each other to offer attractive deals to multi-national corporations. Recently, in Britain, the government has argued that a major problem lies in the restrictions placed on industrial activities and has designated a number of large declining areas as 'Enterprise Zones' where planning controls are relaxed and rates are not levied on new companies.

Developments such as industrial decline and city centre office development have had distinct effects on the structure of local populations. Those people who have moved away have tended to be younger, fitter and more highly skilled, and this migration has split up generations of families, leaving the elderly behind (Willmott 1975). These have also been the sort of areas which have been settled by New

Commonwealth immigrants – that is from Commonwealth countries other than Australia, New Zealand and Canada (Haddon 1975).

The population structure of such inner urban areas and of towns in the declining regions, then, tends to be composed of a relatively high proportion of elderly people born locally, and of younger locally-born with low-paid jobs and high rates of unemployment, together with a rather young population from the New Commonwealth and their children. Such areas also have a distinctive illness profile, with far more people suffering from serious illness than in other areas of the country. Figure 18 shows this for one such area, the London Borough of Newham, and should be compared with Figure 20.

At the heart of the pattern of internal migration in Britain there are cycles of capital investment. Investment which tends to reduce employment prospects (as during the agricultural revolution) forces people out of one area into another where investment is creating jobs and housing opportunities. In time this investment ages, industries and housing stock decline and out-migration begins again. For a temporary period at least this creates some opportunities for people who are even more economically depressed to move into the declining area. The pattern is complicated by government investment in housing, and by the development of transport networks which allow for residence to be widely separated from work.

In terms of modernization theory the transformations noted above

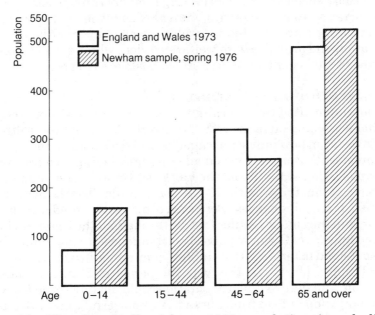

Figure 18 *The chronically sick per 1000 population, in a declining area, compared with the national rate*

SOURCE: Data for England and Wales taken from Scrimshire (1977) and General Household Survey 1973.

correspond with the evolutionary development of a pre-industrial society, through an industrial phase to a post-industrial state. Early industrialization involves a shifting of the workforce out of agriculture and the extractive industries into manufacturing, and a movement from the countryside to the towns. Town life is supposed to create a culture in which people are receptive to change. As time passes so the numbers employed in agriculture continue to decline, and the emphasis on manufacturing gives way to increased employment in service industries: industries such as finance, catering, leisure, government, and communications. Technology is a major engine of change. Thus, for example, technological innovation in agriculture, and automation in industry, both serve to reduce the manpower required: changes in transportation technology allow for the wide separation of work from residence. For the modernization theorist, the decline in the manufacturing sector in a country like Britain is inevitable and, despite the associated unemployment, is not something to be resisted. What is important is to create a climate in which the service industries can develop to compensate for the loss of manufacturing jobs.

From a Marxist viewpoint the same empirical changes are looked upon as phases in the on-going struggle between capital and labour. The current de-industrialization of Britain is viewed as characteristic of advanced capitalism where a few giant multi-national corporations set the employment prospects of the global workforce. De-industrialization is caused by such corporations cutting their operating costs by moving their operations out of countries, or areas of countries, where workers are well-organized and well-paid, well-protected by health and safety legislation and provided with welfare services which entail a tax-cost to employers, into countries where labour costs are cheaper.

Immigration into Britain

The development of Britain cannot be seen sensibly without relating it to what was going on in the rest of the world. Much of the wealth which was invested in new industrial capacity and real estate in the eighteenth and nineteenth centuries was made through slaving, sugar or through the exploitation of India and the Far East. Bristol, for example, rose to prominence on the wealth of the slave trade. The Lancashire and Scottish textile industries were based on cotton produced by slave labour, and they made textiles for sale throughout the Empire. The great dock complexes of Glasgow, Liverpool, Manchester and London have to be understood in terms of Britain's predominance in world trade and its huge Empire. Moreover, this was the period of Britain's population explosion, and the growth in population could not have been fed without the importation of food from abroad. As a powerful nation Britain was able to cope with its population explosion by increasing the area of the globe it exploited for resources, and by exporting people.

Most of these emigrants were volunteers, though criminals were transported, paupers indentured to employers in the colonies, and between 1870 and 1930, a hundred thousand pauper children were shipped overseas by organizations such as Dr Barnardos.

The migration of the British and other Europeans throughout the world set in train other population movements. Millions of Africans had already been transported to the Americas as slaves. American and Canadian Indians were forced ever further westward and northwards as the 'frontier' moved. Australian aborigines were forced into the 'outback' and into reserves of ever-declining size. In Africa, Africans were forced from the lands chosen for settlement by white settlers, and in Latin America and Asia local populations were moved on to make way for ranches and plantations. Everywhere the towns, farms and mines of Europeans became an attraction for indigenous peoples seeking work. As we have seen, the way in which colonized countries were developed was towards serving the needs of the colonizing power. While imperialism raised the standard of health for ordinary people in Britain (mainly by improving the food supply), the population movements it entailed overseas caused widespread epidemics as European diseases were spread to other continents, and as African diseases spread to America and vice versa (Doyal 1979).

There was a small counterflow of colonized people to the British Isles. The slave trade had anyway provided Britain with a small black population, mainly in London and in the western port towns, and this was swelled by black refugees from the American War of Independence. In the eighteenth century probably about 0.11 per cent of the population of England and Wales was black, compared with 3 per cent today. Local black populations were joined by black seamen from the merchant fleet of the Empire, and Chinese communities established themselves in most port towns, both catering for Chinese seamen, and serving the British population with laundries and opium parlours. However, the largest group of colonials were from nearby Ireland – then, of course, wholly part of Britain. In many cities these people came to constitute a significant fraction of the lower working class (Shaw 1979). Many were directly recruited in Ireland as construction workers for roads, railways and canals (or 'navigations'; hence 'navvies'). In addition, throughout the nineteenth century employers faced with labour problems recruited strike-breaking labour direct from Ireland, relying on the absence of any feeling of solidarity between English and Irish workers. Many Irish came on their own initiative to escape the grinding poverty resulting from the English/Scottish colonization and under-development of Ireland (Carefoot and Scott 1969), though far more Irish migrated to the USA. Like other groups of migrants they tended to occupy particular areas of towns, and develop their own community facilities. The Catholic Church was especially important as a welfare agency.

At the end of the nineteenth century poor Jews from Russia and

Eastern Europe began to arrive, driven out by anti-semitism. Many moved on from Britain to the USA, but those who stayed made their first settlements near the docks where they disembarked – in East London especially. The Jewish migration illustrates something much more general about the pattern of settlement of poor immigrants: that poor immigrants tend to settle first in areas which are already in decline.

The old East End of London had been a centre for craft production, but from the middle of the nineteenth century its small workshops had failed to compete with the new mass-production factories of the northern towns. Its heart was the old docklands of the Pool of London. By the middle of the nineteenth century, however, the Pool of London had proved inadequate for the growing Imperial trade, and its watermen too well organized for the liking of the shipowners. The focus of docking had moved downstream, first to Millwall and the Surrey Docks, then to the Royal Docks at Canning Town. With the docks went the dockside industries, and a great many East Enders moved to take advantage of the economic boom further down the river.

Although by twentieth-century standards the old East End of Stepney and Whitechapel and Spitalfields was overcrowded, industrial decline and out-migration from the area left a space for the settlement of Jewish immigrants. Competition for housing between Jews and Gentiles was one source of racial tension in the area, but the violent resistance from well-established working-class areas such as Bethnal Green or Hoxton ensured that few Jews settled outside a limited area. Gentile gangs from such areas often strayed into Jewish streets to attack people and property. The Jews found opportunities in the fiercely competitive world of street trading, which often brought them into conflict with Gentile traders, and in the ailing garment and furniture industries. These they re-vitalized, managing to compete with factory production elsewhere by using tiny workshops (with much work put out to home-workers), low profit margins and low wages. In street trading, wholesaling or manufacturing the Jews coped with the hostile Gentile world by cooperating within their own community in such matters as lines of credit, discounts, and orders. On the whole it was Jewish entrepreneurs who exploited Jewish workers; but the working conditions in the 'sweated trades', and especially the idea that these caused illnesses which might spread more widely, provoked official alarm and added to the anti-Jewish feeling of the turn of the century. This led to Britain's first major Act to restrict immigration, in 1906.

Throughout the nineteenth and early twentieth century Britain exported population, and because migrants were generally young this took a considerable degree of pressure out of Britain's population explosion. Taking the period since 1945 as a whole, Britain has experienced a small positive migration balance, with immigrants exceeding emigrants, though between 1971 and 1983 Britain became a

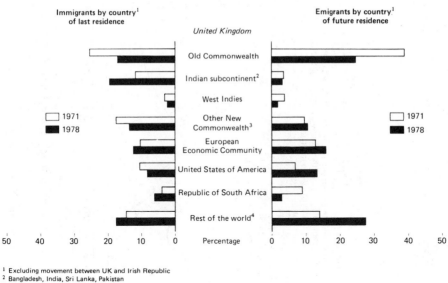

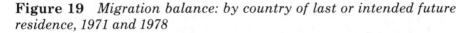

Immigrants by country[1]
of last residence

Emigrants by country[1]
of future residence

United Kingdom

Old Commonwealth

Indian subcontinent[2]

West Indies

☐ 1971
■ 1978

Other New
Commonwealth[3]

European
Economic Community

United States of America

Republic of South Africa

Rest of the world[4]

☐ 1971
■ 1978

50 40 30 20 10 0   Percentage   0 10 20 30 40 50

[1] Excluding movement between UK and Irish Republic
[2] Bangladesh, India, Sri Lanka, Pakistan
[3] Mainly African Commonwealth
[4] Denmark is included in Rest of the world in 1971 and in the EEC in 1978

Source: *Population Trends*, 1980. HMSO

Figure 19 *Migration balance: by country of last or intended future residence, 1971 and 1978*

country of out-migration again. New Commonwealth immigrants have not constituted the majority of immigrants, but it has been New Commonwealth immigration which has caused the most political concern, and we shall focus on that here.

Figure 19 shows the migration balance for 1971 and 1978 in terms of inflows and outflows between the UK and other countries (also refer to Figure 20). Remember, however, that the terms 'immigrant' or 'emigrant' refer simply to people moving across national boundaries who have expressed an intention to settle in another country. The terms do not necessarily designate nationality, citizenship, colour, ethnic group, race or place of birth. Thus in the period 1966–76, about 30 per cent of immigrants into Britain were people born in Britain, and 49 per cent of emigrants from Britain had been born in some other country. The figure for immigration is of course often mistaken as a measure of black people coming to settle permanently in Britain. Even for New Commonwealth immigrants born in the New Commonwealth it has been estimated that more than 20 per cent are actually 'white' (General Household Survey 1971; Lomas 1973). For these sorts of reason, Figure 19 which shows migration to and from other countries is only an inadequate guide to immigration by racial or cultural groups. Moreover, since the way of calculating numbers of immigrants, and the laws of citizenship, have

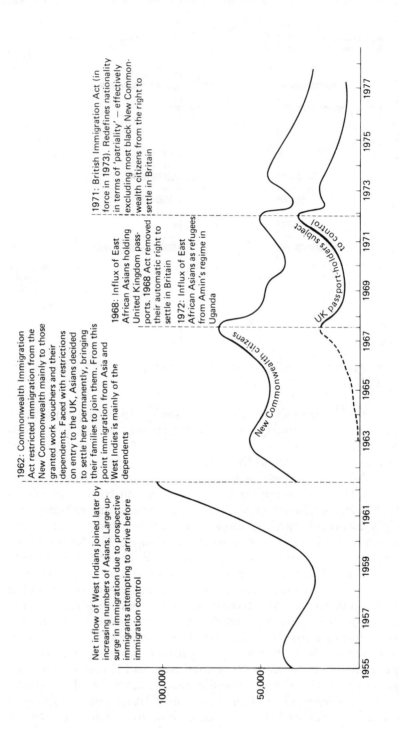

Figure 20 *Net inflow of New Commonwealth citizens and, after 1968, UK passport-holders subject to immigration control, 1955–78.*

Note: New Commonwealth refers to all Commonwealth countries excepting Australia, Canada and New Zealand.

been changed from time to time, the sections between the vertical lines on Figure 20 cannot be compared directly with each other. (For further discussion of the problems with immigration statistics, see Stephenson 1979.)

The period between 1956 and 1965 in Europe is often referred to as the 'post-war economic boom'. Real living standards rose more rapidly during this period than ever before or since. It was a time of rapid economic growth when the demand for labour was very high. European workers were able to exploit the shortage of labour by bidding up their wages through trade union activity,and individuals were able to leave unpleasant and low-paid jobs for better ones. The shortfall in labour was thus mainly in low-paid, unpleasant, public service work with unsocial hours – in hospital, public transport, local authority labouring and so on – or in the more traditional industries which were on the verge of collapse, such as textiles or metals.

The high demand for labour brought many married women into the labour force especially in Britain. But in addition European employers sought labour from poorer countries. Today in Western Europe there are estimated to be some 16 million people of migrant origins. For Continental Europe, North Africa, Greece, Yugoslavia and Turkey provided a reservoir of cheap labour, and within Western Europe, the Southern Italians, Portguese, Spanish and Greeks played the same role. Those European countries with a recent imperial history sought migrant labour from the colonies or ex-colonies: for the French it was Algeria and French-speaking Africa; for Holland, Indonesia and Surinam; and for Britain mainly the West Indies, Asia, Malta and Cyprus. The National Health Service, London Transport and many large private companies had recruiting offices in the West Indies, Asia and elsewhere, or ran advertisements in the newspapers of these countries. Initially there was a very close relationship between immigration and vacancies because so many migrants were recruited for particular jobs, and because there was an efficient information service about vacancies between migrants here and would-be migrants in the homeland.

Most of these early migrants were single people. Those from the Indian sub-continent were almost exclusively male, but there were almost as many West Indian women as men, reflecting the independence of Afro-Caribbean women. There is evidence to suggest that many, perhaps the majority, of early migrants did not come with the intention of permanent settlement, but came to earn enough money to set themselves up in business in their homeland. Immigration laws, passed to restrict immigration, paradoxically may have encouraged permanent settlement.

By the late 1950s black immigration had become an important political issue. There had been so-called race riots in Notting Hill and Nottingham when groups of white youths attacked black people and their homes. It is probably significant that both were areas of high youth unemployment in an otherwise prosperous period. At that time New Commonwealth citizens had an unrestricted right to settle in Britain. Now that they were beginning to exercise these rights the campaign to control immigration gathered pace. The effect of debates about immigration control was to create a rush of migrants from the West Indies and Asia in an attempt to 'beat the ban'. It is probable that most of those who came between 1960 and the early months of 1962 would have come to Britain over a much longer period of time, but many who migrated in haste might not have come to Britain at all without the threat of a ban. One effect was to strengthen the argument of those who were calling for immigration controls.

Asian migrants, especially, seemed to regard themselves as migrant workers rather than as settlers, and as providers for relatives in India, Pakistan or Bangladesh rather than as people striking out on their own. It was not uncommon for older brothers to work for a period in Britain, returning home to marry and to be replaced by a younger kinsman. In parts of India and especially in Bangladesh the earnings of such migrants were the most important 'export earnings'. The 1962 Commonwealth Immigration Act made this kind of migrant labour pattern unworkable, and it is from this date that Asian men begin to settle permanently, bringing their families to join them rather than supporting them in the Indian sub-continent by earnings sent home. It is also from this date that the major flow of immigrants from the Caribbean and Asia is of dependents (spouses, children and elderly relatives), rather than of workers. Since 1962 immigration legislation has become progressively more restrictive, and has discriminated more and more against non-whites (see Figure 20).

The areas to which these migrants came to live were the inner city areas out of which natives were moving. They settled either in the rows of nineteenth-century workmen's cottages from which working-class people were moving to the suburban housing estates, or to the large Victorian family houses vacated by the middle classes in between the wars. It was not so much that these areas offered cheap housing, but that they offered housing which was available to black people at a time when discrimination against them was more widespread then now.

Apart from outright refusals to rent to blacks, West Indians and Asians faced the fact that as newcomers they had low priority on council housing lists. There is some evidence that even when they had waited the necessary number of years they were still discriminated against by council housing departments, and that black families have been most frequently allocated to council slum property: either that acquired for redevelopment, or ageing council property built in the 1930s.

As relatively low-paid workers Asians and Afro-Caribbeans found it difficult to obtain mortgages from building societies to buy the more desirable property in the suburbs, and building societies were very reluctant to loan money for the purchase of cheaper inner urban property. Many did in fact buy small houses with mortgages provided by local councils, and groups of Asians, in particular, pooled their resources to purchase houses for cash. In addition, landlordism offered an opportunity to house oneself and to make a living at the same time. Asians, Maltese, Cypriots and other ethnic minority groups raised loans from finance companies to buy the large Victorian family houses which proved especially suitable for this purpose. Because interest rates were high on such loans, rents had to be high as well, and there has always been a temptation to overcrowd and to skimp on repairs. However, ethnic minority landlords have continued to provide rented accommodation, not only for ethnic minority tenants, but for other groups such as the single poor for whom there is no other provision. More recently much of such housing – in the same ownership – has been converted into 'hotels' to accommodate homeless families whose rents are paid by local authorities or the DHSS.

These areas of New Commonwealth settlement were the areas with the most acute problems of dereliction and, as the years went by, they were among the areas from which job losses were greatest. Many of the industries which recruited black labour had been barely profitable and were unable to modernize – which was why they needed cheap labour – and by the late 1970s they were collapsing. Similarly, by the late 1970s, government policies were reducing the numbers of low-paid public service workers; again an important area of 'immigrant' employment. The kind of areas in which black migrants settled were those in which the competition for housing, education and jobs was most acute. It is difficult to imagine a more fertile ground for ethnic conflict.

The restricted housing and job opportunities for ethnic minority groups has been one reason for concentration in particular areas. In addition concentration allows for development of a supportive community and the provision of religious amenities, shops selling ethnic specialities, newspapers in minority languages and so on. It is a mistake to see the cultural life of ethnic minorities in Britain simply as fossilized versions of the culture in the homeland. Cultures are dynamic entities and the cultures of Asians or Afro-Caribbeans living in the UK have to be read as responses to the experience of minority status. Rastafarianism, for example, was not brought to Britain from the West Indies by the Afro-Caribbean settlers of the 1950s and 1960s, but adopted and developed by their children who were born and educated in Britain.

The attitude of the majority population is a further factor associated with the concentration of ethnic minority groups in particular areas. In areas of the midlands and in East London, physical attacks on Asians and on their houses by whites discourage movement away from an area where they can support each other. Less overt hostility probably has the same effect.

For some functionalist sociologists ethnic minority subcultures are viewed as a problem. They are seen to perpetuate unmodern attitudes and values; and in their terms, since cultural homogeneity is necessary for a stable society, cultural diversity is bound to lead to trouble. Such writers make much of the inevitability of misunderstandings between members of different cultural groups and seek a remedy in the quickest possible assimilation of ethnic minorities to the mainstream culture, i.e. the disappearance of their distinctive way of life. More sophisticated functionalists, writing in the vein of Robert K. Merton (see page 319) see lack of opportunities for social mobility perpetuating ethnic minority subcultures: the more a group is excluded from the wider society the more it is likely to develop and sustain its own distinctive way of life. As noted in Chapter 11, the notion that thwarted talent turns to crime is a common theme in the functionalist theory of deviance. This idea was popular as a diagnosis of the causes of black riots in American cities in the 1960s, and appears in the Scarman report on the riots in British cities in the early 1980s (Scarman 1983).

Marxist writers view matters on a broader canvas. During the imperial period the proletariat of international capitalism was geographically divided: black workers in black countries, white workers in white countries. With imperialism went a popular culture which told white people, however poor, that they were racially superior to 'wogs', and 'coons' and 'niggers'. Racist attitudes which were part and parcel of ordinary life discouraged the development of any conception by white workers that they might share interests with black workers overseas. At a particular point in time (the post-war boom), capital's need for labour was met by the immigration of workers into Britain from the ex-colonies. With the industrial and urban decline of Britain the racism in popular culture encouraged the white working class to blame their problems on immigration rather than on the workings of the capitalist system which exploits black and white alike. Or rather not quite alike, for it is clear that white workers have been able to use their power in the work-place to prevent the employment or promotion of blacks, and to use their political power in local government to skew council housing policy to the advantage of white tenants. The result has been that many black people have been restricted to an 'under-class' of low-paid, casually employed, or unemployed living in the worst housing areas. There has always been such an under-class in British cities, with associated street crime, hustling and a tendency to riot as a way of expressing political grievances. The fact that nowadays many members of this under-class are black has allowed the mass media to focus on 'black crime' or 'black rioting' as if criminality were an inevitable characteristic of black people, and as if the problems of the inner city could be simply solved by the heavy policing of black areas, or the deportation of their inhabitants. The error of such a view is easily seen by considering a city like Glasgow which has very few New Commonwealth immigrants, but is near the top of the European league table for urban dereliction and unemployment, and has a crime rate every bit as serious as cities with large ethnic minority populations.

One of the criticisms which is often levelled at the Marxist view of race relations is that it is too ready to view 'race relations' in terms of class relations, and to see conflicts between ethnic groups as the result of 'false consciousness' perpetuated by and in the interests of capital; as a way of dividing and ruling the working class. Many Marxists have little sympathy with the value ethnic minorities place on their cultural distinctiveness and view this as standing in the way of the development of a more progressive socialist proletarian culture necessary for revolutionary action.

Migration in the Third World

Currently three-quarters of the world's population live in rural areas. If contemporary trends continue, half the world's population will live in towns by the year 2000 and the most rapidly growing are the cities of the Third World.

Third World cities grow both by natural increase and by migration. As in nineteenth-century Britain, rural–urban migrants tend to be young and therefore have a high birth rate. In rural areas a combination of growing population and the commercialization of agriculture has the effect of encouraging migration to the towns.

Outside of Africa and China, in the Third World as a whole, between 70 and 80 per cent of the rural populations are landless. Aid-sponsored agricultural development projects and private enterprise initiatives have tended to increase the size of production units, and the use of machinery and chemicals has reduced the labour requirements in agriculture. In countries such as India, landlords who used to rent land to small tenant farmers now find it profitable to farm it themselves, dispossessing their tenants. In Latin America since the war, millions of peasant farmers have been dispossessed by the granting of lands to North American fruit companies or ranchers, and peasants have often been resettled on marginal lands where they cannot produce an adequate crop. The so-called 'Green Revolution' based on new high-yielding cereals has enormously increased the production of food per acre, especially in Asia. However, since such grains require high inputs of fertilizer and pesticides and allow for mechanized cultivation, the Green Revolution has led to many small farmers losing their land and less work for agricultural labourers. More food has been produced, but average rural incomes have often fallen, encouraging people to move to the towns.

In nineteenth-century Britain much the same happened, but eventually the labour shaken out of the rural economy (and the natural increase in the population) was soaked up by industrial development. The question is whether, or at what speed, industry will develop in Third World countries to provide an alternative source of employment. Time-scale is here very important. The dislocations caused by the agricultural revolution lasted some 150 years, and the British economy rarely grew by more than 2 per cent a year. Industrialization in the Third World has been under way for only 40 years, and although many such countries have experienced growth rates of between 6 and 16 per cent a year, growth rates have fallen dramatically in the 1980s.

As in nineteenth-century Britain, Third World cities tend to be divided into wards which house people from the same rural neighbourhood and/or ethnic group who are able to assist each other and provide personal safety. Again as in Britain in the past, large numbers of children migrate independently to the towns to engage in casual work, petty trading, prostitution and crime.

The rapid uncontrolled growth of Third World cities is often viewed with alarm, and from a northern point of view they are insanitary and poverty stricken. However, it is worth noting that generally in the Third World, average incomes are higher in the towns, and health is better than in the rural areas. For all the problems they pose to governments urban populations are easier to serve with health and welfare facilities than are scattered rural populations.

Just as happened in Britain, governments have attempted to deal with slum accommodation merely by pulling it down without providing alternative accommodation for the poor. Indeed few Third World governments could afford to provide housing for the poor of the quality of an English council house, on the scale required by contemporary urban growth. Some of the more successful policies for dealing with the housing problem have involved providing slum dwellers with basic amenities – such as water supply and sewers – and with materials so that they themselves can erect a reasonable standard of housing. Nonetheless, in cities such as Calcutta or Mexico City 20 per cent of the urban population lives on the streets. A lack of planning control, together with a fear of alienating foreign investors, leads to housing and dangerous industrial processes being located close together. In 1984 the world's largest industrial disaster to date occurred when the Bhopal plant of Union Carbide released poisonous gasses into the atmosphere, poisoning inhabitants of a squatter township built around the plant.

As in nineteenth-century Britain the growth of urban populations in the Third World has had political significance. In Britain the urban masses, with their propensity to riot, became an important political consideration. Similarly in the Third World leaders have had to adjust their policies to keep the urban masses satisfied. One particularly disastrous policy has been the fixing of food prices at a low level. This has lowered the profitability of the food crop sector of agriculture and impoverished food crop farmers, or encouraged them to move into the production of cash crops for export, or themselves to migrate to the towns. This policy has been common in African countries, and Africa is one major area of the world where food production has been outpaced by population growth.

Environmental disasters have also encouraged a movement from the countryside to the cities. As the best land has been taken for commercial farming, peasant farmers have been displaced to areas where the environmental risk is higher. Thus, for example, in the humid tropics where flat lands have been given over to the commercial fruit production or valleys have been flooded for hydro-electricity and irrigation schemes, peasant farmers have cleared the forest from steep hillsides and have become vulnerable to landslips. In the dry tropics peasant cultivation has pushed into semi-arid environments where drought is a hazard, and arable cultivation has forced nomadic herders into environments with even more unreliable rainfall where they become vulnerable to periods of drought. The 1984–5 drought in Africa has led to the migration as refugees of some two and a half million people.

Labour migration is a common feature of the Third World. Wherever there are areas of economic growth there is a demand for migrant labour from less developed areas, within a country or across national borders. America draws from the Caribbean and Mexico; Hong Kong draws in labour from mainland China and the Philippines; Singapore from Malaysia, Indonesia, the Philippines and Thailand; the oil-rich Gulf States and Saudi Arabia from Pakistan, India, Yemen and Sri Lanka; Nigeria from Ghana and elsewhere in West Africa; Zambia from Malawi and the Congo; and South Africa from Malawi, Botswana, Zambia, Mozambique and the Bantustans. As in Continental Europe most of the labour-importing countries have strict laws preventing permanent settlement. In Singapore, for example, migrant workers are deported if they lose their jobs, and are only allowed to marry with the permission of the government after signing a bond that both partners will agree to be sterilized after the birth of two children. Guest worker systems such as this allow the importing country to benefit from migrant labour while it is required, and to export unemployment to a less developed area.

One of the effects of migrant labour, whether temporary or for permanent settlement, is to deprive the area of out-migration of its most vigorous and skilled workers. As Sivanandan says:

Moratuwa, a coastal town in Sri Lanka, once boasted some of the finest carpenters in the world. Today there are none – they are all in Kuwait or in Muscat or Abu Dhabi. And there are no welders, masons, electricians, plumbers, mechanics – all gone. And the doctors, teachers, engineers – they have been long gone – in the first wave of post-war migrations to Britain, Canada, USA,

Australia, and in the second to Nigeria, Zambia, Ghana. Today Sri Lanka, which had the first free health service in the Third World and had some of the finest physicians and surgeons, imports its doctors from Marcos' Philippines. What that must do to the Filipino people is another matter. [Sivanandan 1981]

Modernization theorists lay great store on migrant labour as a way in which the inhabitants of poorer countries can learn skills to take back to their country of origin. Though this must be true to some degree, on balance it appears that the majority of migrant workers do only unskilled or semi-skilled work and therefore learn little of benefit which can be transferred to the home area. And a minority of migrant workers, such as doctors, scientists, engineers and accountants, are trained at the expense of a poorer country, and eventually practise in a richer one. Thus Britain subsidizes the USA in training doctors and scientists, while the National Health Service is heavily subsidized through the training of doctors and midwives in India, Sri Lanka and the Caribbean.

A further effect of migrant labour is to disrupt community life by separating members of families for long periods of time, and to deprive food crop agriculture of labour. In Africa, in particular, migrant workers, whether from Black Africa to Europe or to the South African Republic, or from the countryside to the town, are almost exclusively male. This leaves women with the burden of producing food crops and contributes to the depressed state of African food crop agriculture.

Political strife is a further reason for migration in and from the Third World. Currently 16 million people are listed as refugees by the United Nations. Though political strife cannot be entirely attributed to colonialism, the colonial powers created 'countries' containing widely different ethnic groups, and established borders which often placed members of one ethnic group in two different countries. Apart from insurgencies designed to end colonial rule, as in Namibia, there are wars over boundaries which divide members of the same ethnic group: the Somali in Kenya would prefer that their lands were in Somalia, the Sunni Muslims in Iran would prefer to be Iraqis. Even more common are separatist movements and civil wars over which ethnic group will be the dominant force in the country. In Sri Lanka there is a virtual civil war between the Singhalese and the Tamil descendants of indentured labourers settled there by the British. In Fiji there is considerable friction between the native Fijians and the Indian population shipped there as labourers during the imperial period. In the newly independent Zimbabwe the two largest ethnic groups, the Shona and the Nbebele, cooperated to fight white supremacy, but there is now considerable tension over the dominant political position of Robert Mugabe's Shona people. In the three countries most seriously affected by the 1984–5 Sahelian drought – Ethiopia, Sudan and Chad – civil wars between ethnic groups contributed to the famine and seriously affected the famine relief operation.

Conflicts between ethnic groups almost inevitably become caught up in the global power struggle between greater powers. In the Near East, for example, the Palestinian Arabs, rendered homeless by the granting of their lands to the Jews with the creation of Israel after the Second World War, look to the oil-rich Arab States for financial support, and to Syria which the USA regards as an ally of the Soviet Union. Israel in turn is massively supported by US aid, both because the Palestinians are seen as associated with the Eastern bloc, and because the descendants of Jewish migrants to the USA constitute a powerful political lobby there. What might otherwise be a small-scale conflict is thus continuously supplied with huge quantities of armaments.

Guide to further reading

There are several good introductory texts on development written for A-level students, including Webster (1984), *Introduction to the Sociology of Development*, and Foster-Carter (1985), *The Sociology of Development*. More comprehensive are Hoogvelt (1982), *The Third World in Global Development*, and Alavi and Shanin (1982), *Introduction to the Sociology of Development*.

On world population, see *State of World Population Report 1984* (United Nations Fund for Population Activities 1985) and *Poverty and Population Control*, edited by Bondestam and Bergstrom (1980); and on world food, Tudge (1979), *The Famine Business*.

Aid is well dealt with by Hayter and Watson (1985), *Aid: Rhetoric and Reality*.

For ethnic minorities in Europe, see Castles *et al.* (1984), *Here for Good: Western Europe's New Ethnic Minorities*.

For those who would like to keep up to date with Third World affairs, the magazines *New Internationalist* and *South* are excellent sources.

Bibliography

Abel Smith, B. and Townsend, P. (1965), *The Poor and the Poorest*, Bell

Abercrombie, N., and Urry, J. (1983), *Capital, Labour, and the Middle Classes*, George Allen and Unwin

Abrams, M. (1961), *The Teenage Consumers*, London Press Exchange

Abrams, P., and McCulloch, A. (1975), *Communes, Sociology and Society*, Cambridge University Press

Adams, C., and Laurikietis, K. (1976), *The Gender Trap*, Virago

Alavi, H., and Shanin, T. (eds.) (1982), *Introduction to the Sociology of Development*, Macmillan

Althusser, L. (1971a), *Lenin and Philosophy and Other Essays*, New Left Books

Althusser, L. (1971b), 'Ideology and Ideological State Apparatuses', in Althusser (1971a)

Amsden, A. (ed.) (1980), *The Economics of Women and Work*, Penguin

Anderson, M. (1971), *Family Structure in Nineteenth-Century Lancashire*, Cambridge University Press

Anderson, M. (1971), *Sociology of the Family*, Penguin

Arensberg, C., and Kimball, S. (1940), *Family and Community in Ireland*, Harvard University Press

Aries, P. (1960), *Centuries of Childhood*, Penguin

Armstrong, C., and Wilson, M. (1973), 'City politics and deviancy amplification', in Taylor and Taylor (1973)

Aron, R. (1967), *Eighteen Lectures on Industrial Society*, Weidenfeld and Nicolson

Atkinson, A. B. (1973), 'Low pay and the cycle of poverty', in Field (1973)

Atkinson, J. M. (1978), *Discovering Suicide*, Macmillan

Atkinson, W. M. *et al.* (1975), 'The comparability of suicide rates', *British Journal of Psychiatry*, vol. 66, no. 2

Bachrach, P. (1969), *The Theory of Democratic Elitism*, University of London Press

Ballard, R., and Holden, B. (1975), 'Racial discrimination: no room at the top', *New Society*, (17 April)

Banks J. (1954), *Prosperity and Parenthood*, Routledge and Kegan Paul

Baran, P. A., and Sweezy, P. M. (1968), *Monopoly Capital*, Penguin

Barker, D., and Allen, S. (1976a), *Dependence and Exploitation in Work and Marriage*, Longman

Barker, D., and Allen, S. (1976b), *Sexual Divisions and Society: Process and Change*, Tavistock

Barker, E. (1984), *The Making of a Moonie*, Blackwell

Barker Lunn, J. (1972), *Streaming in the Primary School*, National Foundation for Educational Research

Barrat, D. (1986), *Sociology of the Media*, Tavistock

Bartlett, F. C. (1939), *The Study of Society*, Routledge and Kegan Paul

Becker, H., *et al.* (1961), *Boys in White*, University of Chicago Press

Becker, H. (1963), *Outsiders: Studies in the Sociology of Deviance*, Free Press

Becker, H. (1964). *The Other Side: Perspectives on Deviance*, Collier-Macmillan

Becker, H. (1966), Introduction to C. R. Shaw, *The Jack Roller*, University of Chicago Press (reprinted in Worsley, 1978)

Becker, H. (1971), *Sociological Work*, Allen Lane

Beetham, D. (1977), 'Robert Michels – from socialism to fascism', in *Political Studies*, vol.25, no.1

Bell, C. (1968), *Middle Class Families: Social and Geographical Mobility*, Routledge and Kegan Paul

Bell, C., and Newby, H. (1971), *Community Studies*, Allen and Unwin

Bell, C., and Newby, H. (1974), *The Sociology of Community: A Selection of Readings*, Frank Cass

Bell, C., and Newby, H. (1977), *Doing Sociological Research*, Allen and Unwin

Bell, D. (1974), *The Coming of Post-Industrial Society*, Heinemann

Belotti, E. G. (1975), *Little Girls*, Writers and Readers Publishing perative

Belson, W. (1978), *Television Violence and the Adolescent Boy*, Saxon House

Bendix, R. (1966), *Max Weber: An Intellectual Portrait*, Methuen

Bendix, R. and Lipset, S. (eds.) (1967), *Class, Status and Power*, Routledge and Kegan Paul

Benet, M. K. (1972), *Secretary: an Enquiry into the Female Ghetto*, Sidgwick and Jackson

Berger, P. (1964), *The Human Shape of Work: studies in the sociology of occupations*, Macmillan

Berger, P. (1966), *Invitation to Sociology*, Penguin

Berger, P., *The Social Reality of Religion*, Penguin (1973)

Berger, P., and Luckmann, T. (1963), 'Sociology of religion and sociology of knowledge', *Sociology and Social Research*, vol. 47

Berger, P., and Kellner, H. (1964), 'Marriage and the construction of reality', *Diogenes*, vol. 46 no. 1

Berger, P., and Luckmann, T. (1966), *The Social Construction of Reality*, Penguin

Berger, P., and Berger, B. (1976), *Sociology: a Biographical Approach*, Basic Books

Berle, A., and Means, G. C. (1968), *The Modern Corporation and Private Property*, Harcourt Brace

Bernstein, B., Elvin, H. L. and Peters, R. (1966), 'Ritual in education' (reprinted in Cosin 1971)

Bernstein, B. (1970), 'Education cannot compensate for society', *New Society*, 26.2.70 (reprinted in Cosin 1971)

Bernstein, B. (1971), *Class, Codes and Control*, vol.1, Routledge and Kegan Paul

Bernstein, B. (1975), *Class, Codes and Control*, vol.3, Routledge and Kegan Paul

Bernstein, B. (1971), 'On the classification and framing of educational knowledge', in M. F. D. Young (1971)

Beteille, A. (1969), *Social Inequality*, Penguin

Beynon, H. (1973), *Working for Ford*, Penguin

Blackburn, R. (ed.) (1977), *Revolution and Class Struggle*, Fontana

Blau, P. M. (1963), *The Dynamics of Bureaucracy*, University of Chicago Press

Blauner, R. (1967), *Alienation and Freedom*, University of Chicago Press

Bloor, M. (1976), *Bishop Berkeley and the Adenotonsillectomy Enigma*, Sociology 1976

Board of Education (1926), *The Education of the Adolescent* (Hadow Report), HMSO

Bondestam, L., and Bergstrom, S. (eds.) (1980), *Poverty and Population Control*, Academic Press

Booth, C. (1889), *Life and labour of the people of London*, extracts in Keating (1976)

Bott, E. (1957), *Family and Social Network*, Tavistock

Bottomore, T. (1966), *Elites and Society*, Penguin

Bottomore, T. (1965), *Classes in Modern Society*, Allen and Unwin

Bottomore, T. (1975), *Marxist Sociology*, Macmillan

Bottomore, T., and Rubel, M. (1963), *Karl Marx: Selected Writings*, Penguin

Bourne, R. (1979), 'The snakes and ladders of the British class system', New Society 8 March

Bowlby, J. (1953), *Child Care and the Growth of Love*, Penguin

Bowles, S., and Gintis, H. (1976), *Schooling in Capitalist America*, Routledge and Kegan Paul

Boyd, D. (1973). *Elites and their Education*, National Foundation for Educational Research

Boyers, R., and Orrill, R. (eds) (1972) *Laing and Anti Psychiatry*, Penguin

Braginski, B., *et al.* (1969), *Method in Madness*, Holt, Rinehart and Winston

Braham, P. *et al.* (1981), *Discrimination and Disadvantage in Employment*, Harper & Row

Brake, M. (1980). *The Sociology of Youth Culture and Youth Subcultures*, Routledge and Kegan Paul

Brandt Report (1980), *North, South: a Programme for Survival*, Pan

Braverman, H. (1974), *Labour and Monopoly Capital: the degradation of work in the twentieth century*, Monthly Review Press

Brewster, (1980), 'School days, school days', in Spender, D. and Sarah, E. (1980)

Bronfenbrenner, U. (1968), 'The changing Soviet family', in Gordon (1972)

Bronfenbrenner, U. (1970). *Two Worlds of Childhood: USA and USSR*, Russell Sage Foundation

Broom, L., and Selznick, P. (1968), *Sociology*, Harper

Brown, (1978) 'Depression: a sociological view' in *Basic Readings in Medical Sociology*, Tuckett, D. and Kawfert, J., Tavistock

Brown, C. H. (1979), *Understanding Society*, John Murray

Brown, P., and Jordanova, L. J., (1981), 'Oppressive dichotomies', in Cambridge Women's Study Group (1981)

BSSRS (1979), *A Question of Race*, British Society for Social Responsibility in Science

Budd, S. (1973), *Sociologists and Religion*, Collier-Macmillan

Burgess, E.W. (1925), 'The growth of the city', in Park (1925)

Burgess, R. G. (1982), *Field Research*, George Allen and Unwin

Burgess, R. G. (1983), *Experiencing Comprehensive Education: a study of Bishop McGregor School*, Methuen

Burnham, J. (1945), *The Managerial Revolution*, Penguin

Burns, T., and Stalker, G. M. (1961), *The Management of Innovation*, Tavistock

Butler, D., and Stokes, D. (1974), *Political Change in Britain*, 2nd edn, Macmillan

Butterworth, E., and Weir, D. (1972), *The Social Problems of Modern Britain*, Fontana

Byrne, E. (1978), *Women and Education*, Tavistock

Cambridge Women's Study Group (1981), *Women in Society: Interdisciplinary Essays*, Virago

Carefoot, G., and Sprott, E. (1969), *Famine on the Wind*, Angus and Robertson

Carson, W. and Wiles, P. (eds.) (1971), *Crime and Delinquency in Britain*, Martin Robertson

Cartwright, A. (1967), *Patients and their Doctors*, Routledge and Kegan Paul

Castells, M. (1977), 'The class struggle and urban contradictions', in Cowley (1977)

Castles, S., and Kosack, G. (1973), *Immigrant Workers and Class Structure in Western Europe*, Oxford University Press

Castles, S. *et al.* (1984), *Here for Good: Western Europe's New Ethnic Minorities*, Pluto

CCCS (1981), *Unpopular Education*, Hutchinson

Central Advisory Council for Education (1954), *Early Leaving*, HMSO

Central Advisory Council for Education (1959), *15 to 18* (Crowther Report), HMSO

Central Advisory Council for Education (1963), *Half our Future* (Newsom Report), HMSO

Central Advisory Council for Education (1967), *Children and their Primary Schools* (Plowden Report), HMSO

Central Statistical Office (1980), *Social Trends 1980*, HMSO

Centre for Contemporary Cultural Studies (1977), *On Ideology*, CCCS

Chapman, K. (1986), *Sociology of Schools*, Tavistock

Chibnall, S. (1977), *Law and Order News*, Tavistock

Child Poverty Action Group (1979b), *Poverty*, no. 42 (April)

Cicourel, A.V. (1976), *The Social Organisation of Juvenile Justice*, Heinemann

Cicourel, A., and Kitsuse, J. (1963), *The Educational Decision-makers*, Bobbs-Merrill

Clarke, A. M., and Clarke, A. D. B. (1976), *Early Development: Myth and Evidence*, Open Books

Clinard, M. (1964), *Anomie and Deviant Behaviour*, Free Press

Cloward, R., and Ohlin, L. (1960), *Delinquency and Opportunity: a theory of delinquent groups*, Free Press

Coard, B. (1971), *How the West Indian Child is Made Educationally Subnormal in the British School System*, New Beacon Books

Coates, K., and Silburn, R. (1970), *Poverty: the Forgotten Englishman*, Penguin (rev. edn. 1983, Spokesman Books)

Cochrane, A., St Leger, A.S. and Moore, F. (1978), 'Health Service "Input" and mortality "Output" in developed countries', *Journal of Epidemiology and Community Health*, no. 32, pp. 200-05.

Cohen, A. (1955), *Delinquent Boys: the culture of the gang*, Free Press

Cohen, P. (1972), 'Subcultural conflict and working class community', Working papers in Cultural Studies, no. 2, University of Birmingham, CCCS

Cohen, S. (1971), *Images of Deviance*, Penguin

Cohen, S. (1972), *Folk Devils and Moral Panics*, MacGibbon and Kee

Cohen, S., and Young, J. (1981), *The Manufacture of News*, Constable

Cohen, S., and Taylor, L. (1976), *Escape Attempts: the Theory and Practice of Resistance to Everyday Life*, Allen Lane

Cole, L. C. (1972), 'Playing Russian roulette with biogeochemical cycles', in Dreitzel (1972)

College, M. (1981), *Unemployment and Health*, North Tyneside Community Health Council

Comfort, A. (1968), *The Anxiety Makers*, Panther

Commission for Racial Equality (1978), *Five views on multi-racial Britain*

Committee of the Secondary School Examinations Council (1943), *Curriculum and Examinations in Secondary Schools* (Norwood Report), HMSO

Committee on Higher Education (1963), *Higher Education* (Robbins Report), HMSO

Consultative Committee on Secondary Education (1938), *Secondary Education* (Spens Report), HMSO

Cooper, D. (1968), *Dialectics of Liberation*, Penguin

Cooper, D. (1971), *The Death of the Family*, Allen Lane

Coote, M., and Campbell, B. (1982), *Sweet Freedom; the Struggle for Women's Liberation*, Picador

Coser, L. (1977), *Masters of Sociological Thought*, Harcourt Brace

Cosin, B. (ed.) (1971), *School and Society*, Routledge and Kegan Paul

Cotgrove, S. (1974), 'Objections to Science', *Nature* (August)

Cowley, J. *et al.* (eds.) (1978), *Class Struggle in the Community*, Stage 1

Cox, C. B. and Dyson, A. E. (eds.) (1968), *Fight for Education: a Black Paper*, Critical Quarterly Society

Cox, C. B., and Dyson, A. E. (eds.) (1969), *The Crisis in Education: Black Paper 2*, Critical Quarterly Society

Crewe, I. *et al.* (1977), 'Partisan dealignment in Britain 1964-1974', *British Journal of Political Science*, vol.7

Crompton, R., and Jones, G. (1984), *White Collar Proletariat*, Macmillan

Cuff, E. C., and Payne, G. (1984), *Perspectives in Sociology*, Allen and Unwin

Curran, J., and Seaton, J. (1981), *Power without Responsibility: the Press and Broadcasting in Britain*, Fontana (2nd edn, 1985)

Dahl, R. A. (1961), *Who Governs?*, Yale University Press

Dahrendorf, R. (1957), 'Out of utopia', *American Journal of Sociology*, vol. 64, no. 2 (reprinted in Dahrendorf 1968)

Dahrendorf, R. (1959), *Class and Class Conflict in Industrial Society*, Routledge and Kegan Paul

Dahrendorf, R. (1968), *Essays in the Theory of Society*, Routledge and Kegan Paul

Dahrendorf, R. (1968), 'In praise of Thrasymachus', in Dahrendorf (1968)

Dale, R. *et al.* (eds,) (1976), *Schooling and Capitalism*, Routledge and Kegan Paul

Dale, R. (1977), 'Implications of the rediscovery of the hidden curriculum for the sociology of teaching', in Gleeson (1977)

Davidoff, L. (1973), *The Best Circles: Society, Etiquette and the Season*, Croom Helm

Davies, B. (1976), *Social Control and Education*, Methuen

Davis, F. (1972), *Illness. Interaction and the Self*, Wadsworth

Davis, K. (1948), *Human Society*, Macmillan

Davis, K., and Moore, W. E. (1945), 'Some principles of stratification', *American Sociological Review*, vol. 10 (reprinted in Bendix and Lipset 1967)

Davis, M. L. (1978), *Maternity: Letters from Working Women*, Virago

Deem, R. (1978), *Women and Schooling*, Routledge and Kegan Paul

Delamont, S. (1976), *Interaction in the Classroom*, Methuen

Dennis, N., Henriques, F. and Slaughter, C. (1956), *Coal is Our Life*, Eyre and Spottiswoode

Dept. of Education and Science (1978), *Statistics of Education*, vol. 3, HMSO

Ditton, J. (1972), 'Absent at work: or how to manage monotony', *New Society* (21 December)

Dobash, R. E., and Dobash, R. (1980), *Violence against Wives*, Open Books

Douglas, J. W. B. (1958), *Children Under Five*, Allen and Unwin

Douglas, J. W. B. (1964), *The Home and the School*, MacGibbon and Kee

Downes, D. (1966), *The Delinquent Solution: a study in subcultural theory*, Routledge and Kegan Paul

Doyal, L. (with Pennell, I.) (1979), *The Political Economy of Health*, Pluto

Dreitzel, H. (1972), *The Social Organisation of Health*, Macmillan

Drucker, H. *et al.* (eds.) (1984), *Developments in British Politics*, Macmillan

Du Bois, C. (1944), *The People of Alor*, University of Minnesota Press

Dunnell, K. (1979), *Family Formation in 1976*, OPCS/HMSO

Durkheim, E. (1893), *The Division of Labour in Society*, Free Press, 1933

Durkheim, E. (1895), *The Rules of Sociological Method*, Free Press, 1964

Durkheim, E. (1897), *Suicide: a study in Sociology*, Routledge and Kegan Paul, 1970

Durkheim, E. (1912), *The Elementary Forms of the Religious Life*, Allen and Unwin, 1915

Durkheim, E. (1922), *Education and Sociology*, Free Press, 1956

Durkheim, E. (1938), *Rules of Sociological Method*, University of Chicago Press

Durkheim, E. (1957), *Professional Ethics and Civic Morals*, Routledge and Kegan Paul

Duverger, M. (1972), *Party Politics and Pressure Groups*, Nelson

Education reports, see Central Advisory Council for Education

Eekelaar, J. (1971), *Family Security and Family Breakdown*, Penguin

Eggleston, J. (1974), *Contemporary Research in the Sociology of Education*, Methuen

Ehrenreich, B., and English, D. (1976), *Complaints and Disorders: the sexual politics of illness*, Pluto

Eisenstadt, S.N. (1956), *From Generation to Generation*, Free Press

Elliot, J. (1974), 'Sex role constraints on freedom of discussion: a neglected reality of the classroom', *The New Era*, vol. 55, no. 6

Engels, F. (1844), *The Condition of the Working Class in England*, Oxford University Press, 1958

Engels, F. (1884), *The Origin of the Family, Private Property and the State*, Lawrence and Wishart, 1972

Enzensberger, H. M. (1976), *Raids and Reconstructions*, Pluto Press

Esland, G., Salaman, G., and Speakman, M. (eds.) (1975), *People and Work*, Open University Press

Eysenck, H. (1970), *Crime and Personality*, Paladin

Eysenck, H., and Nias, D. (1978), *Sex, Violence and the Media*, Maurice Temple Smith

Ferrarotti, F. (1979), *An Alternative Sociology*, Halsted

Field, F. (ed.) (1973), *Low Pay*, Arrow Books

Finley, M. I (1973), *Democracy Ancient and Modern*, Chatto and Windus

Firestone, S. (1972), *The Dialectic of Sex*, Paladin

Fiske, J., and Hartley, J. (1978), *Reading Television*, Methuen

Flanders, N. A. (1970), *Analysing Teacher Behaviour*, Addison-Wesley

Fletcher, R. (1966), *The Family and Marriage in Britain*, Penguin

Fletcher, R. (1971), *The Making of Sociology*, Michael Joseph

Floud, J. E., Halsey, A. H. and Martin, F. M. (eds) (1956), *Social Class and Educational Opportunity*, Heinemann

Flude, M., and Ahier, J. (1974), *Educability. Schools and Ideology*, Croom Helm

Ford, J. (1969), *Social Class and the Comprehensive School*, Routledge and Kegan Paul

Foster-Carter, A. (1985), *The Sociology of Development*, Causeway

Fox, A. (1966), *Industrial Society and Industrial Relations*, HMSO

Frank, A. (1969), *Latin America: Underdevelopment or Revolution*, Monthly Review Press

Frankenberg, R. (1957), *Village on the Border*, Cohen and West

Frith, S. (1984), *The Sociology of Youth*, Causeway

Fryer, P. (1984), *Staying Power: the History of Black People in Britain*, Pluto

Galbraith, J. K. (1967), *The New Industrial State*, Hamish Hamilton

Gans, H. (1967), *The Levittowners*, Allen Lane

Gans, H. J. (1971), 'The positive functions of poverty', *Social Policy 2* (July, August)

Garfinkel, H. (1956), 'Conditions of successful degradation ceremonies', *American Journal of Sociology*, vol. 61 (reprinted in Rubington and Weinberg 1968)

Garfinkel, H. (1968a), 'The origins of the term "Ethnomethodology"' in Turner (ed.) (1974)

Garfinkel, H. (1968b), *Studies in Ethnomethodology*, Prentice-Hall

Gavron, H. (1966), *The Captive Wife*, Penguin

George, S. (1976), *How the Other Half Die*, Penguin

Geras, N. (1976), 'Luxemburg and Trotsky on the contradiction of bourgeois democracy', in Blackburn (ed.) (1977)

Gerth, H., and Mills, C. W. (1948), *Essays from Max Weber*, Routledge and Kegan Paul

Giddens, A. (1979), *Central Problems in Social Theory*, Macmillan

Giddens, A., and Mackenzie, G. (eds.) (1983), *Social Class and the Division of Labour*, Cambridge University Press

Giner, S. (1972), *Sociology*, Martin Robertson

Glasgow University Media Group (1976), *Bad News*, Routledge and Kegan Paul

Glasgow University Media Group (1980), *More Bad News*, Routledge and Kegan Paul

Glasgow University Media Group (1982), *Really Bad News*, Writers' and Readers' Cooperative

Glasgow University Media Group (1985), *War and Peace News*, Open University Press

Glass, D. (1954), *Social Mobility in Britain*, Routledge and Kegan Paul

Glazer-Malbin, N., and Waehrer, H.Y. (eds.) (1972), *Women in a Man-Made World*, Rand McNally

Gleeson, D. (1977), *Identity and Structure: Issues in the Sociology of Education*, Nafferton Books

Glover, D. (1984), *The Sociology of the Mass Media*, Causeway

Glover, D., and Strawbridge, S. (1985), *The Sociology of Knowledge*, Causeway

Goffman, E. (1961), *Asylums*, Penguin, 1970

Goffman, E. (1963), *Stigma*, Penguin

Goffman, E. (1969), *The Presentation of Self in Everyday Life*, Penguin

Gold, R. L. (1958), 'Roles in sociological field observations', *Social Forces*, vol. 6

Golding, P., and Middleton, S. (1982), *Images of Welfare*, Martin Robertson

Goldthorpe, J., and Lockwood, D. (1963), 'Affluence and the British class structure', *Sociological Review*, vol. 11

Goldthorpe, J., *et al.* (1968a), *The Affluent Worker: Industrial Attitudes and Behaviour*, Cambridge University Press

Goldthorpe, J., *et al.* (1968b), *The Affluent Worker: Political Attitudes and Behaviour*, Cambridge University Press

Goldthorpe, J., *et al.* (1969), *The Affluent Worker in the Class Structure*, Cambridge University Press

Goldthorpe, J., *et al.* (1980), *Social Mobility and Class Structure in Modern Britain*, Clarendon Press.

Gomm, R., and McNeill, P. (1982), *A Handbook for Sociology Teachers*, Heinemann

Goode, W. (1971), 'A sociological perspective on marital dissolution', in Anderson (1971)

Gordon, M. (ed.) (1972), *The Nuclear Family in Crisis*, Harper and Row

Gough, I. R. (1970), 'Poverty and health', *Social and Economic Administration*, vol. 4 no. 3

Gould, S. J. (1980), 'Dr Down's syndrome', *New Scientist*, vol 86 no. 1205

Gouldner, A. (1954), *Wildcat Strike: a study in worker–management relationship*, Routledge and Kegan Paul

Gouldner, A. (1973), *For Sociology: Renewal and Critique in Sociology To-day*, Penguin

Gross, N. (1953), 'Social class identification in the urban community', *American Sociological Review*, vol. 18

Habermas, J. (1975), 'Technology and science as ideology', in Esland *et al.* (1975)

Haddon, R. (1975), 'The location of West Indians in the London housing market', in Lambert and Weir (1975)

Hacker, H. M. (1972), 'Women as a minority group', in Glazer-Malbin and Waehrer (1972)

Hall, S., and Jefferson, T. (1976), *Resistance through Rituals*, Hutchinson

Hall, S., *et al.* (1978), *Policing the Crisis: Mugging, the State and Law and Order*, Macmillan

Halloran, J. D. (1964), 'Television and violence', *Twentieth Century* (Winter)

Halsey, A. H., Floud, J., and Anderson, C. A. (eds.) (1961), *Education, Economy and Society*, Free Press

Halsey, A. H. (ed.) (1972), *Educational Priority*, HMSO

Halsey, A. H. (1978), *Change in British Society*, Oxford University Press

Halsey, A. H., Heath, A. and Ridge, J. (1980), *Origins and Destinations: Family, Class and Education in Modern Britain*, Clarendon Press

Hammersley, M. (1974), 'The organisation of pupil participation', *Sociological Review*, vol. 22, no. 3

Hammersley, M., and Woods, P. (eds.) (1976), *The Process of Schooling*, Routledge and Kegan Paul

Hammond, P. E. (1964), *Sociologists at Work*, Basic Books

Haralambos, M. (1980), *Sociology: themes and perspectives*, University Tutorial Press

Hargreaves, D. (1967), *Social Relations in a Secondary School*, Routledge and Kegan Paul

Hargreaves, D. (1974), 'Deschoolers and New Romantics', in Flude and Ahier (1974)

Hargreaves, D., Hestor, S., and Mellor, F. (1975), *Deviance in Classrooms*, Routledge and Kegan Paul

Harrington, M. (1963), *The Other America*, Penguin

Harris, C. (1983), *The Family and Industrial Society*, George Allen and Unwin

Harvey, D. (1977), 'Social justice and spatial systems', in Raynor and Harris (1977)

Hayter, T., and Watson, C. (1985), *Aid: Rhetoric and Reality*, Pluto

Hebdige, D. (1979), *Subculture: the meaning of style*, Methuen

Hobsbawm, E. (1969), *Industry and Empire*, Penguin

Hoogvelt, A. (1982), *The Third World in Global Development*, MacMillan

Howe, M. (1976), *Man. Environment and Disease in Britain*, Penguin

Hoyles, M. (1977), *The Politics of Literacy*, Writers' and Readers' Publishing Cooperative

Hyman, R. (1975), *Industrial Relations: a Marxist introduction*, Macmillan

Illich, I. (1971), *Deschooling Society*, Calder and Boyars

Illich, I. (1976), *Medical Nemesis: the Expropriation of Health*, Marion Boyars

Illich, I. (1979), *Tools for Conviviality*, Marion Boyars

Inkeles, A. (1964), *What is Sociology?* Prentice-Hall

Irvine, J., Miles, I., and Evans, J. (1979), *Demystifying Social Statistics*, Pluto Press

Jack, M. (1974), 'Elite theory; ideological, tautology or scientific?', in Crewe (ed.) (1974), *British Political Sociology Yearbook*, vol. 1: *Elites in Western Democracy 1*, Croom Helm

Jackson, B. (1964), *Streaming: an education system in miniature*, Routledge and Kegan Paul

Jackson, B., and Marsden, D. (1962), *Education and the Working Class*, Routledge and Kegan Paul

Jackson, P.W. (1968), *Life in Classrooms*, Holt, Rinehart and Winston

Jacobson, (1982) B. *Smoking is a Feminist Issue*, Pluto Press

Jencks, C. (1972), *Inequality*, Harper and Row

Johnson, R. (1970), 'Educational policy and social control in early Victorian England', *Past and Present*, vol. 49

Johnson, R. (1976), 'Notes on the schooling of the English working class, 1780–1850', in Dale *et al.* (1976)

Johnson, T. (1972), *Professions and Power*, Macmillan

Johnson, T. (1976), *Work and Power*, Course D302, Unit 16, Open University Press

Jordan, Z. A. (ed.) (1971), *Karl Marx*, Michael Joseph

Kanter, R. (1972), *Commitment and Community*, Harvard University Press

Kaplan, A. (1964), *The Conduct of Enquiry*, Chandler

Katz, E., and Lazarsfeld, P. (1955), *Personal Influence*, Free Press

Kaysen, C. (1957), 'The social significance of the modern corporation', *American Economic Review* (May)

Keating, P. (ed.) (1976), *Into Unknown England*, Fontana

Keddie, N. (1971), 'Classroom knowledge' in Young, M. F. D. (1971)

Keddie, N. (1973), *Tinker, Tailor . . . the myth of Cultural Deprivation*, Penguin

Kelsall, R. K. (1955), *Higher Civil Servants in Britain*, Routledge and Kegan Paul

Kelsall, R. K. (1979), *Population*, Longman

Kelsall, R. K., and Kelsall, H. M. (1974), *Stratification*, Longman

Kerr, C. *et al.* (1962), *Industrialism and Industrial Man*, Heinemann (Penguin 1983)

Kerr, M. (1958), *The People of Ship Street*, Routledge and Kegan Paul

Kincaid, J. C. (1973), *Poverty and Equality in Britain*, Penguin

Kitsuse, J., and Cicourel, A. (1963), 'A note on the uses of official statistics', *Social Problems*

Kitzinger, S. (1978), *Women as Mothers*, Fontana

Klapper, J. T. (1960), *The Effects of Mass Communication*, Free Press

Klein, J. (1965), *Samples from English Cultures*, Routledge and Kegan Paul

Knowles, K. G. (1952), *Strikes: a study of industrial conflict*, Blackwell

Krausz, E., and Miller, S. H. (1974), *Social Research Design*, Longman

Kuhn, T. S. (1970), *The Structure of Scientific Revolutions*, University of Chicago Press

Labov, W. (1969), 'The logic of non-standard English', *Georgetown Monographs*, vol. 22 (reprinted in Keddie 1973)

Lacey, C. (1970), *Hightown Grammar*, Manchester University Press

Laing, R. D. (1970), *Politics of Experience*, Penguin

Laing, R. D., and Esterson, A. (1970), *Sanity, Madness and the Family*, Penguin

Lambert, R. (1968), *The Hothouse Society*, Weidenfeld and Nicolson

Lambert, C., and Weir, D. (1975), *Cities in Modern Britain*, Fontana

Land, H. (1975), 'The myth of the male breadwinner', *New Society* (9 October)

Land, H. (1976), 'Women: Supporters or Supported?', in Barker and Allen (1976)

Laing, R.D., and Esterson, A. (1970), *Sanity, Madness and the Family*, Penguin

Laslett, P. (1972), *Household and Family in Past Time*, Cambridge University Press

Laslett, P. (1977), *Family Life and Illicit Love in Earlier Generations*, Cambridge University Press

Laslett, P. (1983), *The World We Have Lost Further Explored*, Methuen

Last, G. (1963), 'The iceberg: completing the clinical picture in general practice', *Lancet*, vol. ii

Lawson, J., and Silver, H. (1973), *A Social History of Education in England*, Methuen

Leeson, J., and Grey, J. (1978), *Women and Medicine*, Tavistock

Lemert, E. (1972), *Human Deviance, Social Problems and Social Control*, Prentice-Hall

Lenin, I. (1915), *Imperialism, the Highest Stage of Capitalism*, Moscow Publishing House

Lenski, G. E. (1966), *Power and Privilege: Theory of Social Stratification*, McGraw-Hill

Levine, D. (1977), *Family Formation in the Age of Nascent Capitalism*, Academic Press

Lewis, O. (1961), *Children of Sanchez*, Random House

Lewis, O. (1966), *La Vida: a Puerto Rican family in the Culture of Poverty*, Random House

Lipset, S. M. (1960), *Political Man*, Heinemann

Little, A. (1978), *'Schools and race'*, Commission for Racial Equality, 1978

Littlejohn, J. (1972), *Social Stratification*, Allen and Unwin

Lobban, G. (1976), *Sexism in Childrens' Books: Facts, Figures and Guidelines*, Writers' and Readers' Publishing Cooperative

Lobban, G. (1977), 'Sexist bias in reading schemes', in Hoyles (1977)

Lockwood, D. (1958), *The Black Coated Worker*, Allen and Unwin

Lockwood, D. (1966), 'Sources of variation in working class images of society', *Sociological Review*, vol. 14

Lomas, E. (1973), *Census 1971: the Coloured Population of Great Britain*, Runnymede Trust

Lombroso, C. (1867), *The Criminal Man*, Putnam, 1911

Lukes, S. (1979), 'Power and authority', in Bottomore and Nisbet (eds.) (1979)

Lundberg, G. A., *et al.* (1963), *Sociology*, Harper and Row

Lydall, H. F., and Tipping, D. G. (1961), 'The distribution of personal wealth in Britain', *Bulletin of the Oxford University Institute of Statistics* (February)

Macfarlane, A. (1978), *The Origins of English Individualism*, Blackwell

Macfarlane, A., and Mugford, M. (1984), *Birth Counts*, HMSO

McKee, L., and O'Brien, M. (1982), *The Father Figure*, Tavistock

McKenzie, R. (1933), *The Metropolitan Community*, McGraw-Hill

McKenzie, R., and Silver, A. (1968), *Angels in Marble*, Heinemann

McKeowen, T. (1976), *The Modern Rise of Population*, Arnold

McLaren, A. (1978), *Birth Control in Nineteenth Century England*, Croom Helm

McNeill, P. (1985), *Research Methods*, Tavistock

McRobbie, A. (1978), *Women Take Issue: Aspects of Women's Subordination*, Hutchinson

Macpherson, C. B. (1966), *The Real World of Democracy*, Oxford University Press

Madge, J. (1953), *The Tools of Social Science*, Longman

Mannheim, K. (1940), *Man and Society in an Age of Reconstruction*, Routledge and Kegan Paul

Mannheim, K. (1929), *Ideology and Utopia*, Routledge and Kegan Paul (1948)

Mannheim, K. (1951), *Freedom, Power and Democratic Planning*, Routledge and Kegan Paul

Marcuse, H. (1964), *One Dimensional Man*, Routledge and Kegan Paul

Margolis, M. (1979), *Viable Democracy*, Penguin

Marsden, D. and Owens, D. (1975), 'The Jekyll and Hyde Marriages', *New Society* (8 May)

Marshall, T. H. (1965), *Social Policy*, Hutchinson

Martin, D. (1967), *A Sociology of English Religion*, Heinemann

Martin, D. (1978), *A General Theory of Secularisation*, Blackwell

Marx, K. (1844), 'Critique of Hegel's philosophy of right', extracts in Bottomore and Rubel (1963)

Marx, K. (1845), *The German Ideology*, Penguin (1974)

Marx, K., and Engels, F. (1848), *Manifesto of the Communist Party*, Progress Publishers 1952

Marx, K. (1859), *Preface to the Critique of Political Economy*, Lawrence and Wishart 1971

Marx, K. (1867) *Capital*, Lawrence and Wishart, 1970

Marx, K. (1867), *Capital* quoted in Bottomore and Rubel (1963)

Marx, K. (1899), *Wages, Price and Profits*, Allen and Unwin

Marx, K. (1849), 'Wage Labour and Capital' in *K. Marx and F. Engels, Selected Works in Three Volumes*, Progress Publishers, 1969

Marx, K., and Engels, F. (1884), 'The origins of the family', in Engels 1884

Massey, D. (1983), 'Industrial restructuring as class restructuring: production centralisation and local uniqueness', *Regional Studies*, vol. 17, no. 2

Mathews, J. (1980), 'Marxism, energy and technological change', in *Politics and Power*, Routledge and Kegan Paul

Matza, D. (1964), *Delinquency and Drift*, Wiley

Mayhew, H. (1849), *London Labour and the London Poor*, Cass 1967

Mead, G. H. (1934), *Mind, Self and Society*, University of Chicago Press

Mead, M. (1950), *Male and Female*, Penguin 1962

Mead, M. (1970), *Culture and Commitment*, Bodley Head

Medvedev, Z., and Medvedev, R. (1969), *A Question of Madness*, Penguin

Meighan, R., Shelton, D. I., and Marks, T. (1979), *Perspectives on Society*, Nelson

Merton, R. K. (1938), 'Social structure and anomie', *American Sociological Review*, vol. 3 (reprinted in Clinard 1964)

Merton, R. K. (1957), *Social Theory and Social Structure*, Free Press

Merton, R. K. (1968), *Social Theory and Social Structure*, Free Press (enlarged edition)

Miliband, R. (1973), *The State in Capitalist Society*, Quartet

Millerson, G. (1964), *The Qualifying Associations: a study in professionalisation*, Routledge and Kegan Paul

Mills, C. Wright (1956), *The Power Elite*, Oxford University Press

Mills C. Wright (1951), *White Collar*, Oxford University Press
Mills, C. Wright (1959), *The Sociological Imagination*, Oxford University Press
Moonman, J. (1973), *The Effectiveness of Fringe Benefits in Industry*, Gower
Morgan, D. (1975), *Social Theory and the Family*, Routledge and Kegan Paul
Morley, D. (1980), *The 'Nationwide' Audience*, British Film Institute
MSHE (1985), *The Educational and Vocational Experience of 15-18 Year Old Young People of Ethnic Minority Groups*, University of Warwick
Murdock, G. P. (1949), *Social Structure*, Macmillan
Myrdal, A., and Klein, V. (1956), *Women's Two Roles*, Routledge and Kegan Paul

Nash, R. (1973), *Classrooms Observed*, Routledge and Kegan Paul
National Food Survey (1980), HMSO
Newby, H. (1977), *The Deferential Worker*, Penguin
Newsom Report (1963), see Central Advisory Council for Education
Newson, J., and Newson, E. (1965), *Patterns of Infant Care in an Urban Community*, Penguin
Newson, J., and Newson, E. (1974), 'Cultural aspects of child rearing in the English speaking world', in Richards (1974)
Nichols, T. (1980), *Capital and Labour*, Athlone Press
Nicholson, J. (1977), *What Society does to Girls*, Virago
Nisbet, R. A. (ed) (1965), *Emile Durkheim*, Prentice-Hall

Oakley, A. (1972), 'Are husbands good housewives?', *New Society* (17 February)
Oakley, A. (1974a), *Housewife*, Penguin
Oakley, A. (1974b), *The Sociology of Housework*, Martin Robertson
O'Donnell, M. (1981), *A New Introduction to Sociology*, Harrap–Nelson
O'Donnell, M. (1983), *A New Introductory Reader in Sociology*, Harrap–Nelson
O'Donnell, M. (1985), *Age and Generation*, Tavistock
Office of Population, Censuses and Surveys (1946), *Special Family Census, 1946*, HMSO
Office of Population, Censuses and Surveys (1961), *Census 1961*, HMSO
Office of Population, Censuses and Surveys (1977), *International Migration 1977* (Series MN No. 4), HMSO
Office of Population, Censuses and Surveys (1979), *Population Projections* (Monitor Series PP2) HMSO
Okely, J. (1983), *The Traveller-Gypsies*, Cambridge University Press
Open University (1976a), *Patterns of Inequality*, Course D302, Open University Press
Open University (1976b), *People and Work*, Course DE351, Open University Press
Ortega y Gasset, J. (1932), *The Revolt of the Masses*, Allen and Unwin
Ortner, S. (1974), 'Is female to male as nature is to culture?', in Rosaldo and Lamphere (eds.) (1974)
Outhwaite, W. (1975), *Understanding Social Life*, Allen and Unwin

Pahl, R. E. (1975), *Whose City? and Further Essays on Urban Society*, Longman
Park, R. E. (1925), *The City, Chicago*, University of Chicago Press
Parker, S. (1971), *The Future of Work and Leisure*, Allen and Unwin
Parker, S. (1976), *The Sociology of Leisure*, Allen and Unwin

Parker, S. *et al.* (1977), *The Sociology of Industry*, Allen and Unwin

Parry, G. (1969), *Political Elites*, Allen and Unwin

Parsons, T. (1952), *The Social System*, Tavistock

Parsons, T. (1957), *Economy and Society*, Free Press

Parsons, T., and Bales, R. F. (1956), *Family, Socialisation, and Interaction Process*, Routledge and Kegan Paul

Parsons, T. (1959), 'The school class as a social system', *Harvard Educational Review*, vol. 29 (reprinted in Halsey, Floud, and Anderson 1961)

Parsons, T. (1969), *Politics and Social Structure*, Free Press

Patrick, J. (1973), *A Glasgow Gang Observed*, Eyre Methuen

Pearce, F. (1973), 'Crime corporations and the American social order', in Taylor and Taylor (eds.) (1973)

Pedley, R. (1963), *The Comprehensive School*, Penguin

Politics of Health Group (1980), *Food and Profit: it makes you sick*, British Society for Social Responsibility in Science

Porter, R. B. (1971), *The Contribution of the Biological and Medical Sciences to Human Welfare* (Presidential address), British Association for the Advancement of Science

Powles, J. (1973), 'On the limitations of modern science', *Science, Medicine and Man*, vol. 1, Pergamon

Pring, R. (1972), 'Knowledge out of control', *Education for Teaching*, no. 89

Pryce, K. (1979), *Endless Pressure*, Penguin

Radcliffe-Brown, A. R. (1952), *Structure and Function in Primitive Society*, Routledge and Kegan Paul

Rakusen, J., and Davidson, N. (1982), *Our Bodies, Ourselves: what technology does to pregnancy*, Pan

Rampton Report (1981), *West Indian Children in Our Schools*, HMSO

Rapoport, R., and R. N. (1977), *Dual-Career Families Re-examined*, Martin Robertson

Rapoport, R. N., Fogarty, M., and Rapoport, R. (eds.) (1982), *Families in Britain*, Routledge and Kegan Paul

Raynor, J., and Harris, E. (eds.) (1977), *The City Experience*, Ward Lock Educational

RCDIW – see Royal Commission

Rees, A. (1950), *Life in a Welsh Countryside*, University of Wales Press

Reid, I. (1977), *Social Class Differences in Britain: a Source Book*, Open Books

Reid, I. (1978), *Sociological Perspectives on School and Education*, Open Books

Revell, J. R. S. (1965), 'Changes in the social distribution of property', *International Conference of Economic History*, vol. 1

Rex, J. (1975), *Approaches to Sociology*, Routledge and Kegan Paul

Rex, J., and Moore, R. (1968), *Race, Community and Conflict*, Routledge and Kegan Paul

Richards, M. (1974), *The Integration of the Child into the Adult World*, Cambridge University Press

Rigby, A. (1974), *Alternative Realities*, Routledge and Kegan Paul

Ritzer, G. *et al.* (1979), *Sociology*, Allyn and Bacon

Roberts, H. (1981), *Women, Health and Reproduction*, Routledge and Kegan Paul

Roemer, M., and Schwarz, J. (1979), 'Doctor slowdown: effects on the population of Los Angeles County', *Social Science and Medicine*, vol. 13, series C. no. 4

Rosaldo, M., and Lamphere, L. (eds.) (1974), *Woman, Culture and Society*, Stanford University Press

Rose, A. (ed.) (1962), *Human Behaviour and Social Processes*, Routledge and Kegan Paul

Rose, H., and Rose. S. (1980), 'The rise of radical science', *New Scientist*, vol. 85 no. 1188

Rosenhan, D. (1973), 'On being sane in insane places', *Science*, no. 179

Rosser, C., and Harris, C. (1965), *The Family and Social Change: a Study of Family and Kinship in a South Wales Town*, Routledge and Kegan Paul

Rostow, W. W. (1960), *The Stages of Economic Growth: a non-Communist manifesto*, Cambridge University Press (2nd edn. 1971)

Roszak, T. (1971), *The Making of a Counter Culture*, Faber and Faber

Roth, J. (1963), *Timetables*, Bobbs Merrill

Rowntree, B. S. (1901), *Poverty: a Study of Town Life*, Macmillan

Rowntree, B. S. (1941), *Poverty and Progress*, Longman

Rowntree, B. S., and Lavers, G. R. (1951), *Poverty and the Welfare State*, Longman

Royal Commission on Distribution of Income and Wealth (1979), *Report no, 7*, HMSO

Rubington, E., and Weinberg, M. (1968), *Deviance: the Interactionist Perspective*, Macmillan

Runciman, W. G. (1966), *Relative Deprivation and Social Justice*, Routledge and Kegan Paul

Runnymede Trust (1975), *Race and Council Housing in Britain*, Runnymede Trust

Rutter, M. *et al.* (1979), *Fifteen Thousand Hours*, Open Books

Ryan, W. (1971), *Blaming the Victim*, Orbach and Chambers

Ryder, J., and Silver, H. (1977), *Modern English Society*, Methuen

Sampson, A. (1965), *Anatomy of Britain Today*, Hodder and Stoughton

Sampson, A. (1971), *New Anatomy of Britain*, Hodder and Stoughton

Scarman, Lord Justice (1983), *The Scarman Report: the Brixton Disorders 10–12th April 1981*, Penguin

Schofield, M. (1965), *The Sexual Behaviour of Young People*, Longman

Schumpeter, J. A. (1943), *Capitalism, Socialism and Democracy*, (5th edn 1976), Allen and Unwin

Scott, J. (1979), *Corporations, Classes and Capitalism*, Hutchinson

Scrimshire, A. (1977), 'Health in Newham', *New Society* (24 February)

Sears, D., and McConohey, J. (1973), *The Politics of Violence: the New Urban Blacks and the Watts Riot*, Houghton Mifflin

Sharpe, S. (1976), *Just like a Girl*, Penguin

Shorter, E. (1976), *The Making of the Modern Family*, Collins

Silver, H. (ed.) (1973), *Equal Opportunity in Education*, Methuen

Silverman, D. (1970), *The Theory of Organisations*, Heinemann

Sivanandan, A. (1981), 'Imperialism and disorganic development in a silicon age', in Braham *et al.* (1981)

Shipman, M. (1981), *The Limitations of Social Research*, Longman

Smith, A. (1976), *Social Change: Social Theories and Historical Processes*, Longman

Smith, D. (1977), *Racial Disadvantage in Britain*, Penguin

Smith, M., Parker, S., and Smith, C. (1973), *Leisure and Society in Britain*, Allen Lane

Social Science Teacher (1979a), 'Royal Commission on Distribution of Income and Wealth', vol. 9, no. 1 (October)

Social Science Teacher (1979b), 'The Conservative inner cabinet', vol. 9, no. 1 (October)

Spender, D. (1978), 'Don't talk: listen', *Times Educational Supplement*, 3 November.

Spender, D. (1980), *Man-made Language*, Routledge and Kegan Paul

Spender, D. (1982), *Invisible Women: the Schooling Scandal*, Writers' and Readers' Publishing Cooperative

Spender, D., and Sarah, E. (1980), *Learning to Lose*, The Women's Press

Spicer, C. C., and Lipworth, (1966), *Regional and Social Factors in Infant Mortality*, HMSO

Squibb, P. G. (1973), 'The concept of intelligence: a sociological perspective', *Sociological Review*, vol. 21

Stacey, M. (1960), *Tradition and Change: a study of Banbury*, Oxford University Press

Stacey, M. (1969), *Methods of Social Research*, Pergamon

Stacey, M., Batstone, E., Bell, C., and Murcott, A. (1975) *Power, Persistence and Change: a Second Study of Banbury*, Routledge and Kegan Paul

Stanworth, M. (1983), *Gender and Schooling: Study of Sexual Divisions in the Classroom*, Hutchinson

Stanworth, P., and Giddens, A. (eds.) (1974), *Elites and Power in British Society*, Cambridge University Press

Stephenson, L. (1979), 'Demography and race: some limitations and some distortions', in Meighan, Shelton and Marks (1979)

Storm, M. (1976), *Urban Growth in Britain*, Arnold

Sudnow, D. (1967), *Passing On: the social organisation of dying*, Prentice Hall

Sugarman, B. (1968), *Sociology*, Heinemann

Sutherland, E. H. (1955), *White Collar Crime*, Holt, Rinehart and Winston, 1961

Sutherland, E., and Cressey, D. (1961), *Principles of Criminology*, Lippincott

Swann, Lord (1985), *Report of the Committee of Enquiry into the Education of Children from Ethnic Minority Groups*, HMSO

Swift, D. F. (1965), 'Educational psychology, sociology and the environment', *British Journal of Sociology*, vol. 16, no. 4

Sykes, G., and Matza, D. (1957), 'Techniques of neutralisation: A theory of delinquency', *American Sociological Review*, vol. 22 (reprinted in Rubington and Weinberg 1968)

Szasz, T. (1972), *Myth of Mental Illness*, Paladin

Tawney, R. H. (1931), *Equality*, Allen and Unwin

Taylor, I., and Taylor, L. (1973), *Politics and Deviance*, Penguin

Taylor, I., Walton, P., and Young, J. (1973), *The New Criminology*, Routledge and Kegan Paul

Taylor, I., Walton, P., and Young, J. (1975), *Critical Criminology*, Routledge and

Kegan Paul

Taylor, L, (1971), *Deviance and Society*, Michael Joseph

Titmuss, R. M. (1962), *Income Distribution and Social Change*, Allen and Unwin

Tönnies, F. (1887), *Gemeinschaft und Gesellschaft*. Published in English as *Community and Association* by Charles P. Loomis, 1955

Townsend, P. (1954), 'Measuring poverty', *British Journal of Sociology*, vol. 5

Townsend, P. (1979), *Poverty in the United Kingdom*, Penguin

Townsend, P., and Davidson, N. (1982), *Inequalities in Health: The Black Report*, Penguin

Tracey, M. (1977), *Production of Political Television*, Routledge and Kegan Paul

Troeltsch, E. (1912), *The Social Teaching of the Christian Church*, Allen and Unwin

Trowler, P. (1984), *Topics in Sociology*, UTP

Trowler, P. (1985), *Further Topics in Sociology*, UTP

Tuckett, D. (1977), *An Introduction to Medical Sociology*, Tavistock

Tudge, C. (1979), *The Famine Business*, Penguin

Tumin, M.W. (1953), 'Some principles of stratification: a critical analysis', *American Sociological Review*, vol. 18 (reprinted in Bendix and Lipset 1967)

Tunstall, J. (1962), *The Fishermen*, MacGibbon and Kee

Tunstall, J. (1983), *The Media in Britain*, Constable

Turner, B. (1975), *Industrialism*, Longman

Turner, R. (1960), 'Sponsored and contest mobility and the school system', *American Sociological Review*, vol. 25

Turner, R. (ed.) (1974), *Ethnomethodology*, Penguin

Tylor, E. B. (1871), *Primitive Culture*, Murray

UCCA (1985), *Twenty-second Report 1983–84*, UCCA

Valentine, C. (1968), *Culture and Poverty*, University of Chicago Press

Van den Haag, W. (1975), *Punishing Criminals*, Basic Books

Vulliamy, G. (1973), *New Perspectives in Sociology*, Association for the Teaching of the Social Sciences

Wakeford, J. (1969), *The Cloistered Elite*, Macmillan

Walliman, I., *et al.* (1980) 'Misreading Weber: the concept of macht', *Sociology*, vol. 14, no. 2

Wallis, R. (1984), *The Elementary Forms of the New Religious Life*, Routledge and Kegan Paul

Walton, P. (1979), Introduction to Goffman, E., *Gender Advertisements*, Macmillan

Watson, J. D. (1968), *The Double Helix*, Weidenfeld and Nicolson

Weber, M. (1904), *The Protestant Ethic and the Spirit of Capitalism*. Allen and Unwin, 1952

Weber, M. (1920), 'The Chinese Literati', in Gerth and Mills (1946)

Weber, M. (1924), 'Class, status and party' in Gerth and Mills (1948)

Weber, M. (1947), *The Theory of Social and Economic Organisations*, Free Press

Webster, A. (1984), *Introduction to the Sociology of Development*, Macmillan

Wedderburn, D. (1962), 'Poverty in Britain Today', *Sociological Review*

Wedderburn, D. (1970), 'Workplace inequality', *New Society* (9 April)

Wedderburn, D. (ed.) (1974), *Poverty, Inequality and Class Structure*, Cambridge University Press

Weinberg, M., and Rubington, E. (1973), *The Solution of Social Problems*, Oxford University Press

Weir, D. (ed.) (1973), *Men and Work in Modern Britain*, Fontana

West, D. J. (1969), *Present Conduct and Future Delinquency*, Heinemann

West, D. J. (1973), 'Are delinquents different:', *New Society* (22 November)

West, J. (ed.) (1982), *Work, Women and the Labour Market*, Routledge and Kegan Paul

Westergaard, J., and Resler, H. (1975), *Class in a Capitalist Society*, Heinemann

Whyte, W. F. (1955), *Street Corner Society*, University of Chicago Press (3rd edn., 1981)

Wilensky, H. (1964), 'The professionalisation of everyone', *American Journal of Sociology*, vol. 69

Williams, F. (1977), *Why the Poor Pay More*, Macmillan

Williams, R. (1983), *Key Words: a Vocabulary of Culture and Society*, Fontana

Williams, W. M. (1956), *The Sociology of an English Village*, Routledge and Kegan Paul

Willis, P. (1977), *Learning to Labour: How Working Class Kids Get Working Class Jobs*, Saxon House

Willmott, P. (1966), *Adolescent Boys of East London*, Routledge and Kegan Paul

Willmott, P. (1974), 'Population and community in London', *New Society* (24 October)

Willmott, P., and Young, M. (1960), *Family and Class in a London Suburb*, Routledge and Kegan Paul

Wilson, A. (1985), *Family*, Tavistock

Wilson, B. (1982), *Religion in Sociological Perspective*, Oxford University Press

Wilson, B. R. (1961), *Sects and Society*, Heinemann

Wilson, B. R. (1966), *Religion in Secular Society*, C. A. Watts and Co.

Wilson, B. R. (1977), 'How religious are we?', *New Society* (27 October)

Wilson, J. Q. (1968), *City Politics and Public Policy*, Wiley

Wilson, J. Q. (1975), *Thinking about Crime*, Wiley

Wirth, L. (1938), 'Urbanism as a way of life', *American Journal of Sociology*, vol. 44

Wood, S. (1973), *The Times*, 25 April

Woods, P. (1980a), *Teacher Strategies: explorations in the sociology of the school*, Croom Helm

Woods, P. (1980b), *Pupil Strategies: explorations in the sociology of the school*, Croom Helm

Woods, P. (1983), *Sociology and the School; an interactionist viewpoint*, Routledge and Kegan Paul

Worsley, P. (1957), *The Trumpet Shall Sound*, MacGibbon and Kee

Worsley, P. (1977), *Introducing Sociology*, Penguin (2nd edition)

Young, J. (1971a), *The Drug Takers: the Social Meaning of Drug Use*, Paladin

Young, J. (1971b), 'The role of the police as amplifiers of deviancy', in Cohen (1971)

Young, M., and Willmott, P. (1956), 'Social grading by manual workers', *British Journal of Sociology*, vol, 4 no. 2

Young, M., and Willmott, P. (1957), *Family and Kinship in East London*, Penguin

Young, M., and Willmott, P. (1973), *The Symmetrical Family*, Routledge and Kegan Paul

Young, M. F. D. (1971), *Knowledge and Control*, Collier Macmillan

Zimmerman, D. H. (1974), 'Fact as practical accomplishment', in Turner (1974)

Zola, I. (1975), 'Medicine as an institution of social control', *Sociological Review*, vol. 20, no. 4

Zweig, F. (1961), *The Worker in an Affluent Society*, Heinemann

Acknowledgements

Thanks are due to the following publishers and authors for permission kindly granted to reproduce from copyright material:

Tables

2 J. Tunstall, *The Media in Britain* (Constable 1983)

5 H. F. Lydall and D. G. Tipping, 'The distribution of wealth in Britain', *The Oxford Bulletin of Economics and Statistics* (February 1961)

6 J. Westergaard and H. Resler, *Class in Capitalist Society* (Heinemann Educational 1975)

7 B. Jackson, *Streaming: an Education System in Miniature* (Routledge and Kegan Paul 1964)

8 P. Stanworth and A. Giddens, *Elites and Power in British Society* (Cambridge University Press 1974)

9 ibid.

10 M. Margolis, *Viable Democracy*, (Penguin 1979)

11 D. Butler and D. Stokes, *Political Change in Britain* (Macmillan, London and Basingstoke 1974)

12 H. Drucker *et al.* (eds.), *Developments in British Politics* (Macmillan 1984)

13 I. Crewe *et al.*, 'Partisan dealignment in Britain 1964-74', *British Journal of Political Science*, vol. 7 (1977)

14 Lord Swann, *Report of the Committee of Enquiry into the Education of Children from Ethnic Minority Groups*, (HMSO 1985)

16 *The Changing Experience of Women*, U221, Unit 2 (Open University)

17 Schools Council, ILEA
19 Her Majesty's Stationery Office, OPCS Series no. 1, 'Occupational mortality',
    Decennial Supplement (1970–2), Crown copyright
20 A. Macfarlane and M. Mugford, *Birth Courts* (HMSO 1984)
22 A. Macfarlane and M. Mugford, *Birth Counts* (HMSO 1984)
23 Her Majesty's Stationery Office, *National Food Survey*, (1980), Crown
    copyright

Figures
 3 P. Worsley, *Introducing Sociology* (Penguin Books Ltd 1977)
 7 'Fewer children in court: a guide to the Children's Acts', *New Society*
12 Her Majesty's Stationery Office, OPCS, 'Census, England and Wales, 1891
    and 1971', Crown copyright
14 J. Powles, 'On the limitations of modern science', in *Science, Medicine and
    Man*, vol. 1 (Pergamon 1973)
15 R. B. Porter, 'The contribution of the biological and medical sciences to
    human welfare', *Presidential Addresses of the British Association for the
    Advancement of Science* (British Association for the Advancement of
    Sciences 1971)
16 A. Macfarlane and M. Mugford, *Birth Counts* (HMSO 1984)
18 A. Scrimshire, 'Health in Newham', *New Society* 24.2.77
19 Her Majesty's Stationery Office, *Population Trends*, No. 18 (1980), Crown
    copyright

The cartoon on page 339 from *The Changing Experience of Women*, U221, Unit 2
    (Open University)

Index